Time Series Analysis on AWS

Learn how to build forecasting models and detect anomalies in your time series data

Michaël Hoarau

BIRMINGHAM—MUMBAI

Time Series Analysis on AWS

Copyright © 2022 Packt Publishing

Publishing Product Manager: Reshma Raman

Senior Editor: Roshan Kumar, David Sugarman

Content Development Editor: Tazeen Shaikh

Technical Editor: Sonam Pandey

Copy Editor: Safis Editing

Project Coordinator: Aparna Ravikumar Nair

Proofreader: Safis Editing

Indexer: Subalakshmi Govindhan

Production Designer: Jyoti Chauhan

Marketing Coordinator: Priyanka Mhatre

First published: February 2022

Production reference: 2240222

Published by Packt Publishing Ltd.
Livery Place
35 Livery Street
Birmingham
B3 2PB, UK.

ISBN 978-1-80181-684-7

www.packt.com

To my parents, Roseline and Philippe, for their life-long dedication to offering the best learning environment I could hope for. To my wife, Nathalie, for her love, support, and inspiration. To my son, as he starts his journey to be a great creative thinker.

– Michaël Hoarau

Contributors

About the author

Michaël Hoarau is an AI/ML specialist **solutions architect (SA)** working at **Amazon Web Services (AWS)**. He is an AWS Certified Associate SA. He previously worked as an AI/ML specialist SA at AWS and the EMEA head of data science at GE Digital. He has experience in building product quality prediction systems for multiple industries. He has used forecasting techniques to build virtual sensors for industrial production lines. He has also helped multiple customers build forecasting and anomaly detection systems to increase their business efficiency.

I want to thank the people who have been close to me and supported me through the many evenings and weekends spent writing this book, especially my wife, Nathalie, and my son, Valentin.

About the reviewers

Subramanian M Suryanarayanan (**Mani**) is head of category marketing and analytics at BigBasket – India's largest online supermarket. He has 23+ years of experience in consulting and analytics. He studied at the University of Madras, IIM-Ahmedabad, and MIT. Mani is a frequent contributor to industry and academic forums. He invests in, advises, and mentors start-ups in the DeepTech space. He is a mentor with the DeepTechClub of NASSCOM. Mani is the co-author of the best-selling book on BigBasket, *Saying No to Jugaad*, which was ranked among the top 5 best business books in India in 2020.

> *I want to thank my wife, Deepa, and my son, Nandan, who showed immense patience when I spent many evenings reviewing this book at the expense of spending time with them.*

Christy Bergman is an AI/ML specialist solutions architect at AWS. Her work involves helping AWS customers be successful using AI/ML services to solve real-world business problems. Prior to joining AWS, Christy built real-time fraud detection at a banking start-up and prior to that was a data scientist in the subscription software industry. In her spare time, she enjoys hiking and bird watching.

Table of Contents

2
An Overview of Amazon Forecast

3
Creating a Project and Ingesting Your Data

4
Training a Predictor with AutoML

5
Customizing Your Predictor Training

6
Generating New Forecasts

7

Improving and Scaling Your Forecast Strategy

Section 2: Detecting Abnormal Behavior in Multivariate Time Series with Amazon Lookout for Equipment

8

An Overview of Amazon Lookout for Equipment

9
Creating a Dataset and Ingesting Your Data

10
Training and Evaluating a Model

14
Creating and Activating a Detector

15
Viewing Anomalies and Providing Feedback

Index

Other Books You May Enjoy

Preface

As a business analyst or data scientist, you will have to use many algorithms and approaches to prepare, process, and build **machine learning** (**ML**)-based applications by leveraging time series data, but you will likely face problems such as not knowing which algorithm to choose or how to combine and interpret these algorithms. **Amazon Web Services** (**AWS**) provides numerous services to help you build applications fueled by **artificial intelligence** (**AI**) capabilities. This book will see you get to grips with three AWS AI/ML managed services and enable you to deliver your desired business outcomes.

The book begins with **Amazon Forecast**, where you'll discover how to use time series forecasting and sophisticated statistical and ML algorithms to deliver business outcomes accurately. You'll then learn how to use **Amazon Lookout for Equipment** to build multivariate time series anomaly detection models geared toward industrial equipment and discover how it provides valuable insights to support teams with predictive maintenance and predictive quality use cases. In the final chapters, you'll explore **Amazon Lookout for Metrics** and automatically detect and diagnose outliers in your business and operational data.

By the end of this AWS book, you'll have learned how to use the three AWS AI services effectively to perform time series analysis.

Who this book is for

This book is for data analysts, business analysts, and data scientists looking to analyze time series data effectively to solve business problems. Basic statistics knowledge would be useful, but no ML knowledge is needed to follow the content in this book. Prior experience with time series data and how they relate to various business problems will help you get the most out of this book. This book will help ML practitioners find new ways to leverage their skills to build effective time series-based applications with the technologies described.

What this book covers

Chapter 1, *An Overview of Time Series Analysis*, will establish how time series data is different from regular tabular data and will hint at why we need different approaches to process them. You will also learn about the different types of time series you may encounter and gain an understanding of the kind of predictive power your time series data contains.

Chapter 2, *An Overview of Amazon Forecast*, will teach you about what Amazon Forecast is designed for, how it works, and the kinds of situations it is suited for. By the end of the chapter, you will also have a good command of the underlying concepts of Amazon Forecast, such as dataset groups, datasets, predictors, and forecasts.

Chapter 3, *Creating a Project and Ingesting Your Data*, will describe how to create and organize multiple datasets within the dataset group construct, how to configure datasets, and how to ingest CSV data. You will also gain a high-level understanding of all the heavy lifting Amazon Forecast performs on your behalf to save as much data preparation effort as possible.

Chapter 4, *Training a Predictor with AutoML*, will use the datasets prepared and ingested previously to train a forecasting model. You will learn how to configure training and discover what impact each feature can have on the training duration and outputs. The evaluation dashboard will be described in depth.

Chapter 5, *Customizing Your Predictor Training*, will go deeper into the different possible configurations that Amazon Forecast has to offer, after you have trained your first predictor using the automated features provided by AWS. From choosing the right algorithm for a given problem to leveraging supplementary features such as weather data, you will learn how you can increase the accuracy of your forecasts while optimizing your training time.

Chapter 6, *Generating New Forecasts*, will help you generate new forecasts and get new insights to support your daily business decisions, by leveraging the predictors you trained previously. This chapter will help you actually generate forecasts, download the results, and visualize them using your favorite spreadsheet software.

Chapter 7, *Improving and Scaling Your Forecast Strategy*, will help you get the most from Amazon Forecast. This chapter will point you in the right direction to monitor your models and compare predictions to real-life data, a crucial task to detect any drift in performance, which could trigger retraining. Last but not least, you will also leverage a sample from the AWS Solutions Library to automate your predictor training, forecast generation, and dashboard visualization.

Chapter 8, An Overview of Amazon Lookout for Equipment, will describe what Amazon Lookout for Equipment can do, how it works, and the kind of applications it's suited for. You will understand at a high level how to prepare your dataset and how you can integrate service results into your business processes.

Chapter 9, Creating a Dataset and Ingesting Your Data, will teach you how to create and organize multiple datasets and how to perform dataset ingestion. You will also gain a high-level understanding of all the heavy lifting AWS performs on your behalf to save as much data preparation effort as possible (in terms of imputation, time series alignment, resampling, and so on).

Chapter 10, Training and Evaluating a Model, will have you use the datasets prepared and ingested previously to train a multivariate anomaly detection model. You will learn about how to configure training and what impact each feature can have on the training output and the training duration. The evaluation and diagnostics dashboard will be described in depth to help you get a good view of the quality of the output.

Chapter 11, Scheduling Regular Inferences, will show you how to configure and run an inference scheduler that will run your data against your trained model. In this chapter, you will learn how to manage such schedulers and how to use the predictions obtained.

Chapter 12, Reducing Time to Insights for Anomaly Detections, will help you improve your model performance and go further in results post-processing. This chapter will also point you in the right direction when it comes to monitoring your models and detecting any drift, which would trigger either retraining or further investigation.

Chapter 13, An Overview of Amazon Lookout for Metrics, will explain what Amazon Lookout for Metrics is designed for, how it works, and the kind of situations it is suited for. By the end of this chapter, you will also have a good command of the underlying concepts of Amazon Lookout for Metrics (datasources, datasets, detectors, alerts, and anomalies).

Chapter 14, Creating and Activating a Detector, will describe the process of creating and activating a detector. You will also learn about the different integration paths that are available to connect Amazon Lookout for Metrics to various data sources and alerts.

Chapter 15, Viewing Anomalies and Providing Feedback, starts with a trained detector and shows you how to dive into detected anomalies and review them, as well as covering other key concepts, such as severity thresholds, how to leverage the impact analysis dashboard to perform root cause analysis, and how to provide feedback to the service.

To get the most out of this book

To get the most out of this book, you must have some basic knowledge about what time series data is and how it can relate to various business problems (sales or demand forecasting, predictive maintenance, and so on). You must also have an understanding of what an anomaly is when dealing with time series data.

More generally, having a high-level understanding of what cloud computing is and how you can leverage cloud services to solve your daily business problems is a good starting point.

AWS services covered in the book	OS required
Amazon Forecast	Any browser (Chrome recommended) running on Windows, Mac OS X, or Linux (Any)
Amazon Lookout for Equipment	Any browser (Chrome recommended) running on Windows, Mac OS X, or Linux (Any)
Amazon Lookout for Metrics	Any browser (Chrome recommended) running on Windows, Mac OS X, or Linux (Any)

To access the cloud services described in this book, you will need an AWS account. Account creation is covered in the *Technical requirements* section of *Chapter 2, An Overview of Amazon Forecast*.

If you are using the digital version of this book, we advise you to type the code yourself or access the code from the book's GitHub repository (a link is available in the next section). Doing so will help you avoid any potential errors related to the copying and pasting of code.

Download the example code files

You can download the example code files for this book from GitHub at `https://github.com/PacktPublishing/Time-series-Analysis-on-AWS`. If there's an update to the code, it will be updated in the GitHub repository.

We also have other code bundles from our rich catalog of books and videos available at `https://github.com/PacktPublishing/`. Check them out!

Download the color images

We also provide a PDF file that has color images of the screenshots and diagrams used in this book. You can download it here: `https://static.packt-cdn.com/downloads/9781801816847_ColorImages.pdf`.

Conventions used

There are a number of text conventions used throughout this book.

`Code in text`: Indicates code words in text, database table names, folder names, filenames, file extensions, pathnames, dummy URLs, user input, and Twitter handles. Here is an example: "Mount the downloaded `WebStorm-10*.dmg` disk image file as another disk in your system."

A block of code is set as follows:

```
START            = '2013-06-01'
END              = '2013-07-31'
DATASET          = 'household_energy_consumption'
FORECAST_PREFIX = 'export_energy_consumption_XXXX'
```

Any command-line input or output is written as follows:

```
python3 -m pip install --quiet s3fs pandas
wget https://raw.githubusercontent.com/PacktPublishing/
Time series-analysis-on-AWS-/main/Chapter09/create_
schema.py
```

Bold: Indicates a new term, an important word, or words that you see onscreen. For instance, words in menus or dialog boxes appear in **bold**. Here is an example: "Click on **Amazon Forecast** to go to the service home page."

> Tips or Important Notes
> Note that *successive import jobs are not aggregated:* only the most recent import will be considered when you use your datasets to train a predictor.

Get in touch

Feedback from our readers is always welcome.

General feedback: If you have questions about any aspect of this book, email us at customercare@packtpub.com and mention the book title in the subject of your message.

Errata: Although we have taken every care to ensure the accuracy of our content, mistakes do happen. If you have found a mistake in this book, we would be grateful if you would report this to us. Please visit www.packtpub.com/support/errata and fill in the form.

Piracy: If you come across any illegal copies of our works in any form on the internet, we would be grateful if you would provide us with the location address or website name. Please contact us at copyright@packt.com with a link to the material.

If you are interested in becoming an author: If there is a topic that you have expertise in and you are interested in either writing or contributing to a book, please visit authors.packtpub.com.

Share Your Thoughts

Once you've read *Time series analysis on AWS*, we'd love to hear your thoughts! Scan the QR code below to go straight to the Amazon review page for this book and share your feedback.

https://packt.link/r/1-801-81684-0

Your review is important to us and the tech community and will help us make sure we're delivering excellent quality content.

Section 1: Analyzing Time Series and Delivering Highly Accurate Forecasts with Amazon Forecast

This section will see you become familiar with time series data, the challenges it poses, and how it can be used to solve real-life business problems. You will learn about the different forms that time series datasets can take and the key use cases they help to address.

In this section, you will also learn about **Amazon Forecast** and how this AI service can help you tackle forecasting challenges. By the end of this section, you will have trained a forecast model and you will know how to generate new forecasts based on new data. You will also learn how to get deep insights from your model results to improve your forecasting strategy or gain a better understanding of the reason why a given prediction was made by your model.

This section comprises the following chapters:

- *Chapter 1, An Overview of Time Series Analysis*
- *Chapter 2, An Overview of Amazon Forecast*
- *Chapter 3, Creating a Project and Ingesting Your Data*
- *Chapter 4, Training a Predictor with AutoML*
- *Chapter 5, Customizing Your Predictor Training*
- *Chapter 6, Generating New Forecasts*
- *Chapter 7, Improving and Scaling Your Forecast Strategy*

1
An Overview of Time Series Analysis

Time series analysis is a technical domain with a very large choice of techniques that need to be carefully selected depending on the business problem you want to solve and the nature of your time series. In this chapter, we will discover the different families of time series and expose unique challenges you may encounter when dealing with this type of data.

By the end of this chapter, you will understand how to recognize what type of time series data you have and select the best approaches to perform your time series analysis (depending on the insights you want to uncover), and you will understand the use cases that **Amazon Forecast**, **Amazon Lookout for Equipment**, and **Amazon Lookout for Metrics** can help you solve, and which ones they are not suitable for.

You will also have a sound toolbox of time series techniques, **Amazon Web Services (AWS)** services, and open source **Python** packages that you can leverage in addition to the three managed services described in detail in this book. Data scientists will also find these tools to be great additions to their time series **exploratory data analysis (EDA)** toolbox.

In this chapter, we are going to cover the following main topics:

- What is a time series dataset?

- Recognizing the different families of time series

- Adding context to time series data

- Learning about common time series challenges

- Selecting an analysis approach

- Typical time series use cases

Technical requirements

No hands-on experience in a language such as **Python** or **R** is necessary to follow along with the content of this chapter. However, for the more technology-savvy readers, we will address some technical considerations (such as visualization, transformation, and preprocessing) and the packages you can leverage in the Python language to address these. In addition, you can also open the **Jupyter notebook** you will find in the following GitHub repository to follow along and experiment by yourself: `https://github.com/PacktPublishing/Time-series-Analysis-on-AWS/blob/main/Chapter01/chapter1-time-series-analysis-overview.ipynb`.

Although following along this chapter with the aforementioned notebook provided is optional, this will help you build your intuition about what insights the time series techniques described in this introductory chapter can deliver.

What is a time series dataset?

From a mathematical point of view, a time series is a **discrete sequence** of data points that are listed **chronologically**. Let's take each of the highlighted terms of this definition, as follows:

- **Sequence**: A time series is a sequence of data points. Each data point can take a single value (usually a binary, an integer, or a real value).

- **Discrete**: Although the phenomena measured by a system can be continuous (the outside temperature is a continuous variable as time can, of course, range over the entire real number line), time series data is generated by systems that capture data points at a certain interval (a temperature sensor can, for instance, take a new temperature reading every 5 minutes). The measurement interval is usually regular (the data points will be equally spaced in time), but more often than not, they are irregular.

- **Chronologically**: The sequence of data points is naturally time-ordered. If you were to perform an analysis of your time series data, you will generally observe that data points that are close together in time will be more closely related than observations that are further apart. This natural ordering means that any time series model usually tries to learn from past values of a given sequence rather than from future values (this is obvious when you try to forecast future values of a time series sequence but is still very important for other use cases).

Machine learning (**ML**) and **artificial intelligence** (**AI**) have largely been successful at leveraging new technologies including **dedicated processing units** (such as **graphics processing units**, or **GPUs**), **fast network channels**, and **immense storage capacities**. Paradigm shifts such as **cloud computing** have played a big role in democratizing access to such technologies, allowing tremendous leaps in novel architectures that are immediately leveraged in production workloads.

In this landscape, time series appear to have benefited a lot less from these advances: what makes time series data so specific? We might consider a time series dataset to be a mere tabular dataset that would be time-indexed: this would be a big mistake. Introducing time as a variable in your dataset means that you are now dealing with the notion of temporality: patterns can now emerge based on the timestamp of each row of your dataset. Let's now have a look at the different families of time series you may encounter.

Recognizing the different families of time series

In this section, you will become familiar with the different families of time series. For any ML practitioner, it is obvious that a single image should not be processed like a video stream and that detecting an anomaly on an image requires a high enough resolution to capture the said anomaly. Multiple images from a certain subject (for example, pictures of a cauliflower) would not be very useful to teach an ML system anything about the visual characteristics of a pumpkin—or an aircraft, for that matter. As eyesight is one of our human senses, this may be obvious. However, we will see in this section and the following one (dedicated to challenges specific to time series) that the same kinds of differences apply to different time series.

There are four different families involved in time series data, which are outlined here:

- **Univariate time series data**
- **Continuous multivariate data**
- **Event-based multivariate data**
- **Multiple time series data**

Univariate time series data

A *univariate time series* is a sequence of single time-dependent values.

Such a series could be the energy output in **kilowatt-hour (kWh)** of a power plant, the closing price of a single stock market action, or the daily average temperature measured in Paris, France.

The following screenshot shows an excerpt of the energy consumption of a household:

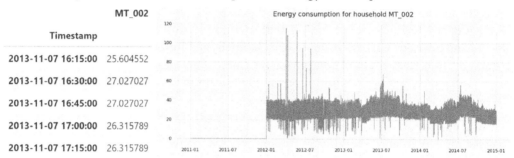

MT_002	
Timestamp	
2013-11-07 16:15:00	25.604552
2013-11-07 16:30:00	27.027027
2013-11-07 16:45:00	27.027027
2013-11-07 17:00:00	26.315789
2013-11-07 17:15:00	26.315789

Figure 1.1 – First rows and line plot of a univariate time series capturing the energy consumption of a household

A univariate time series can be *discrete*: for instance, you may be limited to the single daily value of stock market closing prices. In this situation, if you wanted to have a higher resolution (say, hourly data), you would end up with the same value duplicated 24 times per day.

Temperature seems to be closer to a *continuous* variable, for that matter: you can get a reading as frequently as you would wish, and you can expect some level of variation whenever you have a data point. You are, however, limited to the frequency at which the temperature sensor takes its reading (every 5 minutes for a home meteorological station or every hour in main meteorological stations). For practical purposes, most time series are indeed discrete, hence the definition called out earlier in this chapter.

The three services described in this book (*Amazon Forecast*, *Amazon Lookout for Equipment*, and Amazon *Lookout for Metrics*) can deal with univariate data to perform with various use cases.

Continuous multivariate data

A *multivariate time series dataset* is a sequence of many-valued vector values emitted at the same time. In this type of dataset, each variable can be considered individually or in the context shaped by the other variables as a whole. This happens when complex relationships govern the way these variables evolve with time (think about several engineering variables linked through physics-based equations).

An industrial asset such as an arc furnace (used in steel manufacturing) is running 24/7 and emits time series data captured by sensors during its entire lifetime. Understanding these continuous time series is critical to prevent any risk of unplanned downtime by performing the appropriate maintenance activities (a domain widely known under the umbrella term of **predictive maintenance**). Operators of such assets have to deal with sometimes thousands of time series generated at a high frequency (it is not uncommon to collect data with a 10-millisecond sampling rate), and each sensor is measuring a physical grandeur. The key reason why each time series should not be considered individually is that each of these physical grandeurs is usually linked to all the others by more or less complex physical equations.

Take the example of a centrifugal pump: such a pump transforms rotational energy provided by a motor into the displacement of a fluid. While going through such a pump, the fluid gains both additional speed and pressure. According to Euler's pump equation, the head pressure created by the impeller of the centrifugal pump is derived using the following expression:

$$H = \frac{1}{2}(u_2^2 - u_1^2 + w_2^2 - w_1^2 + c_2^2 - c_1^2) \cdot g$$

In the preceding expression, the following applies:

- H is the head pressure.
- u denotes the peripheral circumferential velocity vector.
- w denotes the relative velocity vector.
- c denotes the absolute velocity vector.
- Subscript 1 denotes the input variable (also called inlet for such a pump). For instance, $w1$ is the inlet relative velocity.
- Subscript 2 denotes output variables (also called peripheral variables when dealing with this kind of asset). For instance, $w2$ is the peripheral relative velocity.
- g is the gravitational acceleration and is a constant value depending on the latitude where the pump is located.

A multivariate time series dataset describing this centrifugal pump could include $u1$, $u2$, $w1$, $w2$, $c1$, $c2$, and H. All these variables are obviously linked together by the law of physics that governs this particular asset and cannot be considered individually as univariate time series.

If you know when this particular pump is in good shape, has had a maintenance operation, or is running through an abnormal event, you can also have an additional column in your time series capturing this state: your multivariate time series can then be seen as a related dataset that might be useful to try and predict the condition of your pump. You will find more details and examples about labels and related time series data in the *Adding context to time series data* section.

Amazon Lookout for Equipment, one of the three services described in this book, is able to perform anomaly detection on this type of multivariate dataset.

Event-based multivariate data

There are situations where data is continuously recorded across several operating modes: an aircraft going through different sequences of maneuvers from the pilot, a production line producing successive batches of different products, or rotating equipment (such as a motor or a fan) operating at different speeds depending on the need.

A multivariate time series dataset can be collected across multiple episodes or events, as follows:

- Each aircraft flight can log a time series dataset from hundreds of sensors and can be matched to a certain sequence of actions executed by the aircraft pilot. Of course, a given aircraft will go through several overlapping maintenance cycles, each flight is different, and the aircraft components themselves go through a natural aging process that can generate additional stress and behavior changes due to the fatigue of going through hundreds of successive flights.

- A beauty-care plant produces multiple distinct products on the same production line (multiple types and brands of shampoos and shower gels), separated by a clean, in-place process to ensure there is no contamination of a given product by a previous one. Each batch is associated with a different recipe, with different raw materials and different physical characteristics. Although the equipment and process time series are recorded continuously and can be seen as a single-flow variable indexed by time, they can be segmented by the batch they are associated with.

In some cases, a multivariate dataset must be associated with additional context to understand which operating mode a given segment of a time series can be associated with. If the number of situations to consider is reasonably low, a service such as Amazon Lookout for Equipment can be used to perform anomaly detection on this type of dataset.

Multiple time series data

You might also encounter situations where you have multiple time series data that does not form a multivariate time series dataset. These are situations where you have multiple independent signals that can each be seen as a single univariate time series. Although full independence might be debatable depending on your situation, there are no additional insights to be gained by considering potential relationships between the different univariate series.

Here are some examples of such a situation:

- **Closing price for multiple stock market actions**: For any given company, the trading stock can be influenced by both exogenous factors (for example, a worldwide pandemic pushing entire countries into shelter-in-place situations) and endogenous decisions (board of directors' decisions; a strategic move from leadership; major innovation delivered by a **research and development** (**R&D**) team). Each stock price is not necessarily impacted by other companies' stock prices (competitors, partners, organizations operating on the same market).

- **Sold items for multiple products on an online retail store**: Although some products might be related (more summer clothes when temperatures are rising again in spring), they do not have an influence on each other and they happen to sport similar behavior.

  Multiple time series are hard to analyze and process as true multivariate time series data as the mechanics that trigger seemingly linked behaviors are most of the time coming from external factors (summer approaching and having a similar effect on many summer-related items). Modern neural networks are, however, able to train global models on all items at once: this allows them to uncover relationships and context that are not provided in the dataset to reach a higher level of accuracy than traditional statistical models that are local (univariate-focused) by nature.

  We will see later on that Amazon Forecast (for forecasting with local and global models) and Amazon Lookout for Metrics (for anomaly detection on univariate business metrics) are good examples of services provided by Amazon that can deal with this type of dataset.

Adding context to time series data

Simply speaking, there are three main ways an ML model can learn something new, as outlined here:

- **Supervised learning** (**SL**): Models are trained using **input data** and **labels** (or targets). The labels are provided as an instructor would provide directions to a student learning a new move. Training a model to approximate the relationship between input data and labels is a supervised approach.

- **Unsupervised learning** (**UL**): This approach is used when using **ML** to uncover and **extract underlying relationships** that may exist in a given dataset. In this case, we only operate on the input data and do not need to provide any labels or output data. We can, however, use labels to assess how good a given unsupervised model is at capturing reality.

- **Reinforcement learning** (**RL**): To train a model with RL, we build an environment that is able to send feedback to an agent. We then let the agent operate within this environment (using a set of **actions**) and react based on the **feedback** provided by the environment in response to each action. We do not have a fixed training dataset anymore, but an environment that sends an input sample (feedback) **in reaction** to an action from the agent.

Whether you are dealing with univariate, multiple, or multivariate time series datasets, you might need to provide extra **context**: location, unique **identification** (**ID**) number of a batch, components from the recipes used for a given batch, sequence of actions performed by a pilot during an aircraft flight test, and so on. The same sequence of values for univariate and multivariate time series could lead to a different interpretation in different contexts (for example, are we cruising or taking off; are we producing a batch of shampoo or shower gel?).

All this additional context can be provided in the form of *labels*, **related time series**, or **metadata** that will be used differently depending on the type of ML you leverage. Let's have a look at what these pieces of context can look like.

Labels

Labels can be used in SL settings where ML models are trained using input data (our time series dataset) and output data (the labels). In a supervised approach, training a model is the process of learning an approximation between the input data and the labels. Let's review a few examples of labels you can encounter along with your time series datasets, as follows:

- **The National Aeronautics and Space Administration** (**NASA**) has provided the community with a very widely used benchmark dataset that contains the remaining useful lifetime of a turbofan measured in cycles: each engine (identified by unit_ number in the following table) has its health measured with multiple sensors, and readings are provided after each flight (or cycle). The multivariate dataset recorded for each engine can be labeled with the remaining useful lifetime (rul) known or estimated at the end of each cycle (this is the last column in the following table). Here, each individual timestamp is characterized by a label (the remaining lifetime measured in a cycle):

	unit_number	cycle	setting_1	setting_2	setting_3	sensor_1	sensor_2	sensor_21	rul
0	1	1	-0.000700	-0.000400	100.000000	518.670000	641.820000	23.419000	191
1	1	2	0.001900	-0.000300	100.000000	518.670000	642.150000	23.423600	190
2	1	3	-0.004300	0.000300	100.000000	518.670000	642.350000	23.344200	189
3	1	4	0.000700	0.000000	100.000000	518.670000	642.350000	23.373900	188
4	1	5	-0.001900	-0.000200	100.000000	518.670000	642.370000	23.404400	187
5	1	6	-0.004300	-0.000100	100.000000	518.670000	642.100000	23.366900	186
6	1	7	0.001000	0.000100	100.000000	518.670000	642.480000	23.377400	185
7	1	8	-0.003400	0.000300	100.000000	518.670000	642.560000	23.310600	184
8	1	9	0.000800	0.000100	100.000000	518.670000	642.120000	23.406600	183
9	1	10	-0.003300	0.000100	100.000000	518.670000	641.710000	23.469400	182

Figure 1.2 – NASA turbofan remaining useful lifetime

- The `ECG200` dataset is another widely used time series dataset as a benchmark for time series classification. The electrical activity recorded during human heartbeats can be labeled as **Normal** or **Ischemia** (myocardial infarction), as illustrated in the following screenshot. Each time series as a whole is characterized by a label:

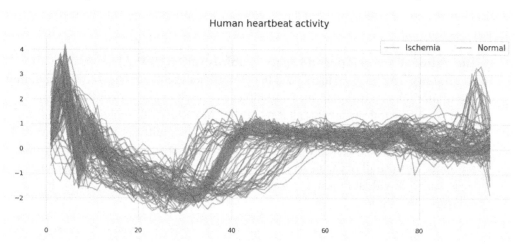

Figure 1.3 – Heartbeat activity for 100 patients (ECG200 dataset)

- **Kaggle** also offers a few time series datasets of interest. One of them contains sensor data from a water pump with known time ranges where the pump is broken and when it is being repaired. In the following case, labels are available as time ranges:

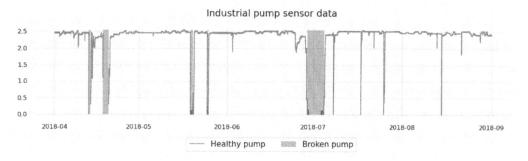

Figure 1.4 – Water pump sensor data showcasing healthy and broken time ranges

As you can see, labels can be used to characterize individual timestamps of a time series, portions of a time series, or even whole time series.

Related time series

Related time series are additional variables that evolve in parallel to the time series that is the target of your analysis. Let's have a look at a few examples, as follows:

- In the case of a manufacturing plant producing different batches of product, a critical signal to have is the unique batch ID that can be matched with the starting and ending timestamps of the time series data.

- The electricity consumption of multiple households from London can be matched with several pieces of weather data (temperature, wind speed, rainfall), as illustrated in the following screenshot:

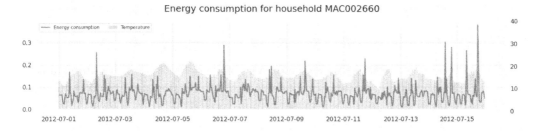

Figure 1.5 – London household energy consumption versus outside temperature in the same period

- In the water pump dataset, the different sensors' data could be considered as related time series data for the pump health variable, which can either take a value of 0 (healthy pump) or 1 (broken pump).

Metadata

When your dataset is multivariate or includes multiple time series, each of these can be associated with parameters that do not depend on time. Let's have a look at this in more detail here:

- In the example of a manufacturing plant mentioned before, each batch of products could be different, and the metadata associated with each batch ID could be the recipe used to manufacture this very batch.

- For London household energy consumption, each time series is associated with a household that could be further associated with its house size, the number of people, its type (house or flat), the construction time, the address, and so on. The following screenshot lists some of the metadata associated with a few households from this dataset: we can see, for instance, that 27 households fall into the ACORN-A category that has a house with 2 beds:

	MAIN CATEGORIES	CATEGORIES	REFERENCE	ACORN-A	ACORN-B	ACORN-E
666	SHOPPING	Furniture & Fittings Stores	Premium	214.000000	209.000000	139.000000
778	LEISURE TIME	Interests & Hobbies	Charity / Voluntary Work	122.000000	122.000000	48.000000
47	HOUSING	House Size	Number of Beds : 2	27.000000	28.000000	124.000000
182	MARKETING CHANNELS	Future Responses	Messages on mobile phone	105.000000	105.000000	126.000000
159	MARKETING CHANNELS	Channels Received	Leaflets - Door or Newspaper	102.000000	103.000000	98.000000
51	HOUSING	House Value	House Value up to 100k	13.000000	17.000000	40.000000
176	MARKETING CHANNELS	Future Responses	Leaflets/Samples handed out in the street or p...	101.000000	101.000000	113.000000
148	TRANSPORT	Public Transport Accessibility Level	6a	101.394783	8.303678	176.905736
356	DIGITAL	Types of internet usage : Laptop or PC	Vote on television shows (e.g. X Factor, Stric...	72.000000	88.000000	84.000000
38	HOUSING	House Type	Semi-detached house	56.000000	70.000000	66.000000

Figure 1.6 – London household metadata excerpt

Now you have understood how time series can be further described with additional context such as labels, related time series, and metadata, let's now dive into common challenges you can encounter when analyzing time series data.

Learning about common time series challenges

Time series data is a very compact way to encode multi-scale behaviors of the measured phenomenon: this is the key reason why fundamentally unique approaches are necessary compared to tabular datasets, acoustic data, images, or videos. Multivariate datasets add another layer of complexity due to the underlying implicit relationships that can exist between multiple signals.

This section will highlight key challenges that ML practitioners must learn to tackle to successfully uncover insights hidden in time series data.

These challenges can include the following:

- Technical challenges
- Visualization challenges

- Behavioral challenges
- Missing insights and context

Technical challenges

In addition to time series data, contextual information can also be stored as separate files (or tables from a database): this includes labels, related time series, or metadata about the items being measured. Related time series will have the same considerations as your main time series dataset, whereas labels and metadata will usually be stored as a single file or a database table. We will not focus on these items as they do not pose any challenges different from any usual tabular dataset.

Time series file structure

When you discover a new time series dataset, the first thing you have to do before you can apply your favorite ML approach is to understand the type of processing you need to apply to it. This dataset can actually come in several files that you will have to assemble to get a complete overview, structured in one of the following ways:

- **By time ranges**: With one file for each month and every sensor included in each file. In the following screenshot, the first file will cover the range in green (April 2018) and contains all the data for every sensor (from sensor_00 to sensor_09), the second file will cover the range in red (May 2018), and the third file will cover the range in purple (June 2018):

timestamp	sensor_00	...	sensor_09	timestamp	sensor_00	...	sensor_09	timestamp	sensor_00	...	sensor_09
2018-04-01	2.445039	...	15.094995	2018-05-01	2.453699	...	14.893017	2018-06-05	2.489018	...	15.014536
2018-04-06	2.424734	...	15.008543	2018-05-06	2.463929	...	15.087628	2018-06-10	2.482078	...	15.044081
2018-04-11	2.191763	...	14.910773	2018-05-11	2.473434	...	15.022479	2018-06-15	2.482272	...	14.970018
2018-04-16	2.102360	...	10.082631	2018-05-16	1.916096	...	14.543209	2018-06-20	2.451048	...	14.975070
2018-04-21	2.411800	...	15.081951	2018-05-21	2.201530	...	14.801671	2018-06-25	1.890748	...	14.213763
2018-04-26	2.462382	...	15.098790	2018-05-26	2.453609	...	15.032157	2018-06-30	0.131959	...	7.611683

Figure 1.7 – File structure by time range (example: one file per month)

- **By variable**: With one file per sensor for the complete time range, as illustrated in the following screenshot:

sensor_00		sensor_01		sensor_03	
timestamp		timestamp		timestamp	
2018-04-01	2.445039	2018-04-01	48.994356	2018-04-01	44.556645
2018-04-06	2.424734	2018-04-06	48.648725	2018-04-06	42.698132
2018-04-11	2.191763	2018-04-11	49.748630	2018-04-11	44.443882
2018-04-16	2.102360	2018-04-16	43.144889	2018-04-16	39.190084
2018-04-21	2.411800	2018-04-21	49.088142	2018-04-21	44.927160
...	...	...	...	...	...
2018-08-09	2.457470	2018-08-09	49.103713	2018-08-09	44.840451
2018-08-14	2.444553	2018-08-14	49.543576	2018-08-14	44.819654
2018-08-19	2.477040	2018-08-19	49.730388	2018-08-19	45.119579
2018-08-24	2.435326	2018-08-24	49.707343	2018-08-24	45.144108
2018-08-29	2.436124	2018-08-29	49.155218	2018-08-29	44.946143

Figure 1.8 – File structure by variable (for example, one sensor per file)

- Or, you could use both the time range and variables, as follows:

	sensor_00		sensor_00		sensor_00
timestamp		timestamp		timestamp	
2018-04-01	2.445039	2018-05-01	2.453699	2018-06-05	2.489018
2018-04-06	2.424734	2018-05-06	2.463929	2018-06-10	2.482078
2018-04-11	2.191763	2018-05-11	2.473434	2018-06-15	2.482272
2018-04-16	2.102360	2018-05-16	1.916096	2018-06-20	2.451048
2018-04-21	2.411800	2018-05-21	2.201530	2018-06-25	1.890748
2018-04-26	2.462382	2018-05-26	2.453609	2018-06-30	0.131959

	sensor_01		sensor_01		sensor_01
timestamp		timestamp		timestamp	
2018-04-01	48.994356	2018-05-01	46.821613	2018-06-05	48.589806
2018-04-06	48.648725	2018-05-06	47.957542	2018-06-10	48.960924
2018-04-11	49.748630	2018-05-11	47.265340	2018-06-15	48.966964
2018-04-16	43.144889	2018-05-16	47.198777	2018-06-20	48.912819
2018-04-21	49.088142	2018-05-21	46.929590	2018-06-25	46.205716
2018-04-26	46.729395	2018-05-26	49.044607	2018-06-30	36.330060

Figure 1.9 – File structure by variable and by time range (for example, one file for each month and each sensor)

When you deal with multiple time series (either independent or multivariate), you might want to assemble them in a single table (or DataFrame if you are a **Python pandas** practitioner). When each time series is stored in a distinct file, you may suffer from misaligned timestamps, as in the following case:

	sensor_00		sensor_01		sensor_02
timestamp		timestamp		timestamp	
2018-04-01	2.445039	2018-04-01	47.950337	2018-04-01	52.096718
2018-04-06	2.424734	2018-04-03	49.848134	2018-04-08	51.030574
2018-04-11	2.191763	2018-04-05	50.218519	2018-04-15	45.722312
2018-04-16	2.102360	2018-04-07	46.951843	2018-04-22	53.278153
2018-04-21	2.411800	2018-04-09	49.127994	2018-04-29	51.743657
2018-04-26	2.462382	2018-04-11	51.358596	2018-05-06	52.873434
2018-05-01	2.453699	2018-04-13	48.911794	2018-05-13	52.524503
2018-05-06	2.463929	2018-04-15	46.597627	2018-05-20	50.782725
2018-05-11	2.473434	2018-04-17	42.765348	2018-05-27	53.944845
2018-05-16	1.916096	2018-04-19	42.595530	2018-06-03	52.533945

Figure 1.10 – Multivariate time series with misaligned timestamps

There are three approaches you can take, and this will depend on the actual processing and learning process you will set up further down the road. You could do one of the following:

- *Leave each time series in its own file with its own timestamps.* This leaves your dataset untouched but will force you to consider a more flexible data structure when you want to feed it into an ML system.

- *Resample every time series to a common sampling rate and concatenate the different files by inserting each time series as a column in your table.* This will be easier to manipulate and process but you won't be dealing with your raw data anymore. In addition, if your contextual data also provides timestamps (to separate each batch of a manufactured product, for instance), you will have to take them into account (one approach could be to slice your data to have time series per batch and resample and assemble your dataset as a second step).

- *Merge all the time series and forward fill every missing value created at the merge stage* (see all the NaN values in the following screenshot). This process is more compute-intensive, especially when your timestamps are irregular:

timestamp	sensor_00	timestamp	sensor_01	timestamp	sensor_02
2018-04-01	2.445039	2018-04-01	47.950337	2018-04-01	52.096718
2018-04-06	2.424734	2018-04-03	49.848134	2018-04-08	51.030574
2018-04-11	2.191763	2018-04-05	50.218519	2018-04-15	45.722312
2018-04-16	2.102360	2018-04-07	46.951843	2018-04-22	53.278153
2018-04-21	2.411800	2018-04-09	49.127994	2018-04-29	51.743657
2018-04-26	2.462382	2018-04-11	51.358596	2018-05-06	52.873434
2018-05-01	2.453699	2018-04-13	48.911794	2018-05-13	52.524503
2018-05-06	2.463929	2018-04-15	46.597627	2018-05-20	50.782725
2018-05-11	2.473434	2018-04-17	42.765348	2018-05-27	53.944845
2018-05-16	1.916096	2018-04-19	42.595530	2018-06-03	52.533945

timestamp	sensor_00	sensor_01	sensor_02
2018-04-01	2.445039	47.950337	52.096718
2018-04-03	NaN	49.848134	NaN
2018-04-05	NaN	50.218519	NaN
2018-04-06	2.424734	NaN	NaN
2018-04-07	NaN	46.951843	NaN
2018-04-08	NaN	NaN	51.030574
2018-04-09	NaN	49.127994	NaN
2018-04-11	2.191763	51.358596	NaN
2018-04-13	NaN	48.911794	NaN
2018-04-15	NaN	46.597627	45.722312

Figure 1.11 – Merging time series with misaligned timestamps

Storage considerations

The format used to store the time series data itself can vary and will have its own benefits or challenges. The following list exposes common formats and the Python libraries that can help tackle them:

- **Comma-separated values** (**CSV**): One of the most common and—unfortunately— least efficient formats to deal with when it comes to storing time series data. If you need to read or write time series data multiple times (for instance, during EDA), it is highly recommended to transform your CSV file into another more efficient format. In Python, you can read and write CSV files with pandas (read_csv and to_csv), and **NumPy** (genfromtxt and savetxt).

- **Microsoft Excel** (**XLSX**): In Python, you can read and write Excel files with pandas (read_excel and to_excel) or dedicated libraries such as openpyxl or xlsxwriter. At the time of this writing, Microsoft Excel is limited to 1,048,576 rows (2^{20}) in a single file. When your dataset covers several files and you need to combine them for further processing, sticking to Excel can generate errors that are difficult to pinpoint further down the road. As with CSV, it is highly recommended to transform your dataset into another format if you plan to open and write it multiple times during your dataset lifetime.

- **Parquet**: This is a very efficient column-oriented storage format. The **Apache Arrow** project hosts several libraries that offer great performance to deal with very large files. Writing a 5 **gigabyte** (**GB**) CSV file can take up to 10 minutes, whereas the same data in Parquet will take up around 3.5 GB and be written in 30 seconds. In Python, Parquet files and datasets can be managed by the `pyarrow.parquet` module.

- **Hierarchical Data Format 5** (**HDF5**): HDF5 is a binary data format dedicated to storing huge amounts of numerical data. With its ability to let you slice multi-terabyte datasets on disk to bring only what you need in memory, this is a great format for data exploration. In Python, you can read and write HDF5 files with `pandas` (`read_hdf` and `to_hdf`) or the `h5py` library.

- **Databases**: Your time series might also be stored in general-purpose databases (that you will query using standard **Structured Query Language** (**SQL**) languages) or may be purpose-built for time series such as **Amazon Timestream** or **InfluxDB**. Column-oriented databases or scalable key-value stores such as **Cassandra** or **Amazon DynamoDB** can also be used while taking benefit from anti-patterns useful for storing and querying time series data.

Data quality

As with any other type of data, time series can be plagued by multiple data quality issues. **Missing data** (or Not-a-Number values) can be filled in with different techniques, including the following:

- **Replace missing data points by the mean or median of the whole time series**: the `fancyimpute` (`http://github.com/iskandr/fancyimpute`) library includes a `SimpleFill` method that can tackle this task.

- **Using a rolling window of a reasonable size before replacing missing data points by the average value**: the `impyute` module (`https://impyute.readthedocs.io`) includes several methods of interest for time series such as `moving_window` to perform exactly this.

- **Forward fill missing data points by the last known value**: This can be a useful technique when the data source uses some compression scheme (an industrial historian system such as **OSIsoft PI** can enable compression of the sensor data it collects, only recording a data point when the value changes). The `pandas` library includes functions such as `Series.fillna` whereby you can decide to backfill, forward fill, or replace a missing value with a constant value.

- **You can also interpolate values between two known values**: Combined with a resampling to align every timestamp for multivariate situations, this yields a robust and complete dataset. You can use the `Series.interpolate` method from `pandas` to achieve this.

For all these situations, we highly recommend plotting and comparing the original and resulting time series to ensure that these techniques do not negatively impact the overall behavior of your time series: imputing data (especially interpolation) can make outliers a lot more difficult to spot, for instance.

Important note

Imputing scattered missing values is not mandatory, depending on the analysis you want to perform—for instance, scattered missing values may not impair your ability to understand a trend or forecast future values of a time series. As a matter of fact, wrongly imputing scattered missing values for forecasting may bias the model if you use a constant value (say, zero) to replace the holes in your time series. If you want to perform some anomaly detection, a missing value may actually be connected to the underlying reason of an anomaly (meaning that the probability of a value being missing is higher when an anomaly is around the corner). Imputing these missing values may hide the very phenomena you want to detect or predict.

Other quality issues can arise regarding timestamps: an easy problem to solve is the supposed monotonic increase. When timestamps are not increasing along with your time series, you can use a function such as `pandas.DataFrame.sort_index` or `pandas.DataFrame.sort_values` to reorder your dataset correctly.

Duplicated timestamps can also arise. When they are associated with duplicated values, using `pandas.DataFrame.duplicated` will help you pinpoint and remove these errors. When the sampling rate is lesser or equal to an hour, you might see duplicate timestamps with different values: this can happen around daylight saving time changes. In some countries, time moves forward by an hour at the start of summer and back again in the middle of the fall—for example, Paris (France) time is usually **Central European Time** (**CET**); in summer months, Paris falls into **Central European Summer Time** (**CEST**). Unfortunately, this usually means that you have to discard all the duplicated values altogether, except if you are able to replace the timestamps with their equivalents, including the actual time zone they were referring to.

> **Data quality at scale**
>
> In production systems where large volumes of data must be processed at scale, you may have to leverage distribution and parallelization frameworks such as `Dask`, `Vaex`, or `Ray`. Moreover, you may have to move away from Python altogether: in this case, services such as **AWS Glue**, **AWS Glue DataBrew**, and **Amazon Elastic MapReduce** (**Amazon EMR**) will provide you a managed platform to run your data transformation pipeline with **Apache Spark**, **Flink**, or **Hive**, for instance.

Visualization challenges

Taking a sneak peek at a time series by reading and displaying the first few records of a time series dataset can be useful to make sure the format is the one expected. However, more often than not, you will want to visualize your time series data, which will lead you into an active area of research: how to transform a time series dataset into a relevant visual representation.

Here are some key challenges you will likely encounter:

- Plotting a high number of data points
- Preventing key events from being smoothed out by any resampling
- Plotting several time series in parallel
- Getting visual cues from a massive amount of time series
- Uncovering multiple scales behavior across long time series
- Mapping labels and metadata on time series

Let's have a look at different techniques and approaches you can leverage to tackle these challenges.

Using interactive libraries to plot time series

Raw time series data is usually visualized with line plots: you can easily achieve this in Microsoft Excel or in a Jupyter notebook (thanks to the `matplotlib` library with Python, for instance). However, bringing long time series in memory to plot them can generate heavy files and images difficult or long to render, even on powerful machines. In addition, the rendered plots might consist of more data points than what your screen can display in terms of pixels. This means that the rendering engine of your favorite visualization library will smooth out your time series. How do you ensure, then, that you do not miss the important characteristics of your signal if they happen to be smoothed out?

On the other hand, you could slice a time series to a more reasonable time range. This may, however, lead you to inappropriate conclusions about the seasonality, the outliers to be processed, or potential missing values to be imputed on certain time ranges outside of your scope of analysis.

This is where **interactive visualization** comes in. Using such a tool will allow you to load a time series, zoom out to get the big picture, zoom in to focus on certain details, and pan a sliding window to visualize a movie of your time series while keeping full control of the traveling! For Python users, libraries such as `plotly` (`http://plotly.com`) or `bokeh` (`http://bokeh.org`) are great options.

Plotting several time series in parallel

When you need to plot several time series and understand how they evolve with regard to each other, you have different options depending on the number of signals you want to visualize and display at once. What is the best representation to plot several time series in parallel? Indeed, different time series will likely have different ranges of possible values, and we only have two axes on a line plot.

If you have just a couple of time series, any static or interactive line plot will work. If both time series have a different range of values, you can assign a secondary axis to one of them, as illustrated in the following screenshot:

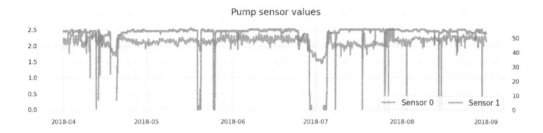

Figure 1.12 – Visualizing a low number of plots

If you have more than two time series and fewer than 10 to 20 that have similar ranges, you can assign a line plot to each of them in the same context. It is not too crowded yet, and this will allow you to detect any level shifts (when all signals go through a sudden significant change). If the range of possible values each time series takes is widely different from one another, a solution is to normalize them by scaling them all to take values comprised between `0.0` and `1.0` (for instance). The `scikit-learn` library includes methods that are well known by ML practitioners for doing just this (check out the `sklearn.preprocessing.Normalizer` or the `sklearn.preprocessing.StandardScaler` methods).

The following screenshot shows a moderate number of plots being visualized:

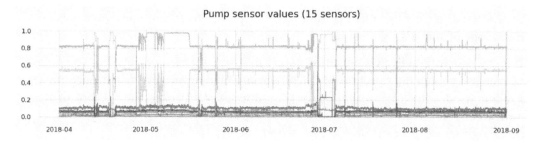

Figure 1.13 – Visualizing a moderate number of plots

Even though this plot is a bit too crowded to focus on the details of each signal, we can already pinpoint some periods of interest.

Let's now say that you have *hundreds of time series*. Is it possible to visualize hundreds of time series in parallel to identify shared behaviors across a multivariate dataset? Plotting all of them on a single chart will render it too crowded and definitely unusable. Plotting each signal in its own line plot will occupy a prohibitive real estate and won't allow you to spot time periods when many signals were impacted at once.

This is where **strip charts** come in. As you can see in the following screenshot, transforming a single-line plot into a strip chart makes the information a lot more compact:

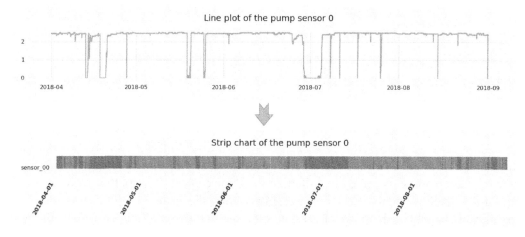

Figure 1.14 – From a line plot to a strip chart

The trick is to bin the values of each time series and to assign a color to each bin. You could decide, for instance, that low values will be red, average values will be orange, and high values will be green. Let's now plot the 52 signals from the previous water pump example over 5 years with a 1-minute resolution. We get the following output:

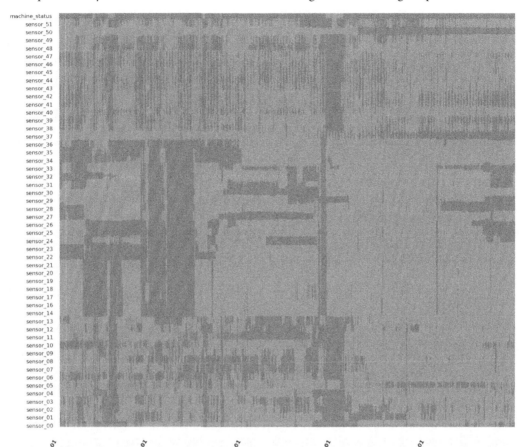

Figure 1.15 – 11.4 million data points at a single glance

Do you see some patterns you would like to investigate? I would definitely isolate the red bands (where many, if not all, signals are evolving in their lowest values) and have a look at what is happening between early May or at the end of June (where many signals seem to be at their lowest). For more details about strip charts and in-depth demonstration, you can refer to the following article: https://towardsdatascience.com/using-strip-charts-to-visualize-dozens-of-time series-at-once-a983baabb54f

Enabling multiscale exploration

If you have very long time series, you might want to find interesting temporal patterns that may be harder to catch than the usual weekly, monthly, or yearly seasonality. Detecting patterns is easier if you can adjust the time scale at which you are looking at your time series and the starting point. A great multiscale visualization is the **Pinus view**, as outlined in this paper: `http://dx.doi.org/10.1109/TVCG.2012.191`.

The approach of the author of this paper makes no assumption about either time scale or the starting points. This makes it easier to identify the underlying dynamics of complex systems.

Behavioral challenges

Every time series encodes multiple underlying behaviors in a sequence of measurements. Is there a trend, a seasonality? Is it a chaotic random walk? Does it sport major shifts in successive segments of time? Depending on the use case, we want to uncover and isolate very specific behaviors while discarding others.

In this section, we are going to review what time series stationarity and level shifts are, how to uncover these phenomena, and how to deal with them.

Stationarity

A given time series is said to be stationary if its statistical mean and variance are constant and its covariance is independent of time when we take a segment of the series and shift it over the time axis.

Some use cases require the usage of parametric methods: such a method considers that the underlying process has a structure that can be described using a small number of parameters. For instance, the **autoregressive integrated moving average** (**ARIMA**) method (detailed later in *Chapter 7, Improving and Scaling Your Forecast Strategy*) is a statistical method used to forecast future values of a time series: as with any parametric method, it assumes that the time series is stationary.

How do you identify if your time series is non-stationary? There are several techniques and statistical tests (such as the **Dickey-Fuller test**). You can also use an **autocorrelation plot**. Autocorrelation measures the similarity between data points of a given time series as a function of the time lag between them.

You can see an example of some autocorrelation plots here:

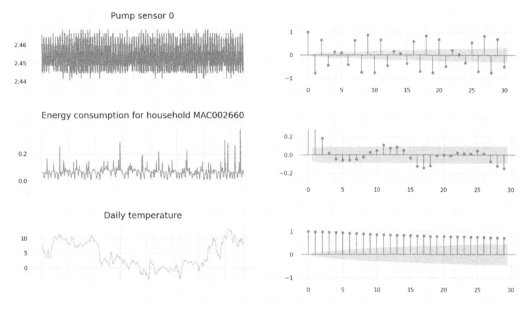

Figure 1.16 – Autocorrelation plots (on the left) for different types of signal

Such a plot can be used to do the following:

- **Detect seasonality**: If the autocorrelation plot has a sinusoidal shape and you can find a period on the plot, this will give you the length of the season. Seasonality is indeed the periodic fluctuation of the values of your time series. This is what can be seen on the second plot in *Figure 1.16* and, to a lesser extent, on the first plot (the pump sensor data).

- **Assess stationarity**: Stationary time series will have an autocorrelation plot that drops quickly to zero (which is the case of the energy consumption time series), while a non-stationary process will see a slow decrease of the same plot (see the daily temperature signal in *Figure 1.16*).

If you have seasonal time series, an **STL procedure** (which stands for **seasonal-trend decomposition based on Loess**) has the ability to split your time series into three underlying components: a seasonal component, a trend component, and the residue (basically, everything else!), as illustrated in the following screenshot:

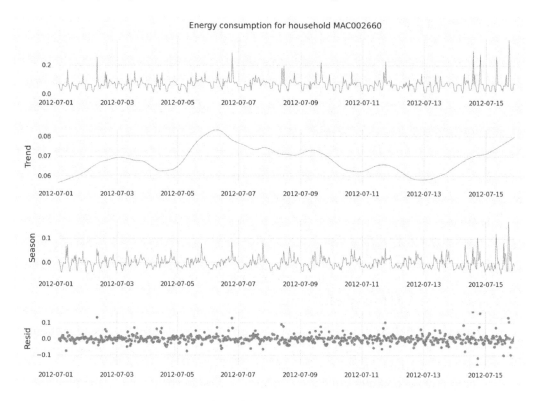

Figure 1.17 – Seasonal trend decomposition of a time series signal

You can then focus your analysis on the component you are interested in: characterizing the trends, identifying the underlying seasonal characteristics, or performing raw analysis on the residue.

If the time series analysis you want to use requires you to make your signals stationary, you will need to do the following:

- **Remove the trend**: To stabilize the mean of a time series and eliminate a trend, one technique that can be used is **differencing**. This simply consists of computing the differences between consecutive data points in the time series. You can also fit a linear regression model on your data and subtract the trend line found from your original data.

- **Remove any seasonal effects**: Differencing can also be applied to seasonal effects. If your time series has a weekly component, removing the value from 1 week before (lag difference of 1 week) will effectively remove this effect from your time series.

Level shifts

A **level shift** is an event that triggers a shift in the statistical distribution of a time series at a given point in time. A time series can see its mean, variance, or correlation suddenly shift. This can happen for both univariate and multivariate datasets and can be linked to an underlying change of the behavior measured by the time series. For instance, an industrial asset can have several operating modes: when the machine switches from one operating mode to another, this can trigger a level shift in the data captured by the sensors that are instrumenting the machine.

Level shifts can have a very negative impact on the ability to forecast time series values or to properly detect anomalies in a dataset. This is one of the key reasons why a model's performance starts to drift suddenly at prediction time.

The `ruptures` Python package offers a comprehensive overview of different change-point-detection algorithms that are useful for spotting and segmenting a time series signal as follows:

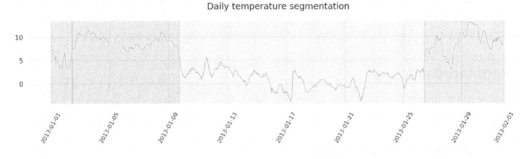

Figure 1.18 – Segments detected on the weather temperature with a binary segmentation approach

It is generally not suitable to try to remove level shifts from a dataset: detecting them properly will help you assemble the best training and testing datasets for your use case. They can also be used to label time series datasets.

Missing insights and context

A key challenge with time series data for most use cases is the missing context: we might need some labels to associate a portion of the time series data with underlying operating modes, activities, or the presence of anomalies or not. You can either use a manual or an automated approach to label your data.

Manual labeling

Your first option will be to manually label your time series. You can build a custom labeling template on **Amazon SageMaker Ground Truth** (https://docs.aws. amazon.com/sagemaker/latest/dg/sms-custom-templates.html) or install an open source package such as the following:

- **Label Studio** (https://labelstud.io): This open source project hit the 1.0 release in May 2021 and is a general-purpose labeling environment that happens to include time series annotation capabilities. It can natively connect to datasets stored in **Amazon S3**.

- **TRAINSET** (https://github.com/geocene/trainset): This is a very lightweight labeling tool exclusively dedicated to time series data.

- **Grafana** (https://grafana.com/docs/grafana/latest/dashboards/ annotations): Grafana comes with a native annotation tool available directly from the graph panel or through their **hyper text transfer protocol** (**HTTP**) **application programming interface** (**API**).

- **Curve** (https://github.com/baidu/Curve): Currently archived at the time of writing this book.

Providing reliable labels on time series data generally requires significant effort from **subject-matter experts** (**SMEs**) who may not have enough availability to perform this task. Automating your labeling process could then be an option to investigate.

Automated labeling

Your second option is to perform automatic labeling of your datasets. This can be achieved in different ways depending on your use cases. You could do one of the following:

- You can use change-point-detection algorithms to detect different activities, modes, or operating ranges. The ruptures Python package is a great starting point to explore the change-point-detection algorithms.

- You can also leverage unsupervised anomaly scoring algorithms such as **scikit-learn Isolation Forest** (sklearn.ensemble.IsolationForest), the **Random Cut Forest** built-in algorithm from **Amazon SageMaker** (https://docs.aws. amazon.com/sagemaker/latest/dg/randomcutforest.html), or build a custom **deep learning** (**DL**) neural network based on an autoencoder architecture.

- You can also transform your time series (see the different analysis approaches in the next section): tabular, symbolic, or imaging techniques will then let you cluster your time series and identify potential labels of interest.

Depending on the dynamics and complexity of your data, automated labeling can actually require additional verification to validate the quality of the generated labels. Automated labeling can be used to kick-start a manual labeling process with prelabelled data to be confirmed by a human operator.

Selecting an analysis approach

By now, we have met the different families of time series-related datasets, and we have listed key potential challenges you may encounter when processing them. In this section, we will describe the different approaches we can take to analyze time series data.

Using raw time series data

Of course, the first and main way to perform time series analysis is to use the raw time sequences themselves, without any drastic transformation. The main benefit of this approach is the limited amount of preprocessing work you have to perform on your time series datasets before starting your actual analysis.

What can we do with these raw time series? We can leverage *Amazon SageMaker* and leverage the following built-in algorithms:

- **Random Cut Forest**: This algorithm is a robust cousin from the **scikit-learn Isolation Forest algorithm** and can compute an anomaly score for each of your data points. It considers each time series as a univariate one and cannot learn any relationship or global behavior from multiple or multivariate time series.

- **DeepAR**: This probabilistic forecasting algorithm is a great fit if you have hundreds of different time series that you can leverage to predict their future values. Not only does this algorithm provide you with point prediction (several single values over a certain forecast horizon), but it can also predict different quantiles, making it easier to answer questions such as: *Given a confidence level of 80% (for instance), what boundary values will my time series take in the near future?*

In addition to these built-in algorithms, you can of course bring your favorite packages to Amazon SageMaker to perform various tasks such as forecasting (by bringing in `Prophet` and `NeuralProphet` libraries) or change-point detection (with the `ruptures` Python package, for instance).

The following three AWS services we dedicate a part to in this book also assume that you will provide raw time series datasets as inputs:

- **Amazon Forecast**: To perform time series forecasting

- **Amazon Lookout for Equipment**: To deliver anomalous event forewarning usable to improve predictive maintenance practices

- **Amazon Lookout for Metrics**: To detect anomalies and help in **root-cause analysis (RCA)**

Other open source packages and AWS services can process transformed time series datasets. Let's now have a look at the different transformations you can apply to your time series.

Summarizing time series into tabular datasets

The first class of transformation you can apply to a time series dataset is to compact it by replacing each time series with some metrics that characterize it. You can do this manually by taking the mean and median of your time series or computing standard deviation. The key objective in this approach is to simplify the analysis of a time series by transforming a series of data points into one or several metrics. Once summarized, your insights can be used to support your EDA or build classification pipelines when new incoming time series sequences are available.

You can perform this summarization manually if you know which features you would like to engineer, or you can leverage Python packages such as the following:

- `tsfresh`: (`http://tsfresh.com`)

- `hctsa`: (`https://github.com/benfulcher/hctsa`)

- `featuretools`: (`https://www.featuretools.com`)

- `Cesium`: (`http://cesium-ml.org`)

- `FATS`: (`http://isadoranun.github.io/tsfeat`)

These libraries can take multiple time series as input and compute hundreds, if not thousands, of features for each of them. Once you have a traditional tabular dataset, you can apply the usual ML techniques to perform dimension reduction, uncover feature importance, or run classification and clustering techniques.

By using Amazon SageMaker, you can access well-known algorithms that have been adapted to benefit from the scalability offered by the cloud. In some cases, they have been rewritten from scratch to enable linear scalability that makes them practical on huge datasets! Here are some of them:

- **Principal Component Analysis** (**PCA**): This algorithm can be used to perform dimensionality reductions on the obtained dataset (`https://docs.aws.amazon.com/sagemaker/latest/dg/pca.html`).

- **K-Means**: This is an unsupervised algorithm where each row will correspond to a single time series and each computed attribute will be used to compute a similarity between the time series (`https://docs.aws.amazon.com/sagemaker/latest/dg/k-means.html`).

- **K-Nearest Neighbors** (**KNN**): This is another algorithm that benefits from a scalable implementation. Once your time series has been transformed into a tabular dataset, you can frame your problem either as a classification or a regression problem and leverage KNN (`https://docs.aws.amazon.com/sagemaker/latest/dg/k-nearest-neighbors.html`).

- **XGBoost**: This is the Swiss Army knife of many data scientists and is a well-known algorithm to perform supervised classification and regression on tabular datasets (`https://docs.aws.amazon.com/sagemaker/latest/dg/xgboost.html`).

You can also leverage Amazon SageMaker and bring your custom preprocessing and modeling approaches if the built-in algorithms do not fit your purpose. Interesting approaches could be more generalizable dimension reduction techniques (such as **Uniform Manifold Approximation and Projection** (**UMAP**) or **t-distributed stochastic neighbor embedding** (**t-SNE**) and other clustering techniques such as **Hierarchical Density-Based Spatial Clustering of Applications with Noise** (**HDBSCAN**)). Once you have a tabular dataset, you can also apply and neural network-based approaches for both classification and regression.

Using imaging techniques

A time series can also be transformed into an image: this allows you to leverage the very rich field of computer vision approaches and architectures. You can leverage the `pyts` Python package to apply the transformation described in this chapter (`https://pyts.readthedocs.io`) and, more particularly, the `pyts.image` submodule.

Once your time series is transformed into an image, you can leverage many techniques to learn about it, such as the following:

- Use **convolutional neural networks** (**CNN**) architectures to learn valuable features and build such custom models on Amazon SageMaker or use its built-in **image classification** algorithm.

- Leverage **Amazon Rekognition Custom Labels** to rapidly build models that can rapidly classify different behaviors that would be highlighted by the image transformation process.

- Use **Amazon Lookout for Vision** to perform anomaly detection and classify which images are representative of an underlying issue captured in the time series.

Let's now have a look at the different transformations we can apply to our time series and what they can let you capture about their underlying dynamics. We will deep dive into the following:

- **Recurrence plots**
- **Gramian angular fields**
- **Markov transition fields** (**MTF**)
- **Network graphs**

Recurrence plots

A recurrence is a time at which a time series returns back to a value it has visited before. A recurrence plot illustrates the collection of pairs of timestamps at which the time series is at the same place—that is, the same value. Each point can take a binary value of 0 or 1. A recurrence plot helps in understanding the dynamics of a time series and such recurrence is closely related to dynamic non-linear systems. An example of recurrence plots being used can be seen here:

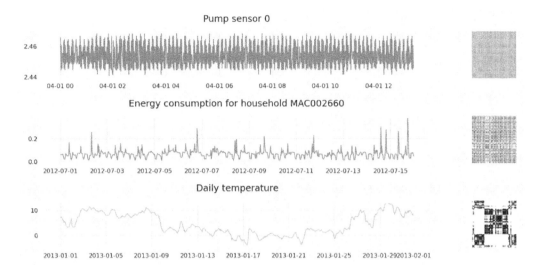

Figure 1.19 – Spotting time series dynamics with recurrence plots

A recurrence plot can be extended to multivariate datasets by taking the Hadamard product of each plot (matrix multiplication term by term).

Gramian angular fields

This representation is built upon the Gram matrix of an encoded time series. The detailed process would need you to scale your time series, convert it to polar coordinates (to keep the temporal dependency), and then you would compute the Gram matrix of the different time intervals.

Each cell of a Gram matrix is the pairwise dot-products of every pair of values in the encoded time series. In the following example, these are the different values of the scaled time series T:

$$X = \{x_1, \dots, x_n\}$$

In this case, the same time series encoded in polar coordinates will take each value and compute its angular cosine, as follows:

$$\tilde{X} = \{\varphi_1 = \arccos(x_1), \dots, \varphi_n = \arccos(x_n)\}$$

Then, the Gram matrix is computed as follows:

$$G = \begin{bmatrix} cos(\varphi_1 + \varphi_1) & cos(\varphi_1 + \varphi_2) & \cdots & cos(\varphi_1 + \varphi_n) \\ cos(\varphi_2 + \varphi_1) & cos(\varphi_2 + \varphi_2) & \cdots & cos(\varphi_2 + \varphi_n) \\ \vdots & \vdots & \ddots & \vdots \\ cos(\varphi_n + \varphi_1) & cos(\varphi_n + \varphi_2) & \cdots & cos(\varphi_n + \varphi_n) \end{bmatrix}$$

Let's plot the Gramian angular fields of the same three time series as before, as follows:

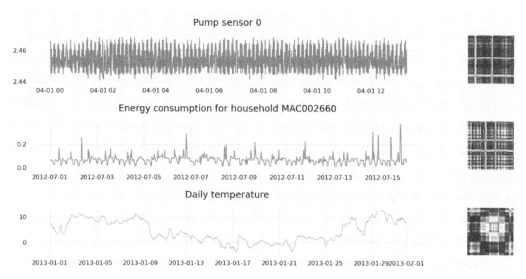

Figure 1.20 – Capturing period with Gramian angular fields

Compared to the previous representation (the recurrence plot), the Gramian angular fields are less prone to generate white noise for heavily period signals (such as the pump signal below). Moreover, each point takes a real value and is not limited to 0 and 1 (hence the colored pictures instead of the grayscale ones that recurrence plots can produce).

MTF

MTF is a visualization technique to highlight the behavior of time series. To build an MTF, you can use the `pyts.image` module. Under the hood, this is the transformation that is applied to your time series:

- Discretization of the time series along with the different values it can take.

- Build a Markov transition matrix.

- Compute the transition probabilities from one timestamp to all the others.

- Reorganize the transition probabilities into an MTF.

- Compute an aggregated MTF.

The following screenshot shows the MTF of the same three time series as before:

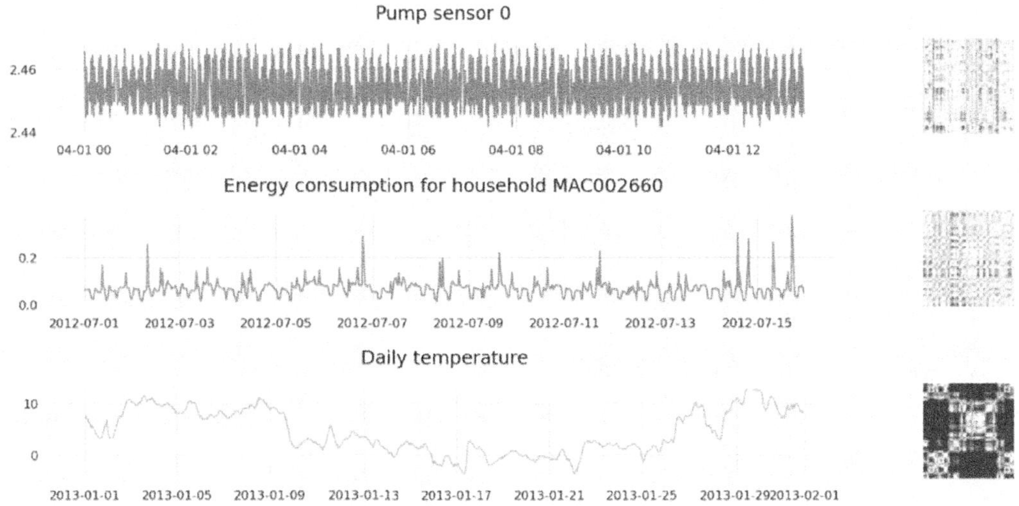

Figure 1.21 – Uncovering time series behavior with MTF

If you're interested in what insights this representation can bring you, feel free to dive deeper into it by walking through this GitHub repository: https://github. com/michaelhoarau/mtf-deep-dive. You can also read about this in detail in the following article: https://towardsdatascience.com/advanced- visualization-techniques-for-time series-analysis-14eeb17ec4b0

Modularity network graphs

From an MTF (see the previous section), we can generate a graph $G = (V, E)$: we have a direct mapping between vertex V and the time index i. From there, there are two possible encodings of interest: flow encoding or modularity encoding. These are described in more detail here:

- **Flow encoding**: This representation helps us observe where the big information flow occurs.

  We map the flow of time to the vertex, using a color gradient from $T0$ to TN to color each node of the network graph.

  We use the MTF weight to color the edges between the vertices.

- **Modularity encoding**: Modularity is an important pattern in network analysis to identify specific local structures. This is the encoding that I find most useful in time series analysis.

We map the module label (with the community ID) to each vertex with a specific color attached to each community.

We map the size of the vertices to a clustering coefficient.

We map the edge color to the module label of the target vertex.

To build a network graph from the MTF, you can use the `tsia` Python package. You can check the deep dive available as a Jupyter notebook in this GitHub repository: `https://github.com/michaelhoarau/mtf-deep-dive`.

A network graph is built from an MTF following this process:

- We compute the MTF for the time series.

- We build a network graph by taking this time series as an entry.

- We compute the partitions and modularity and encode these pieces of information into a network graph representation.

Once again, let's take the three time series previously processed and build their associated network graphs, as follows:

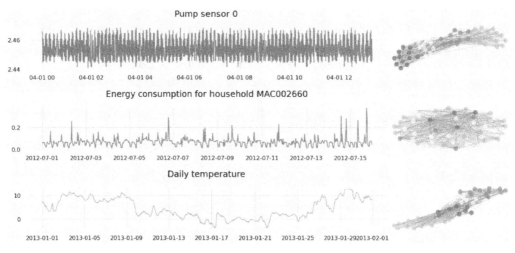

Figure 1.22 – Using network graphs to understand the structure of the time series

There are many features you can engineer once you have a network graph. You can use these features to build a numerical representation of the time series (an embedding). The characteristics you can derive from a network graph include the following:

- Diameter

- Average degree and average weighted degree

- Density

- Average path length

- Average clustering coefficient

- Modularity

- Number of partitions

All these parameters can be derived thanks to the `networkx` and `python-louvain` modules.

Symbolic transformations

Time series can also be discretized into sequences of text: this is a symbolic approach as we transform the original real values into symbolic strings. Once your time series are successfully represented into such a sequence of symbols (which can act as an embedding of your sequence), you can leverage many techniques to extract insights from them, including the following:

- You can use embedding for indexing use cases: given the embedding of a query time series, you can measure some distance to the collection of embeddings present in a database and return the closest matching one.

- Symbolic approaches transform real-value sequences of data into discrete data, which opens up the field of possible techniques—for instance, using suffix trees and Markov chains to detect novel or anomalous behavior, making it a relevant technique for anomaly detection use cases.

- Transformers and self-attention have triggered tremendous progress in **natural language processing** (**NLP**). As time series and natural languages are sometimes considered close due to their sequential nature, we are seeing a more and more mature implementation of the transformer architecture for time series classification and forecasting.

You can leverage the `pyts` Python package to apply the transformation described in this chapter (`https://pyts.readthedocs.io`) and Amazon SageMaker to bring the architecture described previously as custom models. Let's now have a look at the different symbolic transformations we can apply to our time series. In this section, we will deep dive into the following:

- **Bag-of-words representations** (**BOW**)

- **Bag of symbolic Fourier approximations** (**BOSS**)

- **Word extraction for time series classification** (**WEASEL**)

BOW representations (BOW and SAX-VSM)

The BOW approach applies a sliding window over a time series and can transform each subsequence into a word using **symbolic aggregate approximation (SAX)**. SAX reduces a time series into a string of arbitrary lengths. It's a two-step process that starts with a dimensionality reduction via **piecewise aggregate approximation (PAA)** and then a discretization of the obtained simplified time series into SAX symbols. You can leverage the `pyts.bag_of_words.BagOfWords` module to build the following representation:

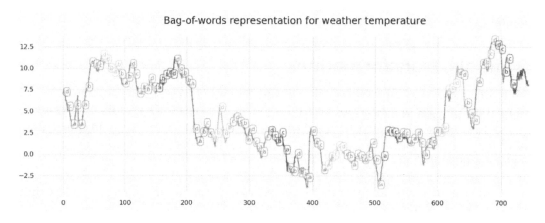

Figure 1.23 – Example of SAX to transform a time series

The BOW approach can be modified to leverage **term frequency-inverse document frequency (TF-IDF)** statistics. TF-IDF is a statistic that reflects how important a given word is in a corpus. SAX-VSM (**SAX in vector space model**) uses this statistic to link it to the number of times a symbol appears in a time series. You can leverage the `pyts.classification.SAXVSM` module to build this representation.

Bag of SFA Symbols (BOSS and BOSS VS)

The BOSS representation uses the structure-based representation of the BOW method but replaces PAA/SAX with a **symbolic Fourier approximation (SFA)**. It is also possible to build upon the BOSS model and combine it with the TF-IDF model. As in the case of SAX-VSM, BOSS VS uses this statistic to link it to the number of times a symbol appears in a time series. You can leverage the `pyts.classification.BOSSVS` module to build this representation.

Word extraction for time series classification (WEASEL and WEASEL-MUSE)

The WEASEL approach builds upon the same kind of bag-of-pattern models as BOW and BOSS described just before. More precisely, it uses SFA (like the BOSS method). The windowing step is more flexible as it extracts them at multiple lengths (to account for patterns with different lengths) and also considers their local order instead of considering each window independently (by assembling bigrams, successive words, as features).

WEASEL generates richer feature sets than the other methods, which can lead to reduced signal-to-noise and high-loss information. To mitigate this, WEASEL starts by applying Fourier transforms on each window and uses an **analysis of variance** (**ANOVA**) f-test and information gain binning to choose the most discriminate Fourier coefficients. At the end of the representation generation pipeline, WEASEL also applies a Chi-Squared test to filter out less relevant words generated by the bag-of-patterns process.

You can leverage the `pyts.transformation.WEASEL` module to build this representation. Let's build the symbolic representations of the different time series of the heartbeats time series. We will keep the same color code (red for ischemia and blue for normal). The output can be seen here:

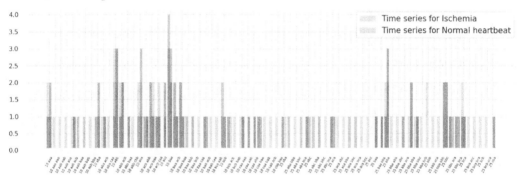

Figure 1.24 – WEASEL symbolic representation of heartbeats

The WEASEL representation is suited to univariate time series but can be extended to multivariate ones by using the **WEASEL+MUSE** algorithm (**MUSE** stands for **Multivariate Unsupervised Symbols and dErivatives**). You can leverage the `pyts.multivariate.transformation.WEASELMUSE` module to build this representation.

This section comes now to an end, and you should now have a hint on how rich time series analysis methodologies can be. With that in mind, we will now see how we can apply this fresh knowledge to solve different time series-based use cases.

Typical time series use cases

Until this point, we have exposed many different considerations about the types, challenges, and analysis approaches you have to deal with when it comes to processing time series data. But what can we do with time series? What kind of insights can we derive from them? Recognizing the purpose of your analysis is a critical step in designing an appropriate approach for your data preparation activities or understanding how the insights derived from your analysis can be used by your end users. For instance, removing outliers from a time series can improve a forecasting analysis but makes any anomaly detection approach a moot point.

Typical use cases where time series datasets play an important—if not the most important role—can be any of these:

- **Forecasting**
- **Anomaly detection**
- **Event forewarning** (anomaly prediction)
- **Virtual sensors**
- **Activity detection** (pattern analysis)
- **Predictive quality**
- **Setpoint optimization**

In the next three parts of this book, we are going to focus on forecasting (with Amazon Forecast), anomaly detection (with Amazon Lookout for Metrics), and multivariate event forewarning (using Amazon Lookout for Equipment to output detected anomalies that can then be analyzed over time to build anomaly forewarning notifications).

The remainder of this chapter will be dedicated to an overview of what else you can achieve using time series data. Although you can combine the AWS services exposed in this book to achieve part of what is necessary to solve these problems, a good rule of thumb is to consider that it won't be straightforward, and other approaches may yield a faster time to gain insights.

Virtual sensors

Also called **soft sensors**, this type of model is used to infer the calculation of a physical measurement with an ML model. Some harsh environments may not be suitable to install actual physical sensors. In other cases, there are no reliable physical sensors to measure the physical characteristics you are interested in (or a physical sensor does not exist altogether). Last but not least, sometimes you need a real-time measurement to manage your process but can only get one daily measure.

A virtual sensor uses a multivariate time series (all the other sensors available) to yield current or predicted values for the measurement you cannot get directly, at a useful granularity.

On AWS, you can do the following:

- Build a custom model with the *DeepAR* built-in algorithm from Amazon SageMaker (https://docs.aws.amazon.com/sagemaker/latest/dg/deepar.html)

- Leverage the DeepAR architecture or the DeepVAR one (a multivariate variant of DeepAR) from the GluonTS library (http://ts.gluon.ai), a library open sourced and maintained by AWS

Activity detection

When you have segments of univariate or multivariate time series, you may want to perform some pattern analysis to derive the exact actions that led to them. This can be useful to perform human activity recognition based on accelerometer data as captured by your phone (sports mobile applications automatically able to tell if you're cycling, walking, or running) or to understand your intent by analyzing brainwave data.

Many DL architectures can tackle this motif discovery task (long short-term memory (**LSTM**), CNN, or a combination of both): alternative approaches let you transform your time series into tabular data or images to apply clustering and classification techniques. All of these can be built as custom models on Amazon SageMaker or by using some of the built-in scalable algorithms available in this service, such as the following:

- PCA: https://docs.aws.amazon.com/sagemaker/latest/dg/pca.html

- XGBoost

- Image classification

If you choose to transform your time series into images, you can also leverage Amazon Rekognition Custom Labels for classification or Amazon Lookout for Vision to perform anomaly detection.

Once you have an existing database of activities, you can also leverage an indexing approach: in this case, building a symbolic representation of your time series will allow you to use it as an embedding to query similar time series in a database, or even past segments of the same time series if you want to discover potential recurring motifs.

Predictive quality

Imagine that you have a process that ends up with a product or service with a quality that can vary depending on how well the process was executed. This is typically what can happen on a manufacturing production line where equipment sensors, process data, and other tabular characteristics can be measured and matched to the actual quality of the finished goods.

You can then use all these time series to build a predictive model that tries to predict if the current batch of products will achieve the appropriate quality grade or if it will have to be reworked or thrown away as waste.

Recurring neural networks (**RNNs**) are traditionally what is built to address this use case. Depending on how you shape your available dataset, you might however be able to use either Amazon Forecast (using the predicted quality or grade of the product as the main time series to predict and all the other available data as related time series) or Amazon Lookout for Equipment (by considering bad product quality as anomalies for which you want to get as much forewarning as possible).

Setpoint optimization

In process industries (industries that transform raw materials into finished goods such as shampoo, an aluminum coil, or a piece of furniture), setpoints are the target value of a process variable. Imagine that you need to keep the temperature of a fluid at 50°C; then, your setpoint is 50°C. The actual value measured by the process might be different and the objective of process control systems is to ensure that the process value reaches and stays at the desired setpoint.

In such a situation, you can leverage the time series data of your process to optimize an outcome: for instance, the quantity of waste generated, the energy or water used, or the change to generate a higher grade of product from a quality standpoint (see the previous predictive quality use case for more details). Based on the desired outcome, you can then use an ML approach to recommend setpoints that will ensure you reach your objectives.

Potential approaches to tackle this delicate optimization problem include the following:

- **Partial least squares** (**PLS**) and **Sparse PLS**
- DL-based **model predictive control** (**MPC**), which combines neural-network-based controllers and RNNs to replicate the dynamic behavior of an MPC.
- RL with fault-tolerant control through **quality learning** (**Q-learning**)

The output expected for such models is the setpoint value for each parameter that controls the process. All these approaches can be built as custom models on Amazon SageMaker (which also provides an RL toolkit and environment in case you want to leverage Q-learning to solve this use case).

Summary

Although every time series looks alike (a tabular dataset indexed by time), choosing the right tools and approaches to frame a time series problem is critical to successfully leverage ML to uncover business insights.

After reading this chapter, you understand how time series can vastly differ from one another and you should have a good command of the families of preprocessing, transformation, and analysis techniques that can help derive insights from time series datasets. You also have an overview of the different AWS services and open source packages you can leverage to help you in your endeavor. After reading this chapter, you can now recognize how rich this domain is and the numerous options you have to process and analyze your time series data.

In the next three parts of this book, we are going to abstract away most of these choices and options by leveraging managed services that will do most of the heavy lifting for you. However, it is key to have a good command of these concepts to develop the right understanding of what is going on under the hood. This will also help you make the right choices whenever you have to tackle a new use case.

We will start with the most popular time series problem we want to solve with time series forecasting, with Amazon Forecast.

2
An Overview of Amazon Forecast

Time series forecasting is a very popular and widely used technique to deliver insights to a large variety of business stakeholders. Although the values predicted by a forecast can be used as they are (this is, for instance, what you do when you use spreadsheet formulas to feed financial planning practices and predict a **business unit's** (**BU's**) results to inform the appropriate business development decisions), they are usually a means to an end: forecasting then becomes an essential cog that feeds other models or business processes (forecasting product demand to optimize the production of manufactured goods).

Time series forecasting was around before **machine learning** (**ML**) and **artificial intelligence** (**AI**) became so pervasive. In this book, you are going to leverage several services built thanks to ML: these technologies are usually at their best when a massive amount of data is available or when the relationships between this data become impossible to tackle with a mere spreadsheet. When a retailer is building a demand forecast as part of their supply chain planning, the number of **stock-keeping units** (**SKUs**) and location combinations is often in the millions, making it valuable to leverage the latest AI technologies.

Amazon Forecast is the first **Amazon Web Services** (**AWS**)-managed service that we will explore in detail in this book. By the end of this chapter, you will understand how to frame a forecasting problem that is suitable for Amazon Forecast and will be ready to dive into the next chapters of of this book to develop a sound understanding of the key steps necessary to build your first forecast.

In this chapter, we're going to cover the following main topics:

- What kinds of problems can we solve with forecasting?
- What is Amazon Forecast?
- How does Amazon Forecast work?
- Choosing the right applications

Technical requirements

No hands-on experience of a language such as **Python** or **R** is necessary to follow along with the content from this chapter. However, we highly recommend that you follow along in the **AWS console**, from where you can access the Amazon Forecast service.

If you already have an AWS account, you can connect to the AWS console, click on the search bar at the top, and enter `Forecast`. In the **Services** section, click on **Amazon Forecast** to bring up the landing page of the service console.

If you don't have an AWS account, you will need to create one before you can log in to your console. To create an AWS account, proceed as follows:

1. Open `https://portal.aws.amazon.com/billing/signup` and follow the online instructions. You will receive a phone call to obtain a verification code for signing up.

2. Create an **Identity and Access Management** (**IAM**) administrator user: when you create an AWS account, you get a root user account that gives you complete access to all of the AWS resources in your account. It is strongly recommended to adhere to the best practice of creating individual IAM users. To create such a secure user, see the *Creating your first IAM admin user and user group* section of the IAM service documentation, at `https://docs.aws.amazon.com/IAM/latest/UserGuide/getting-started_create-admin-group.html`.

You are now ready to use Amazon Forecast!

What kinds of problems can we solve with forecasting?

Forecasting is the science of predicting the future values of a time series as accurately as possible, given all the available information (including historical values of the very time series of interest, other related time series, and knowledge of any events that can impact your forecast). After reading the previous chapter, you might understand why it can also be considered an art!

Forecasting is a regular task required by many activities: most of the time, a forecast is a means to an end and not an actual objective in itself—except for financial planning, as mentioned in the introduction, although you could argue that financial planning is also a means to ensure good business decision-making. Here are a few examples of situations where you can leverage forecasting to achieve better business outcomes:

- Forecasting future demand for a product *to decide how much a plant will have to manufacture and by when*. Failing to predict high demand in a given region can cause missed revenue opportunities while manufacturing too much of a product in another region will generate more inventory and increase the capital cost.

- Forecasting the sale of thousands of items in hundreds of stores *so that a retailer will know how much inventory to stock* in stores or warehouses to serve local clients or reduce delivery delays and costs.

- Predicting the electricity demand for households at an hourly level so that energy providers can *make the cheapest electricity trading decision while maintaining the balance of the electricity grid.*

- *Improve workforce planning* by predicting transactional quantities (rendezvous at bank tellers; customer traffic at supermarket checkouts…).

- Predicting replacement parts' demand so that planners can *pre-order parts ahead of time*, as part of predictive maintenance planning.

- Provide equipment failure probability, with a confidence level, based on sensor data installed on subsystems of the industrial equipment. Linked to replacement parts' prediction, the outcome of this forecast helps plant managers *optimize their inventory, limiting the impact of reactive maintenance and reinforcing their predictive maintenance practice.*

- Predict a company website's traffic to *scale the underlying infrastructure* and predict the associated cost of serving content to its audience.

- Predict memory, **central processing unit (CPU)**, **input/output (I/O)** throughput, storage, and other operational loads so that cloud services such as **Amazon Redshift** (for hosting data warehouses) or **Amazon DynamoDB** (NoSQL database) can *provision and scale their underlying infrastructures.*

In a nutshell, the outputs of any forecasting activities are critical to ensure any operations continue to run smoothly or to take the appropriate actions. Some activities are easy to forecast, while others are just plain random walks (new values taking a random value with seemingly no link to previous ones, such as stock prices' evolution). When deciding to forecast a time series, you should assess whether the following apply:

- **You have enough data available**: The amount of data necessary to achieve a good forecast will depend both on the type of algorithm you leverage and on the underlying dynamic of your time series.

- **You understand the contributing factors**: This is how much you understand the underlying factors that impact how a time series evolves.

When using predictions in a real-life system, you should also assess *how likely it is that the results of your forecasts will impact the behavior of its environment.* Let's take a few examples, as follows:

- If an energy provider predicts the energy consumption for a city, this will likely have no impact on the actual electricity consumption of the said city.

- On the other hand, if you provide individual electricity consumption predictions to all households of the same city for the days to come, they might adjust their behavior to reduce their consumption (for example, turning down the heating to waste less energy and save money). This will make your energy prediction forecast less good, but you will have achieved your business objective to reduce the energy consumption of the local population.

- As a major financial institution, if you provide advice on stock market investment to your customers, you will influence this market and have an effect on the stock price quantitative analysis another department may be trying to forecast.

In other words, *understanding how much your forecasts can become self-fulfilling prophecies* is key to ensuring the overall dynamic stability of your predictions and the environment they are part of. In addition, understanding this helps you explain what degraded performance looks like for a forecasting model. At the early stages, providing forecasts to end users could be performed using an **A/B testing** approach (for example, sending an energy forecast to part of the city over a period of time): this will allow you to measure the impact your forecasts can have on the overall dynamic system and build better performance metrics.

Now that you understand the types of problems forecasting can solve, let's take some time to properly frame a given forecasting problem.

Framing your forecasting problem

As hinted in *Chapter 1, An Overview of Time Series Analysis*, there are many ways to frame a problem dealing with time series data, and forecasting is only one type of these problems. As its name suggests, Amazon Forecast is suitable for solving **forecasting problems**: problems where you want to know *what will happen, when it will happen,* and—possibly—*why it happened.*

Time series can be found in many areas and situations, and it is easy to find forecasting problems everywhere. In ML, forecasting is one of the most challenging problems to solve (after all, we are trying to predict the future!), and deciding to go down that path may prove difficult—if not impossible—depending on the actual forecasting predictive power the available data contains. Let's take two examples where forecasting is not the best path to take, as follows:

- You own a video-on-demand service, and based on past views and collected interests from your users, you would like to predict what they will likely watch next. You could structure your data to try to forecast the next views so that you can expose these shows on a personalized home page for your users. Although this approach can be rich (it does take the time dimension into consideration), it is very hard to solve efficiently as your time series will be very sparse (a few data points for each user every day at most). *This kind of problem is better solved with a recommendation engine* (check out **Amazon Personalize** for more details on how you could build a recommendation engine, for instance).

- You are operating a shampoo production plant and you want to predict the quality of any given batch in production. On your manufacturing line, you collect the product recipe, the characteristics of the raw material that are part of the chemical formulation, and the process parameters you apply with the setpoints you configure on each piece of equipment of the product line. You could use all these time series to try to predict the quality of a given batch; however, the underlying assumption is that the predictive power contained in the time series and tabular data collected is high enough to predict the appearance of the defects you are looking for.

These defects might come from the environmental conditions (hygrometry of the factory; external temperature; rainfall; raw material supplier; bad programming sequence entered by an operator). *This kind of problem might be better framed as an anomaly detection problem*: in this case, a service such as **Amazon Lookout for Equipment** (which will be our focus in *Part 3, Detecting Abnormal Behavior in Multivariate Time Series with Amazon Lookout for Equipment*, of this book) might be better suited to provide the insights you are looking for.

After deciding that *forecasting is indeed what you want to leverage to solve your problem*, there are several questions you need to address in the early stages of your forecasting project, as follows:

- What would you like to forecast?

- What is the frequency of the available data (hourly, daily, monthly…)?

- What is the desired forecast horizon?

- How frequently do you need to forecast?

- What is the expected output of the forecasting exercise?

- How will you evaluate the accuracy of your forecasts?

- How will the forecast outputs be used further down the road?

Moreover, a key task is obviously to collect, assemble, and prepare the historical data needed to build your forecasting model. You will also need to identify whether related data known at the same time can lend some statistical power to your model to improve your forecast accuracy; as time series forecasting practitioners, you might have used approaches such as Granger predictive causality tests to validate whether a given time series can be used to forecast another one.

Collecting and preparing this related data will be an additional step before you can build your model. You might also need to collect and prepare non-time-related relationships between your time series (such as hierarchies, where some locations are in the same region, or some items are in the same product groups, or some items share the same color).

The following screenshot summarizes the forecasting problem scope:

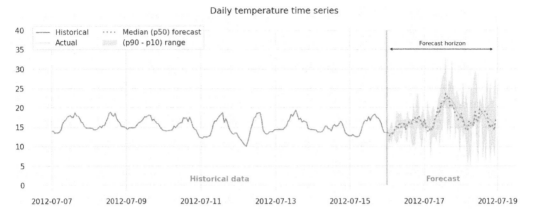

Figure 2.1 – Time series forecasting components

Let's dive into several of the key areas of this screenshot, as follows:

- **Historical data**: The historical data is the part of your time series that will be used to train a forecasting model. In *Figure 2.1*, this is the regular line plot located on the left of the graph.

- **Historical data frequency**: Your historical time series data can be available at a regular or irregular sampling rate. If your raw data is not regularly sampled or if its frequency is different from the forecast granularity, you may have to aggregate your data at the desired unit. In retail, each product sale is recorded when it happens, but not every product is sold every day, leading to a sparse time series with spikes that correspond to days when a sale has happened. Aggregated sales for each product at a weekly or monthly level will smooth out the original signal.

- **Forecast horizon**: This is the prediction length you can expect for a forecast. This is usually measured in the number of time steps using the desired unit, which might be different from the original time series. If you expect daily data as a result of your forecast and need predictions for the coming week, your sampling unit will be at the daily level and your forecast horizon will be 7 days.

- **Expected output**: You can request a point-in-time forecast. In the plot shown in *Figure 2.1*, this is the dotted line located in the forecast horizon and it helps answer this type of question: *What will the value of the time series be by tomorrow?* A forecast can also emit a value for several time steps at once. This helps answer questions such as: *Which value will the time series take for every day of the coming week?* Your forecast may also be consumed by organizations or systems that expect a range of possible values; in this case, you will replace the point values with probabilistic forecasts that emit a range of possible values at each predicted time step (in the previous plot, this is represented by the area plot around the median forecast denoted by a dotted line, delimited by the lower bound and upper bound of the requested quantiles—p10 and p90 in this case).

You now know how to frame a good forecasting problem, so let's apply this fresh knowledge to Amazon Forecast!

What is Amazon Forecast?

Amazon Forecast is one of the AI-/ML-managed services available on the AWS cloud platform. Flexible and accurate forecasts are key in many business areas to predict demand and ensure inventory or raw material are stocked accordingly or predict wait times and ensure your counters are staffed accordingly. While all organizations use some form of forecasting process today, traditional methods cannot leverage the increasing quantity and complexity of time series signals available to us.

Managed services are services where the end users only bring their data and configure some parameters to suit their needs. All other tasks, *considered as undifferentiated heavy lifting*, are performed on the users' behalf by the service. This includes the automation of all the infrastructure management: as an Amazon Forecast user, you don't have to provision and manage **virtual machines** (**VMs**), configure user accounts, manage security, plan for scalability if your request volume increases, decommission unused resources, and so on.

In the case of **AI-/ML-managed services**, some *data preparation, ingestion tasks, and model management activities are also performed under the hood*, allowing you to focus primarily on the problem to solve. Amazon Forecast is a scalable managed service that automates the whole **end-to-end** (**E2E**) forecasting pipeline, from data ingestion to model deployment and serving forecasts. The service also deals with data preparation under the hood. Amazon Forecast can do the following:

- Fill missing values in your datasets while letting you customize the parameters to use to replace them.

- Prepare the time series so that it can be ingested by multiple algorithms—Amazon Forecast can prepare time series sequences to feed **deep learning** (**DL**) models or generate multiple random sequences to output probabilistic forecasts for proprietary algorithms such as **non-parametric time series** (**NPTS**).

- Pick the best algorithms depending on your datasets—Amazon Forecast can use AutoML to automatically choose between statistical forecasting algorithms (such as **AutoRegressive Integrated Moving Average** (**ARIMA**), **Exponential Smoothing** (**ETS**), NPTS, or Prophet) and more advanced data-hungry neural network-based architectures (such as DeepAR+ or **Convolutional Neural Network-Quantile Regression** (**CNN-QR**) **deep neural networks** (**DNNs**)). You will have an overview of the different algorithms used by Amazon Forecast, along with the advantages and disadvantages of using each of them, in *Chapter 5, Customizing Your Predictor Training*.

- Segment your data and automatically apply the best ensemble of algorithms for each segment.

- Provide confidence intervals thanks to probabilistic forecast generation—traditional algorithms only output point forecasts (usually the mean value) with a confidence interval, relying on strong assumptions about the data distribution.

- Provide explainability scores to help you understand which factors influence the forecast of specific items and for which time duration.

- Manage multiple local statistical models for each of your time series—using ARIMA, ETS, NPTS, or Prophet to train on 100 time series means that you would have to manage 100 models on your own. Amazon Forecast transparently manages all these models for you and lets you easily export all forecasts at once as a single **comma-separated values** (**CSV**) file after inference as if it were just one model.

- Perform model evaluation on multiple time windows and provide evaluation results for all your time series data at once in a single CSV file digestible by the usual spreadsheet or **business intelligence** (**BI**) visualization software. Amazon Forecast uses backtesting techniques on your behalf (you will deep dive into this feature and how to customize it to suit your needs in *Chapter 5, Customizing Your Predictor Training*).

- Automatically compute multiple accuracy metrics when evaluating and selecting the best models, including traditional point forecast metrics such as **Weighted Absolute Percentage Error** (**WAPE**) and unbiased error metrics for probabilistic forecasts (namely, **Weighted Quantile Loss** (**wQL**)). You will discover the details behind these accuracy metrics in *Chapter 4, Training a Predictor with AutoML*.

- Perform hyperparameter optimization to find the best parameters to train your models.

- Add built-in features such as public holidays or weather data to improve your forecast accuracy. When relevant, Amazon Forecast also feeds features such as lagged values to capture seasonality in your datasets. For instance, if your samples are taken at an hourly frequency, Amazon Forecast will feed values from the last 1, 2, and 3 days to algorithms such as DeepAR+ that can benefit from these additional insights to build more accurate models.

Based on the same technology used at *Amazon.com*, Amazon Forecast drills down the extensive experience Amazon has on forecasting techniques to make it available to every developer and data scientist. It's a fully managed service that uses statistical and DL-based algorithms to deliver accurate time series forecasts. Although an ML practitioner or a data scientist will be able to leverage their skills to improve the service results and make the best of it, Amazon Forecast does not require any ML experience to deliver future time series predictions based on your historical data.

Amazon Forecast also includes the latest advances in DL to provide DL algorithms (namely **DeepAR+** and **CNN-QR**) that are able to learn more complex models and serve situations where you might need to build forecasts for millions of time series, address cold start situations, or easily build what-if scenarios. Amazon Forecast is also able to automatically segment your data and build an ensemble of models, increasing forecast accuracy with no additional heavy analysis at your end.

Up to now, you have seen how to frame a forecasting problem and how the Amazon Forecast service can help you solve this. You will now see how Amazon Forecast works, which will give you the keys to successfully apply this service to your business problems.

How does Amazon Forecast work?

To build forecasting models, Amazon Forecast deals with the following concepts and resources:

- **Datasets**: A dataset is a container to host your data. Amazon Forecast algorithms use these datasets to train its models. Each dataset is defined by a schema whereby you can define the columns and their types. Amazon Forecast includes several domains with predefined schemas to help you get started.

- **Dataset groups**: Amazon Forecast algorithms can leverage several datasets to train a model. A dataset group is a container that packages a group of datasets used together to train a forecasting model.

- **Featurization**: The featurization configuration lets you specify parameters to transform the data. This is where you specify a null-value filling strategy to apply to the different variables of your dataset.

- **Algorithms**: Amazon Forecast has access to multiple algorithms including statistical algorithms (ARIMA, ETS, Prophet, and NPTS) and DL algorithms (DeepAR+ and CNN-QR). Algorithm choice can be abstracted away from the user when choosing AutoML at training time while giving the more advanced practitioner the ability to select and configure the algorithm of their choice.

- **Training parameters**: Some algorithms can be further customized by providing specific hyperparameter values. Another common training parameter to all algorithms is the forecast horizon.

- **Recipes**: A recipe is a combination of several ingredients: an algorithm, a featurization configuration, and evaluation parameters

- **Predictors**: This is a trained model. To create a predictor, you provide a dataset group and a forecasting recipe (which includes an algorithm, although you can let Amazon Forecast choose the algorithm on your behalf and work in **AutoML** mode). The **AutoPredictor** feature lets Amazon Forecast build an ensemble of algorithms to better adapt to the different segments your data may enclose.

- **Metrics**: Amazon Forecast uses several accuracy metrics to evaluate the predictors built into the service and help you choose which one to use to generate forecasts that will serve your business purpose. These metrics are evaluated through a backtesting technique that you can configure to split your data between training and testing parts.

- **Forecasts**: You can run inference (that is, generate new predictions) to generate forecasts based on an existing predictor. Amazon Forecast outputs probabilistic forecasts instead of point forecasts of mean values—for instance, Amazon Forecast can tell you if there is a 10% chance that the actual values of your time series are below the values predicted by the model. By default, forecasts will be generated at 10%, 50%, and 90% probabilities, giving you more insights for sound decision-making.

- **Explainability insights**: In ML, explainability allows you to better understand how the different attributes in your dataset impact your predictions. With Amazon Forecast, you can request forecast explainability insights—this feature will be exposed both in a dashboard and as a downloadable report, and will help you understand how the different features of your datasets impact forecast results for individual time series and at which points in time.

Let's now have a look at how these concepts are integrated into an Amazon Forecast typical workflow.

Amazon Forecast workflow overview

Any forecasting process involves two steps, as outlined here:

1. We start by looking backward in the historical data to establish a baseline and uncover trends that may continue in the future.

2. We then use these trends to predict the future values of your time series data.

   As illustrated in the following diagram, Amazon Forecast provides an approach to tackle these two steps:

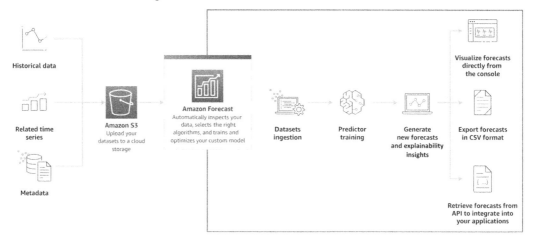

Figure 2.2 – Amazon Forecast overview

Let's dive into this diagram to explain the different steps you will have to go through to use Amazon Forecast, as follows:

- **Uploading and ingesting data** into the service—this will be thoroughly detailed in the next chapter. Amazon Forecast can use data that is located in Amazon **Simple Storage Service (S3)**, a scalable data storage infrastructure used to store any kind of object and dataset. At ingestion time, Amazon Forecast inspects your data and identifies valuable features that will be used at training time.

- **Training a predictor**, as described in *Chapter 4, Training a Predictor with AutoML*. Depending on the performance obtained, you can iterate over the data ingestion and training steps a few times to achieve the desired performance. Under the hood, Amazon Forecast can train multiple models using a variety of algorithms, select the best parameters for each of the models, optimize them, and select the most accurate one.

- Once you have a predictor that you are happy with, you can start **generating new forecasts** that will also be time series (although they may contain only one data point, depending on the prediction length you ask for). When you ask Amazon Forecast to generate a forecast, it will actually deploy and host your model so that you can export all predictions at once.

- If you enable the **AutoPredictor** mode, Amazon Forecast will also allow you to generate explainability insights that you will be able to visualize in the console **user interface** (**UI**). You will also have the opportunity to download a detailed report in CSV format.

A good understanding of the Amazon Forecast workflow would not be complete without a presentation of the key drivers of the pricing model of this service. In the next section, you will match the different steps of this workflow with the different pricing dimensions of Amazon Forecast.

Pricing

As with many AWS services, you only pay for what you use, with no upfront commitment. Although the cost of the service is minimal to build a **proof of concept** (**PoC**)—especially if you can benefit from the Free Tier—there are four dimensions to consider for operationalizing a forecasting pipeline with Amazon Forecast, as outlined here:

- **Storage**: The data is ingested and prepared to ensure the fastest training time by Amazon Forecast. Storage is priced for each **gigabyte** (**GB**) ingested in the service.

- **Training hours**: Each time you train a new custom model based on your data, you are billed for the number of hours of training.

- **Generated forecast data points**: You are billed for each unit of 1,000 forecast data points generated by the service. A forecast data point is a combination of the number of unique time series, the number of quantiles, and the time points within the forecast horizon.

- **Forecast explanations**: You are also billed for any explanation generated by the service to explain the impact of different attributes or related variables of your dataset on your forecasts.

If this is the first time you are using Amazon Forecast with any given account, you have access to a Free Tier, which will allow you to use the service for free for 2 months. During this period, you will not be charged if you use the following:

- **Storage**: Less than 10 GB per month
- **Training hours**: Fewer than 10 hours per month
- **Generated forecast data points**: Fewer than 100,000 forecast data points per month

AWS service developers work relentlessly to reduce the operational costs of services, and price reductions happen regularly. At the time this book was written, these components were priced as follows:

- **Storage**: $0.088 per GB.
- **Training hours**: $0.24 per hour.
- **Generated forecasts**: Starts at $2.00 per 1,000 forecasts for the first 100,000 data points. Pricing then decreases according to a tiered pricing table.

For the most up-to-date pricing, you can check the Amazon Forecast pricing page:

```
https://aws.amazon.com/forecast/pricing/
```

Up to now, you have read about how to find and frame a proper forecasting problem. You have also learned how Amazon Forecast works. You are now ready to dive into the choices you will need to make to select applications that will benefit the most from Amazon Forecast's capabilities.

Choosing the right applications

You have successfully framed your ML project as a forecasting problem and you have collected some historical time series datasets. Is Amazon Forecast a good candidate to deliver the desired insights? Let's review some considerations that will help you understand whether Amazon Forecast is suitable for your forecasting scenario—namely, the following:

- Latency requirements
- Dataset requirements
- Use-case requirements

All in all, reading through these requirements will help you define when Amazon Forecast is best suited for a given problem. You will also understand when it is not likely to be a good candidate for this. You will have some pointers on what you need to do to adjust your problem framework so that it matches Amazon Forecast's native capabilities.

Latency requirements

With Amazon Forecast, the *training must happen in the cloud*—if your data is not available in cloud storage such as Amazon S3, the first step will be to transfer it there.

At prediction time, the *inference will also happen in the cloud*—you will need to send your freshest data to the cloud, and a trained model (the predictor) will be generated and also stored in the cloud. As inference happens in the cloud, you will depend on network latency between your local systems and the internet. If you need forecasting predictions in near real time to feed optimization algorithms in a factory, Amazon Forecast will likely be the wrong candidate and you should explore building a custom forecasting model that you will deploy at the edge (for instance, leveraging Amazon SageMaker and its **Edge Manager** feature to compile, deploy, and manage ML models on local machines).

Dataset requirements

Although Amazon Forecast includes some statistical methods that have been successfully used on small datasets, large datasets with dense time series are likely more valuable to deliver a business **return on investment** (**ROI**) perspective.

The underlying DL algorithms included in the services start to shine when you have at least *several hundred time series* (the service can scale to millions of distinct time series) and a *long historical period* to train on (ideally, more than 1,000 data points per time series).

The more advanced algorithms leveraged by Amazon Forecast are also able to capture relationships between multiple related time series and shared non-time related attributes.

Depending on the available length from your time series data, you will also be limited in the maximum forecast horizon you can actually request. This horizon will be the lesser of 500 time steps or one-third of the dataset length. Here are a couple of examples to illustrate this:

- If your historical time series contains 1,000 days of data at a daily granularity (1,000 time steps), your maximum forecast horizon will be 333 days.

- If your historical time series contains 1,000 days of data but at an hourly granularity (24 x 1,000 = 24,000 time steps), your maximum forecast horizon will be 500 hours (if you decide to keep the same sampling rate of 1 hour per time step).

Amazon Forecast is a univariate forecasting service—the target dataset that contains the metrics of interest can only include a single field to forecast for. If you have a multivariate dataset and want to deliver predictions for multiple fields in parallel, you would have to build several individual models with Amazon Forecast. Depending on your use case, this may not be suitable, as dependency between different variables may contain valuable insights to forecast future values for all these variables.

Last but not least, your data must have a compatible time interval—although Amazon Forecast can deal with datasets that have a time interval ranging from 1 minute to 1 year, the more common intervals are hours, days, and weeks. *High-frequency datasets* (for example, sensor data collected at a 10-millisecond sampling rate) will require you to aggregate the data at a minimum of 1 minute. If you are looking at predictive fast events, this is not a suitable approach (I would argue that a forecasting formulation might not be the right one). On the other end of the spectrum, *long periods* of time—such as decades—in environmental science will lead to a sparsity of your dataset, which may generate a low-quality forecast.

Use-case requirements

Throughout this chapter, you have read through multiple forecasting examples. You have also seen how much heavy lifting Amazon Forecast performs on your behalf. There are, however, situations and use cases for which Amazon Forecast is not the best match, such as the following:

- **Small data**: Use cases similar to financial planning, where you need to forecast monthly revenue for a company for the next 5 years based on the last 3 years (36 data points).

- **Long periods of time with sparse data**: This generally yields small data.

- **Random walk**: Random processes such as stock market indices where future values are heavily impacted by external factors with low (to no) predictive power in past historical data alone.

- **High-frequency data**: Datasets with a sampling rate of less than 1 minute or even less than 1 second are not suitable for Amazon Forecast.

- **Multivariate data**: Although Amazon Forecast can forecast univariate data while leveraging insights coming from related time series data, the service is not built to provide multivariate forecasts in parallel for several interdependent time series.

Summary

Amazon Forecast is an AI-/ML-managed service running in the cloud and provides a one-stop shop to solve many forecasting problems.

In this chapter, you learned how to frame your problem as a forecasting one and discovered the key concepts manipulated by the Amazon Forecast service (for instance, datasets, predictors, forecasts, and explainability insights).

This chapter was important to help you develop a good understanding of which applications will be good candidates to be solved with Amazon Forecast. You also read about how you can improve your forecasting problem-framing approach, should you want to benefit the most from all the undifferentiated heavy lifting that this service can deliver on your behalf.

In the next chapter, we are going to create our first forecasting project by creating a dataset group and ingesting some time series data.

3
Creating a Project and Ingesting Your Data

In the previous chapter, we identified a **forecasting** problem of interest. In this chapter, we are taking a dive into using Amazon Forecast with a dataset that contains the energy consumption of a few thousand households located in London. This dataset is hosted publicly by Kaggle and you will have the opportunity to either prepare it yourself or fast-track your journey by using an already prepared one.

By the end of this chapter, you will have a good understanding of this dataset and you will know how to **ingest** it into the service.

In this chapter, we're going to cover the following main topics:

- Understanding the components of a dataset group
- Preparing a dataset for forecasting purposes
- Creating an Amazon Forecast dataset group
- Ingesting data in Amazon Forecast

Technical requirements

No hands-on experience in a language such as **Python** or **R** is necessary to follow along with the content from this chapter. However, we highly recommend that you read this chapter while connected to your own AWS account and open the Amazon Forecast console to run the different actions on your end.

To create an AWS account and log in to the Amazon Forecast console, you can refer yourself to the technical requirements of *Chapter 2, An Overview of Amazon Forecast*.

In the companion GitHub repository of this book, you will find a notebook that will show you the detailed steps to prepare the dataset we are going to use from now on. *This preparation is optional* to follow along with this chapter. At your first reading, I recommend that you download the prepared dataset from the following link:

```
https://packt-publishing-timeseries-on-aws-michaelhoarau.
s3-eu-west-1.amazonaws.com/part1-amazon-forecast/energy_
consumption.zip
```

From there, you can log in to AWS Console and follow along with this chapter without writing a single line of code.

At a later reading, feel free to go through the preparation code to understand how to prepare a dataset ready to be consumed by Amazon Forecast. You will find a notebook with all this preparation on the companion GitHub repository of this book:

```
https://github.com/PacktPublishing/Time-series-Analysis-on-
AWS/blob/main/Chapter03/chapter3-dataset-preparation.ipynb
```

This notebook will help you to understand the format expected to build a successful model. You will need to download the raw dataset from Kaggle: the preparatory notebook will detail all the steps necessary to create a Kaggle account and download the data.

Understanding the components of a dataset group

When creating a dataset in Amazon Forecast, you can specify its type. It can be one of the following:

- A mandatory **target time series**
- An optional **related time series**
- An optional **metadata** dataset

These three dataset types help you organize your whole dataset in a format that is compatible with Amazon Forecast.

When you define a dataset group, you also specify its **domain**: a domain specifies a schema for a common use case but does not impact the algorithms or hyperparameters used at training time. A domain is merely a convenient way to organize your dataset. Amazon Forecast provides the following predefined domains: RETAIL, INVENTORY_ PLANNING, EC2_CAPACITY, WORK_FORCE, WEB_TRAFFIC, and METRICS. If none of these suit your use case, you can use the CUSTOM domain and define your custom fields at dataset creation time.

When you want to train a predictor, you create up to three datasets, one of each of the types described previously, with only the target time series being mandatory. You will add your datasets to a **dataset group**, which is a logical way of regrouping the data necessary to train a predictor: let's dive deeper into each dataset type.

Target time series

If your dataset is a time series and it contains the **target** one you want to train a forecasting model for, you will use the *target* type for your time series dataset. This dataset type is mandatory; it must always be provided to train a predictor.

This dataset must contain the target field and *can contain up to 10 other variables* called **attributes** (or dimensions). At forecast time, you can use these attributes to specify the aggregation level for which you want to make a prediction.

By definition, your target time series must include historical data and won't provide any data in the forecast horizon.

Related time series

When you have time series data that does not contain your target measure, but other time-oriented variables that may have an impact on the way your target field evolves, you can use the optional *related* time series dataset. The related time series you collected may have some correlation with the variable you are trying to predict: if you are familiar with the **Granger causality test**, this can be used to assess the predictive capability of a given variable to predict another one. As such, using related time series *may* reinforce the statistical strength of the underlying algorithms used by Amazon Forecast.

> **Important Note about Granger Causality**
>
> This method is probabilistic in essence: it uses the observed time series data to find patterns of correlation. Granger causality helps you assess whether using the past values of a given time series helps you to improve the forecast of your target time series of interest. It does not prove causality between two time series, but only the possible improvement of a forecast performance

The related time series dataset is optional and each variable enclosed in it is used to give more context to your forecast. The related dataset and the target dataset must be joinable by a timestamp.

A related time series dataset *can contain up to 13 related features*. You can also specify up to 10 additional forecast **attributes**; however, they must be consistent with the attributes you defined for the target time series.

Unlike the target time series, related time series can contain historical values (past values) *and* forward-looking values (values present in the forecast horizon). For most of the underlying algorithms leveraged by Amazon Forecast, the forward-looking values of every related time series are mandatory. One of the latest algorithms implemented in the service (CNN-QR, see *Chapter 5, Customizing Your Predictor Training*, for more details on each algorithm used by Amazon Forecast) can deal with related time series that only contain historical data, but it is the only one at the time of writing this book.

Item metadata

Use this dataset type for every other variable that does not vary over time, anything that is not a time series, but includes information about the items you are predicting for. Metadata should apply to more than one item to be useful from a forecasting perspective. For instance, the name of each item is not useful metadata, whereas a product category for an e-commerce website can help group together items that may have similar demand-level patterns.

As we will see in *Chapter 7, Improving and Scaling Your Forecast Strategy*, the item metadata dataset is also leveraged in **cold-start** situations: this happens when you want to obtain a forecast for a new item. If you provide an item metadata dataset, Amazon Forecast can derive some level of similarities with known items to suggest a forecast until enough actual data has been collected.

Each row *can include up to 10 metadata fields*: one of them must be the identification field matching the item from the target time series.

Preparing a dataset for forecasting purposes

Throughout this chapter and the remaining chapters of this part, we are going to focus on an energy consumption dataset. The problem we want to solve is the following:

Predicting the daily electricity consumption of a household in London for the following month.

In this section, we are going to detail the following steps:

1. Preparing the raw dataset in a format ready to be used by Amazon Forecast. If you have downloaded the already prepared dataset as mentioned in the technical requirements at the beginning of this chapter, *this part is optional* and you can go directly to the second step.

2. Upload your prepared CSV files to Amazon **Simple Storage Service** (**S3**) for storage: Amazon S3 lets you store files and is often used as a file data store for many AWS services such as Amazon Forecast.

3. Authorize Amazon Forecast to access your data in Amazon S3: this is optional as you can let Amazon Forecast do it for you while you ingest new data. However, this will give you better control over the authorization aspects and can help debug permission errors in your future work with Amazon Forecast.

Preparing the raw dataset (optional)

In this section, we are going to go through the different preparation steps that will allow us to prepare the raw data from the London household electricity consumption dataset (as it is available from Kaggle) until it is ready to be ingested and consumed by Amazon Forecast.

When you build a forecast model based on a new dataset, you will likely partner with your favorite data scientist team to help you extract and isolate the relevant information from your raw data. You would then work with a data engineering team to automate all these preparation steps so that you can feed new data to your trained model.

At your first reading, you can skip this more advanced section, download the already prepared dataset directly (refer to the *Technical requirements* section at the beginning of this chapter), and continue working directly from AWS Console by jumping to the *Authorizing Amazon Forecast to access your S3 bucket (optional)* section.

Collecting the dataset

The dataset we are going to use is the smart meters dataset from London hosted on Kaggle:

```
https://www.kaggle.com/jeanmidev/smart-meters-in-london
```

This dataset contains the energy readings for a sample of more than 5,500 households in London, between November 2011 and February 2014. The smart meters only measure electrical consumption and do not tackle any other energy source. The dataset also contains customer segmentation information available as classification from Acorn (a segmentation tool used to categorize the United Kingdom's population into very detailed demographic types). For more details about the Acorn segmentation, you can find a detailed user guide on their website:

```
https://acorn.caci.co.uk/downloads/Acorn-User-guide.pdf
```

Dataset overview

There are 19 files in total in this dataset, but we are only going to use the following ones:

- `informations_households.csv`: This file is the main index and entry point into the dataset. It contains the customer segmentation category and tells you in which files you can find the electricity consumption data. For instance, the household referenced by the **MAC002543** identifier is in the **ACORN-E** segment and its electricity consumption can be found in a file named `block_12.csv`.

	LCLid	stdorToU	Acorn	Acorn_grouped	file
2	MAC000002	Std	ACORN-A	Affluent	block_0
3	MAC003613	Std	ACORN-A	Affluent	block_0
4	MAC003597	Std	ACORN-A	Affluent	block_0
5	MAC003579	Std	ACORN-A	Affluent	block_0
6	MAC003566	Std	ACORN-A	Affluent	block_0

Figure 3.1 – London household index file overview

- `halfhourly_dataset.zip`: This archive contains the block files with the energy consumption sampled every half-hour. *We are going to use this data for our target time series dataset.* Here is an excerpt from the `block_12.csv` file that contains the energy consumption of household **MAC002543**.

	LCLid	tstp	energy(kWh/hh)
342953	MAC002543	2012-07-09 11:30:00.0000000	0.054
342954	MAC002543	2012-07-09 12:00:00.0000000	0.053
342955	MAC002543	2012-07-09 12:30:00.0000000	0.053
342956	MAC002543	2012-07-09 13:00:00.0000000	0.053
342957	MAC002543	2012-07-09 13:30:00.0000000	0.053

Figure 3.2 – London household energy consumption extract

- `weatherhourlydarksky.csv`: This contains the hourly weather data in London for the same time period as the electricity measurements. It contains weather information such as temperature, pressure, and wind speed. *This data will go in our related time series dataset.*

time	visibility	windBearing	temperature	dewPoint	pressure	apparentTemperature	windSpeed	humidity
2012-07-01 00:00:00	13.24	231	13.44	10.25	1011.33	13.44	4.14	0.81
2012-07-01 01:00:00	13.37	232	13.25	10.20	1011.61	13.25	4.07	0.82
2012-07-01 02:00:00	13.08	229	12.28	9.62	1011.81	12.28	3.76	0.84
2012-07-01 03:00:00	13.79	229	11.77	9.23	1011.90	11.77	3.75	0.84
2012-07-01 04:00:00	13.68	223	11.26	9.06	1012.28	11.26	3.88	0.86
...	...	...	...	...	...	...	...	...
2013-06-30 19:00:00	15.50	245	21.03	12.39	1018.59	21.03	5.23	0.58
2013-06-30 20:00:00	16.09	248	19.67	12.34	1018.53	19.67	4.30	0.63
2013-06-30 21:00:00	14.31	254	18.46	11.99	1018.86	18.46	4.84	0.66
2013-06-30 22:00:00	13.58	267	16.25	11.40	1019.10	16.25	4.49	0.73
2013-06-30 23:00:00	14.08	265	15.10	10.67	1018.91	15.10	4.34	0.75

Figure 3.3 – London weather data extract

- `acorn_details.csv`: This file contains the segmentation details for each household segment. Once preprocessed, this data will go in our item metadata dataset.

	MAIN CATEGORIES	CATEGORIES	REFERENCE	ACORN-A	ACORN-B	ACORN-E
714	COMMUNITY SAFETY	Crime Survey for England	Lack of discipline from school	89.000000	96.000000	90.000000
499	DIGITAL	Regularly research on the internet	Tickets for events/cinema/theatre	116.000000	129.000000	134.000000
212	FINANCE	Credit Cards	Always pays credit card balance in full	180.000000	167.000000	124.000000
116	EDUCATION	England: Pupils at the end of KS1	Achieving expected level in maths	106.000000	105.000000	103.000000
810	LEISURE TIME	Visit Pubs for a Meal - Evening	Value	97.000000	100.000000	111.000000
675	SHOPPING	High Street Retailers	H&M	51.470695	114.117308	116.712311
311	DIGITAL	Social Media Activity (at least weekly)	Visit the profile/fan page of a product/brand ...	91.000000	95.000000	122.000000
130	HEALTH	Behaviours & Lifestyle	I am perfectly happy with my standard of living	125.000000	124.000000	100.000000
707	ENVIRONMENT	Action	Rarely leave the mobile phone charger in the s...	109.000000	109.000000	95.000000
532	DIGITAL	Purchased on the internet	Local Government Services	108.000000	109.000000	124.000000

Figure 3.4 – London household customer segmentation

Preparing the target time series dataset

As the energy consumption dataset we are using does not match any of the predefined domains from Amazon Forecast, we are going to use the **CUSTOM** domain. When using the **CUSTOM** domain Amazon Forecast expects a CSV file with the following fields:

- `timestamp`: The energy consumption data is available at 30-minute granularity. We are going to resample this dataset to have daily data.

- `item_id`: In our case, this will correspond to the household ID (the MACxxxxxx number).

- `target_value`: The value associated with a given household (`item_id`) at each timestamp. This will be our energy consumption in kWh.

The different steps necessary to prepare the raw electricity consumption data will be the following:

1. Read the `informations_households.csv` file and keep only the household IDs associated with a given customer segment (the Acorn field must be different than `ACORN-U`, which means an *unknown* segment). We do want to leverage some of the Acorn segmentation data in our metadata dataset.

2. Loop through each selected household ID, open the associated `block_XX.csv` file (located in the `halfhourly_dataset.zip` archive), and consolidate an *energy dataframe* that will have the energy consumption for each household over the available time period.

3. Resample the energy dataframe to a one-day granularity (from the raw 30 minutes available). The related dataset that we will use later has a one-hour granularity and Amazon Forecast requires that both datasets have the same underlying frequency. We will also resample the related dataset to one-day granularity, to ensure that the energy consumption data frequency will match the London weather data.

4. Limit the scope of our analysis to a time ranging from 2012-07-01 to 2013-06-30 (one full year of data): this will limit the training time and any processing or visualization you want to run on the dataset. This will also leave us with a whole section of the data ranging from 2013-07-01 to the end of the available time (2014-02-28) to use as a test dataset our models will have never seen.

To Dive Deeper...

As an exercise, you can run this tutorial with the whole dataset (instead of one year) and compare how the forecast performance evolves when adding more historical data to the training set. You can also select another granularity down to one hour.

The final dataset is a CSV file structured as follows:

	item_id	timestamp	target_value
0	MAC000003	2012-07-01	12.359
1	MAC000003	2012-07-02	12.775
2	MAC000003	2012-07-03	11.584
3	MAC000003	2012-07-04	12.700
4	MAC000003	2012-07-05	13.724
...	...	...	...
1301432	MAC005562	2013-06-26	7.466
1301433	MAC005562	2013-06-27	10.738
1301434	MAC005562	2013-06-28	11.128
1301435	MAC005562	2013-06-29	9.363
1301436	MAC005562	2013-06-30	9.491

Figure 3.5 – Prepared target time series dataset

Each household is linked to a single `item_id` value that has a time range between 2012-07-01 and 2013-06-30. The target value corresponds to the energy consumed.

No additional forecast **attributes** are available. Attributes of interest for an energy provider could be the ZIP code of each household: as several households share the same ZIP code, this would allow forecasts to be requested at the item level (getting forecasts for each household) or at this aggregation level (getting energy consumption forecasts at the ZIP code level).

Preparing the related time series dataset

In the related time series dataset, we are going to position our weather data (see *Figure 3.3 – London weather data extract* from earlier). For energy consumption forecasting purposes, we are going to keep the following fields: temperature, windspeed, and humidity.

As we selected the **CUSTOM** domain, the schema expected by Amazon Forecast for the related time series will contain the following fields: `item_id`, `timestamp`, `temperature`, `wind_speed`, and `humidity`.

> **Important Note**
>
> Each `item_id` *must have its own related time series.* For instance, the temperature for every timestamp must be provided for household **MAC002543**, and another set of temperatures must be provided by household **MAC002556**. In a real situation, these temperatures might be slightly different as each household may be associated with a different weather station depending on their location. In this tutorial, we will duplicate the same data and simplify the problem by considering that only one weather station covers the whole London metropolitan area.

After extracting the features of interest and duplicating them for each household, the final related time series dataset will look like this:

	item_id	timestamp	temperature	wind_speed	humidity		item_id	timestamp	temperature	wind_speed	humidity
0	MAC000003	2012-07-01	14.862500	5.138750	0.703333	1303780	MAC005562	2012-07-01	14.862500	5.138750	0.703333
1	MAC000003	2012-07-02	15.229583	4.557500	0.832917	1303781	MAC005562	2012-07-02	15.229583	4.557500	0.832917
2	MAC000003	2012-07-03	16.927917	3.710833	0.895833	1303782	MAC005562	2012-07-03	16.927917	3.710833	0.895833
3	MAC000003	2012-07-04	18.426250	3.368750	0.853333	1303783	MAC005562	2012-07-04	18.426250	3.368750	0.853333
4	MAC000003	2012-07-05	18.496667	2.000833	0.707083	1303784	MAC005562	2012-07-05	18.496667	2.000833	0.707083
...	...	...	...	...	...	...	...	...	...	...	...
360	MAC000003	2013-06-26	16.252083	2.269583	0.632083	1304140	MAC005562	2013-06-26	16.252083	2.269583	0.632083
361	MAC000003	2013-06-27	15.173750	2.925833	0.700417	1304141	MAC005562	2013-06-27	15.173750	2.925833	0.700417
362	MAC000003	2013-06-28	16.288750	3.616667	0.867917	1304142	MAC005562	2013-06-28	16.288750	3.616667	0.867917
363	MAC000003	2013-06-29	17.214583	3.434583	0.603333	1304143	MAC005562	2013-06-29	17.214583	3.434583	0.603333
364	MAC000003	2013-06-30	19.741250	4.401667	0.676667	1304144	MAC005562	2013-06-30	19.741250	4.401667	0.676667

Figure 3.6 – Prepared related time series dataset

As expected, the preceding figure shows how each weather time series is repeated for each household: on the left-hand side of this diagram, you can see an excerpt of the related time series data that can be linked to the **MAC000003** household and, on the right, you can see the ones linked to the **MAC005562** household.

> **Important Note**
>
> All the items from the target dataset must be included in the related time series data. In our case, this means that every household present in the target time series must have its own set of related time series. If not, any model trained on this dataset group will *only be built on the households that are present in both datasets.*

Preparing the item metadata dataset

The item metadata dataset is optional. When provided, Amazon Forecast only expects the `item_id` field to be present in this CSV file. You are free to choose the name of any additional column that you would like to provide.

The `acorn_details.csv` file provides more than 800 characteristics for each customer segment. The metadata dataset can only include 9 fields on top of the `item_id` field. While sifting through the categories available, you may build an intuition that some of them could have something to do with the energy consumption of the household. One approach could be to select the ones that match your intuition (or provided by a subject matter expert if you have access to one!) and add them to your item metadata dataset. You could then build a model with and without this data to assess how valuable they are to provide better energy consumption prediction (if any).

For this exercise, we arbitrarily kept the following ones:

- Geography: England, Northern Ireland, Scotland, or Wales.

- Family: 1, 2, 3-4, or 5+ persons are living in the household.

- Working from home.

The different steps necessary to prepare the metadata will be the following:

1. From the original `acorn_details.csv` file, we will only keep the desired categories (*Household Size, Geography*) and restrict the *Travel To Work* category to the *Work mainly at or from home* segment.

2. We will then merge the household ID with the appropriate customer segment (`ACORN-{X}`)

The final item metadata dataset will look something like this:

	item_id	geography_england	geography_northern_ireland	...	family_3_4_persons	family_5_more_persons	transport_work_from_home
0	MAC000246	107.0	30.0	...	114.0	128.0	230.0
1	MAC004431	107.0	30.0	...	114.0	128.0	230.0
2	MAC004387	107.0	30.0	...	114.0	128.0	230.0
3	MAC004319	107.0	30.0	...	114.0	128.0	230.0
4	MAC004247	107.0	30.0	...	114.0	128.0	230.0
...	...	...	...	...	...	...	...
3535	MAC002345	97.0	43.0	...	85.0	76.0	62.0
3536	MAC002185	97.0	43.0	...	85.0	76.0	62.0
3537	MAC002347	97.0	43.0	...	85.0	76.0	62.0
3538	MAC002331	97.0	43.0	...	85.0	76.0	62.0
3539	MAC000318	97.0	43.0	...	85.0	76.0	62.0

Figure 3.7 – Prepared item metadata tabular dataset

Households that are part of the same customer segment (the same Acorn group) will share the same metadata as you can see in *Figure 3.7 – Prepared item metadata tabular dataset* for households **MAC000246** and **MAC004431**, for instance. As expected, this dataset is tabular as metadata is not time-dependent.

Uploading your data to Amazon S3 for storage

If you went through the data collection and preparation from the previous subtopic, you should have three CSV files that we are going to push on an Amazon S3 bucket. If you skipped the previous data preparation, you can download this archive directly from the following location:

```
https://packt-publishing-timeseries-on-aws-michaelhoarau.
s3-eu-west-1.amazonaws.com/part1-amazon-forecast/energy_
consumption.zip
```

Download this archive and unzip it: you should have three CSV files containing the target time series data, the related time series data, and the item metadata.

Amazon S3 bucket creation

Equipped with our prepared datasets, let's create a bucket on Amazon S3 and upload our data there:

1. If you went through the technical requirements prerequisites at the beginning of this chapter, you should already be logged in to your AWS console, otherwise, fire up your favorite browser and log in to your AWS console.

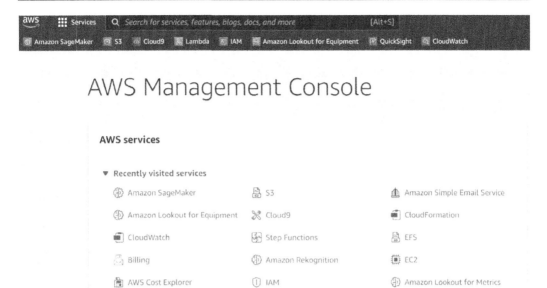

Figure 3.8 – AWS Console home page

2. At the top left of your console, you will see a **Services** drop-down menu that will display all the available AWS services. In the **Storage** section, look at the **S3** service and click on its name to go to the S3 console. If you are using a fresh account, your bucket listing might still be empty.

Figure 3.9 – Amazon S3 console landing page

3. From here, you are going to click on the **Create bucket** button located at the top of your buckets list section. You are taken to the bucket creation page.

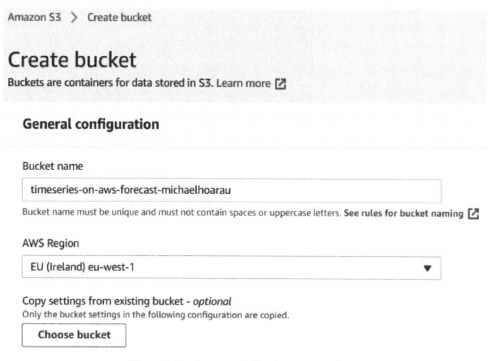

Figure 3.10 – Amazon S3 bucket creation form

4. Choose a name for your bucket. This name must be unique across the whole S3 service. I will call mine `timeseries-on-aws-forecast-michael-hoarau`. That should be unique enough.

5. Select an AWS Region where your data will be fetched from by Amazon Forecast. I selected the `Europe (Ireland)` Region for mine.

> **Important Note**
>
> At the time of writing this book, Amazon Forecast is only available in the following Regions: US East (N. Virginia), US East (Ohio), US West (Oregon), Asia Pacific (Mumbai), Asia Pacific (Seoul), Asia Pacific (Singapore), Asia Pacific (Sydney), Asia Pacific (Tokyo), Europe (Frankfurt), and Europe (Ireland). Make sure you select one of these Regions to create your bucket or you won't be able to ingest your data into Amazon Forecast.

6. You can keep all the other fields as their default values and click on **Create bucket**. You are brought back to the S3 home page and you should see your newly created bucket in the buckets listing. A green message at the top of the window will confirm that your bucket was successfully created.

Figure 3.11 – Amazon S3 successful bucket creation message

Your Amazon S3 bucket is now created and we can start uploading our CSV files in this location.

Uploading your dataset to Amazon S3

To upload your dataset, complete the following steps:

1. Click on the name of the bucket you just created in the buckets list that appears on the S3 home page:

Figure 3.12 – Amazon S3 empty objects listing from your new bucket

This page lists all the objects available in this bucket: it is empty for now.

2. From here, click on the **Upload** button at the top of the objects list. You will be brought to the upload page where you can either click on the **Add files** button or drag and drop the CSV files unpacked from the archive you previously downloaded.

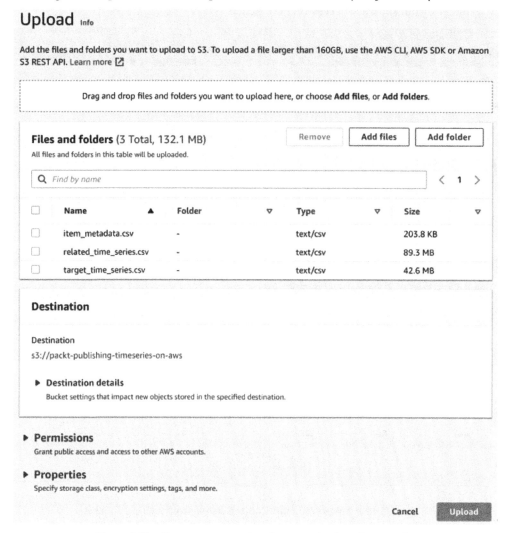

Figure 3.13 – Energy consumption dataset upload on Amazon S3

3. Leave all the other fields as their default values, scroll to the bottom of the screen, and click on **Upload** to start uploading the files. These files total 132 MB and it may take a while depending on your internet upload bandwidth. An upload status page is displayed while the transfer is in progress.

4. Once this is done, you can click on the **Exit** button to be brought back to the objects list at the root of your bucket.

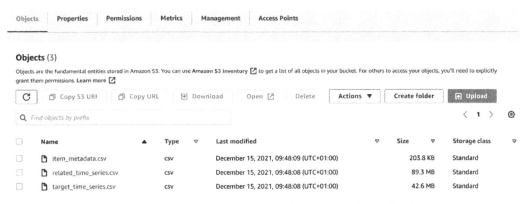

Figure 3.14 – Energy consumption dataset upload completed

Once your upload is complete, you should see three CSV files in the objects list, one for each dataset type.

5. Click on each of the dataset names and copy and paste their S3 URI (their address in Amazon S3).

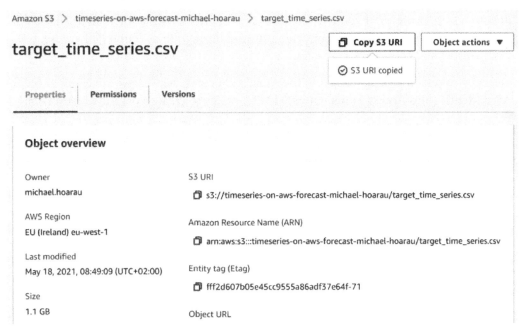

Figure 3.15 – Energy consumption dataset S3 URI

In our case, the S3 URI of an object in Amazon S3 takes the following format:

```
s3://BUCKET_NAME/FILENAME
```

For instance, my target time series data URI is the following:

```
s3://timeseries-on-aws-forecast-michael-hoarau/target_time_
series.csv
```

We will need these three links later at ingestion time. Let's now give access to this S3 bucket to Amazon Forecast.

Authorizing Amazon Forecast to access your S3 bucket (optional)

By default, the security mechanisms enforced between different AWS services will prohibit any service other than Amazon S3 from accessing your data. From your account, you can upload, delete, or move your data from the bucket you just created. Amazon Forecast, however, is a different service and will not be able to access this data. We need to specify that Amazon Forecast can access any data in this bucket.

You can configure this access directly from the Amazon Forecast console, during the ingestion step. However, if you want to have more control over the roles and the different accesses created within your account, you can read through this section. Otherwise, feel free to skip it and come back here later.

To enable access to your S3 bucket to the Amazon Forecast service, we are going to use the AWS **Identity and Access Management (IAM)** service to create a dedicated **IAM role:**

1. At the top left of your console, click on the **Services** drop-down menu and search for the **Security, Identity, and Compliance** section: click on the IAM service name to go to this service console.

2. In the left panel menu, click on **Roles** and click on the **Create role** button on the top left of this screen.

3. On the **Create role** screen, select **AWS service** as the type of trusted entity:

Figure 3.16 – IAM role creation – trusted entity type selection

4. In the following section (**Choose a use case**), locate **Forecast** and click on the service name.

5. In the last section (**Select your use case**), select **Allows Amazon Forecast to access data in S3**.

6. Click on the **Next** button until you reach the last step (**Review**): provide a name and a description for your role (I called it `AmazonForecastEnergyConsumption`).

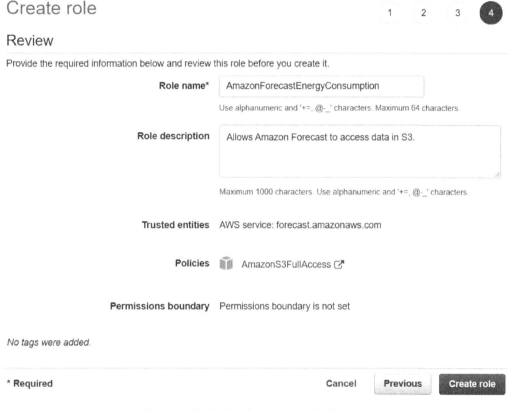

Figure 3.17 – IAM role creation – Review step

7. Click on **Create role**: your role is created and you are presented with a summary of your role. At the top of this screen, you will see a role **ARN** (**Amazon Resource Name**) field: copy this ARN and paste it somewhere handy. We will need it when we ingest our data into the service.

When Amazon Forecast attempts to read the datasets you just uploaded in S3, it will request permissions from IAM by using the role we just created. You are now ready to ingest your dataset into Amazon Forecast.

Creating an Amazon Forecast dataset group

As mentioned earlier, dataset groups are a convenient way to organize your datasets for each of your use cases or projects. Each dataset group is a collection of up to three datasets (one for each type: target time series, related time series, and metadata). For our energy consumption tutorial, we will have all three types of dataset present in the dataset group. To create your first forecasting project with Amazon Forecast, complete the following steps:

1. Log in to your AWS console and search for `Forecast` in the search bar at the top.
2. Click on **Amazon Forecast** to go to the service home page.

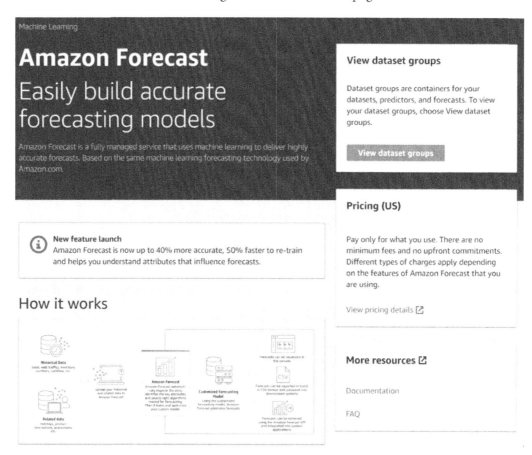

Figure 3.18 – Amazon Forecast home page

3. On this page, you can either click on the **View dataset groups** button on the right side of the screen or click the hamburger icon (the one with three horizontal lines) on the top left to open the left panel, where you can click on **Dataset groups**. You will land on a page listing all the dataset groups visible from your AWS account. If this is your first time using the service, your list will be empty.

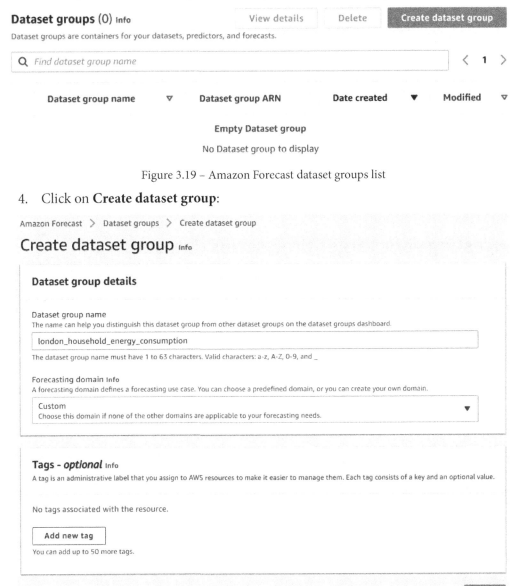

Figure 3.19 – Amazon Forecast dataset groups list

4. Click on **Create dataset group**:

Figure 3.20 – Amazon Forecast dataset group creation screen

5. On this screen, you are just asked to give a name to your dataset group (let's call it `london_household_energy_consumption`) and a forecasting domain. As mentioned earlier, we are going to use the **CUSTOM** domain. Note that the domain is defined at the dataset group level. Every dataset associated with this dataset group later will have the same domain: you cannot mix a **CUSTOM** domain for a target time series and a **RETAIL** domain for the related time series.

6. Then, click **Next** to create your target time series dataset (the only one mandatory for the **CUSTOM** domain).

The dataset group will be created, and you will be brought to the target time series ingestion screen.

Ingesting data in Amazon Forecast

We are going to ingest our three datasets one by one to populate a complete dataset group: a target dataset that we are going to forecast for, a related time series dataset, and an item metadata dataset.

Ingesting your target time series dataset

At the end of the dataset group creation, you are automatically brought to the target time series dataset creation. If you stop the process after the dataset group creation and want to access this ingestion screen later from the Amazon Forecast home page, you just need to click on your dataset group name to view this dashboard.

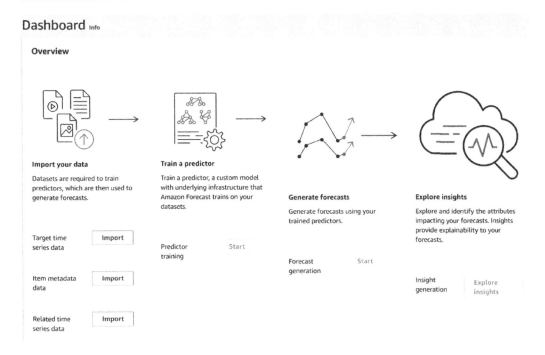

Dashboard Info

Overview

Import your data

Datasets are required to train predictors, which are then used to generate forecasts.

Train a predictor

Train a predictor, a custom model with underlying infrastructure that Amazon Forecast trains on your datasets.

Generate forecasts

Generate forecasts using your trained predictors.

Explore insights

Explore and identify the attributes impacting your forecasts. Insights provide explainability to your forecasts.

Target time series data   Import

Item metadata data   Import

Related time series data   Import

Predictor training   Start

Forecast generation   Start

Insight generation   Explore insights

Figure 3.21 – Initial dataset group dashboard

From there, you can click on the **Import** button next to the **Target time series data** label. To create your target time series dataset, you will need to feed in dataset details and the import details.

Configuring dataset details

We are going to name our target dataset `energy_consumption_data` as it only contains the energy consumption for each household. The remaining parameters will be as follows:

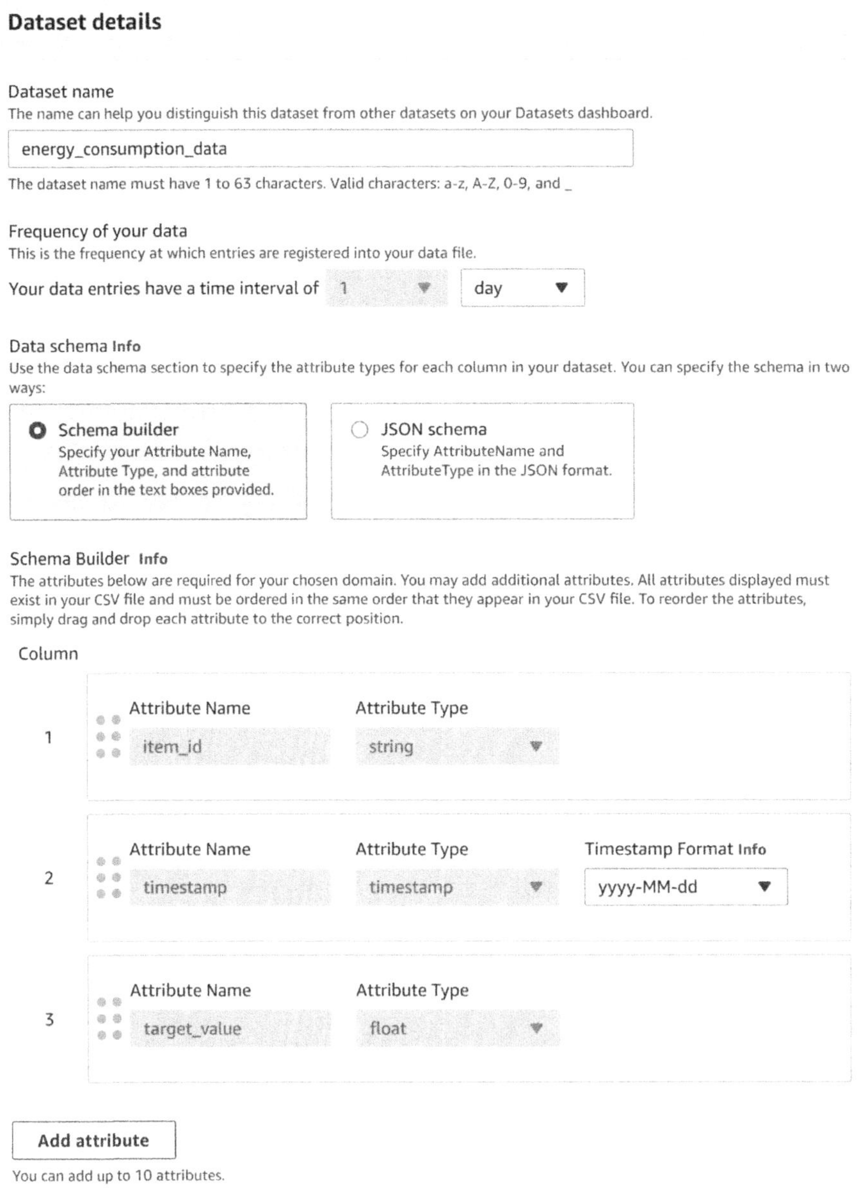

Dataset details

Dataset name
The name can help you distinguish this dataset from other datasets on your Datasets dashboard.

> energy_consumption_data

The dataset name must have 1 to 63 characters. Valid characters: a-z, A-Z, 0-9, and _

Frequency of your data
This is the frequency at which entries are registered into your data file.

Your data entries have a time interval of   1   ▼   day   ▼

Data schema Info
Use the data schema section to specify the attribute types for each column in your dataset. You can specify the schema in two ways:

⦿ Schema builder
  Specify your Attribute Name,
  Attribute Type, and attribute
  order in the text boxes provided.

◯ JSON schema
  Specify AttributeName and
  AttributeType in the JSON format.

Schema Builder Info
The attributes below are required for your chosen domain. You may add additional attributes. All attributes displayed must exist in your CSV file and must be ordered in the same order that they appear in your CSV file. To reorder the attributes, simply drag and drop each attribute to the correct position.

Column

	Attribute Name	Attribute Type	
1	item_id	string ▼	

	Attribute Name	Attribute Type	Timestamp Format Info
2	timestamp	timestamp ▼	yyyy-MM-dd ▼

	Attribute Name	Attribute Type	
3	target_value	float ▼	

> **Add attribute**

You can add up to 10 attributes.

Figure 3.22 – Target dataset details

When configuring your dataset, you must define the following:

- The *frequency* with which your data is recorded in your file. Frequency can be set with the two drop-down lists, one defining the unit of the interval (which can either be minute, hour, day, week, month, or year) and the number of units (only applicable when you select the minute interval). For instance, your time series can have data recorded every 15 minutes or every month. In our case, we are selecting 1 day.

- The *data schema*: This schema will initially be populated with the fields that are mandatory for the domain you selected when you created the dataset group. You can only configure the timestamp format, which can either be yyyy-MM-dd HH:mm:ss (example: 2021-05-19 07:00:00) or yyyy-MM-dd (2021-05-19). If you chose hour or minute for the interval frequency, you must select the long format (yyyy-MM-dd HH:mm:ss). For our daily dataset, we are selecting yyyy-MM-dd.

On the drag-and-drop schema builder, you can reorder the fields by using the handles next to each attribute name.

> **Important Note**
> The order of the fields *must match* the order of your CSV file.

You can add other attributes by clicking on the **Add attribute** button at the bottom of the schema builder. Each new attribute needs a name and a type.

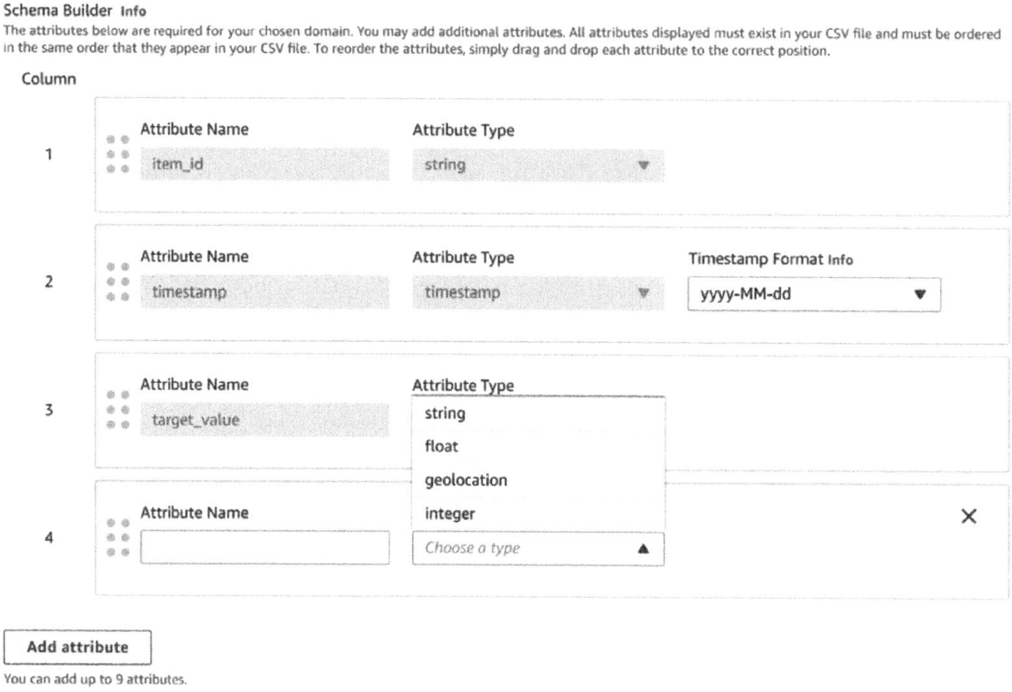

Schema Builder Info

The attributes below are required for your chosen domain. You may add additional attributes. All attributes displayed must exist in your CSV file and must be ordered in the same order that they appear in your CSV file. To reorder the attributes, simply drag and drop each attribute to the correct position.

Column

1   Attribute Name   Attribute Type
    item_id   string

2   Attribute Name   Attribute Type   Timestamp Format Info
    timestamp   timestamp   yyyy-MM-dd

3   Attribute Name   Attribute Type
    target_value   string
                     float
                     geolocation
4   Attribute Name   integer   ✕
                     Choose a type

Add attribute

You can add up to 9 attributes.

Figure 3.23 – Adding an attribute with the schema builder

An attribute can take the following type: **string**, **float**, **integer**, or **geolocation**. Geolocation is used by Amazon Forecast to match your location with the internal weather data feature. At the time of writing, the geolocation attributes can only accept locations in Europe, the US (excluding Hawaii and Alaska), Canada, South America, and Asia Pacific. To get an up-to-date list of geolocations supported by Amazon Forecast, you can refer yourself to the weather index documentation:

```
https://docs.aws.amazon.com/forecast/latest/dg/weather.
html#geolocation-bounds
```

The geolocation format can either be a ZIP code (for US locations only) or a latitude/longitude decimal degree (for all locations):

- ZIP codes must be entered by specifying US_#####, followed by the five-digit ZIP code (US_98121). Only US ZIP codes are supported at the time of writing.

- The latitude/longitude must be a string following this format: ##.####_##.####
(for instance, 47.4922_-2.3639 will be used to store a location with a 47.4922
latitude and a -2.3639 longitude).

As an alternative to the schema builder, you can also select the JSON schema and
specify all the attributes (mandatory and optional ones) in a JSON format. Note that the
timestamp format must be configured in a separate control below the JSON specification.

Figure 3.24 – Specifying a schema in JSON format

For this tutorial, you can keep the default values and field order in the schema builder

Configuring dataset import details

In the **Dataset import details** screen, you can fill in the following fields:

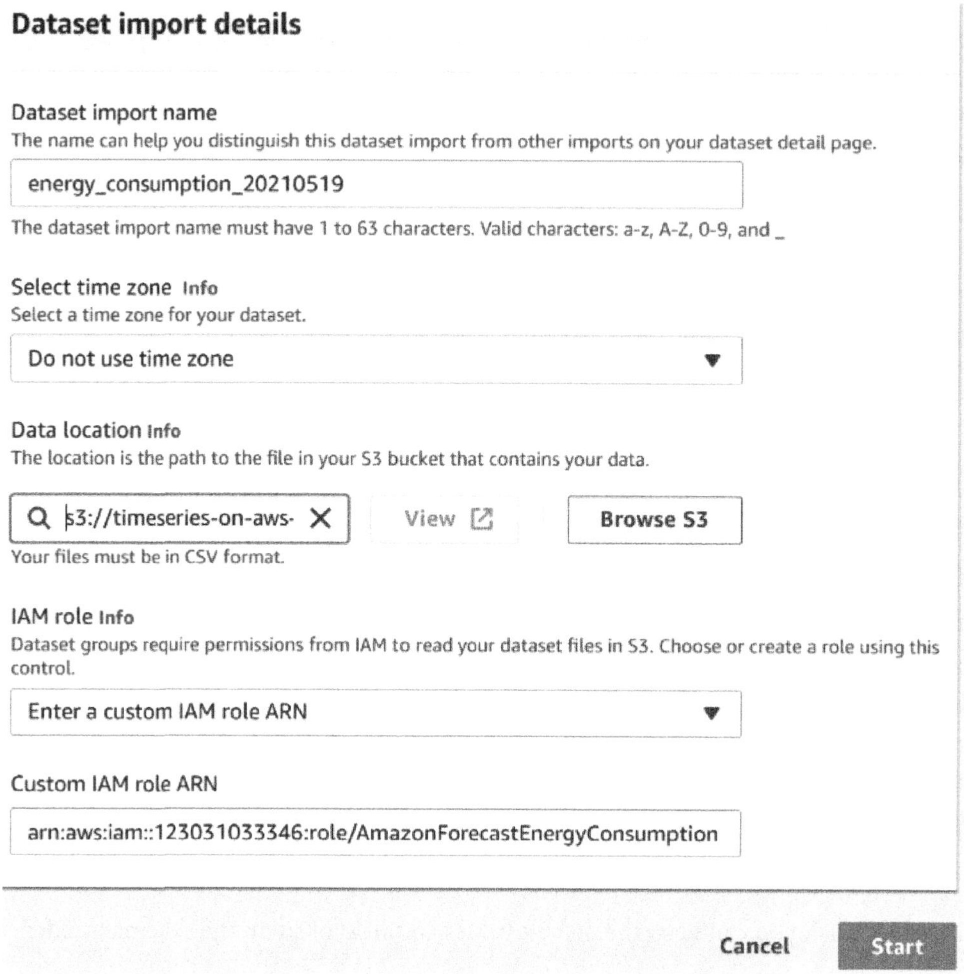

Dataset import details

Dataset import name
The name can help you distinguish this dataset import from other imports on your dataset detail page.

energy_consumption_20210519

The dataset import name must have 1 to 63 characters. Valid characters: a-z, A-Z, 0-9, and _

Select time zone Info
Select a time zone for your dataset.

Do not use time zone   ▼

Data location Info
The location is the path to the file in your S3 bucket that contains your data.

🔍 s3://timeseries-on-aws- ✕   View ⧉   Browse S3

Your files must be in CSV format.

IAM role Info
Dataset groups require permissions from IAM to read your dataset files in S3. Choose or create a role using this control.

Enter a custom IAM role ARN   ▼

Custom IAM role ARN

arn:aws:iam::123031033346:role/AmazonForecastEnergyConsumption

Cancel   **Start**

Figure 3.25 – Specifying the import details

You will need to do the following:

- Give a *name* to your import. This will help you distinguish between different import jobs. We will call it `energy_consumption_20210519` (I added a timestamp to know when I imported it).

> **Important Note**
> Note that *successive import jobs are not aggregated*: only the most recent import will be considered when you use your datasets to train a predictor.

- Enter the *S3 URI for the target time series* that you copied earlier when you uploaded the CSV file to Amazon S3.
- Select **Enter a custom IAM role ARN** and paste the ARN of the `AmazonForecastEnergyConsumption` role that you created earlier in the IAM service. The format of the ARN should be `arn:aws:iam::<ACCOUNT-NUMBER>:role/AmazonForecastEnergyConsumption`, where `<ACCOUNT-NUMBER>` needs to be replaced by your AWS account number.

Once you're done, you can click on **Start** to start the ingestion process. Your ingestion process begins.

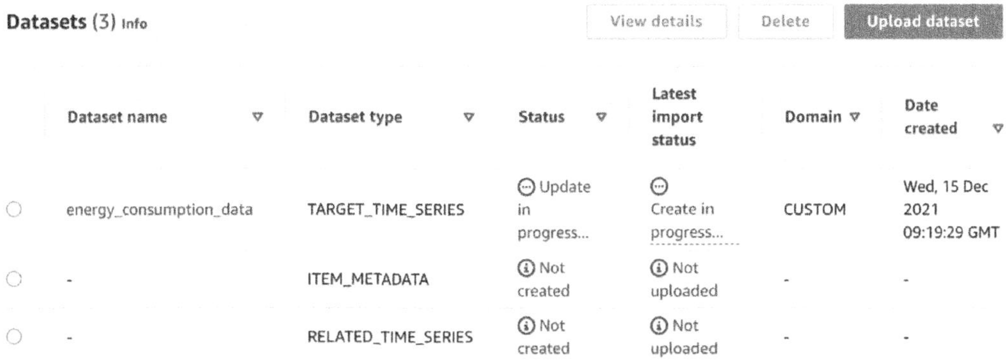

Datasets (3) Info

Dataset name		Dataset type		Status		Latest import status	Domain	Date created	
○ energy_consumption_data	▽	TARGET_TIME_SERIES	▽	⊖ Update in progress...	▽	⊙ Create in progress...	CUSTOM	Wed, 15 Dec 2021 09:19:29 GMT	▽
○ -		ITEM_METADATA		ⓘ Not created		ⓘ Not uploaded	-	-	
○ -		RELATED_TIME_SERIES		ⓘ Not created		ⓘ Not uploaded	-	-	

Figure 3.26 – Target time series ingestion in progress

If you click on your dataset name, you can get the status with an estimated time remaining for ingestion. You also have the ability to stop or delete the ingestion if you made a mistake and don't want to wait for the process to finish before you can actually restart it.

Ingesting related time series

Let's go back to our dataset group dashboard: we can see that our target time series data is active.

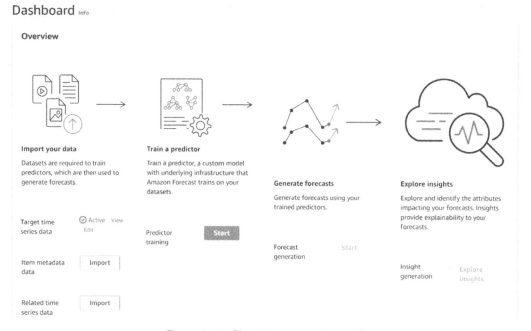

Figure 3.27 – Target time series ingested

> **Important Note**
> In your case, the dataset ingestion might still be in progress, but you don't have to wait for an ingestion job to finish before starting another one. Several ingestion jobs can run in parallel.

From the previous screen, you can click on the **Import** button next to the **Related time series data** label. To create your related time series dataset, you will need to feed the same details as for the target time series dataset. We will use the following information to configure it:

- *Dataset name*: `london_weather_data` (as the related time series are weather data).

- *Frequency of your data*: `1 day`.

- *Dataset import name*: `london_weather_20210519`.

- *Data location*: Here, enter the S3 URI for the related time series that you copied earlier when you uploaded the CSV file to Amazon S3.

- *IAM role*: Select **Enter a custom IAM role ARN** and paste the ARN of the `AmazonForecastEnergyConsumption` role that you created earlier in the IAM service. The format of the ARN should be `arn:aws:iam::<ACCOUNT-NUMBER>:role/AmazonForecastEnergyConsumption`, where `<ACCOUNT-NUMBER>` needs to be replaced by your AWS account number.

In **Schema Builder**, you will have to respect the same order as the header in your CSV file.

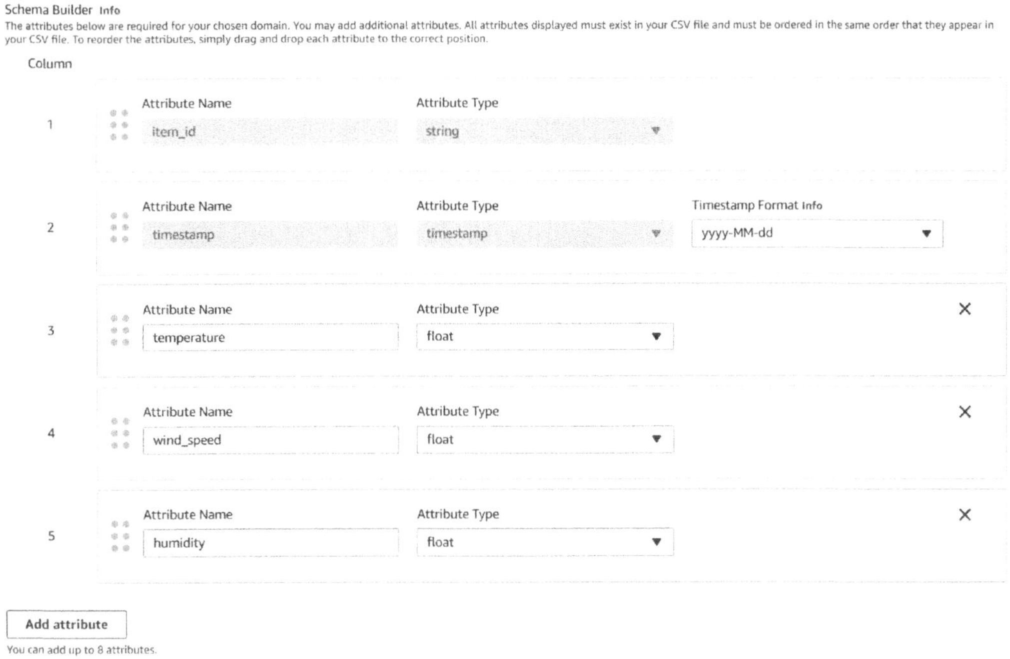

Figure 3.28 – Related time series schema definition

Once you're done, you can click on **Start** to start the ingestion process. Your ingestion process begins.

If you click on your dataset name, you can get the status with an estimated time remaining for ingestion. You also have the ability to stop or delete the ingestion if you made a mistake and don't want to wait for the process to finish before you can actually restart it.

Ingesting metadata

Let's go back to our dataset group dashboard: after a while, you will see that both your target and related time series datasets are active.

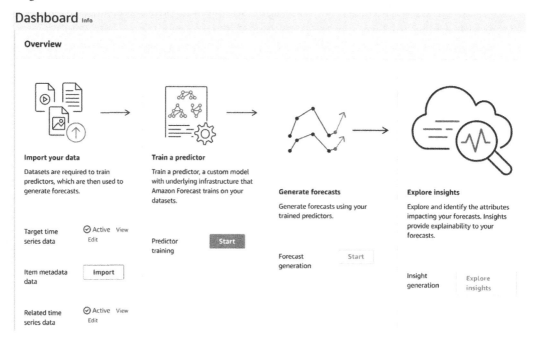

Figure 3.29 – Target and related time series ingested

As mentioned earlier, yours might still be in progress, but you can launch an item metadata ingestion job even if this is still the case (several ingestion jobs can run in parallel).

From the previous screen, you can click on the **Import** button next to the **Item metadata data** label. To create your related time series dataset, you will need to feed the same details as for the target time series dataset. We will use the following information to configure it:

- *Dataset name*: household_segment (as the metadata concerns the customer segmentation associated with each household).

- *Dataset import name*: household_segment_20210519.

- *Data location*: Here, enter the S3 URI for the item metadata that you copied earlier when you uploaded the CSV file to Amazon S3.

- *IAM role*: Select **Enter a custom IAM role ARN** and paste the ARN of the `AmazonForecastEnergyConsumption` role that you created earlier in the IAM service. The format of the ARN should be `arn:aws:iam::<ACCOUNT-NUMBER>:role/AmazonForecastEnergyConsumption`, where `<ACCOUNT-NUMBER>` needs to be replaced by your AWS account number.

In **Schema Builder**, you will have to respect the same order as the header in your CSV file and all the attribute types will be set to string: `geography_england`, `geography_northern_ireland`, `geography_scotland`, `geography_wales`, `family_1_person`, `family_2_persons`, `family_3_4_persons`, `family_5_more_persons`, and `transport_work_from_home`.

Once you're done, you can click on **Start** to start the ingestion process. Your ingestion process begins.

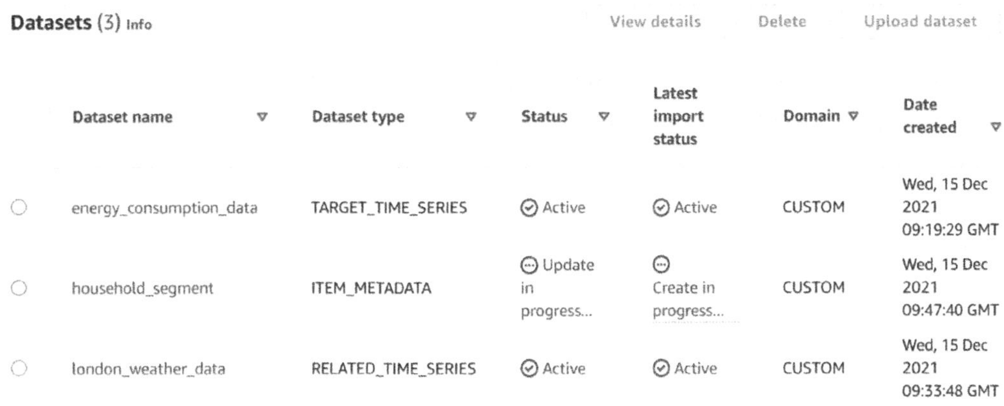

Datasets (3) Info   View details   Delete   Upload dataset

Dataset name ▽	Dataset type ▽	Status ▽	Latest import status	Domain ▽	Date created ▽
○ energy_consumption_data	TARGET_TIME_SERIES	⊘ Active	⊘ Active	CUSTOM	Wed, 15 Dec 2021 09:19:29 GMT
○ household_segment	ITEM_METADATA	⊝ Update in progress...	⊝ Create in progress...	CUSTOM	Wed, 15 Dec 2021 09:47:40 GMT
○ london_weather_data	RELATED_TIME_SERIES	⊘ Active	⊘ Active	CUSTOM	Wed, 15 Dec 2021 09:33:48 GMT

Figure 3.30 – Metadata ingestion in progress

If you click on your dataset name, you can get the status with an estimated time remaining for ingestion. You also have the ability to stop or delete the ingestion if you made a mistake and don't want to wait for the process to finish before you can actually correct and restart it.

What's happening behind the scenes?

You may be wondering what is happening behind the scenes when you ingest your CSV files in an Amazon Forecast dataset. As you noticed, this process lasts longer than what a mere data transfer would take. When you trigger the ingestion from Amazon S3, Amazon Forecast will perform many operations on your behalf, including the following:

- Provisioning the necessary AWS infrastructure to transfer the data from S3
- Loading the data into the service
- Inspecting the data and fixing missing values
- Performing time aggregation if required

Some algorithms (such as DeepAR+) will also build additional lagged features: a **lagged value** is a value from a past period. For instance, if your data has an hourly frequency, Amazon Forecast will also generate lagged values for the past 1, 2, and 3 days. If your data has a daily frequency, the lagged values are coming from the previous 1, 2, 3, and 4 weeks (basically, every week of the past month) and the previous year. This allows Amazon Forecast to better capture seasonality patterns consistent with the time series frequency.

As a data scientist, if you ever had to prepare robust time series sequences to feed a recurring neural network such as an **LSTM deep learning architecture**, you know how tedious, error-prone and long this process can be. Once your data conforms to the CSV format expected by Amazon Forecast, the service manages all this undifferentiated heavy lifting on your behalf.

In addition, under the hood, Amazon Forecast will also automatically provision (and clean) the necessary resources to perform all these steps.

Summary

In this chapter, you learned how Amazon Forecast organizes the datasets it needs to train a model. You also developed a good understanding of the dataset we are going to use throughout this part dedicated to forecasting and got your first hands-on experience of Amazon Forecast, as you learned how to create a forecasting project (called a dataset group in the service terminology) and how to ingest your CSV files into the appropriate datasets. You also got to learn how to use some related services, such as Amazon S3 (where we stored our CSV datasets) and AWS IAM (where we define a role to securely give access to your data to Amazon Forecast).

After reading this chapter, you will have developed a good understanding of the way Amazon Forecast requires the different datasets it needs to be structured. I recommend that you spend time understanding how each type of dataset is used by the service and which fields are actually expected from each file.

In the next chapter, we are going to train our first predictor and evaluate its performance on our London energy consumption dataset.

4
Training a Predictor with AutoML

In *Chapter 3, Creating a Project and Ingesting Your Data*, you learned how a raw dataset obtained from a public data source could be prepared and ingested in a suitable format for **Amazon Forecast**. Additionally, you created your first forecasting project (which, in the service, is called a dataset group) and populated it with three datasets. These datasets included the very time series that you want to forecast and several related time series that, intuitively, will lend some predictive power to the model you are going to train.

In this chapter, you will use these ingested datasets to train a forecasting model in Amazon Forecast; this construct is called a **Predictor**. Following this, you will learn how to configure the training along with the impact that each configuration can have on the training duration and the quality of the results. By the end of the chapter, you will also have a sound understanding of the evaluation dashboard.

In this chapter, we're going to cover the following main topics:

- Using your datasets to train a predictor
- How Amazon Forecast leverages automated machine learning
- Understanding the predictor evaluation dashboard
- Exporting and visualizing your predictor backtest results

Technical requirements

No hands-on experience in a language such as **Python** or **R** is necessary to follow along with the content from this chapter. However, I highly recommend that you read this chapter while connected to your own AWS account and open the Amazon Forecast console to run the different actions at your end.

To create an AWS account and log in to the Amazon Forecast console, you can refer to the *Technical requirements* section of *Chapter 2, An Overview of Amazon Forecast.*

Using your datasets to train a predictor

By the end of *Chapter 3, Creating a Project and Ingesting Your Data,* you had ingested three datasets in a dataset group, called `london_household_energy_consumption`, as follows:

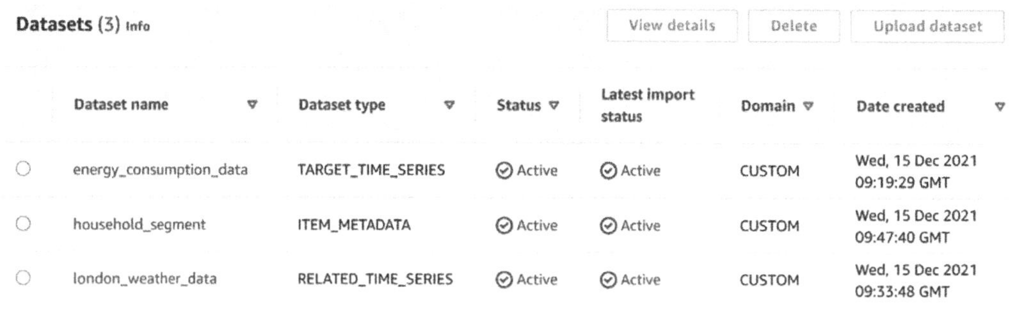

Datasets (3) Info

	Dataset name ▽	Dataset type ▽	Status ▽	Latest import status	Domain ▽	Date created ▽
○	energy_consumption_data	TARGET_TIME_SERIES	⊘ Active	⊘ Active	CUSTOM	Wed, 15 Dec 2021 09:19:29 GMT
○	household_segment	ITEM_METADATA	⊘ Active	⊘ Active	CUSTOM	Wed, 15 Dec 2021 09:47:40 GMT
○	london_weather_data	RELATED_TIME_SERIES	⊘ Active	⊘ Active	CUSTOM	Wed, 15 Dec 2021 09:33:48 GMT

Figure 4.1 – The London household dataset group overview

From here, you are now going to train a predictor using these three datasets. To do so, from the Amazon Forecast home page, locate the **View dataset groups** button on the right-hand side and click on it. Then, click on the name of your project. This will display the main dashboard of your dataset group. From here, click on the **Start** button under the **Predictor training** label:

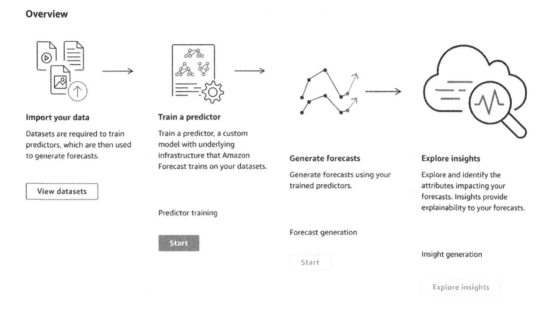

Figure 4.2 – The London household dataset group dashboard

This will bring you to the predictor configuration screen. The first two sections are dedicated to the predictor's settings: in this chapter, you are only going to modify a few of these parameters, while the other ones will be further explored in *Chapter 5, Customizing Your Predictor Training*:

Predictor name
The name can help you distinguish this predictor from your other predictors.

london_energy_automl

The predictor name must have 1 to 63 characters. Valid characters: a-z, A-Z, 0-9, and _

Forecast configuration

Forecast frequency
This is the frequency at which your forecasts are generated.

Your forecast frequency is   1   ▼   day   ▼

Forecast horizon Info
This number tells Amazon Forecast how far into the future to predict your data at the specified forecast frequency.

30

Figure 4.3 – The basic predictor settings

You can fill in the following parameters:

- **Predictor name**: Let's call our predictor `london_energy_automl`

- **Forecast frequency**: We want to keep the same frequency as our original ingested data. So, let's set this parameter to `1 day`.

- **Forecast horizon**: This is `30`. As the selected forecast horizon is 1 day, this means that we want to train a model that will be able to generate the equivalent of 30 days worth of data points in the future.

You can leave the forecast dimension and forecast quantiles as their default values.

> **Note**
>
> It is not mandatory to have a forecast frequency that matches your dataset frequency. You can have your ingested data available hourly and then decide that you will generate a daily forecast.

In the second part of the predictor settings, you are going to disable **AutoPredictor** and then configure the following parameters:

- **Algorithm selection**: Select **Choose for me (AutoML)** to let Amazon Forecast choose the best algorithm given your dataset.

- **Optimization metric**: Select **Default** (by default, Amazon Forecast uses the **Average wQL** option. For more information regarding this, please refer to the *How Amazon Forecast leverages automated machine learning* section).

For reference, take a look at the following screenshot:

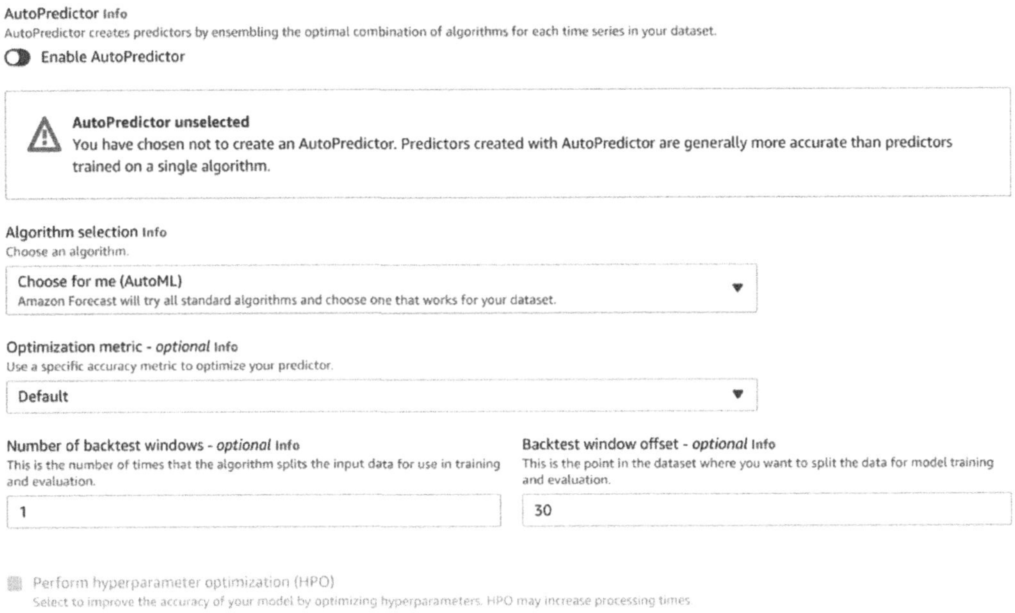

AutoPredictor Info
AutoPredictor creates predictors by ensembling the optimal combination of algorithms for each time series in your dataset.

⬤ Enable AutoPredictor

⚠ **AutoPredictor unselected**
You have chosen not to create an AutoPredictor. Predictors created with AutoPredictor are generally more accurate than predictors trained on a single algorithm.

Algorithm selection Info
Choose an algorithm.

| Choose for me (AutoML) ▼ |
| Amazon Forecast will try all standard algorithms and choose one that works for your dataset. |

Optimization metric - *optional* Info
Use a specific accuracy metric to optimize your predictor.

| Default ▼ |

Number of backtest windows - *optional* Info
This is the number of times that the algorithm splits the input data for use in training and evaluation.

| 1 |

Backtest window offset - *optional* Info
This is the point in the dataset where you want to split the data for model training and evaluation.

| 30 |

▦ Perform hyperparameter optimization (HPO)
Select to improve the accuracy of your model by optimizing hyperparameters. HPO may increase processing times.

Figure 4.4 – The basic predictor settings

Leave all the other parameters with their default values, as you will explore them later in *Chapter 5, Customizing Your Predictor Training*.

> **Important Note**
>
> At the time of writing this book, the **AutoPredictor** option was not available. At that time, Amazon Forecast would apply a single algorithm to all the time series in your dataset. You will discover in *Chapter 5, Customizing Your Predictor Training*, that this might not be a good option when different segments of your dataset have significantly different behaviors.
>
> With the AutoPredictor option, Amazon Forecast can now automatically assemble the best combination of algorithms for each time series in your dataset. In general, this creates predictors that are more accurate than single-algorithm ones, and it is now the default option when you configure a new predictor.
>
> In addition to this, when selecting the AutoPredictor path, you can also enable **Explainability** to allow Amazon Forecast to provide more insights into the predictions it makes at forecast time. AutoPredictor also comes with a built-in retraining capability, which makes it easier to retrain a predictor when the underlying dataset is updated. Both the explainability feature and the retraining feature are *not* available for legacy predictors (predictors trained with AutoPredictor disabled).

Scroll down to the bottom of the predictor creation screen and click on the **Start** button. Your predictor will start training:

> ⓘ **Predictor training for london_energy_automl has started.**
> **We will let you know when your predictor has been trained.**

Figure 4.5 – Your first predictor starting to train

You can click on the **View predictors** button present on the dataset group dashboard to inspect the progress of your predictor training.

Following this, Amazon Forecast will give you the estimated time remaining and the ability to stop your training should you want to change your training parameters or cut the training cost of a predictor that is taking too long to train, as shown in the following screenshot:

Figure 4.6 – The predictor training is in progress

> **Important Note**
> When you stop a training job, the predictor is not deleted: you can still preview its metadata. In addition, you *cannot resume a stopped job*.

Additionally, you have the option to upgrade a standard predictor to an AutoPredictor (as you can see in the **AutoPredictor** column).

Once your predictor has been trained, the **Predictors** list from your dataset group is updated with the key characteristics (for example, the forecast types, the **WAPE** metrics, and the **RMSE** metrics) of the trained model:

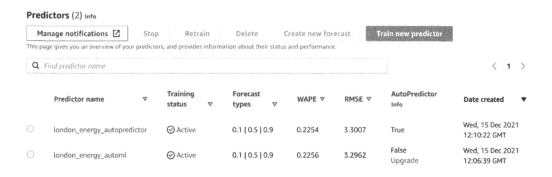

Figure 4.7 – Overview of the trained predictor

In the preceding table, you can directly access the following information:

- **Training status**: The trained predictors will be marked as **Active**.

- **Forecast types**: These are the different **quantiles** requested for your predictor. We will dive deeper into what quantiles are and when you would need to customize them in *Chapter 5, Customizing Your Predictor Training*. By default, Amazon Forecast will train a predictor to emit three values for each prediction point in the forecast horizon: a median value (this is also called p50 or percentile 50, which is marked here as forecast type **0.5**) and an interval with a low boundary at p10 (forecast type **0.1**) and a high boundary at p90 (forecast type **0.9**).

- **WAPE**: This is one of the metrics used in forecasting to assess the quality of a prediction model. **WAPE** stands for **Weighted Absolute Percentage Error** and measures the deviation of the forecasted values from the actual values. The lower the WAPE, the better the model. Our first model, **WAPE**, is **0.2254**.

- **RMSE**: This is another useful metric to assess the quality of a forecasting model. It stands for **Root Mean Square Error** and also measures the deviation of the forecasted values from the actual ones. The **RMSE** value of the model is **3.2904**.

- **AutoPredictor**: This states whether the current predictor has been trained with AutoPredictor enabled or not, and gives you the ability to upgrade a legacy predictor to the more feature-rich AutoPredictor.

We will describe the metrics, in detail, in the *Understanding the predictor evaluation dashboard* section.

How Amazon Forecast leverages automated machine learning

During the training of your first predictor, you disabled AutoPredictor and then allowed the algorithm to choose its default value, which is AutoML. In **Automated Machine Learning** (**AutoML**) mode, you don't have to understand which algorithm and configuration to choose from, as Amazon Forecast will run your data against all of the available algorithms (at the time of writing, there are six) and choose the best one.

So, how does Amazon Forecast rank the different algorithms? It computes the **weighted quantile loss** (**wQL**; to read more about wQL, please check the *Algorithm metrics* section) for the forecast types you selected. By default, the selected forecast types are the median (p10) and the boundaries of the 80% confidence interval (p10 and p90). Amazon Forecast computes the wQL for these three quantiles. To determine the winning algorithm, it then takes the average over all of the wQL values that have been calculated: the algorithm with the lowest value will be the winning one.

My predictor obtained the following results for each algorithm:

	wQL[0.1]	wQL[0.5]	wQL[0.9]	WAPE	RMSE
CNN-QR (Winner)	0.0993	0.2254	0.1183	0.2254	3.2904
Deep_AR_Plus	0.1100	0.2353	0.1253	0.2364	3.4374
ARIMA	0.1196	0.2456	0.1430	0.2456	3.6026
Prophet	0.1243	0.2636	0.1305	0.2617	3.8997
NPTS	0.1107	0.3329	0.1813	0.3618	5.1994
ETS	0.1636	0.2866	0.2084	0.2866	4.6343

Figure 4.8 – Algorithm metrics comparison

The CNN-QR algorithm is the winner with an average **wQL** value of **0.1477**. This value is obtained by taking the average of the wQL values for the three quantiles selected:

(wQL[0.1] + wQL[0.5] + wQL[0.9]) / 3 =

(0.0993 + 0.2254 + 0.1183) / 3 = 0.1477

Note that these metrics are computed for each backtest window. For our first training session, we set the default value to one backtest window. If you select more backtest windows (Amazon Forecast allows you to specify up to five), AutoML will average these metrics across all of them before selecting the winning algorithm.

Important Note

When running each algorithm in AutoML, Amazon Forecast uses the default parameters of each algorithm. You will see in *Chapter 5, Customizing Your Predictor Training*, that you can customize some of the algorithms by adjusting their hyperparameters when they are available. AutoML does not give you this option. You will have to choose between the automatic model selection (with AutoML) or hyperparameter optimization of a given algorithm that you manually select.

Understanding the predictor evaluation dashboard

When you click on a predictor name on the list of trained models that are available for your dataset group, you get access to a detailed overview screen where you can get a better understanding of the quality of your model. This screen also serves as a reminder of how your training was configured. In this section, we are going to take a detailed look at the different sections of this screen, including the following:

- Predictor overview
- Predictor metrics
- Predictor backtest results

Predictor overview

The **Predictor overview** section is the first section of the predictor details page:

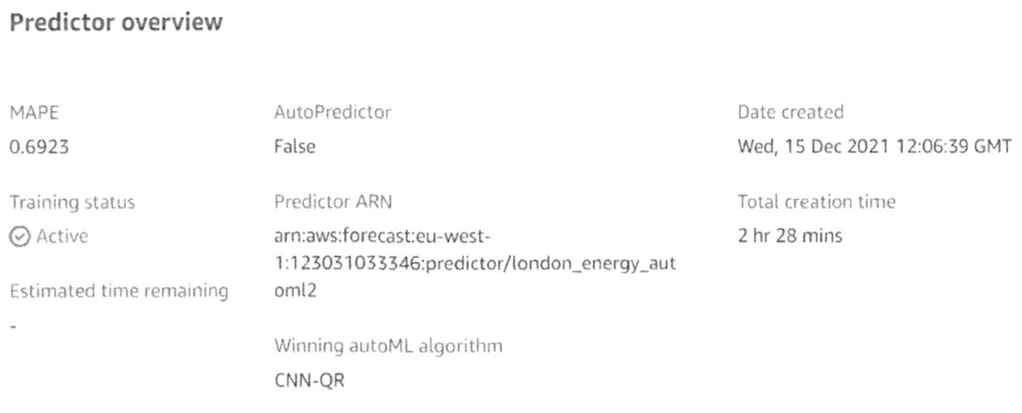

Predictor overview

MAPE	AutoPredictor	Date created
0.6923	False	Wed, 15 Dec 2021 12:06:39 GMT
Training status	Predictor ARN	Total creation time
⊘ Active	arn:aws:forecast:eu-west-1:123031033346:predictor/london_energy_aut	2 hr 28 mins
Estimated time remaining	oml2	
-		
	Winning autoML algorithm	
	CNN-QR	

Figure 4.9 – The results page: Predictor overview

You can find three types of information in this section:

- *Training parameters*: These remind you how the predictor was trained. For instance, you can check whether **AutoPredictor** was set to `True` or `False` when training this particular predictor.

- *Training results:*

  a) **MAPE**: The **Mean Absolute Percentage Error** (**MAPE**) is one of the performance metrics of a forecasting model (in our case, the MAPE value is **0.6923**).

  > **Important Note**
  >
  > To train a predictor, Amazon Forecast will provision and use the resources deemed necessary to deliver the results in a reasonable amount of time. During this training time, multiple compute instances might be used in parallel: the training time will be multiplied by this number of instances to compute the total cost of your training.

  b) **Winning AutoML algorithm**: If **AutoML** is set to `True`, this field will tell you which of the underlying algorithms fared better. **CNN-QR** is one of the six algorithms that you will learn about, in detail, in *Chapter 5, Customizing Your Predictor Training*.

- *Predictor attributes:*

  - **Predictor ARN**: This is useful when you use the API and want to precisely point to a particular predictor. This is a unique identifier (**ARN** stands for **Amazon Resource Number**).

  - **Date created**: This is the date at which you created the predictor and started the training process.

  - **Total creation time**: Training my predictor took **2 hr 28 mins**. This will be the training time used to compute my bills at the end of the billing cycle.

The **Estimated time remaining** field is only populated while the predictor is in progress. Once a predictor is active, this field becomes empty.

Predictor metrics

The next section of interest on the predictor page is the **Predictor metrics** one. This section shows the predictor metrics for each backtest window and each algorithm. When the predictor is trained with AutoML on, the sections open with the winning algorithm results by default (in our case, **CNN-QR**):

Predictor metrics Info   CNN-QR (Winner) ▼   [Export backtest results]

Weighted Absolute Percentage Error (WAPE)   Root Mean Squared Error (RMSE)   Mean Absolute Percentage Error (MAPE)
0.2256   3.2962   0.6923

Mean Absolute Scaled Error (MASE)
3.7655

Weighted quantile loss values (wQL)

Average wQL	wQL[0.1]	wQL[0.5]	wQL[0.9]
0.1477	0.0991	0.2256	0.1185

Figure 4.10 – The results page: algorithm metrics

Using the drop-down menu in the upper-right corner of this section, you can select the algorithm that you want to see the results for. As demonstrated earlier, our predictor obtained the following results for each algorithm:

	wQL[0.1]	wQL[0.5]	wQL[0.9]	WAPE	RMSE
CNN-QR (Winner)	0.0993	0.2254	0.1183	0.2254	3.2904
Deep_AR_Plus	0.1100	0.2353	0.1253	0.2364	3.4374
ARIMA	0.1196	0.2456	0.1430	0.2456	3.6026
Prophet	0.1243	0.2636	0.1305	0.2617	3.8997
NPTS	0.1107	0.3329	0.1813	0.3618	5.1994
ETS	0.1636	0.2866	0.2084	0.2866	4.6343

Figure 4.11 – Comparing algorithm metrics

When AutoML is enabled, Amazon Forecast selects the algorithm that delivers the best average **wQL** value across every forecast type (these are **0.1, 0.5**, and **0.9** when you use the default quantiles). In the preceding table, CNN-QR has an average **wQL** value of the following:

(0.0993 + 0.2254 + 0.1183) / 3 = 0.1477

The second-best algorithm is Deep_AR_Plus with an average **wQL** value of the following:

(0.1100 + 0.2353 + 0.1253) / 3 = 0.1569

So, how are these metrics computed? How do you interpret them? How do you know if a value is a good one? To know more about the metrics in detail, please head over to *Chapter 7, Improving and Scaling Your Forecast Strategy*. You will find a dedicated section that will detail the ins and outs of these metrics and how to use them.

Note that visualizing the predicted values and the associated metrics for a few `item_id` time series is crucial to get the big picture and complement this high-level aggregated analysis. In the next section, we are going to export the actual backtest results and plot them for a few households.

Exporting and visualizing your predictor backtest results

In this section, you are going to explore how you can visualize the performance of the predictor that you trained by exporting and visualizing the backtest results. I will start by explaining what backtesting is and then show you how you can export and visualize the results associated with your predictor.

In the **Predictor metrics** section, you might have noticed an **Export backtest results** button in the upper-right corner of the section, as shown in the following screenshot:

Figure 4.12 – The results page: Predictor metrics

Before we click on this button, first, let's define what **backtesting** is in the next section.

What is backtesting?

Backtesting is a technique used in time series-oriented machine learning to tune your model parameters during training and produce accuracy metrics. To perform backtesting, Amazon Forecast splits the data that you provide into two datasets:

- A **training dataset**, which is used to train a model
- A **testing dataset**, which is used to generate forecasts for data points within the testing set

Then, Amazon Forecasts computes the different accuracy metrics, as described earlier, by comparing how close the forecasted values are when compared with the actual values in the testing set. In the following diagram, you can see how a single backtest window is defined:

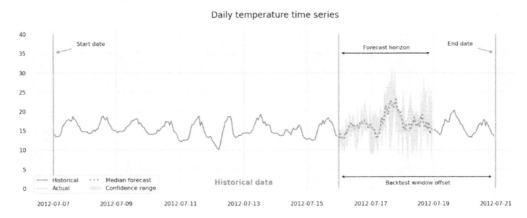

Figure 4.13 – Defining the backtest window length

In the preceding plot, you can see how Amazon Forecast would split your dataset to build a training dataset out of the historical data and a testing dataset out of data present in the forecast horizon. Note that in the preceding plot, the forecast horizon is shorter than the backtest window width: the latter is used to define the time split at which the forecast horizon starts. In this case, only part of the data present in the backtest window is used to build the testing dataset. If you want the testing dataset to leverage as much data as possible, you will have to set the backtest window to a width that is equal to the forecast horizon (which is the default value suggested by Amazon Forecast).

To train your first predictor, we leave the backtesting parameters at their default values. They are as follows:

- The *number of backtest windows* is 1.
- The *length of the backtest window* is equal to the forecast horizon. If you remember well, we selected a 30-day horizon, so our default backtest window length was also set to 30. You can adjust this value to request Amazon Forecast to use a larger backtest window than the forecast horizon. However, the backtest window length cannot be smaller than the requested forecast horizon.

In *Chapter 5, Customizing Your Predictor Training*, you will learn how you can adjust these parameters to improve your forecasting accuracy.

Exporting backtest results

Now, let's click on the **Export backtest results** button. You are brought to the following **Export details** screen:

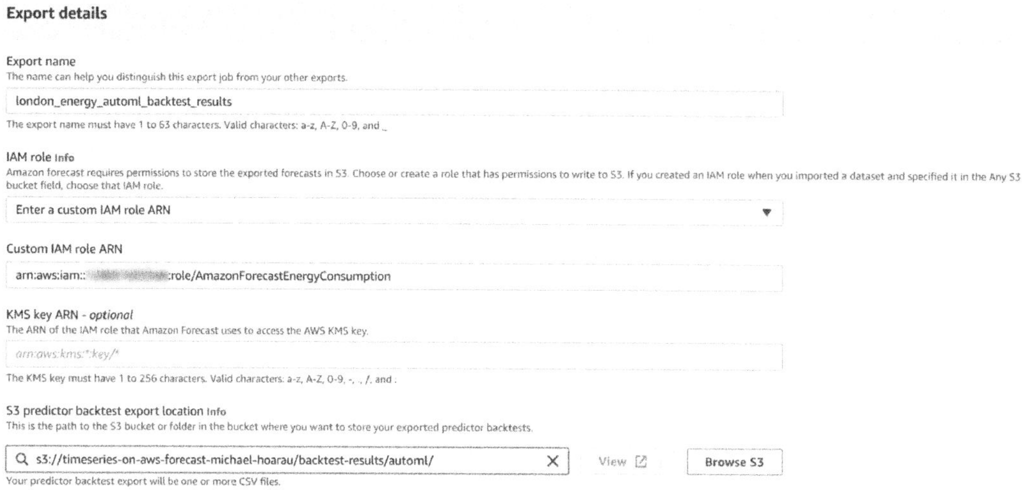

Export details

Export name
The name can help you distinguish this export job from your other exports.

london_energy_automl_backtest_results

The export name must have 1 to 63 characters. Valid characters: a-z, A-Z, 0-9, and _

IAM role Info
Amazon forecast requires permissions to store the exported forecasts in S3. Choose or create a role that has permissions to write to S3. If you created an IAM role when you imported a dataset and specified it in the Any S3 bucket field, choose that IAM role.

Enter a custom IAM role ARN   ▼

Custom IAM role ARN

arn:aws:iam:: ░░░░░ ░░░░░ :role/AmazonForecastEnergyConsumption

KMS key ARN - *optional*
The ARN of the IAM role that Amazon Forecast uses to access the AWS KMS key.

arn:aws:kms:*:key/*

The KMS key must have 1 to 256 characters. Valid characters: a-z, A-Z, 0-9, -, ., /, and :

S3 predictor backtest export location Info
This is the path to the S3 bucket or folder in the bucket where you want to store your exported predictor backtests.

🔍 s3://timeseries-on-aws-forecast-michael-hoarau/backtest-results/automl/   ✕   View ↗   Browse S3

Your predictor backtest export will be one or more CSV files.

Figure 4.14 –Export details of backtest results

> **Important Note**
> In AutoML mode, backtest results are only available for the winning algorithm.

As you can see in the preceding screenshot, you need to fill in the following parameters:

- **Export name**: london_energy_automl_backtest_results

- **IAM role**: Select **Enter a custom IAM role ARN** and paste the ARN of the AmazonForecastEnergyConsumption role that you created in *Chapter 3, Creating a Project and Ingesting Your Data,* in the IAM service. As a reminder, the format of the ARN should be arn:aws:iam::<ACCOUNT-NUMBER>:role/AmazonForecastEnergyConsumption, where <ACCOUNT-NUMBER> needs to be replaced by your AWS account number.

- **S3 predictor backtest export location**: We are going to export our results in the same location where we put the datasets to be ingested. Fill in the following S3 URL: `s3://<BUCKET>/backtest-results/automl/`. Here, `<BUCKET>` should be replaced by the name of the bucket you created in *Chapter 3, Creating a Project and Ingesting Your Data*. Mine was called `timeseries-on-aws-forecast-michael-hoarau`, and the full URL where I want my backtest results to be exported will be `s3:// timeseries-on-aws-forecast-michael-hoarau/backtest-results/automl/`.

Click on the **Start** button to initiate the backtest results export. A blue ribbon at the top of the window informs you that a predictor backtest export is in progress. This process can take up to 15 to 20 minutes, after which we can go to the Amazon S3 console to collect our results.

In the upper-left corner of your AWS console, you will see a **Services** drop-down menu that will display all of the available AWS services. In the **Storage** section, look for the **S3** service and click on its name to navigate to the S3 console. Click on the name of the bucket you used to upload your datasets to visualize its content:

Figure 4.15 – Backtest results location on Amazon S3

On this screen, you will see a `backtest-results/` folder. Click on it, and then click on the `automl` folder name. In this folder, you will find an `accuracy-metrics-values` folder and a `forecasted-values` folder.

We are going to take a look at the content of each of these folders next.

Backtest predictions overview

In the S3 listing of the `backtest-results/` folder, click on the `forecasted-values/` folder. You will end up inside a directory with a collection of CSV files:

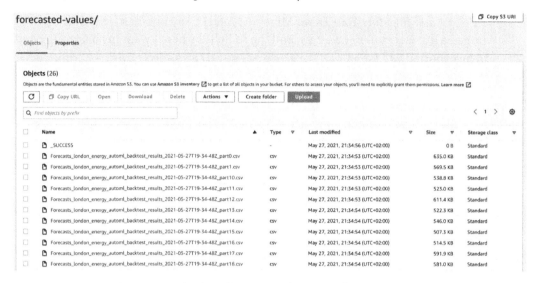

Figure 4.16 – Backtest forecast results as stored on Amazon S3

Each CSV file has a name that follows this pattern:

```
Forecasts_<export_name>_<yyyy-mm-ddTHH-MM-SSZ>_part<NN>
```

Here, `export_name` is the label you chose to name your backtest export job followed by a `timestamp` label (time at which the export was generated) and a `part number` label.

Each CSV file contains the backtest results for a subset of `item_id` (which, in our case, corresponds to the household ID). In the dataset we used, we had slightly more than 3,500 households and Amazon Forecast generated 25 files (from `part0` to `part24`), each containing the backtest results for approximately 140 households.

Click on the checkbox next to the first CSV file and click on **Download**. This action will download the CSV file locally where you can open it with any spreadsheet software such as Excel or process it with your favorite programming language. I am going to open this file with Excel and plot the different time series available in these files for a few households. Click on the following link to download my Excel file and follow along with my analysis: `https://packt-publishing-timeseries-on-aws-michaelhoarau.s3-eu-west-1.amazonaws.com/part1-amazon-forecast/london_energy_automl_backtest_results.xlsx`

The raw data is located in the first tab (**raw**) and looks like this:

	A	B	C	D	E	F	G	H	I
1	item_id	timestamp	target_value	backtestwindow_start_time	backtestwindow_end_time	p10	p50	p90	
2	MAC001803	2013-06-01T00:00:00Z	0,979	2013-06-01T00:00:00	2013-06-30T00:00:00	0,729440629	1,187367916	2,354403019	
3	MAC001803	2013-06-02T00:00:00Z	0,973	2013-06-01T00:00:00	2013-06-30T00:00:00	0,756773293	1,231862664	2,560441971	
4	MAC001803	2013-06-03T00:00:00Z	1,019	2013-06-01T00:00:00	2013-06-30T00:00:00	0,675655723	1,015442014	1,886719108	
5	MAC001803	2013-06-04T00:00:00Z	0,963	2013-06-01T00:00:00	2013-06-30T00:00:00	0,685590744	1,062819719	2,100817919	
6	MAC001803	2013-06-05T00:00:00Z	0,981	2013-06-01T00:00:00	2013-06-30T00:00:00	0,838173687	1,125506639	2,016360044	
7	MAC001803	2013-06-06T00:00:00Z	0,995	2013-06-01T00:00:00	2013-06-30T00:00:00	0,550817728	0,992931962	1,930458546	
8	MAC001803	2013-06-07T00:00:00Z	1,076	2013-06-01T00:00:00	2013-06-30T00:00:00	0,495151103	1,090229869	2,358493805	
9	MAC001803	2013-06-08T00:00:00Z	0,985	2013-06-01T00:00:00	2013-06-30T00:00:00	0,493359029	1,192526102	2,307828426	
10	MAC001803	2013-06-09T00:00:00Z	0,998	2013-06-01T00:00:00	2013-06-30T00:00:00	0,857026815	1,066516161	1,914440274	
11	MAC001803	2013-06-10T00:00:00Z	1,001	2013-06-01T00:00:00	2013-06-30T00:00:00	0,70153451	0,90643245	1,68554759	
12	MAC001803	2013-06-11T00:00:00Z	0,982	2013-06-01T00:00:00	2013-06-30T00:00:00	0,719361961	0,950176835	1,926070452	
13	MAC001803	2013-06-12T00:00:00Z	1,025	2013-06-01T00:00:00	2013-06-30T00:00:00	0,699070096	0,987177074	1,925270796	
14	MAC001803	2013-06-13T00:00:00Z	1,037	2013-06-01T00:00:00	2013-06-30T00:00:00	0,600809157	0,77252233	1,76926136	
15	MAC001803	2013-06-14T00:00:00Z	1,042	2013-06-01T00:00:00	2013-06-30T00:00:00	0,568310201	0,835910082	2,065519333	
16	MAC001803	2013-06-15T00:00:00Z	1,117	2013-06-01T00:00:00	2013-06-30T00:00:00	0,604528546	1,000369668	2,225152493	
17	MAC001803	2013-06-16T00:00:00Z	0,964	2013-06-01T00:00:00	2013-06-30T00:00:00	0,733091593	1,200875521	2,672187805	
18	MAC001803	2013-06-17T00:00:00Z	1	2013-06-01T00:00:00	2013-06-30T00:00:00	0,708183587	0,777950823	1,734839916	
19	MAC001803	2013-06-18T00:00:00Z	1,157	2013-06-01T00:00:00	2013-06-30T00:00:00	0,758836746	0,942750812	2,161010981	
20	MAC001803	2013-06-19T00:00:00Z	2,799	2013-06-01T00:00:00	2013-06-30T00:00:00	0,710776389	0,965316236	2,157253981	
21	MAC001803	2013-06-20T00:00:00Z	1,079	2013-06-01T00:00:00	2013-06-30T00:00:00	0,657781005	0,76887846	1,792552233	
22	MAC001803	2013-06-21T00:00:00Z	1,082	2013-06-01T00:00:00	2013-06-30T00:00:00	0,641253829	1,058848619	2,340186596	
23	MAC001803	2013-06-22T00:00:00Z	1,429	2013-06-01T00:00:00	2013-06-30T00:00:00	0,840278029	1,244062662	2,676504612	
24	MAC001803	2013-06-23T00:00:00Z	1,003	2013-06-01T00:00:00	2013-06-30T00:00:00	0,498462141	1,210797787	2,870205879	
25	MAC001803	2013-06-24T00:00:00Z	1,007	2013-06-01T00:00:00	2013-06-30T00:00:00	0,864430487	1,044870496	2,558401108	
26	MAC001803	2013-06-25T00:00:00Z	0,923	2013-06-01T00:00:00	2013-06-30T00:00:00	0,639360249	1,109704733	2,325706244	
27	MAC001803	2013-06-26T00:00:00Z	0,964	2013-06-01T00:00:00	2013-06-30T00:00:00	0,580239654	0,954522312	2,355161667	
28	MAC001803	2013-06-27T00:00:00Z	1,006	2013-06-01T00:00:00	2013-06-30T00:00:00	0,586509109	0,798478007	1,96077013	

Figure 4.17 – Raw data from the backtest result

The different columns generated by Amazon Forecast are as follows:

- `item_id`: This column contains the ID of each household.

- `timestamp`: For each household, there will be as many data points as the length of the backtest window, as configured in the predictor training parameters. With a forecast frequency of 1 day and a backtest window length of 30, we end up with 30 data points. The timestamps from these columns will include 30 days worth for each household.

- `target_value`: This is the actual value as observed in the known historical time series data. This is the value that our predictions will be compared to in order to compute the error made by the model for a given data point.

- `Backtestwindow_start_time` and `Backtestwindow_end_time`: This is the start and end of the backtest window. At training time, you can request up to five backtest windows (we will see this in the advanced configuration in *Chapter 5*, *Customizing Your Predictor Training*). Backtest results will be available for all of the backtest windows.

- `p10`, `p50`, and `p90`: These are the values for each forecast type as requested at training time. You can request up to five forecast types, and they will all appear as individual columns in this file.

Now let's navigate to the second tab of the Excel file (called **analysis**): this tab leverages the raw data located in the first tab to plot the predictions obtained in the backtest window and offers a comparison with the actual data:

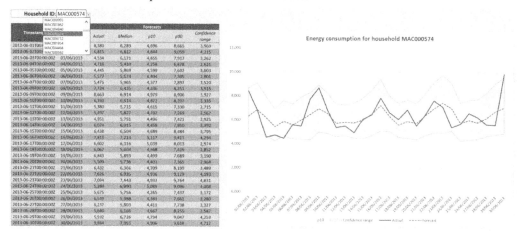

Figure 4.18 – The backtest analysis tab

Use the drop-down menu in the upper-left corner to select the household you want to analyze. The backtest result for this household is updated and the plot on the right reflects this change. Let's zoom into the backtest plot:

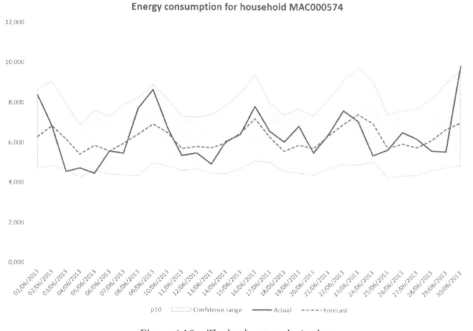

Figure 4.19 – The backtest analysis plot

On this plot, you can see three pieces of information:

- The *actual* energy consumption in the thick solid line.

- The *predicted values* in a dotted line: This is the median forecast (also called forecast type 0.5 or p50). This forecast type estimates a value that is lower than the observed value 50% of the time.

- The *80% confidence interval* is represented as a shaded area around the median forecast. The lower bound of this confidence interval is the p10 forecast (the actual values are expected to be lower than this value 10% of the time), and the upper bound is the p90 forecast (for which the actual values are expected to be lower 90% of the time).

Feel free to explore further by selecting a different household to see what the backtest results look like.

Backtest accuracy overview

In the S3 listing of the `backtest-results/` folder, click on the `accuracy-metrics-values/` folder. You will end up inside a directory with a collection of CSV files with names that follow this pattern: `Accuracy_<export_name>_<yyyy-mm-ddTHH-MM-SSZ>_part<NN>`. Here, `export_name` is the label you chose to name your backtest export job followed by a `timestamp` label (the time at which the export was generated) and a `part number` label:

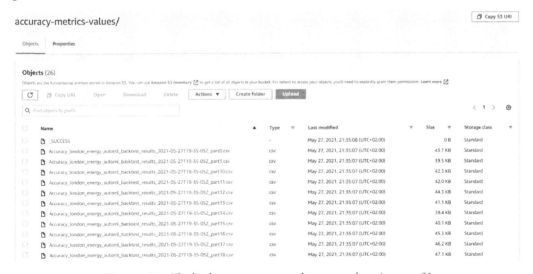

Figure 4.20 – The backtest accuracy results as stored on Amazon S3

Each CSV file contains the backtest accuracy results for a subset of `item_id` (which, in our case, corresponds to the household ID). In the dataset we used, we had slightly more than 3,500 households, and Amazon Forecast generated 25 files (from part0 to part24) with each containing the backtest results for approximately 140 households. If you want to have a complete overview of the accuracy metrics for all `item_id` types of your dataset, you will have to download and concatenate all the CSV files (or perform this action programmatically).

Click on the checkbox next to the first CSV file and click on **Download**. This action will download the CSV file locally where you can open it with any spreadsheet software such as Excel or process it with your favorite programming language.

For the analysis we just performed, I concatenated all of the accuracy metrics files and made them available in the following link. Feel free to download and open this file to follow along with my analysis: `https://packt-publishing-timeseries-on-aws-michaelhoarau.s3-eu-west-1.amazonaws.com/part1-amazon-forecast/london_energy_automl_backtest_accuracy_metrics.csv`

The raw data provided by Amazon Forecast is located in the first tab and contains the accuracy metric computed for each `item_id` time series, as shown in the following screenshot:

item_id	backtest_window	backtestwindow_start_time	backtestwindow_end_time	wQL[0.1]	wQL[0.5]	wQL[0.9]	RMSE	WAPE	
MAC000020	Summary	2013-06-01T00:00:00	2013-06-30T00:00:00	0,07414	0,19804	0,12587	1,52925	33,76336	
MAC000018	Summary	2013-06-01T00:00:00	2013-06-30T00:00:00	0,06577	0,11320	0,05907	1,34468	30,53381	
MAC000008	Summary	2013-06-01T00:00:00	2013-06-30T00:00:00	0,07243	0,10849	0,05311	2,58491	57,46529	
MAC000006	Summary	2013-06-01T00:00:00	2013-06-30T00:00:00	0,04567	0,11154	0,07230	0,36281	8,72251	
MAC000013	Summary	2013-06-01T00:00:00	2013-06-30T00:00:00	0,03081	0,15374	0,08589	0,68018	17,83491	
MAC000019	Summary	2013-06-01T00:00:00	2013-06-30T00:00:00	0,10165	0,20377	0,11995	1,47651	35,23587	
MAC000004	Summary	2013-06-01T00:00:00	2013-06-30T00:00:00	0,05626	0,20836	0,19347	0,56884	10,80964	
MAC000003	Summary	2013-06-01T00:00:00	2013-06-30T00:00:00	0,05663	0,08374	0,04852	1,39297	30,02842	
MAC000021	Summary	2013-06-01T00:00:00	2013-06-30T00:00:00	0,06364	0,06904	0,07309	1,63683	39,07425	
MAC000020	Computed	2013-06-01T00:00:00	2013-06-30T00:00:00	0,07414	0,19804	0,12587	1,52925	33,76336	
MAC000018	Computed	2013-06-01T00:00:00	2013-06-30T00:00:00	0,06577	0,11320	0,05907	1,34468	30,53381	
MAC000008	Computed	2013-06-01T00:00:00	2013-06-30T00:00:00	0,07243	0,10849	0,05311	2,58491	57,46529	
MAC000006	Computed	2013-06-01T00:00:00	2013-06-30T00:00:00	0,04567	0,11154	0,07230	0,36281	8,72251	
MAC000013	Computed	2013-06-01T00:00:00	2013-06-30T00:00:00	0,03081	0,15374	0,08589	0,68018	17,83491	
MAC000019	Computed	2013-06-01T00:00:00	2013-06-30T00:00:00	0,10165	0,20377	0,11995	1,47651	35,23587	
MAC000004	Computed	2013-06-01T00:00:00	2013-06-30T00:00:00	0,05626	0,20836	0,19347	0,56884	10,80964	
MAC000003	Computed	2013-06-01T00:00:00	2013-06-30T00:00:00	0,05663	0,08374	0,04852	1,39297	30,02842	
MAC000021	Computed	2013-06-01T00:00:00	2013-06-30T00:00:00	0,06364	0,06904	0,07309	1,63683	39,07425	

Figure 4.21 – The backtest accuracy metrics raw data

> **Note**
>
> If you open the CSV file with spreadsheet software such as Microsoft Excel, you will have to transform the text into columns and select comma as the separator (you will find this feature in the **Data** tab of Microsoft Excel). Depending on the regional parameters of your local stations, you might also have to explicitly specify the decimal separator you want to use for all the wQL columns. This is so that Excel treats them as numerical values and not strings of text.

For each `item_id` time series, you will find the metrics computed for the following:

- Each backtest window (we can have up to five, which will yield five rows for each `item_id` time series in this file)

- The summary (this is the average over all of the requested backtest windows, the grayed-out area in the previous diagram)

The metrics computed for each household are the ones shown in the console: the weighted quantile for each forecast type (if you kept the default parameters, this will be `wQL[0.1]`, `wQL[0.5]`, and `wQL[0.9]`), the RMSE, and the WAPE.

Summary

Congratulations! In this chapter, you trained your first predictor with Amazon Forecast. You learned how to configure a predictor with the default training parameters and developed a sound command regarding how a trained predictor can be evaluated through different metrics such as the wQL, the WAPE, or the RMSE. Additionally, you learned how to download the evaluations of a trained model to finely analyze your predictor results with your favorite spreadsheet tool.

In the next chapter, you will learn how to leverage all the flexibility Amazon Forecast can provide you to customize and further enhance your predictors to better suit your data.

5

Customizing Your Predictor Training

In the previous chapter, you trained your first predictor on a household energy consumption dataset. You used the fully **automated machine learning** (**AutoML**) approach offered by default by Amazon Forecast, which let you obtain an accurate forecast without any ML or statistical knowledge about time series forecasting.

In this chapter, you will continue to work on the same datasets, but you will explore the flexibility that **Amazon Forecast** gives you when training a predictor. This will allow you to better understand when and how you can adjust your forecasting approach based on specificities in your dataset or specific domain knowledge you wish to leverage.

In this chapter, we're going to cover the following main topics:

- Choosing an algorithm and configuring the training parameters
- Leveraging **hyperparameter optimization** (**HPO**)
- Reinforcing your backtesting strategy
- Including holiday and weather data
- Implementing featurization techniques
- Customizing quantiles to suit your business needs

Technical requirements

No hands-on experience of a language such as **Python** or **R** is necessary to follow along with the content from this chapter. However, we highly recommend that you read this chapter while being connected to your own **Amazon Web Services** (**AWS**) account and open the Amazon Forecast console to run the different actions on your end.

To create an AWS account and log in to the Amazon Forecast console, you can refer to the *Technical requirements* section of *Chapter 2, An Overview of Amazon Forecast*.

The content in this chapter assumes that you have a dataset already ingested and ready to be used to train a new predictor. If you don't, I recommend that you follow the detailed process detailed in *Chapter 3, Creating a Project and Ingesting your Data*. You will need the **Simple Storage Service** (**S3**) location of your three datasets, which should look like this (replace <YOUR_BUCKET> with the name of the bucket of your choice):

- **Target time series**: s3://<YOUR_BUCKET>/target_time_series.csv
- **Related time series**: s3://<YOUR_BUCKET>/related_time_series.csv
- **Item metadata**: s3://<YOUR_BUCKET>/item_metadata.csv

You will also need the **Identity and Access Management** (**IAM**) role you created to let Amazon Forecast access your data from Amazon S3. The unique **Amazon Resource Number** (**ARN**) of this role should have the following format: arn:aws:iam::<ACCOUNT-NUMBER>:role/AmazonForecastEnergyConsumption. Here, you need to replace <ACCOUNT-NUMBER> with your AWS account number.

With this information, you are now ready to dive into the more advanced features offered by Amazon Forecast.

Choosing an algorithm and configuring the training parameters

In *Chapter 4, Training a Predictor with AutoML*, we let Amazon Forecast make all the choices for us and left all the parameters at their default values, including the choice of algorithm. When you follow this path, Amazon Forecast applies every algorithm it knows on your dataset and selects the winning one by looking at which one achieves the best average **weighted absolute percentage error** (**WAPE**) metric in your backtest window (if you kept the default choice for the optimization metric to be used).

At the time of writing this chapter, Amazon Forecast knows about six algorithms. The AutoML process is great when you don't have a precise idea about the algorithm that will give the best result with your dataset. The `AutoPredictor` settings also give you the flexibility to experiment easily with an **ensembling** technique that will let Amazon Forecast devise the best combination of algorithms for each time series of your dataset. However, both these processes can be quite lengthy as they will, in effect, train and evaluate up to six models to select only one algorithm at the end (for AutoML) or a combination of these algorithms for each time series (for `AutoPredictor`).

Once you have some experience with Amazon Forecast, you may want to cut down on this training time (which will save you both time and training costs) and directly select the right algorithm among the ones available in the service.

When you open the Amazon Forecast console to create a new predictor and disable the AutoPredictor setting, you are presented with the following options in an **Algorithm selection** dropdown:

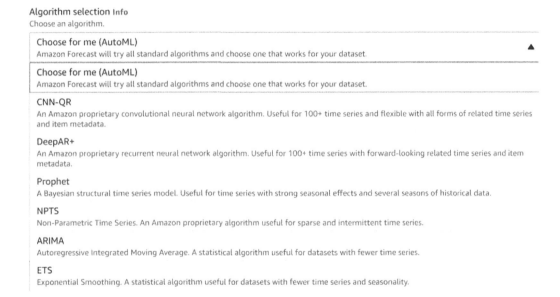

Figure 5.1 – Manual algorithm selection

In this chapter, we will dive into each of the following algorithms:

- **Exponential smoothing (ETS)**
- **Autoregressive integrated moving average (ARIMA)**
- **Non-parametric time series (NPTS)**

- **Prophet**
- **DeepAR+**
- **Convolutional Neural Network-Quantile Regression (CNN-QR)**

For each of these, I will give you some theoretical background that will help you understand the behaviors these algorithms are best suited to capture. I will also give you some pointers about when your use case will be a good fit for any given algorithm.

ETS

ETS stands for **Error, Trend, and Seasonality**: ETS is part of the exponential smoothing family of statistical algorithms. These algorithms work well when the number of time series is small (fewer than `100`).

The idea behind exponential smoothing is to use a weighted average of all the previous values in a given time series, to forecast future values. This approach approximates a given time series by capturing the most important patterns and leaving out the finer-scale structures or rapid changes that may be less relevant for forecasting future values.

The ETS implementation of Amazon Forecast performs exponential smoothing accounting for trends and seasonality in your time series data by leveraging several layers of smoothing.

Theoretical background

Trend and seasonal components can be additive or multiplicative by nature: if we consume 50% more electricity during winter, the seasonality is **multiplicative**. On the other hand, if we sell 1,000 more books during Black Friday, the seasonality will be **additive**.

Let's call y_t the raw values of our initial time series and let's decompose the different smoothing layers *in the case of additive trend and seasonality*, as follows:

1. We first start by applying a **moving average** (**MA**) on our time series. If W is the width of the rolling window and y_t the different timesteps of our time series, then the MA computed at time t will give us the predicted forecast F_{t+1} at time t+1 and is given by the following formula:

$$F_{t+1} = MA_t = \frac{y_{t-W+1} + y_{t-W+2} + \cdots + y_{t-1} + y_t}{W}$$

2. The MA step gives the same importance (weight) to each of the previous timesteps that fall in the rolling window width. Adding a smoothing constant will give more weight to recent values while reducing the impact of the window width choice. Let's call our smoothing constant α: this value, set between 0 and 1, will be a parameter telling our model how fast we want to forget the previous values of the time series. This can also be called a baseline factor as it's used to model the **base behavior** our forecast will have. In the following formula, you will notice that the previous timesteps are now weighted with a weight that is exponentially decreasing. Our forecast baseline at time t+1 can be derived from the series level at the previous timestep, L_t:

$$F_{t+1} = L_t$$
$$L_t = \alpha y_t + (1 - \alpha)L_{t-1}$$
$$F_{t+1} = \alpha y_t + \alpha(1 - \alpha)y_{t-1} + \alpha(1 - \alpha)^2 y_{t-2} + \cdots$$

3. When a **trend component** is present in our time series, the previous approach does not do well: to counter this, we add a trend smoothing parameter, generally called β, that we apply in a similar fashion on the difference between successive timesteps on our series. β is also set between 0 and 1. This yields to the double exponential smoothing, and the point forecast k periods ahead can be derived from both the series level and the series slope at the previous timestep L_t and B_t, as illustrated in the following formula:

$$F_{t+k} = L_t + k \cdot B_t$$
$$L_t = \alpha y_t + (1 - \alpha) \cdot (L_{t-1} + B_{t-1})$$
$$B_t = \beta \cdot (L_t - L_{t-1}) + (1 - \beta) \cdot B_{t-1}$$

4. If our signal also contains additional **high-frequency (HF)** signals such as a **seasonality component**, we need to add a third exponential smoothing parameter, usually called γ, and call the seasonal smoothing parameter (also set between 0 and 1 as α and β). If m denotes the number of seasons to capture our new point forecast k periods ahead, this can now be derived with the triple exponential smoothing, using the series level L_t, the series slope B_t, and the seasonal component S_t at the previous timestep, as follows:

$$F_{t+k} = L_t + k \cdot B_t + S_{t+k-m}$$
$$L_t = \alpha(y_t - S_{t-m}) + (1 - \alpha) \cdot (L_{t-1} + B_{t-1})$$
$$B_t = \beta \cdot (L_t - L_{t-1}) + (1 - \beta) \cdot B_{t-1}$$
$$S_t = \gamma \cdot (y_t - L_{t-1} + B_{t-1}) + (1 - \gamma) \cdot S_{t-m}$$

5. The ETS algorithm is also able to apply a **damping** parameter φ when there is a trend in a time series. When computing several periods ahead (in other words, when predicting a forecast horizon of several timesteps), we use the same slope as determined at the end of the historical time series for each forecast period. For long forecast periods, this may seem unrealistic, and we might want to dampen the detected trend as the forecast horizon increases. Accounting for this damping parameter (strictly set between β and 1), the previous equations become these:

$$F_{t+k} = L_t + (1 + \varphi + \cdots + \varphi^{k-1}) \cdot B_t + S_{t+k-m}$$
$$L_t = \alpha(y_t - S_{t-m}) + (1 - \alpha) \cdot (L_{t-1} + B_{t-1})$$
$$B_t = \beta \cdot (L_t - L_{t-1}) + (1 - \beta) \cdot B_{t-1}$$
$$S_t = \gamma \cdot (y_t - L_{t-1} + B_{t-1}) + (1 - \gamma) \cdot S_{t-m}$$

Implementation in Amazon Forecast

When Amazon Forecast trains a model with ETS, it uses the default parameters of the `ets` function available in the R `forecast` package. This means that all the `ets` parameters are automatically estimated. In addition, Amazon Forecast also automatically selects the model type according to the following criteria:

- With or without trend or seasonality

- Additive or multiplicative trend and seasonality

- Applying damping or not

All of these choices are abstracted away from you: multiple models are run behind the scenes and the best one is selected.

Amazon Forecast will create a local model for each time series available in your dataset. In the energy consumption example we have been running, each household electricity consumption would be modeled as a single ETS model.

If you want to get more in-depth details about the different exponential smoothing methods (including details of the equations when considering damping, and multiplicative trends and seasonality), how all these parameters are automatically computed, and which variation is automatically selected, I recommend you deep dive into this paper by Rob Hyndman et. al: *A state space framework for automatic forecasting using exponential smoothing methods*. Here is a persistent link to this paper: `https://doi.org/10.1016/S0169-2070(01)00110-8`.

ARIMA

With ETS, ARIMA is another very well-known family of flexible statistical forecasting models. ARIMA is a generalization of the ARMA family of models, where ARMA describes a time series with two polynomials: one for autoregression and the other for the MA.

Although all these family of models involves inputting many parameters and computing coefficients, Amazon Forecast leverages the `auto.arima` method from the `forecast` R package available on the **Comprehensive R Archive Network** (**CRAN**). This method conducts a search over the possible values of the different ARIMA parameters to identify the best model of this family.

Theoretical background

Let's call y_t the raw values of our initial time series and let's decompose the different steps needed to estimate an ARIMA model, as follows:

1. We start by making the time series stationary by using differencing. In statistics, this transformation is applied to non-stationary time series to remove non-constant trends. In the ARIMA implementation of Amazon Forecast, differencing is applied once (first-order differencing y_t') or twice (second-order differencing y_t'') and is the reason why the model is called **integrated** (the *I* in ARIMA stands for *integrated*). The formula is provided here:

$$y_t' = y_t - y_{t-1}$$
$$y_t'' = y_t' - y_{t-1}' = y_t - 2 \cdot y_{t-1} + y_{t-2}$$

2. We then use this differenced data to build an **autoregressive** (**AR**) model that specifies that our prediction depends linearly on the previous timesteps and on a random term. Let's call Y_t (with a capital Y) the differenced data obtained after the integrated step of the algorithm (Y_t will either be y_t' or y_t'', depending on the differencing order retained in the previous step). An AR model of order p can be written as a function of previous terms of the series and of a series of coefficients φ_1 to φ_p, as shown in the following formula:

$$Y_t = c + \varepsilon_t + \varphi_1 Y_{t-1} + \varphi_2 Y_{t-2} + \cdots + \varphi_p Y_{t-p}$$

3. Once we have an AR model, we use an MA model to capture the dependency of our prediction on the current and previous values of the random term. An MA model of order q can be written as a function of the mean μ of the series and of a list of parameters θ_1 to θ_q applied to random error terms ε_t to $\varepsilon_{t\text{-}q}$, as shown in the following formula:

$$Y_t = \mu + \varepsilon_t + \theta_1 \varepsilon_{t-1} + \cdots + \theta_q \varepsilon_{t-q}$$

4. When putting together an AR model and an MA model after differencing, we end up with the following estimation for the ARIMA model:

$$Y_t = c + \varepsilon_t + \varphi_1 Y_{t-1} + \varphi_2 Y_{t-2} + \cdots + \varphi_p Y_{t-p} + \theta_1 \varepsilon_{t-1} + \cdots + \theta_q \varepsilon_{t-q}$$

Implementation in Amazon Forecast

When Amazon Forecast trains a model with ETS, it uses the default parameters of the `arima` function available in the R `forecast` package. Amazon Forecast also uses the `auto.arima` method, which conducts a search of the parameter space to automatically find the best ARIMA parameters for your dataset. This includes exploring a range of values for the following:

- The differencing degree
- The AR order
- The MA order

This means that all these `arima` parameters are automatically estimated and that the model type is also automatically selected: all of these choices are abstracted away from you as multiple models are run behind the scenes, and the best one is selected.

Amazon Forecast will create a local model for each time series available in your dataset. In the energy consumption example we have been running, each household electricity consumption would be modeled as a single ARIMA model.

If you want to get more in-depth details about the automatic parameter choice from ARIMA, I recommend that you deep dive into this paper by Hyndman and Khandakar: *Automatic Time Series Forecasting: The forecast Package for R*. Here is a persistent link to this paper: https://doi.org/10.18637/jss.v027.i03.

NPTS

A simple forecaster is an algorithm that uses one of the past observed values as the forecast for the next timestep, as outlined here:

- A naïve forecaster takes the immediately previous observation as the forecast for the next timestep.

- A seasonal naïve forecaster takes the observation of the past seasons as the forecast for the next timestep.

NPTS falls into this class of simple forecaster.

Theoretical background

As just mentioned, NPTS falls in the simple forecasters' category. However, it does not use a fixed time index as the last value: rather, it samples randomly one of the past values to generate a prediction. By sampling multiple times, NPTS is able to generate a predictive distribution that Amazon Forecast can use to compute prediction intervals.

Let's call y_t the raw values of our initial time series, with t ranging from 0 to T − 1 and T being the time step for which we want to deliver a prediction $\widehat{y_T}$, as follows:

$$\widehat{y_T} = y_t$$

And the time index t is actually sampled from a sampling distribution q_T. NPTS uses the following sampling distribution:

$$q_T(t) = \frac{e^{-\alpha|T-t|}}{\sum_{t'=0}^{T-1} e^{-\alpha|T-t|}}$$

Here, α is a kernel weight hyperparameter that should be adjusted based on the data and helps you control the amount of decay in the weights. This allows NPTS to sample recent past values with a higher probability than observations from a distant past.

This hyperparameter can take values from 0 to infinitum. Here are the meanings of these extreme values:

- When α if 0, then all the weights are uniform: this leads to the **climatological forecaster**. The predicted value is sampled uniformly from the past, only accounting for the statistical distribution of values a given time series can time, without considering the dynamical implications of the current behavior.

- If α is set to infinitum, you get the **naïve forecaster**, which always predicts the last observed value.

Once you have generated a prediction for the next step, you can include this prediction in your past datasets and generate subsequent predictions while giving the ability to NPTS to sample past predicted data.

If you want to get in-depth details about this algorithm and, more generally, about intermittent data forecasting, you can dive deeper into the following articles:

- *GluonTS: Probabilistic Time Series Models in Python* (`https://arxiv.org/pdf/1906.05264.pdf`)

- *Intermittent Demand Forecasting with Renewal Processes* (`https://arxiv.org/pdf/2010.01550.pdf`)

Let's now have a look at how this algorithm has been implemented in Amazon Forecast.

Implementation in Amazon Forecast

Here are the key parameters the NPTS algorithm lets you select:

- `context_length`: This is the number of data points in the past NPTS uses to make a prediction. By default, Amazon Forecast uses all the points in the training range.

- `kernel_type`: This is the method used to define weights to sample past observations. This parameter can either be `uniform` or `exponential`. The default value is `exponential`.

- `exp_kernel_weights`: When you choose an `exponential` kernel type, you can specify the α parameter to control how fast the exponential decay is applied to past values. The default value for this parameter is `0.01`. This parameter should always be a positive number.

- You can also choose to sample only the past seasons instead of sampling from all the available observations. This behavior is controlled by the `use_seasonal_model` parameter, which can be set to `True` (which is the default value) or `False`.

When a seasonal model is used, you also have the ability to request Amazon Forecast to automatically provide and use seasonal features that depend on the forecast granularity by setting the `use_default_time_features` parameter to `True`. Let's say, for instance, that your data is available at the hourly level: if this parameter is set to `True` and you want to give a prediction for 3 p.m., then the NPTS algorithm will only sample past observations that also happened at 3 p.m.

Prophet

Prophet is a forecasting algorithm that was open sourced by Facebook in February 2017.

Theoretical background

The Prophet algorithm is similar to generalized additive models with four components, as follows:

$$y(t) = g(t) + s(t) + h(t) + \varepsilon_t$$

Here, the following applies:

- $g(t)$ is the trend function: trends are modeled with a piecewise logistic growth model. Prophet also allows trends to change through automatic changepoint selection (by defining a large number of changepoints—for instance, one per month). The logistic growth model is defined using the capacity $C(t)$ (what the maximum market size is in terms of the number of events measured), the growth rate k, and an offset parameter m, as follows:

$$g(t) = \frac{C(t)}{1 + e^{-k \cdot (t-m)}}$$

- $s(t)$ represents periodic changes such as yearly or weekly seasonal components. If P is the regular period you expect your time series to have ($P = 365.25$ for yearly seasonal effect and $P = 7$ for weekly periods), an approximate arbitrary smooth seasonal effect can be defined, such as this:

$$s(t) = \sum_{n=1}^{N} \left(a_n cos \left(\frac{2\pi n t}{P} \right) + b_n sin \left(\frac{2\pi n t}{P} \right) \right)$$

  By default, Prophet uses $N = 10$ for yearly seasonality and $N = 3$ for weekly seasonality.

- $h(t)$ represents the effect of holidays or, more generally, irregular events over 1 or more days. Amazon Forecast feeds this field with a list of holidays when you decide to use the **Holidays** supplementary feature (see the *Including holidays and weather data* section later in this chapter).

- ε_t is an error term accounting for everything that is not accommodated by the model.

If you want to know more about the theoretical details of Prophet, you can read through the original paper published by Facebook available at the following link: https://peerj.com/preprints/3190/.

Implementation in Amazon Forecast

Amazon Forecast uses the `Prophet` class of the Python implementation of Prophet using all the default parameters.

Amazon Forecast will create a local model for each time series available in your dataset. In the energy consumption example we have been running, each household electricity consumption would be modeled as a single Prophet model.

If you want to get more in-depth details about the impact of the default parameter choice from Prophet, I recommend that you read through the comprehensive Prophet documentation available at the following link: `https://facebook.github.io/prophet/`.

DeepAR+

Classical methods we have been reviewing—such as ARIMA, ETS, or NPTS—fit a single model to every single time series provided in a dataset. They then use each of these models to provide a prediction for the desired time series. In some applications, you may have hundreds or thousands of similar time series that evolve in parallel. This will be the case of the number of units sold for each product on an e-commerce website or the electricity consumption of every household served by an energy provider. For these cases, leveraging global models that learn from multiple time series jointly may provide more accurate forecasting. This is the approach taken by DeepAR+.

Theoretical background

DeepAR+ is a supervised algorithm for univariate time series forecasting. It uses **recurrent neural networks (RNNs)** and a large number of time series to train a single global model. At training time, for each time series ingested into the target time series dataset, DeepAR+ generates multiple sequences (time series snippets) with different starting points in the original time series to improve the learning capacity of the model.

The underlying theoretical details are beyond the scope of this book: if you want to know more about the theoretical details of the DeepAR algorithm, you can do the following:

- You can head over to this YouTube video to understand how artificial networks can be adapted to sequences of data (such as time series): `https://www.youtube.com/watch?v=WCUNPb-5EYI`. This video is part of a larger course about ML and **artificial neural networks (ANNs)**.

- You can read through the original published paper, *DeepAR: Probabilistic Forecasting with Autoregressive Recurrent Networks* by David Salinas, Valentin Flunkert, Jan Gasthaus, available at the following link: `https://arxiv.org/abs/1704.04110`.

- The DeepAR+ section of the Amazon Forecast documentation is very detailed, with many illustrations. You can directly follow this link: `https://docs.aws.amazon.com/forecast/latest/dg/aws-forecast-recipe-deeparplus.html`.

Implementation in Amazon Forecast

The key parameters the DeepAR+ algorithm lets you select are listed here:

- `context_length`: This is the number of data points in the past DeepAR+ uses to make a prediction. Typically, this value should be equal to the forecast horizon. DeepAR+ automatically feeds lagged values from the target time series data, so your context length can be much smaller than the seasonality present in your dataset.

- `number_of_epochs`: In ML, the learning process goes over the training data a certain number of times. Each pass is called an epoch. `number_of_epochs` has a direct impact on the training time, and the optimal number will depend on the size of the dataset and on the `learning_rate` parameter.

- `likelihood`: Amazon Forecast generates probabilistic forecasts and provides quantiles of the distribution. To achieve this, DeepAR+ uses different likelihoods (these can be seen as "noise" models) to estimate uncertainty, depending on the behavior of your data. The default value is `student-T` (which is suitable for real-valued data or sparse spiky data). Other possible values are `beta` (real values between 0 and 1), `deterministic-L1` (to generate point forecasts instead of probabilistic ones), `gaussian` (for real-valued data), `negative-binomial` (for non-negative data such as count data), or `piecewise-linear` (for flexible distributions).

DeepAR+ also lets you customize the learning parameters, as follows:

- `learning_rate`: In ML-based algorithms, the learning rate is used to define the step size used at each iteration to try to reach an optimum value for a loss function. The greater the learning rate, the faster newly learned information overrides past learnings. Setting a value for the learning rate is a matter of compromise between moving too fast at the risk of missing optimal values of the model parameters or moving too slowly, making the learning too long. The default value for DeepAR+ is `0.001`.

- `max_learning_rate_decays`: ML model learning can be nonlinear. At the beginning of the process, you can explore faster and have a high learning rate, whereas you may need to reduce the learning speed when you're approaching an optimal value of interest. This parameter defines the number of times the learning rate will be decayed during training. This is disabled by default (0). If this parameter is set to 3 (for instance), and you train your model over 100 epochs, then the learning rate will be decayed once after 25, 50, and 75 epochs (3 decaying episodes).

- `learning_rate_decay`: This parameter defines the factor used to multiply the current learning rate when a decay is triggered. This decay will be applied a number of times, defined by the `max_learning_rate_decays` parameter. The default value is 0.5. In the previous example, where 3 decaying episodes occurred over the course of 100 epochs, if the `learning_rate` parameter starts at 0.1, then it will be reduced to 0.05 after 25 epochs, to 0.025 after 50 epochs, and to 0.0125 after 75 epochs.

The architecture of the model can be customized with the following two parameters:

- The hidden layers of the RNN model from DeepAR+ can be configured by the number of layers (`num_layers`), and each layer can contain a certain number of **long short-term memory** (**LSTM**) cells (`num_cells`).

- `num_averaged_models`: During a given training process, DeepAR+ can encounter several models that have a close overall performance but different accuracy at the individual time series level. DeepAR+ can average (ensemble) different model behaviors to take advantage of the strength of up to five models.

CNN-QR

CNN-QR leverages a similar approach to DeepAR+, as it also builds a global model, learning from multiple time series jointly to provide more accurate forecastings.

Theoretical background

CNN-QR is a **sequence-to-sequence** (**Seq2Seq**) model that uses a large number of time series to train a single global model. In a nutshell, this type of model tests how well a prediction reconstructs a decoding sequence conditioned on an encoding sequence. It uses a quantile decoder to make multi-horizon probabilistic predictions.

The underlying theoretical details are beyond the scope of this book, but if you want to know more about some theoretical work leveraged by algorithms such as CNN-QR, you can read through the following sources:

- *A Multi-Horizon Quantile Recurrent Forecaster* (`https://arxiv.org/pdf/1711.11053.pdf`).

- The Amazon Forecast documentation, which is very detailed with many illustrations. You can directly follow this link: `https://docs.aws.amazon.com/forecast/latest/dg/aws-forecast-algo-cnnqr.html`.

Implementation in Amazon Forecast

The key parameters the DeepAR+ algorithm lets you select are these:

- `context_length`: This is the number of data points in the past CNN-QR uses to make a prediction. Typically, this value should be within 2 and 12 times the forecast horizon. Contrary to DeepAR+, CNN-QR does not automatically feed lagged values from the target time series data, so this parameter will usually be larger than with DeepAR+. Context length can be much smaller than the seasonality present in your dataset.

- `number_of_epochs`: In ML, the learning process goes over the training data a certain number of times. Each pass is called an epoch. `number_of_epochs` has a direct impact on the training time, and the optimal number will depend on the size of the dataset.

- `use_related_data`: This parameter will tell Amazon Forecast to use all the related time series data (`ALL`), none of them (`NONE`), only related data that does not have values in the forecast horizon (`HISTORICAL`), or only related data present both in the past and in the forecast horizon (`FORWARD_LOOKING`).

- `use_item_metadata`: This parameter will tell Amazon Forecast to use all provided item metadata (`ALL`) or none of it (`NONE`).

When should you select an algorithm?

The Amazon Forecast documentation includes a table to help you compare the different built-in algorithms used by this service. I recommend you refer yourself to it, as new approaches and algorithms may have been included in the service since the time of writing this book. You can find it at this link: `https://docs.aws.amazon.com/forecast/latest/dg/aws-forecast-choosing-recipes.html`.

Based on the algorithms available at the time of writing, I expanded this table to add a few other relevant criteria. The following table summarizes the best algorithm options you can leverage, depending on the characteristics of your time series datasets:

CRITERIA	CNN-QR	DEEPAR+	PROPHET	NPTS	ARIMA	ETS
Accepts historical related time series	✓	✗	✗	✗	✗	✗
Accept forward looking related time series	✓	✓	✓	✗	✗	✗
Accepts item metadata	✓	✓		✗	✗	✗
Accepts weather index	✓	✓	✓	✗	✗	✗
Suitable for sparse datasets	✓	✓	✗	✓	✗	✗
Performs HPO	✓	✓	✗	✗	✗	✗
Allows overriding default hyperparameters values	✓	✓	✗	✓	✗	✗
Suitable for what-if analysis	✓	✓	✓	✗	✗	✗
Suitable for cold start scenarios	✓	✓	✗	✗	✗	✗
Suitable for up to 10 time series	✗	✗	✗	✓	✓	✓
Suitable for up to 100 time series	✗	✗	✓	✗	✗	✗
Suitable for hundreds or more time series	✓	✓	✗	✗	✗	✗
Suitable for time series with 300+ data points	✓	✓	✓	✓	✗	✗
Suitable for short time series (less than 300 data points per time series)	✗	✗	✓	✗	✓	✓
Local model (one model is fit to each time series)			✓	✓	✓	✓
Global model	✓	✓				

Figure 5.2 – Algorithm selection cheat sheet

Let's now expand beyond this summary table and dive into some specifics of each of these algorithms, as follows:

- **ARIMA**, **ETS**, and **NPTS**: These algorithms are quite low-computationally-intensive and can give you a robust baseline for your forecasting problem.

- **ARIMA**: The ARIMA algorithm parameters are not tunable by the HPO process, as the `auto.arima` method from the Forecast R package takes care of it to identify the most suitable parameters.

- **NPTS**: Amazon Forecast AutoML sometimes chooses NPTS when you know it is not the best fit. What happens is that your data may appear sparse at a certain granularity: if you train a predictor with AutoML, it may select NPTS, even though you have hundreds of individual time series that a **deep neural network** (**DNN**) could learn better from. One approach to let AutoML select an algorithm with a larger learning capacity is to aggregate your data at high granularity (for instance, summing hourly data to build a daily dataset).

- **Prophet**: This algorithm is a great fit for datasets that exhibit multiple strong seasonal behaviors at different scales and contain an extended time period (preferably at least a year for hourly, daily, or weekly data). Prophet is also very good at capturing the impact of important holidays that occur at irregular intervals and that are known in advance (yearly sporting events at varying dates). If your datasets include large periods of missing values or large outliers, have non-linear growth trends, or saturate values while approaching a limit, then Prophet can also be an excellent candidate.

Now that you know how to select an algorithm suitable for your business needs, let's have a look at how you can customize each of them and override the default parameters we left as is when you trained your first predictor in the previous chapter.

Leveraging HPO

Training an ML model is a process that consists of finding parameters that will help the model to better deal with real data. When you train your own model without using a managed service such as Amazon Forecast, you can encounter three types of parameters, as follows:

- **Model selection parameters**: These are parameters that you have to fix to select a model that best matches your dataset. In this category, you will find the α, β, γ, and φ parameters from the ETS algorithm, for instance. Amazon Forecast implements these algorithms to ensure that automatic exploration is the default behavior for ETS and ARIMA so that you don't have to deal with finding the best values for these by yourself. For other algorithms (such as NPTS), good default parameters are provided, but you have the flexibility to adjust them based on the inner knowledge of your datasets.

- **Coefficients**: These are values that are fitted to your data during the very training of your model. These coefficients can be the weights and biases of a neural network or the θ_1 to θ_q coefficients of the MA part of ARIMA. Once these values have been fitted to your training data, their values define your model, and this set of values constitutes the main artifact that Amazon Forecast saves in the `Predictor` construct.

- **Hyperparameters**: These parameters control the learning process itself. The number of iterations (epochs) to train a **deep learning** (**DL**) model or the learning rate are examples of hyperparameters you can tweak to adjust your training process.

Amazon Forecast endorses the responsibility to manage the model selection parameters and coefficients for you. In the AutoML process, it also uses good default values for the hyperparameters of each algorithm and applies HPO for the DL algorithms (DeepAR+ and CNN-QR) to make things easier for you.

When you manually select an algorithm that can be tuned, you can also enable an HPO process to fine-tune your model and reach the same performance as with AutoML, but without the need to train a model with each of the available algorithms.

What is HPO?

In learning algorithms such as the ones leveraged by Amazon Forecast, HPO is the process used to choose the optimal values of the parameters that control the learning process.

Several approaches can be used, such as grid search (which is simply a parameter sweep) or random search (selecting hyperparameter combinations randomly). Amazon Forecast uses Bayesian optimization.

The theoretical background of such an optimization algorithm is beyond the scope of this book, but simply speaking, HPO matches a given combination of parameter values with the learning metrics (such as WAPE, **weighted quantile loss (wQL)**, or **root mean square error (RMSE)**, as mentioned in *Chapter 4, Training a Predictor with AutoML*). This matching is seen as a function by Bayesian optimization, which tries to build a probabilistic model for it. The Bayesian process iteratively updates hyperparameter configuration and gathers information about the location of the optimum values of the matching functions modeled.

To learn more about HPO algorithms, you can read through the following article: `https://proceedings.neurips.cc/paper/2011/file/86e8f7ab32cfd12 577bc2619bc635690-Paper.pdf`.

If you want to read more about Bayesian optimization and why it is better than grid search or random search, the following article will get you started:

Practical Bayesian Optimization of ML Algorithms (`https://arxiv.org/ abs/1206.2944`)

Let's now train a new predictor, but explicitly using HPO.

Training a CNN-QR predictor with HPO

In this section, we are going to train a second predictor, using the winning algorithm found in *Chapter 4, Training a Predictor with AutoML*. As a reminder, the winning algorithm was CNN-QR and we achieved the following performance:

								Export backtest results
Algorithm metrics Info								CNN-QR (Winner) ▼
Evaluation type	Test window start	Test window end	Items	wQL[0.1]	wQL[0.5]	wQL[0.9]	WAPE	RMSE
Backtest window	Sat, 01 Jun 2013 00:00:00 GMT	Mon, 01 Jul 2013 00:00:00 GMT	3573	0.0993	0.2254	0.1183	0.2254	3.2904

Figure 5.3 – Winning algorithm performance with AutoML

To train a new predictor, log in to the AWS console, navigate to the Amazon Forecast console, and click on the **View dataset groups** button. There, you can click on the name of the dataset group you created in *Chapter 3, Creating a Project and Ingesting your Data*. Check out this chapter if you need a reminder on how to navigate through the Amazon Forecast console. You should now be on the dashboard of your dataset group, where you will click on the **Train predictor** button, as illustrated in the following screenshot:

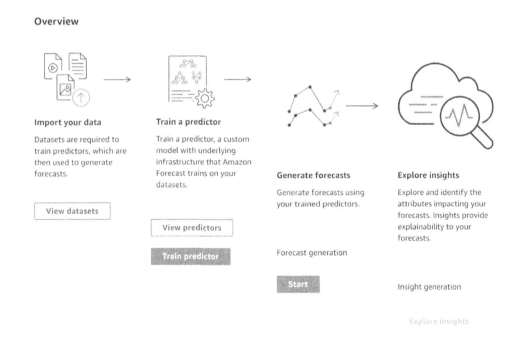

Figure 5.4 – Dataset group initial dashboard

Once you click the **Train predictor** button, the following screen will open up to let you customize your predictor settings:

Predictor settings

Predictor name
The name can help you distinguish this predictor from your other predictors.

The predictor name must have 1 to 63 characters. Valid characters: a-z, A-Z, 0-9, and _

Forecast horizon Info
This number tells Amazon Forecast how far into the future to predict your data at the specified forecast frequency.

Forecast frequency
This is the frequency at which your forecasts are generated.

Your forecast frequency is   1   ▼   day   ▼

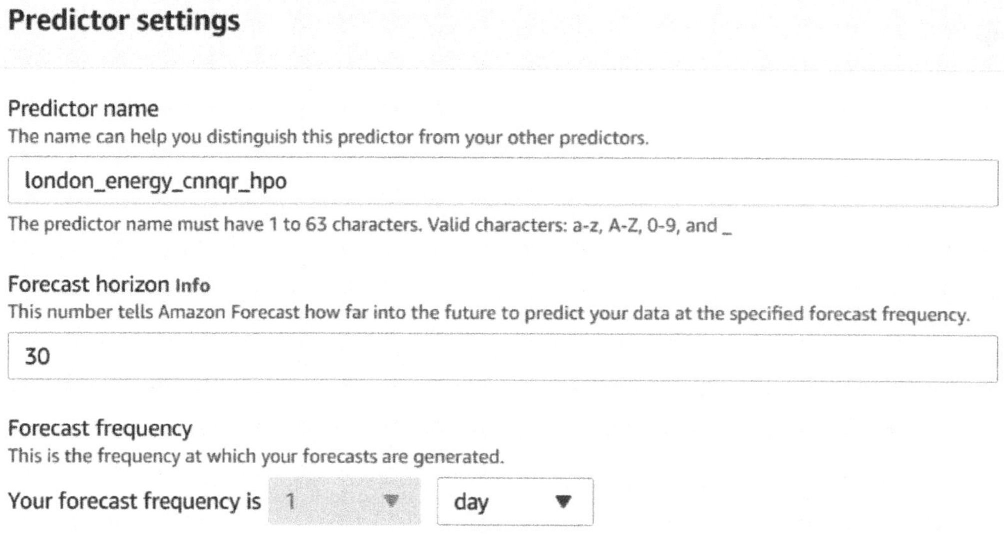

Figure 5.5 – Predictor settings

For your **Predictor settings** options, we are going to fill in the following parameters:

- **Predictor name**: `london_energy_cnnqr_hpo`.

- **Forecast frequency**: We will keep the same frequency as before, which is also the original frequency of the ingested data. Let's set this parameter to `1 day`.

- **Forecast horizon**: `30`. As the selected forecast horizon is `1 day`, this means that we want to train a model that will be able to generate the equivalent of 30 days' worth of data points in the future. We want to compare the performance of our initial predictor with this new one, so let's keep the same horizon to make this comparison more relevant.

- **Forecast quantiles**: Leave the settings at their default values, with three quantiles defined at `0.10`, `0.50`, and `0.90`. We will detail this setting later in this chapter.

In the next section, disable the **AutoPredictor** toggle and select **CNN-QR** in the **Algorithm selection** dropdown.

Click on **Perform hyperparameter optimization (HPO)**. A new section called **HPO Config** appears, where you can decide the range of values you want Amazon Forecast to explore for the different tunable hyperparameters of CNN-QR. This configuration must be written in **JavaScript Object Notation (JSON)** format.

Let's enter the following JSON document into the **HPO Config** widget:

```
{
  "ParameterRanges": {
    "IntegerParameterRanges": [
      {
        "MaxValue": 360,
        "MinValue": 60,
        "ScalingType": "Auto",
        "Name": "context_length"
      }
    ]
  }
}
```

With this configuration, we are telling Amazon Forecast that we want it to explore a hyperparameter space defined by these potential values:

- `context_length` will evolve between `MinValue=60` days and `MaxValue=360` days.

- The HPO process will also automatically try four different configurations of *related datasets*: no related dataset used (`NONE`), all of them (`ALL`), use the related dataset that only contains historical values (`HISTORICAL`), or use the related datasets that contain both past historical values and future values (`FORWARD_LOOKING`).

- It will also automatically try two different configurations of *item metadata*: no metadata used (`NONE`) or all metadata used (`ALL`).

In the **Training parameters** section, we will leave the `epochs` number at `100` (a similar number to the default value used by the AutoML procedure) for comparison purposes, as follows:

```
{
  "epochs": "100"
  [...]
}
```

Leave all the other parameters at their default values and click **Create** to start the training of our new predictor with the HPO procedure. Our predictor will be created with the **Create in progress** status, as illustrated in the following screenshot:

	Predictor name ▽	Training status ▽	Forecast types ▽	WAPE ▽	RMSE ▽	AutoPredictor Info
○	london_energy_cnnqr_hpo2	⊖ Create in progress... 1 hr 36 mins est. remaining	-	-	-	False Upgrade
○	london_energy_autopredictor	⊘ Active	0.1 | 0.5 | 0.9	0.2254	3.3007	True
○	london_energy_automl2	⊘ Active	0.1 | 0.5 | 0.9	0.2256	3.2962	False Upgrade

Figure 5.6 – CNN-QR predictor training with HPO in progress

After a while (a little less than 2 hours, in my case), our new predictor is trained and ready to be used, as can be seen here:

Predictor overview

MAPE	AutoPredictor	Date created
0.2281	False	Fri, 11 Jun 2021 05:42:04 GMT
Training status	Predictor ARN	Total creation time
⊘ Active	arn:aws:forecast:eu-west-1:123031033346:predictor/london_e	1 hr 54 mins
Estimated time remaining	nergy_cnnqr_hpo	Message
-		-
	Algorithm used	
	CNN-QR	

Figure 5.7 – Trained CNN-QR predictor

In your case, the **mean-absolute percentage error** (**MAPE**) metric may be slightly different but will be close to the number you see here. You can see that in my case, I obtained a **MAPE** value of 0.2281, which is extremely close to the value obtained in the AutoML process (which was 0.2254). As explained in the *What is HPO?* section, the slight differences come from the random nature of the Bayesian procedure.

You now know how to configure HPO to your predictor training. However, not all algorithms can be fine-tuned using this process, and not all parameters can be defined as targets with ranges to explore. In the next section, we will look at the options you have for each algorithm.

Introducing tunable hyperparameters with HPO

When you know which algorithm will give the best results for your datasets, you may want to ensure that you get the most out of this algorithm by using HPO. Let's have a look at what is feasible for each algorithm, as follows:

- **ETS**: HPO is not available in Amazon Forecast. However, the service leverages the default parameters from the `ets` module from the `forecast` R package: the latter takes an argument called `model` that is set to `ZZZ` by default. When this is the case, the `model` argument is automatically selected to provide the best-performing ETS model.

- **NPTS**: HPO is not available for NPTS. To train different types of NPTS models, you can train separate predictors with different training parameters on the same dataset group.

- **ARIMA**: HPO is not available in Amazon Forecast. However, Amazon Forecast leverages the `auto.arima` module from the `forecast` R package: this package uses an automatic forecasting procedure to identify the ARIMA parameters that yield the best performance, and the final ARIMA model selected is, in fact, already optimized.

- **Prophet**: HPO is not available for Prophet.

- **DeepAR+**: HPO is available for DeepAR+ and the following parameters can be leveraged and tuned during the process: `context_length` and `learning_rate`.

- **CNN-QR**: When selecting HPO for this algorithm, the following parameters will be tuned during the optimization process: `context_length`, whether or not to use the **related time series** data, and whether or not to use the **item metadata**.

In conclusion, HPO is a process that is available for DL models (DeepAR+ and CNN-QR). The other algorithms do not take advantage of HPO. Now that you know how to override the default hyperparameters of the algorithms leveraged by Amazon Forecast, we are going to look at how you can use a stronger backtesting strategy to improve the quality of your forecasts.

Reinforcing your backtesting strategy

In ML, **backtesting** is a technique used in forecasting to provide the learning process with two datasets, as follows:

- A **training dataset** on which the model will be trained

- A **testing dataset** on which we will evaluate the performance of the model on data that was not seen during the training phase

As a reminder, here are the different elements of backtesting in Amazon Forecast, as outlined in *Chapter 4, Training a Predictor with AutoML*:

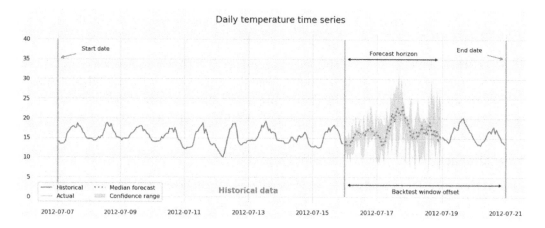

Figure 5.8 – Backtesting elements

When dealing with time series data, the split must mainly be done on the temporal axis (and, to a lesser extent, on the item population) to prevent any data leak from the past data to the future. This is paramount to make your model robust enough for when it will have to deal with actual production data.

By default, when you leave the default parameter as is (when selecting AutoML or when selecting an algorithm manually), Amazon Forecast uses one backtest window with a length equal to the forecast horizon. However, it is a good practice to provide multiple start points to remove any dependency of your predictions on the start date of your forecast. When you select multiple backtest windows, Amazon Forecast computes the evaluation metrics of your models for each window and averages the results. Multiple backtest windows also help deal with a different level of variability in each period, as can be seen here:

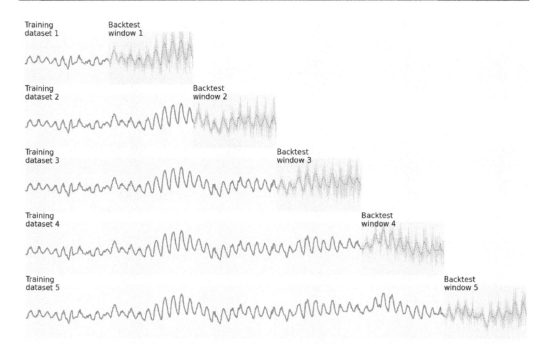

Figure 5.9 – Multiple backtest windows strategy

In the previous screenshot, you can see what Amazon Forecast will do when you select five backtest windows that have the same length as the forecast horizon. This is essentially what happens:

- In the first scenario, the service will train the predictor on a small portion of the data and evaluate it in roughly the same time span.

- Then, each backtest scenario will extend the training dataset and train on additional data while evaluating on a backtest window further in the future (with the same window width).

- At the end of the process, Amazon Forecast will train a new model on the whole dataset so that it's ready to be used for inference and generate new forecasts (this will be described in the next chapter).

Configuring your backtesting strategy happens in the **Predictor settings** section when you wish to create a new predictor without using the AutoPredictor settings, as illustrated in the following screenshot:

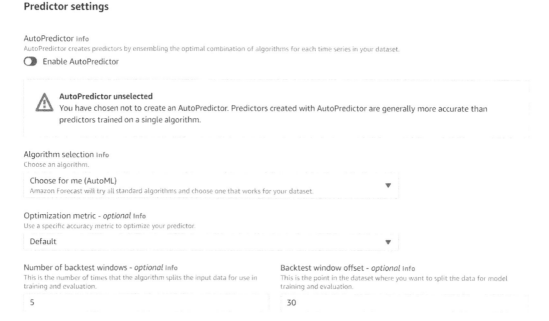

Figure 5.10 – Backtesting configuration for a new predictor

After you make your algorithm selection, you can choose from the following options:

- **Number of backtest windows**: This number can range from 1 to 5.
- **Backtest window offset**: This is the width of the window. By default, it is equal to the forecast horizon and has the same unit.

Let's create a new predictor with the following parameters:

- **Predictor name**: london_energy_cnnqr_backtest
- **Forecast horizon**: 30 (days)
- **Algorithm selection**: Manual
- **Algorithm**: CNN-QR
- **Number of backtest windows**: 5
- **Backtest window offset**: 30

Leave all the other parameters at their default values and click **Start** to create a new predictor with these settings. After an hour or so of training, you can explore the accuracy metric of this new predictor, as illustrated in the following screenshot:

Accuracy metrics Info   Export backtest results

Evaluation type	Test window start	Test window end	Items	wQL[0.1]	wQL[0.5]	wQL[0.9]	WAPE	RMSE
Backtest average	-	-	-	0.1128	0.2590	0.1369	0.2590	4.7961
Backtest window 1	Sat, 01 Jun 2013 00:00:00 GMT	Mon, 01 Jul 2013 00:00:00 GMT	3573	0.0990	0.2287	0.1193	0.2287	3.3035
Backtest window 2	Thu, 02 May 2013 00:00:00 GMT	Sat, 01 Jun 2013 00:00:00 GMT	3573	0.1028	0.2575	0.1366	0.2575	3.9830
Backtest window 3	Tue, 02 Apr 2013 00:00:00 GMT	Thu, 02 May 2013 00:00:00 GMT	3573	0.1591	0.3222	0.1504	0.3222	6.0529
Backtest window 4	Sun, 03 Mar 2013 00:00:00 GMT	Tue, 02 Apr 2013 00:00:00 GMT	3573	0.0976	0.2219	0.1214	0.2219	5.0981
Backtest window 5	Fri, 01 Feb 2013 00:00:00 GMT	Sun, 03 Mar 2013 00:00:00 GMT	3573	0.1056	0.2645	0.1567	0.2645	5.5431

Figure 5.11 – Backtesting accuracy metrics

You will notice that Amazon Forecast computes the accuracy metrics for each backtest window and also gives you the average of these metrics over five windows. You may note some fluctuations of the metrics, depending on the backtest window: this can be a good indicator of the variability of your time series across different time ranges, and you may run some more thorough investigation of your data over these different periods to try to understand the causes of these fluctuations.

You now know how to customize your backtesting strategy to make your training more robust. We are now going to look at how you can customize the features of your dataset by adding features provided by Amazon Forecast (namely, holidays and weather data).

Including holiday and weather data

At the time of writing this book, Amazon Forecast includes two built-in datasets that are made available as engineered features that you can leverage as **supplementary features**: **Holidays** and the **Weather** index.

Enabling the Holidays feature

This supplementary feature includes a dataset of national holidays for 66 countries. You can enable this feature when you create a new predictor: on the predictor creation page, scroll down to the optional **Supplementary features** section and toggle on the **Enable holidays** button, as illustrated in the following screenshot:

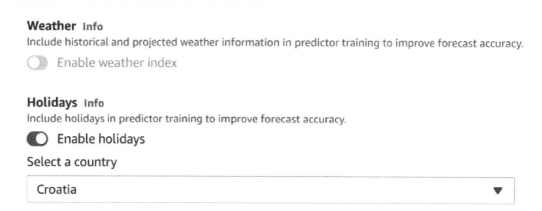

Figure 5.12 – Enabling the Holidays supplementary feature

Once enabled, a drop-down list appears, to let you select the country for which you want to enable holidays. Note that you can only select one country: your whole dataset must pertain to this country. If you have several countries in your dataset and wish to take different holidays into account, you will have to split your dataset by country and train a predictor on each of them.

When this parameter is selected, Amazon Forecast will train a model with and without this parameter: the best configuration will be kept based on the performance metric of your model.

Enabling the Weather index

This supplementary feature includes 2 years of historical weather data and 2 weeks of future weather information for 7 regions covering the whole world, as follows:

- **US** (excluding Hawaii and Alaska), with latitude ranging from 24.6 to 50.0 and longitude between -126.0 and -66.4

- **Canada**, with latitude ranging from 41.0 to 75.0 and longitude from -142.0 and 52.0

- **Europe**, with latitude ranging from 34.8 to 71.8 and longitude from -12.6 to 44.8

- **South America**, with latitude ranging from -56.6 to 14.0 and longitude from -82.2 to -33.0

- **Central America**, with latitude ranging from 6.8 to 33.20 and longitude from -118.80 to -58.20

- **Africa & Middle East**, with latitude ranging from -35.60 to 43.40 and longitude from -18.8 to -58.20

- **Asia Pacific**, with latitude ranging from -47.8 to 55.0 and longitude from -67.0 to 180.60

To leverage weather data in Amazon Forecast, you need to perform the following actions:

- Ensure your dataset has data pertaining exclusively to one single region (for instance, all your data must be linked to locations that are all in Europe). If you have several regions in your data, you will have to create a dataset per region and train one predictor per region.

- Add geolocation information to your dataset.

- Include a geolocation attribute when creating and ingesting your target dataset.

- Select AutoPredictor or AutoML when creating your predictor or manually select an algorithm.

Adding geolocation information to your dataset

Once you have a dataset with data from a single region (**US**, **Canada**, **Europe**, **Central America**, **Africa & Middle East**, or **South America**), you must add a location feature to your dataset. This feature can be one of the following:

- A ZIP code (if your locations are in the **United States (US)**). The column must follow this format: US, followed by an underscore character (_), followed by the 5-digit ZIP code. For instance, US_98121 is a valid postal code to be used.

- Latitude and longitude coordinates in decimal format, both coordinates being separated by an underscore character (_)—for instance, 47.61_-122.33 is a valid string. Amazon Forecast takes care of rounding to the nearest 0.2 degrees if you input raw values with more precision. This format is available for every region.

Our household electricity consumption dataset is from London and the coordinates of London are respectively 51.5073509 (latitude) and -0.1277583 (longitude). If we wanted to add weather data to our dataset, we could add a column called location to our dataset and set its value to 51.5073509_-0.1277583 for every row (as all our households are located in this city).

> **Important Tip**
>
> As mentioned previously, the **Weather** index is only available for the past 2 years. If you want to get some practice with this feature, make sure the availability of weather data is compatible with the recording time of your time series data. If your time series data includes data points before July 1, 2018, the `weather_index` parameter will be disabled in the **user interface** (**UI**).

Including a geolocation attribute

When ingesting a target time series data into a dataset group, you will have the opportunity to select a location type attribute. Follow these next steps:

1. After signing in to the AWS Management Console, open the Amazon Forecast console and click on the **View dataset group** button.

2. On the dataset group list screen presented to you, select an empty dataset group (or create a brand new one: you can refer back to *Chapter 3, Creating a Project and Ingesting your Data,* in case you need some guidance to create and configure a new dataset group).

3. When you're on your dataset group dashboard, click on the **Import** button that is next to the **Target time series data** label. You will arrive at the data ingestion wizard.

4. In the **Schema Builder** section, click on **Add attribute**, name your attribute `location`, and select `geolocation` for the **Attribute Type** value, as follows:

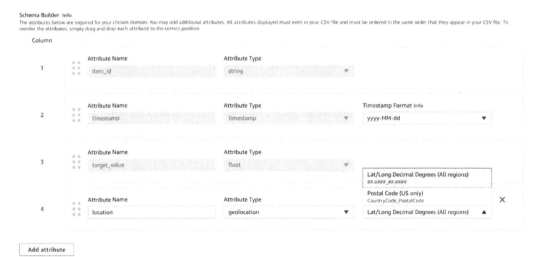

Figure 5.13 – Ingesting data with location information

5. For the **Geolocation format** option, you have a choice between **Lat/Long Decimal Degrees** or **Postal Code** (if your location data is in the US).

You can then continue with the ingestion process, as explained in *Chapter 3, Creating a Project and Ingesting your Data*. If you have other datasets, you can also ingest them in the related time series data and item metadata dataset. You can then train a new predictor based on this dataset group.

Creating a predictor with the Weather index

Once you have a dataset group with location data, you can enable the **Weather** index feature while creating a new predictor based on this dataset, as follows:

1. On the Amazon Forecast console, click on **View dataset groups** to bring up a list of existing dataset groups and choose a dataset group where your location-aware dataset has been ingested.

2. In the navigation pane, choose **Predictors** and click on **Train new predictor**.

3. On the predictor creation page, scroll down to the optional **Supplementary features** section and toggle on the **Enable weather index** button, as illustrated in the following screenshot:

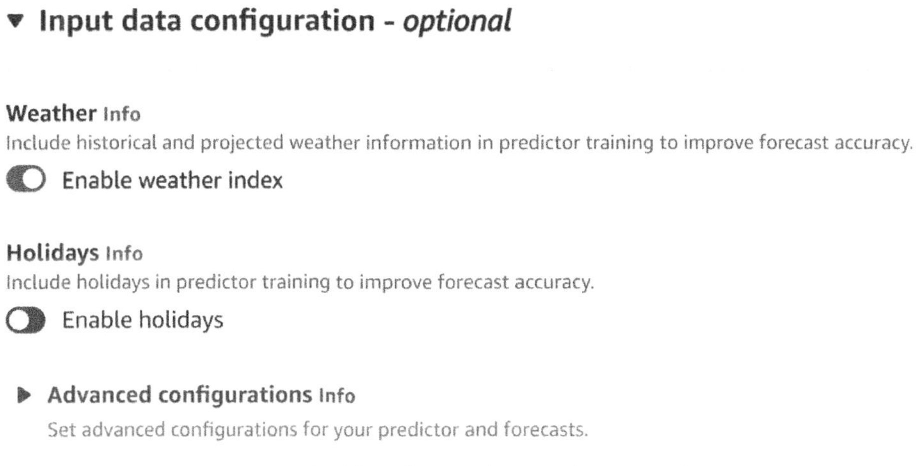

▼ **Input data configuration -** *optional*

Weather Info
Include historical and projected weather information in predictor training to improve forecast accuracy.

🔘 Enable weather index

Holidays Info
Include holidays in predictor training to improve forecast accuracy.

🔘 Enable holidays

▶ **Advanced configurations** Info
Set advanced configurations for your predictor and forecasts.

Figure 5.14 – Enabling the Weather supplementary feature

When you're ready to train a predictor, click on the **Create** button at the bottom of the prediction creation screen to start training a predictor with weather data.

When this parameter is selected, Amazon Forecast will train a model with and without this parameter: the best configuration for each time series will be kept based on the performance metric of your model. In other words, if supplementing weather data to a given time series does not improve accuracy during backtesting, Amazon Forecast will disable the weather feature for this particular time series.

You have now a good idea of how to take weather data and holiday data into account in your forecasting strategy. In the next chapter, you are going to see how you can ask Amazon Forecast to preprocess the features you provide in your own dataset.

Implementing featurization techniques

Amazon Forecast lets you customize the way you can transform the input datasets by filling in missing values. The presence of missing values in raw data is very common and has a deep impact on the quality of your forecasting model. Indeed, each time a value is missing in your target or related time series data, the true observation is not available to assess the real distribution of historical data.

Although there can be multiple reasons why values are missing, the featurization pipeline offered by Amazon Forecast assumes that you are not able to fill in the values based on your domain expertise and that missing values are actually present in the raw data you ingested into the service. For instance, if we plot the energy consumption of the household with the **identifier (ID)** MAC002200, we can see that some values are missing at the end of the dataset, as shown in the following screenshot:

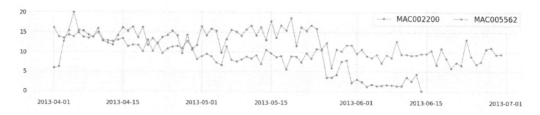

Figure 5.15 – Missing values for the energy consumption of the MAC002200 household

As we are dealing with the energy consumption of a household, this behavior is probably linked to a household that left this particular house. Let's see how you can configure the behavior of Amazon Forecast to deal with this type of situation.

Configuring featurization parameters

Configuring how to deal with missing values happens in the **Advanced configuration** settings of the **Predictor details** section when you wish to create a new predictor.

After logging in to the AWS console, navigate to the Amazon Forecast console and click on the **View dataset groups** button. There, you can click on the name of the dataset group you created in *Chapter 3, Creating a Project and Ingesting your Data*. You should now be on the dashboard of your dataset group, where you can click on **Train predictor**. Scroll to the bottom of the **Predictor details** section and click on **Advanced configurations** to unfold additional configurations. In this section, you will find the **Hyperparameter optimization** configuration, the **Training parameter** configuration (when available for the selected algorithm), and the **Featurizations** section, as illustrated in the following screenshot:

▼ **Advanced configurations** Info
   Set advanced configurations for your predictor and forecasts.

▢ Perform hyperparameter optimization (HPO)
   Select to improve the accuracy of your model by optimizing hyperparameters. HPO may increase processing times.

Featurizations

```
1  [
2    {
3      "AttributeName": "target_value",
4      "FeaturizationPipeline": [
5        {
6          "FeaturizationMethodName": "filling",
7          "FeaturizationMethodParameters": {
8            "aggregation": "sum",
9            "frontfill": "none",
10           "middlefill": "zero",
11           "backfill": "zero"
12         }
13       }
14     ]
15   }
16 ]
```

Figure 5.16 – Featurization configuration

The featurization is configured with this small JSON snippet, and you will have a similar section for every attribute you want to fill in missing values for.

By default, Amazon Forecast only fills in missing values in the target time series data and does not apply any transformation to the related time series data. There are three parameters you can configure, as follows:

- `AttributeName`: This can be either the target field of your target time series data or one of the fields of your related time series data. Depending on the domain selected, this can be `demand`, `target_value`, `workforce_demand`, `value`, `metric_value`, or `number_of_instances`. You can refer back to the schema of your target and related datasets to find which values you can use. In the energy consumption case you have been running, you initially selected the custom domain: the target field for this domain is `target_value`.

- `FeaturizationMethodName`: At the time of writing this book, only the filling method is available. The only value this field can take is `filling`.

- `FeaturizationMethodParameters`: For the filling method, there are two parameters you can configure for both related and target time series (`middlefill` and `backfill`). For the target time series, the `frontfill` parameter is set to `none`, and you can also specify an `aggregation` parameter. For the related time series, you can also specify the filling behavior to apply within the forecast horizon with the `futurefill` parameter.

The following screenshot illustrates these different handling strategies Amazon Forecast can leverage for filling missing values:

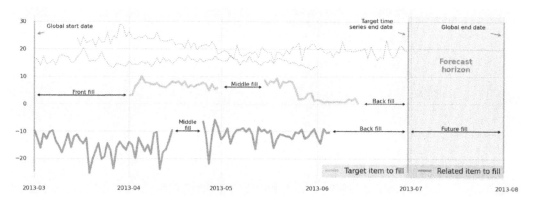

Figure 5.17 – Missing values handling strategies

The global start date is the earliest start date of all the items (illustrated in the preceding screenshot by the top two lines) present in your dataset, while the global end date is the last end date of all the items augmented by the forecast horizon.

Introducing featurization parameter values

The following table illustrates the possible values these parameters can take, depending on the dataset:

PARAMETER	TARGET TIME SERIES	RELATED TIME SERIES
aggregation	**sum**, avg, first, min or max	*Not applicable*
frontfill	**none**	*Not applicable*
middlefill	**zero**, value, median, mean, min or max	zero, value, median, mean, min or max
backfill	**zero**, value, median, mean, min or max	zero, value, median, mean, min or max
futurefill	*Not applicable*	zero, value, median, mean, min or max

Figure 5.18 – Parameters and their possible values

Let's have a look at these parameters in more detail, as follows:

- aggregation: When the forecast frequency requested to create a predictor is different than the raw frequency of your dataset, Amazon Forecast will apply this parameter. By default, it aggregates your raw data by summing the values (sum). If your raw data was available at an hourly level and you request a predictor at the daily level, it will sum all the hourly data available to build a daily dataset. You have the option to alter this behavior by requesting Amazon Forecast to replace the sum by the average (avg), by taking the first value available (first) or by taking the minimum (min) or maximum (max) value over each considered period.

- **Filling parameters**: When applicable, the different filling behaviors available are zero (replace every missing value by zeros), value (replace by a given value), median (replace by the median of the whole time series), mean (replace by the mean), min, or max (replace by the minimum or maximum value of the whole time series).

There are no default values when applying filling methods to related time series (as you can have several series with different expected behavior). Values in bold in the preceding table are the default values applied to the target time series dataset.

When you select a value for one of the filling parameters, you have to define the desired value as a real value with an additional parameter obtained by adding `_value` to the name of the parameter, as follows:

- `middlefill_value` defines the replacement value when you select `middlefill = value`.

- `backfill_value` defines the replacement value when you select `backfill = value`.

- `futurefill_value` defines the replacement value when you select `futurefill = value`.

In this section, you discovered how you can rely on Amazon Forecast to preprocess your features and maintain the consistent data quality necessary to deliver robust and accurate forecasts. In the next section, you are going to dive deeper into how you can put the probabilistic aspect of Amazon Forecast to work to suit your own business needs.

Customizing quantiles to suit your business needs

Amazon Forecast generates probabilistic forecasts at different quantiles, giving you prediction intervals over mere point forecasts. Prediction quantiles (or intervals) let Amazon Forecast express the uncertainty of each prediction and give you more information to include in the decision-making process that is linked to your forecast exercise.

As you have seen earlier in this chapter, Amazon Forecast can leverage different forecasting algorithms: each of these algorithms has a different way to estimate probability distributions. For more details about the theoretical background behind probabilistic forecasting, you can refer to the following papers:

- *GluonTS: Probabilistic Time Series Models in Python* (`https://arxiv.org/pdf/1906.05264.pdf`), which gives you some details about the way the ARIMA, ETS, NPTS, and DeepAR+ algorithms generate these predictions' intervals.

- *A Multi-Horizon Quantile Recurrent Forecaster* (`https://arxiv.org/pdf/1711.11053.pdf`) gives details about how the neural quantile family of models (which include similar architectures to CNN-QR) generates these distributions while directly predicting given timesteps in the forecast horizon.

- The Prophet algorithm is described in detail in the original paper from Facebook and can be found here: `https://peerj.com/preprints/3190/`.

Let's now see how you can configure different forecast types when creating a new predictor.

Configuring your forecast types

Configuring the forecast types you want Amazon Forecast to generate happens on the **Predictor details** section when you wish to create a new predictor. By default, the quantiles selected are 10% (p10), 50% (the median, p50) and 90% (p90). When configuring a predictor, the desired quantiles are called **forecast type** and you can choose up to five of them, including any percentile ranging from 0.01 to 0.99 (with an increment of 0.01). You can also select mean as a forecast type.

> **Important Note**
>
> CNN-QR cannot generate a mean forecast, as this type of algorithm directly generates predictions for a particular quantile: when selecting mean as a forecast type, CNN-QR will fall back to computing the median (p50).

In the following screenshot, I configured my forecast types to request Amazon Forecast to generate the mean forecast and three quantiles (p10, p50, and p99):

Forecast type - *optional* Info
Specify the quantiles used to create forecasts and evaluate predictors. Choose up to 5 quantiles between 0.01 and 0.99 (by increments of 0.01). You can also include the mean forecast with 'mean'.

Forecast types	Value	
Forecast type 1	0.10	Remove
Forecast type 2	mean	Remove
Forecast type 3	0.50	Remove
Forecast type 4	0.99	Remove

Add new forecast type

You can add up to 1 more forecast types.

Figure 5.19 – Selecting forecast types to generate

You can click on **Remove** to remove a forecast and request up to five forecast types by clicking on the **Add new forecast type** button.

> **Important Note**
>
> Amazon Forecast bills you for each time series forecast is generated: each forecast type counts for a billed item and they will always bill you for a minimum of three quantiles, even if you only intend to use one. It is hence highly recommended to customize the default quantiles to suit your business needs and benefit from the probabilistic capability of Amazon Forecast.

Amazon Forecast will compute a quantile loss metric for each requested quantile. In the following screenshot, you can see the default wQL metrics computed for the default quantiles generated by the service: wQL [0.1] is the quantile loss for the p10 forecast type, wQL [0.5] is for the median, and so on:

Accuracy metrics Info   Export backtest results

Evaluation type	Test window start	Test window end	Items	wQL.[0.1]	wQL.[0.5]	wQL.[0.9]	WAPE	RMSE
Backtest average	-	-	-	0.1128	0.2590	0.1369	0.2590	4.7961
Backtest window 1	Sat, 01 Jun 2013 00:00:00 GMT	Mon, 01 Jul 2013 00:00:00 GMT	3573	0.0990	0.2287	0.1193	0.2287	3.3035
Backtest window 2	Thu, 02 May 2013 00:00:00 GMT	Sat, 01 Jun 2013 00:00:00 GMT	3573	0.1028	0.2575	0.1366	0.2575	3.9830
Backtest window 3	Tue, 02 Apr 2013 00:00:00 GMT	Thu, 02 May 2013 00:00:00 GMT	3573	0.1591	0.3222	0.1504	0.3222	6.0529
Backtest window 4	Sun, 03 Mar 2013 00:00:00 GMT	Tue, 02 Apr 2013 00:00:00 GMT	3573	0.0976	0.2219	0.1214	0.2219	5.0981
Backtest window 5	Fri, 01 Feb 2013 00:00:00 GMT	Sun, 03 Mar 2013 00:00:00 GMT	3573	0.1056	0.2645	0.1567	0.2645	5.5431

Figure 5.20 – Quantile loss metrics per forecast type

Let's now see how to choose the right quantiles depending on the type of decision you are expecting to make based on these predictions.

Choosing forecast types

Choosing a forecast type to suit your business need is a trade-off between the cost of over-forecasting (generating higher capital cost or higher inventory) and the cost of under-forecasting (missing revenue because a product is not available when a customer wishes to order it, or because you cannot produce finished goods to meet the actual market demand).

In *Chapter 4*, *Training a Predictor with AutoML*, you met the weighted quantile loss (wQL) metric. As a reminder, computing this metric for a given quantile τ can be done with the following formula:

$$wQL[\tau] = 2 \cdot \frac{\sum_{i,t} \left[\tau \cdot max \left(y_{i,t} - q_{i,t}^{(\tau)}, 0 \right) + (1 - \tau) \cdot max \left(q_{i,t}^{(\tau)} - y_{i,t}, 0 \right) \right]}{\sum_{i,t} |y_{i,t}|}$$

Here, the following applies:

- $y_{i,t}$ is the actual value observed for a given item_id parameter at a point in time t (with t ranging over the time range from the backtest period and i ranging over all items).

- $q_{i,t}^{(\tau)}$ is the t quantile predicted for a given item_id parameter at a point in time t.

- τ is a quantile that can take of one the following values: 0.01, 0.02…, 0.98, or 0.99.

If you are building a sound vaccine strategy and want to achieve global immunity as fast as possible, you must meet your population demand at all costs (meaning that doses must be available when someone comes to get their shot). To meet such imperative demand, a p99 forecast may be very useful: this forecast type expects the true value to be lower than the predicted value 99% of the time. If we use τ = 0.99 in the previous formula, we end up with the following:

- A larger penalty weight to under-forecasting: $0.99 \cdot max\left(y_{i,t} - q_{i,t}^{(0.99)}, 0\right)$
- A smaller penalty weight to over-forecasting: $(1 - 0.99) \cdot max\left(q_{i,t}^{(0.99)} - y_{i,t}, 0\right)$

Let's have a look at another example, as follows:

- If you own a garment store, you don't want to be out of stock of winter articles in winter: the capital cost of overstocking is cheaper (less chance to have many products stuck in your inventory) and a p90 forecast is useful to prevent you from running out of stock.

- On the other hand, when summer comes, you may take your stock decision for winter garments based on the p10 forecast (someone may buy this warm scarf, but there is a high probability that it may stay longer in your inventory before this happens).

As you can see, combining different forecast types gives you the ability to adjust your strategy depending on fluctuations over the year.

Summary

In this chapter, you discovered the many possibilities Amazon Forecast gives you to customize your predictor training to your datasets. You learned how to choose the best algorithm to fit your problem and how to customize different parameters (quantiles, the missing values' filling strategy, and supplementary features usage) to try to improve your forecasting models.

The AutoML capability of Amazon Forecast is a key differentiator when dealing with a new business case or a new dataset. It gives you good directions and reliable results with a fast turnaround. However, achieving higher accuracy to meet your business needs means that you must sometimes be able to override Amazon Forecast decisions by orienting its choice of algorithms, deciding how to process the features of your dataset, or simply requesting a different set of outputs by selecting forecast types that match the way your decision process is run from a business perspective.

In the next chapter, you will use a trained predictor to generate new forecasts (in ML terms, we will use new data to run inferences on a trained model).

6
Generating New Forecasts

In the previous two chapters, you focused on training a few predictors, first using **AutoML** and letting **Amazon Forecast** make all the decisions for you, and then by customizing different aspects of your model.

In this chapter, you are going to use the AutoML predictor you trained in *Chapter 4, Training a Predictor with AutoML*, and you are going to request new predictions by generating a forecast. By the end of this chapter, you will be ready to use a trained forecasting model and understand how to integrate new data and generate new predictions.

In this chapter, we're going to cover the following main topics:

- Generating a forecast
- Using lookup to get your items forecast
- Exporting and visualizing your forecasts
- Generating explainability for your forecasts

Technical requirements

No hands-on experience in a language such as **Python** or **R** is necessary to follow along with the content from this chapter. However, we highly recommend that you read this chapter while connected to your AWS account and open the Amazon Forecast console to run the different actions on your end.

To create an AWS account and log into the Amazon Forecast console, you can refer to the *Technical requirements* of *Chapter 2, An Overview of Amazon Forecast*.

The content in this chapter assumes that you have a predictor already trained and ready to be used to generate new forecasts: if you don't, we recommend that you follow the detailed process explained in *Chapter 4, Training a Predictor with AutoML*. Once you have a trained predictor, you are ready to generate new predictions.

Generating a forecast

In *Chapter 4, Training a Predictor with AutoML*, and *Chapter 5, Customizing Your Predictor Training*, we focused on the first step of the forecasting process: looking back in historical data to establish a baseline and uncover trends that may continue in the future. In Amazon Forecast, this is done by training a predictor (your trained model). Once you have a model ready to be used, you can use Amazon Forecast to generate predictions for your time series: this is the highlighted area on the right side in the following figure:

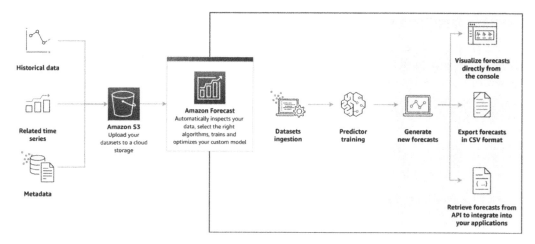

Figure 6.1 – Amazon Forecast overview

In other words, you will use Amazon Forecast to generate future values in a timeframe beyond the last date available in your ingested dataset. In *Chapter 3, Creating a Project and Ingesting Your Data*, you ingested data from 2012-07-01 to 2013-06-30. You are now going to generate predictions for data starting on 2013-07-01.

In the next section, you are going to learn how to create a forecast from a trained predictor and how to update your dataset with fresh values to keep forecasting new values at regular intervals.

Creating your first forecast

Based on the predictor that you trained in *Chapter 4, Training a Predictor with AutoML*, you are going to generate your first forecast. To do so, complete the following steps:

1. Log in to the AWS console and search for Forecast in the search bar at the top.

2. Click on **Amazon Forecast** to go to the service home page.

3. On this page, as shown in the previous figure, you can either click on the **View dataset groups** button on the right side of the screen or click the hamburger icon (the one with three horizontal lines) at the top left to open the left panel, where you can click on **Dataset groups**. You will land on a page listing all the dataset groups visible from your AWS account. As you already trained a predictor, your list should contain at least one item:

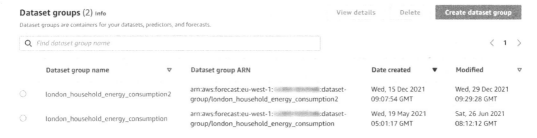

Figure 6.2 – Amazon Forecast dataset groups list

4. Click on your dataset group name (mine is called london_household_energy_ consumption as shown in the previous figure). You are now on your dataset group's dashboard. Click on **Create a forecast** in the **Generate forecasts** column on the right.

5. You are presented with the **Forecast details** screen:

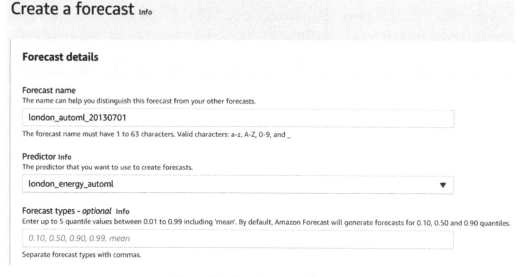

Figure 6.3 – Creating a new forecast

6. On this screen, you need to enter a **Forecast name** (you can generate multiple forecasts with a given model). Let's call it `london_automl_20130701`. The predictor to be used to generate the forecast is already populated for you if you have only one trained predictor associated with the dataset group you selected earlier. Otherwise, you can make a choice in the **Predictor** drop-down list.

7. You can also specify the quantiles you want to forecast for in the **Forecast quantiles** field. You can leave this field to its default values (`0.10, 0.50, 0.90`)

8. Scroll down the screen and click on **Start**: your forecast generation starts.

9. During this step, Amazon Forecast provisions the underlying necessary resources and runs inference using your existing data and your trained predictor. It also prepares the inference results to allow them to be queried further down the road. This process can take up to 40 minutes. Once it's finished, your screen is updated to show the forecast as **Active** and ready to be used.

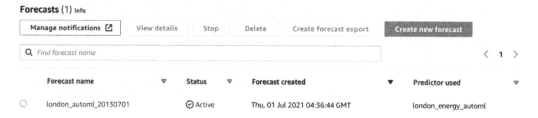

Figure 6.4 – Forecast ready to be queried

Your forecast is now ready: you can now export it (see *Exporting and visualizing your forecasts* later in the chapter) or query it (see *Using lookup to get your items forecast*) to investigate the model predictions for the time series present in your dataset.

Generating new subsequent forecasts

So far, you have trained a predictor between 2012-07-01 and 2013-06-30 and you have generated a forecast for the period ranging from 2013-07-01 to 2013-07-30.

The process to generate the subsequent forecast for future values is the following:

1. When you receive the new values for the month of July 2013, add them to your initial dataset and upload them in the same location as your original data in Amazon S3.

2. Log in to your AWS console and search for Forecast in the search bar at the top.

3. Click on **Amazon Forecast** to go to the service home page.

4. On this page, you click on the **View dataset groups** button on the right side of the screen.

5. Then, on the dataset group list screen displayed, click on your dataset group name (mine is called london_household_energy_consumption): you are now on your dataset group dashboard. Now click on **View datasets**.

6. Click on the target time series dataset name (mine is called energy_consumption_data).

7. On the following screen, scroll down to the **Dataset imports** section and click on the **Create dataset import** button:

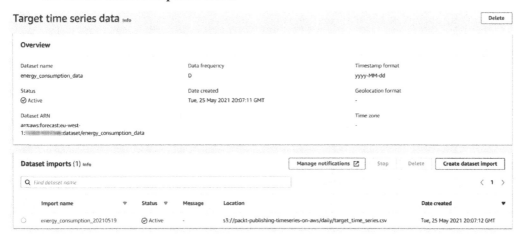

Figure 6.5 – Create new dataset import

8. You will end up on the **Create target time series dataset** screen that you encountered in *Chapter 3, Creating a Project and Ingesting Your Data*, when you ingested the data the first time. Many fields are now grayed out and disabled. Scroll down to **Dataset import details**:

Dataset import details

Dataset import name
The name can help you distinguish this dataset import from other imports on your dataset detail page.

energy_consumption_20130730

The dataset import name must have 1 to 63 characters. Valid characters: a-z, A-Z, 0-9, and _

Select time zone Info
Select a time zone for your dataset.

Do not use time zone ▼

Data location Info
The location is the path to the file in your S3 bucket that contains your data.

🔍 s3://timeseries-on-aws-forecast-michael-hoarau/target_time_series_july_2013.csv   ✕   View 🗗   Browse S3
Your files must be in CSV format.

IAM role Info
Dataset groups require permissions from IAM to read your dataset files in S3. Choose or create a role using this control.

Enter a custom IAM role ARN ▼

Custom IAM role ARN

arn:aws:iam:: ▓▓▓▓ ▓▓▓▓▓▓ :role/AmazonForecastEnergyConsumption

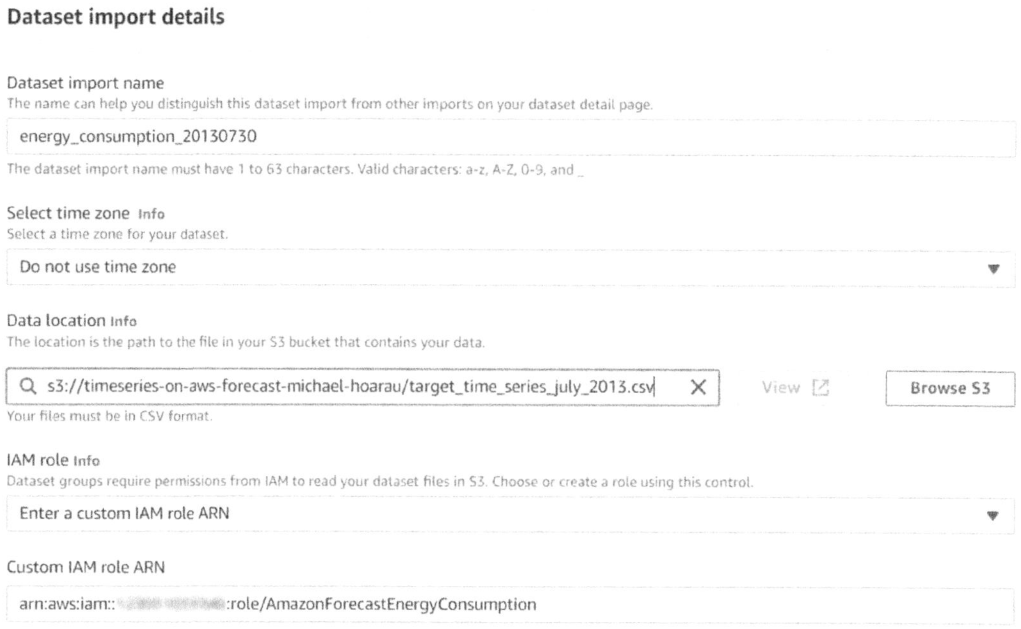

Figure 6.6 – Configuring a new dataset import

On this screen, you will need to do the following:

I. Give a name to your import. This will help you distinguish between different import jobs. We will call it `energy_consumption_20130730` (I added the timestamp of the last date available in the new data).

> **Important Note**
> Note that successive import jobs are not aggregated: only the most recent import will be considered when you use your datasets to train a predictor.

II. Enter the S3 URL for the target time series where you uploaded your new dataset earlier in Amazon S3.

III. Select **Enter a custom IAM role ARN** and paste the ARN of the `AmazonForecastEnergyConsumption` role that you created earlier in the IAM service. The format of the ARN should be `arn:aws:iam::<ACCOUNT-NUMBER>:role/AmazonForecastEnergyConsumption`, where `<ACCOUNT-NUMBER>` needs to be replaced by your AWS account number.

9. Click on the **Start** button at the bottom right of this screen to start updating your target time series. You may have to perform the same actions from steps 6 to 9 for your related time series data.

Your new target time series data and related time series data will now range from `2012-07-01` to `2013-07-30` (one additional month added).

You can now follow two paths:

- *Generate a new forecast without retraining a new predictor*: The new forecast will consider the new data you just added for additional context, but your model doesn't get retrained with the updated data. This is the recommended way if your data has a low risk of drifting from its original statistics distribution (see *Chapter 7*, *Improving and Scaling Your Forecast Strategy*, for additional insights about model drift and model monitoring).

- *Train a new predictor on updated data*: You can retrain your predictor to let it consider the new data. Once your predictor is retrained, you can generate a new forecast with the additional context from a retrained model. However, this will take a longer time and incur additional training costs.

Now that you know how to generate a new forecast from either an original or an updated model, you can start using your predictions.

Using lookup to get your items forecast

When you have at least one forecast with an **Active** status, the **Forecast lookup** feature becomes available:

1. From the dashboard of **Dataset groups**, click on the **Query forecast** button located in the **Generate forecasts** column on the right.

2. Once you click on **Query forecast**, you are presented with the following **Forecast lookup** query interface:

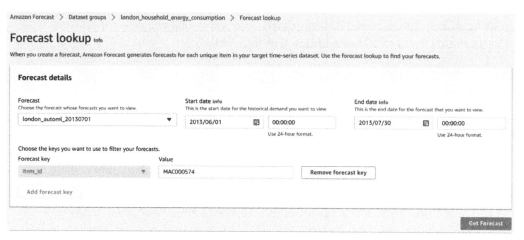

Figure 6.7 – Forecast lookup query interface

3. On this screen, you need to fill in the following values:

    - **Forecast**: The name of one of the forecasts you generated. I will choose the `london_automl_20130701` one.

    - **Start date**: The start date must start *before* your historical data end date and cannot be earlier than your historical data end date minus the forecast horizon used to train your initial predictor. In your case, you trained a predictor with a 30-day forecast horizon and your historical data ends on 2013-06-30. For this forecast, the start date must be between 2013-06-01 00:00:00 and 2013-06-30 00:00:00. Use `2013-06-01` as the start date and leave the time to `00:00:00`.

    - **End date**: The end date must start after the forecast start date and earlier than the forecast start date augmented by the forecast horizon. For this forecast, the end date must be between 2013-07-01 00:00:00 and 2013-07-30 00:00:00. Use `2013-07-30` as the start date and leave the time as `00:00:00`.

- **Forecast key**: When you defined the schema for your target dataset at ingestion time (see *Chapter 3, Creating a Project and Ingesting Your Data*), you defined a target key named `item_id`. This is the key you can use to filter your forecast. Fill in `MAC000574` to request an energy consumption forecast for this particular household.

> **Note**
>
> If you had other dimensions in your target time series data, they would also appear in the forecast key to let you query an aggregated forecast along the selected dimensions.

4. Click on the **Get Forecast** button at the bottom right of the form to visualize your forecast:

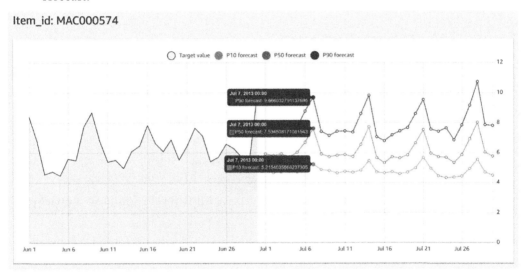

Figure 6.8 – Predictions for household MAC000574

5. On this plot, you can visualize the last part of the historical data associated with `item_id` MAC000574 (in gray on the left) in particular and the predictions for each quantile (or forecast type) you selected when you generated the forecast:

- The bottom line is the **p10 forecast**. If you hover your mouse over the first peak, you can read a value of **5.215**, meaning that there is a 10% chance that the actual value at this date will be below **5.215**.

- The middle line is the **p50 forecast**. If you hover your mouse over the first peak, you can read a value of **7.595**, meaning that there is a 50% chance that the actual energy consumption at this date will be below **7.595**.

- The top line is the **p90 forecast**. If you hover your mouse over the first peak again, you can read a value of **9.666**, meaning that there is a 90% chance that the actual value at this date will be below **9.666**.

6. Feel free to select other household IDs to further explore the predictions generated by your model.

If you want to perform deeper analysis and comparisons, you will need to export the data for the forecast you generated. This is what you are going to do in the next section.

Exporting and visualizing your forecasts

In this section, you will export your forecasts in CSV format and then visualize them on a spreadsheet.

Exporting the predictions

To export all the predictions associated with a generated forecast, you can follow these steps:

1. Log in to your AWS console and search for `Forecast` in the search bar at the top.
2. Click on **Amazon Forecast** to go to the service home page:
3. Click on the **View dataset groups** button on the right side of the screen. You will land on a page listing all the dataset groups visible from your AWS account.
4. Click on the name of the predictor you trained. Mine is called **london_household_energy_consumption**.
5. On the left menu bar, click on **Forecasts** to bring up the list of forecasts generated with this dataset group.
6. Click on the name of one of the forecasts you generated earlier. I will click on **london_automl_20130701**:

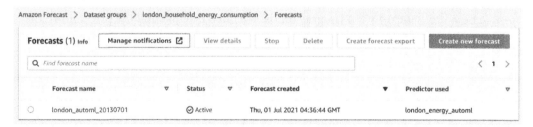

Figure 6.9 – List of available forecasts

7. You are now on the details page of the forecast you generated earlier. In the second section of this page, you have an **Exports** section. The number **(0)** after the section title is the number of exports you requested for this particular forecast. At the top right of this section, click on **Create forecast export**.

8. You are presented with a **Export details** form:

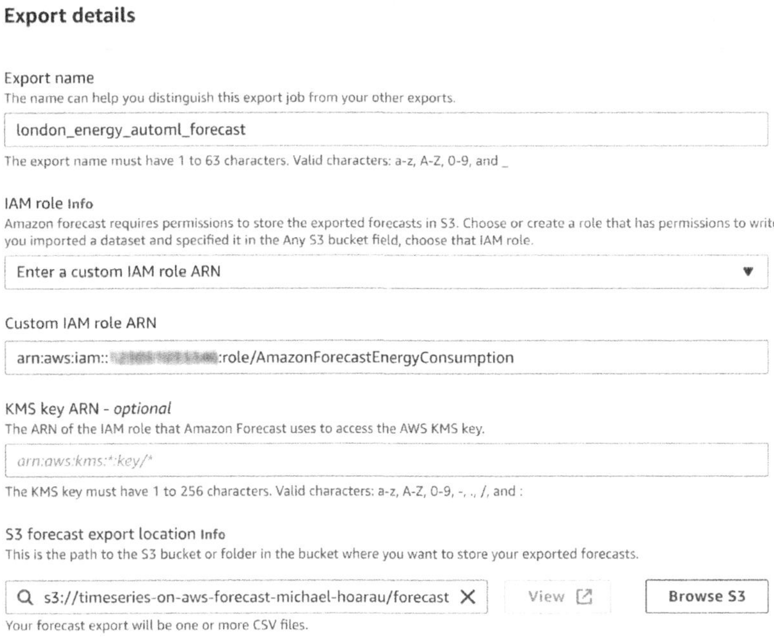

Export details

Export name
The name can help you distinguish this export job from your other exports.

> london_energy_automl_forecast

The export name must have 1 to 63 characters. Valid characters: a-z, A-Z, 0-9, and _

IAM role Info
Amazon forecast requires permissions to store the exported forecasts in S3. Choose or create a role that has permissions to write to S3. If you created an IAM role when you imported a dataset and specified it in the Any S3 bucket field, choose that IAM role.

> Enter a custom IAM role ARN   ▼

Custom IAM role ARN

> arn:aws:iam:: ▓▓▓▓▓▓▓▓▓▓:role/AmazonForecastEnergyConsumption

KMS key ARN - *optional*
The ARN of the IAM role that Amazon Forecast uses to access the AWS KMS key.

> arn:aws:kms:*:key/*

The KMS key must have 1 to 256 characters. Valid characters: a-z, A-Z, 0-9, -, ., /, and :

S3 forecast export location Info
This is the path to the S3 bucket or folder in the bucket where you want to store your exported forecasts.

> 🔍 s3://timeseries-on-aws-forecast-michael-hoarau/forecast ✕   View ↗   Browse S3

Your forecast export will be one or more CSV files.

Figure 6.10 – Create forecast export

9. In **Export details**, fill in the following parameters and leave all the other parameters as their default values:

- **Export name**: london_energy_automl_forecast.

- **IAM role**: Select Enter a custom IAM role ARN.

- **Custom IAM role ARN**: Paste the ARN of the AmazonForecastEnergyConsumption role that you created earlier in the IAM service (see *Chapter 3, Creating a Project and Ingesting Your Data*). The format of the ARN should be arn:aws:iam::<ACCOUNT-NUMBER>:role/ AmazonForecastEnergyConsumption, where <ACCOUNT-NUMBER> needs to be replaced by your AWS account number.

- **S3 forecast export location**: Paste an S3 location from the bucket you also created in *Chapter 3, Creating a Project and Ingesting Your Data*. The format of this S3 path should be `s3://BUCKET_NAME/forecasts/automl/` where `BUCKET_NAME` should be replaced by the name of your bucket.

10. Click on the **Start** button located at the bottom right of this form to launch the forecast export job. Your export creation is now started.

After a while, your data is available in the S3 bucket you selected earlier. Let's now fetch these files and visualize their content.

Visualizing your forecast's results

The forecast export process output the predictions in Amazon S3. Let's open this service to collect these results and visualize them:

1. At the top left of the AWS console, you will see a **Services** drop-down menu that will display all the available AWS services. In the **Storage** section, look for the **S3** service and click on its name to go to the S3 console.

2. Click on the name of the bucket you used to upload your datasets to visualize its content.

3. On this screen, you will see a `forecasts/` folder, click on it, and then click on the `automl` folder name. You will end up in a directory with a collection of CSV files:

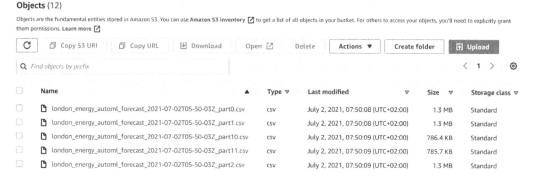

Figure 6.11 – Forecast export results as stored on Amazon S3

Each CSV file has a name that follows this pattern:

`<export_name>_<yyyy-mm-ddTHH-MM-SSZ>_part<NN>`

`export_name` is the label you chose to name your backtest export job followed by a `timestamp` (the time at which the export was generated) and a `part number`.

Each CSV file contains the forecasts for a subset of `item_id` (which corresponds to household ID in our case). In the dataset we used, we had a bit more than 3,500 households and Amazon Forecast generated 12 files (from `part0` to `part11`), each containing the backtest results for approximately 300 households.

4. Click on the checkbox near the first CSV file and click on **Download**. This action will download the CSV file locally where you can open it with any spreadsheet software, such as Excel, or process it with your favorite programming language. You can open this file with Excel and analyze the different time series available in these files for a few households to have a better understanding of your forecast's behavior.

Let's have a look inside one of these files:

item_id	family_1_per son	family_2_per sons	family_3_4_p ersons	geography_e ngland	geography_sc otland	geography_w ales	transport_work_fro m_home	date	p10	p50	p90
mac002252	65	102	116	106	46	84	66	2013-07-01T00:00:00Z	7,17	10,35	14,46
mac002252	65	102	116	106	46	84	66	2013-07-02T00:00:00Z	7,02	10,02	14,24
mac002252	65	102	116	106	46	84	66	2013-07-03T00:00:00Z	7,10	10,72	14,95
mac002252	65	102	116	106	46	84	66	2013-07-04T00:00:00Z	7,66	11,19	15,55
mac002252	65	102	116	106	46	84	66	2013-07-05T00:00:00Z	6,70	10,57	15,10
mac002252	65	102	116	106	46	84	66	2013-07-06T00:00:00Z	6,94	11,44	16,40
mac002252	65	102	116	106	46	84	66	2013-07-07T00:00:00Z	7,56	12,44	17,42
mac002252	65	102	116	106	46	84	66	2013-07-08T00:00:00Z	6,76	9,65	14,04
mac002252	65	102	116	106	46	84	66	2013-07-09T00:00:00Z	6,72	9,74	13,91
mac002252	65	102	116	106	46	84	66	2013-07-10T00:00:00Z	6,87	10,46	14,93

Figure 6.12 – Forecast export results file content

The different columns generated by Amazon Forecast are as follows:

- `item_id`: This column contains the ID of each household.

- `date`: For each household, there will be as many data points as the length of the forecast horizon window as configured in the forecast generation parameters. With a forecast frequency of `1` day and a forecast horizon of `30`, we end up with 30 data points. The timestamps from these columns will include 30 days' worth for each household.

- `p10`, `p50`, and `p90`: The values for each forecast type as requested at training time. You can request up to 5 forecast types and they will all appear as individual columns in this file.

- Item metadata (`family_1_person`, `geography_england`, `transport_ work_from_home`, and so on): You will also get the item metadata columns associated with each `item_id`. If you obtain low performance for the forecast of some of your time series, you will be able to check whether your forecast performance is linked to some categories of items.

To dive further into our forecast results, I concatenated all the forecast files together. Click on the following link to download my Excel file and follow along with my analysis:

```
https://packt-publishing-timeseries-on-aws-michaelhoarau.
s3.eu-west-1.amazonaws.com/part1-amazon-forecast/london_
energy_automl_forecast_results.xlsx
```

In the next section, you will use this file to derive useful information from your predictions.

Performing error analysis

You have been using a dataset with 3,573 unique time series (one for the electricity consumption of each household) to train a predictor and in the previous paragraph, you downloaded the predictions obtained for these. As you generated the predictions for a period for which you still have some actual data, you can compute the same forecast metrics as in the backtesting evaluation:

1. Open the file you downloaded previously. The first tab contains the time series for your items:

	A	B	C	D	E	F
1	item_id	date	p10	p50	p90	actual
183	MAC000003	01/07/2013	10,36	11,80	13,80	13,43
184	MAC000003	02/07/2013	9,91	11,47	13,11	11,16
185	MAC000003	03/07/2013	10,14	11,48	13,02	10,80
186	MAC000003	04/07/2013	10,10	11,59	13,44	10,85
187	MAC000003	05/07/2013	10,07	11,61	13,18	11,65
188	MAC000003	06/07/2013	9,67	11,26	13,10	11,03
189	MAC000003	07/07/2013	10,14	12,55	14,56	10,95

Figure 6.13 – Forecast export results – time series data

In particular, for each `item_id`, you will find the following:

- `date`: For your convenience, I included a copy of the historical data starting on 2013-01-01. The date goes up to the end of the forecast horizon (2013-07-30).

- `p10`, `p50`, and `p90`: The values for each forecast type as requested when you generated the forecast.

- `actual`: The actual value of the time series as available in the original dataset.

We will use these time series to plot them later on. In the second tab, you have the computation results for the **mean absolute percentage error** (**MAPE**) metric for each household:

	A	B	C
1	item_id	MAPE	MAPE (%)
2	MAC002136	154,10	15 410%
3	MAC002594	3,27	327%
4	MAC000636	0,72	72%
5	MAC001309	0,51	51%
6	MAC001269	0,49	49%
7	MAC000037	0,48	48%
8	MAC002072	0,46	46%

Figure 6.14 – Forecast export results – MAPE metrics

I already ordered the file by decreasing MAPE and you can already see that some items are definitely worth further investigation!

In this file, you will see that out of 3,573 items, 35 items obtained a MAPE greater than or equal to 10%. In *Chapter 4, Training a Predictor with AutoML*, the evaluation dashboard from your predictor mentioned that the overall MAPE for the predictor was 22.54%. You now know that for more than 99% of your items, the predictions are off by less than 10%. Depending on your business sensitivity to forecast accuracy, you will of course adjust this threshold of 10% and your analysis scope accordingly.

2. Let's now visually compare a random item with a good forecast (I will select household ID MAC000574 with a MAPE of 2.44%) with a random item that has a bad forecast (household ID MAC000636 with a MAPE of 72.0%). The following plot illustrates the time series for household MAC000574:

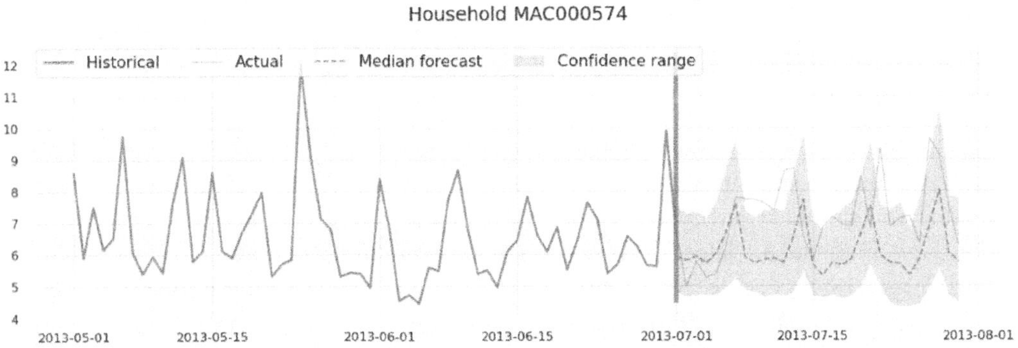

Figure 6.15 – Example of a good forecast

You can verify that most of the time, the actual values (the thin solid line on the right part of the plot) stay within the 80% confidence range. In addition, if you were to compute the average and standard deviation of the energy consumption of this household during the training period and within the forecast horizon, you would find that they are very close: in the training period, the average energy consumption is 7.62 kWh (7.15 kWh in the forecast horizon) while the standard deviation is 1.66 kWh (1.17 kWh in the forecast horizon).

3. Let's now check out what is going on with household MAC000636:

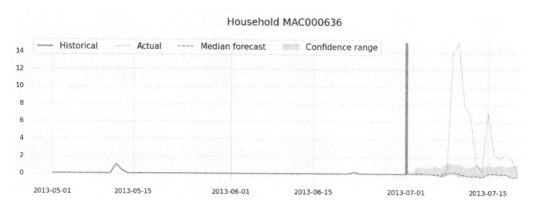

Figure 6.16 – Example of a bad forecast

You can immediately spot that the predictions are nowhere near the actual results. But more importantly, you can see that the behavior of the time series is wildly different between the two periods. We can observe a major data drift, which you can materialize by looking at the statistical properties of this time series over time: in the training period, the energy consumption of this household had an average of 0.14 kWh (versus 3.05 kWh in the forecast horizon) and a standard deviation of 0.19 kWh (versus 4.54 kWh in the forecast horizon).

Analyzing these results after you have trained the first model is critical to understanding whether you should segment your time series into a different population. Combined with the item metadata dataset, this will allow you to refine your training strategy. For instance, you might decide to train two predictors to predict the energy consumption of the households you have been processing. This will increase the accuracy of each segment, at the expense of additional work to build and maintain the predictors that are suitable to cover the whole range of behavior your dataset includes.

> **Important Note**
>
> Since this chapter was written, Amazon Forecast deployed the **AutoPredictor** feature: as mentioned in earlier chapters, when training a predictor with this feature, Amazon Forecast will analyze your data on your behalf to ensemble multiple algorithms and build better forecasts for each individual time series. However, depending on your data, you may still have to perform the type of error analysis we just went through in this paragraph: this practice will always be critical whichever forecasting tool, algorithm, and approaches you select in your line of business.

Generating explainability for your forecasts

Since this chapter was written, Amazon Forecast has also deployed a new feature to provide some level of explainability for your predictions. In the previous paragraph, we walked through an error analysis to understand what can be done to improve the forecast accuracy. In this paragraph, we are going to explore this new explainability feature. Explainability is a set of practices and capabilities that help you understand the predictions made by a statistical, machine learning, or deep learning model. In essence, the goal of explainability is to open what can be perceived as a black box to the end users.

Amazon Forecast computes a specific metric (called the **impact score**) to quantify the impact (does it increase or decrease a given forecast value?) each attribute of your dataset has on your time series. In this paragraph, we are going to look at how to generate such insights and then how to interpret them.

> **Note**
>
> As this was a rather new feature at the time of writing, the dataset we selected won't be the best example to explore the outputs from these new insights provided by Amazon Forecast. However, I will walk you through the process to generate and visualize them. Feel free to have a look at the explainability documentation (`https://docs.aws.amazon.com/forecast/latest/dg/forecast-explainability.html`) or this step-by-step guide if you're comfortable with running Python code in a Jupyter notebook: `https://github.com/aws-samples/amazon-forecast-samples/blob/main/notebooks/advanced/Item_Level_Explainability/Item_Level_Explanability.ipynb`.

Generating forecast explainability

When you have at least one forecast with an **Active** status, the **Explore insights** feature becomes available.

> **Important Note**
>
> Explainability is only available for forecasts generated for predictors trained with the `AutoPredictor` feature. You can also convert your legacy predictor to `AutoPredictor` to enable this feature.

1. The first step is to specify which time series you would like to gain some insights for. To do this, you will write a simple CSV file with a structure that must match the target time series data schema. In your case, we only provided `item_id` without any additional dimensions. If you want to request explainability for the `mac002252`, `mac004141`, `mac000267`, and `mac005293` items, you will fill a text file with one item per line as follows:

    ```
    mac002252
    mac004141
    mac000267
    mac005293
    ```

2. Save this file as `timeseries_explainability.csv`, log into the AWS console, and navigate to Amazon S3.

3. Search for the S3 bucket you have been using and upload this file at the root of your bucket (or any other desired location: just take note of this location as you will need it in the next steps).

4. From the dashboard of **Dataset Groups**, click on the **Explore insights** button located in the last column on the right:

Overview

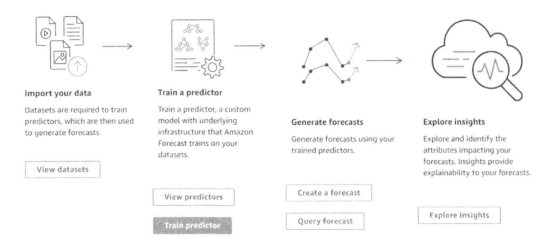

Import your data

Datasets are required to train predictors, which are then used to generate forecasts.

View datasets

Train a predictor

Train a predictor, a custom model with underlying infrastructure that Amazon Forecast trains on your datasets.

View predictors

Train predictor

Generate forecasts

Generate forecasts using your trained predictors.

Create a forecast

Query forecast

Explore insights

Explore and identify the attributes impacting your forecasts. Insights provide explainability to your forecasts.

Explore insights

Figure 6.17 – Accessing the explainability feature from the main dashboard

5. You will be presented with a list of insights previously generated. Click on the **Create explainability** button at the top right of the screen.

6. On the **Create explainability** screen, you will need to enter the following information:

- **Explainability name**: `london_energy_explainability`

- **Select forecast**: From the drop-down list, select the name of the forecast you previously created. If you don't see your forecast in the list and only see a **Forecast not supported** message, this means that your forecast is associated with a model which was not trained with the AutoPredictor (P-Code)feature. You will need to convert your legacy predictor to an AutoPredictor (P-Code) one and return to this screen to generate your explainability insights.

- **Time duration details**: You can either request explainability for the whole forecast horizon or for specific time ranges.

- **S3 location**: Fill in the S3 location of the CSV file you uploaded previously. The format of this S3 path should be `s3://BUCKET_NAME/timeseries_explainability.csv` where `BUCKET_NAME` should be replaced by the name of your bucket.

- **IAM Role**: Select `Enter a custom IAM role ARN`.

- **Custom IAM role ARN**: Paste the ARN of the `AmazonForecastEnergyConsumption` role that you created earlier in the IAM service (see *Chapter 3*, *Creating a Project and Ingesting Your Data*). The format of the ARN should be `arn:aws:iam::<ACCOUNT-NUMBER>:role/AmazonForecastEnergyConsumption`, where `<ACCOUNT-NUMBER>` needs to be replaced by your AWS account number.

- **Data schema**: This schema should be the same as the target time series dataset schema (you should see `item_id` with a `string` type already filled in on your behalf). If you have other dimensions, you can add them here.

7. Scroll down to the bottom of the screen and click on the **Create** button to launch the explainability generation process.

You are brought back to the list of insights screen where you can see the explainability requests in progress. Once the report is ready, you can click on its name to visualize it.

Visualizing forecast explainability

After an explainability report is ready, you will see its status as **Active** on the insights screen:

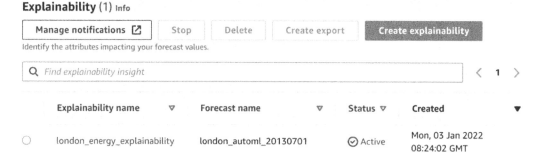

Figure 6.18 – List of available explainability reports

Click on the name of the report to bring up a detailed page. After the **Explainability details** section (where you can find the name of your report, how long it took to generate it, and when it was created), you will find the key section of interest, **Attribute increasing impact score**. This section includes two horizontal bar charts:

1. At the top, you will find the attributes that increase the normalized impact scores for a selected time series and time points. You can select an aggregated view to display the impact scores for either all the time series and/or all the time points. The following screenshot is extracted from step-by-step notebooks mentioned earlier. On this screenshot, you can see, for instance, that the `Customer_Request` attribute has twice the impact than `Loss_Rate`:

Attribute increasing impact score

Figure 6.19 – Attribute increasing impact score

Important Note

The impact scores only measure the relative impact of the scores and cannot be used to improve model accuracy. They can only be used to explain the contribution each attribute has on a given forecast value.

---

2. At the bottom, you will see a similar bar chart but including only the attributes that decrease the impact scores.

Note that the console plots only display *normalized* impact scores (between -1 and 1) whereas direct API calls can also give you raw impact scores (based on Shapley values). Raw impact scores can be used to combine or compare scores across different time series and time points. However, these scores cannot be compared or combined when they come from different forecasts.

Congratulations, with this last feature, you have reached the end of this chapter! It's time to conclude and move on to the last chapter, dedicated to Amazon Forecast.

Summary

In this chapter, you learned how to generate, export, and visualize the predictions for the models you trained in the previous chapters. You also learned how you could use the forecast export features to monitor the performance of your predictions at the time series level (and not only at the aggregated level as provided by the predictor evaluation dashboard).

Generating forecasts will be your key activity once a model is trained. It's important that you practice this step, which includes establishing a sound error analysis process. Using error analysis at the item level is indeed critical to understand the areas where your forecasts can be improved and where a significant change in your data distribution impacts its performance.

In the next chapter, you will set up fully automated solutions that will perform even more heavy lifting for you so that you can focus on improving your forecast accuracy over time. You will also have a look at how you can put together the key components of a sound model monitoring strategy.

7
Improving and Scaling Your Forecast Strategy

To get the most out of **Amazon Forecast**, you can partner with your favorite data engineer or data scientist to help you improve your predictor accuracy and go further in the results postprocessing. This chapter will point you in the right direction to monitor your models and compare the predictions to real-life data; this is crucial to detect any drift in performance that would invite you to trigger retraining. Last but not least, you will also use a sample from the **AWS Solutions Library** to automate all your predictor training, forecast generation, and dashboard visualizations.

In this chapter, we're going to cover the following main topics:

- Deep diving into forecasting model metrics
- Understanding your model accuracy
- Model monitoring and drift detection
- Serverless architecture orchestration

Technical requirements

In this chapter, we will be tackling more advanced topics and as such, you will need need some hands-on experience in a language such as Python to follow along in more detail. You will also need broader skills in several AWS cloud services that are beyond the scope of this book (such as **AWS CloudFormation** or **Amazon SageMaker**).

We highly recommend that you read this chapter while connected to your own AWS account and open the different service consoles to run the different actions on your end.

To create an AWS account and log into the Amazon Forecast console, you can refer to the *Technical requirements* section of *Chapter 2, An Overview of Amazon Forecast.*

The content in this chapter assumes that you have a predictor already trained; if you don't, we recommend that you follow the detailed process presented in *Chapter 4, Training a Predictor with AutoML.*

This chapter also assumes you have already generated a forecast from a trained predictor; if you haven't already, we recommend that you follow the detailed process presented in *Chapter 6, Generating New Forecasts.*

To follow along with the last section of this chapter (*Serverless architecture orchestration*), you will also need to download the following archive and unzip it:

```
https://packt-publishing-timeseries-on-aws-michaelhoarau.
s3-eu-west-1.amazonaws.com/part1-amazon-forecast/energy_
consumption_serverless.zip
```

Deep diving into forecasting model metrics

When training a forecasting model, Amazon Forecast will use different machine learning metrics to measure how good a given model and parameters are at predicting future values of a time series. In this section, we are going to detail what these metrics are, why they are important, and how Amazon Forecast uses them.

In *Chapter 4, Training a Predictor with AutoML*, you trained your first predictor and obtained the following results:

Accuracy metrics Info				CNN-QR (Winner) ▼		Export backtest results		
Evaluation type	Test window start	Test window end	Items	Weighted quantile loss [wQL]			Metrics based on mean	
				wQL[0.1]	wQL[0.5]	wQL[0.9]	WAPE	RMSE
Backtest window	Sat, 01 Jun 2013 00:00:00 GMT	Mon, 01 Jul 2013 00:00:00 GMT	3573	0.0993	0.2254	0.1183	0.2254	3.2904

Figure 7.1 – Results page: Accuracy metrics

Using the dropdown on the top right of this section, you can select the algorithm for which you want to see the results. The results you obtained from your first predictor should be similar to the following ones:

	wQL[0.1]	wQL[0.5]	wQL[0.9]	WAPE	RMSE
CNN-QR (Winner)	0.0993	0.2254	0.1183	0.2254	3.2904
Deep_AR_Plus	0.1100	0.2353	0.1253	0.2364	3.4374
ARIMA	0.1196	0.2456	0.1430	0.2456	3.6026
Prophet	0.1243	0.2636	0.1305	0.2617	3.8997
NPTS	0.1107	0.3329	0.1813	0.3618	5.1994
ETS	0.1636	0.2866	0.2084	0.2866	4.6343

Figure 7.2 – Algorithm metrics comparison

At the top of this table, you can see several metric names, such as **wQL[0.1]**, **wQL[0.5]**, **wQL[0.9]**, **WAPE**, and **RMSE**. How are these metrics computed? How do you interpret them? How do you know whether a value is a good one? Let's dive deeper into each of these metrics.

Weighted absolute percentage error (WAPE)

This accuracy metric is a method that computes the error made by the forecasting algorithm with regard to the actual values (the real observations). As this metric is averaged over time and over different items (household items in our case), this metric doesn't differentiate between these items. In other words, the WAPE does not assume any preference between which point in time or item the model predicted better. The WAPE is always a positive number and the smaller it is, the better the model.

The formula to derive this metric over a given backtesting window is as follows:

$$WAPE = \frac{\sum_{i,t}|y_{i,t} - \hat{y}_{i,t}|}{\sum_{i,t}|y_{i,t}|}$$

Here, we have the following:

- $y_{i,t}$ is the actual value observed for a given `item_id` at a point in time, t (with t ranging over the time range from the backtest period and i ranging over all items).

- $\hat{y}_{i,t}$ is the mean forecast predicted for a given `item_id` at a point in time, t.

Let's have a look at the following plot, where we have drawn the forecast and the observations for the energy consumption of a given household from our dataset:

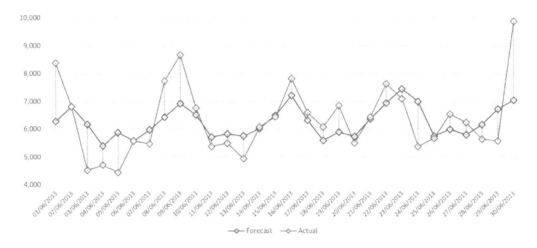

Figure 7.3 – WAPE metric

In the preceding plot, the vertical dotted lines illustrate the difference between the actual values and the forecasted values for a given household. To compute the WAPE metric, you can follow the steps listed here:

1. Take the length of every dotted line in this plot (each line length is the absolute value of the difference between the actual and forecasted values).

2. Sum all these lengths together and sum across all `item_id` in the dataset.

3. Divide this number by the sum of the observed values for every `item_id` over this backtest window.

This will give you an absolute value measured in percentage. For instance, a value of 10.0 could be read as *on average, the forecasted values are ±10% away from the observed values.* Reading this, you might notice one of the disadvantages of this metric, which is that with the WAPE being a percentage, it can be overly influenced by large percentage errors when forecasting small numbers. In addition, this metric is symmetrical: it does not penalize under-forecasting or over-forecasting more.

Note that the absolute error (the denominator in the previous formula) is normalized by the sum of all the values of all your time series. If you're a retailer and deal with the total demand of multiple products, this means that this metric puts more emphasis on the products that are sold frequently. From a business perspective, it makes sense to have a more accurate forecast for your best sellers. In an energy consumption use case (such as the one we have been using), this means that households with significantly higher consumption will have more impact on this metric. Although this makes sense to ensure you deliver the right amount of electricity through your grid, this may not be useful if you want to deliver personalized recommendations to each household.

Mean absolute percentage error (MAPE)

Like the WAPE, this metric computes the error made by the forecasting algorithm with regard to the real observations. The formula to derive this metric over a given backtesting window is as follows:

$$MAPE_i = \frac{1}{n} \sum_t \left| \frac{y_{i,t} - \hat{y}_{i,t}}{y_{i,t}} \right|$$

Here, we have the following:

- $y_{i,t}$ is the actual value observed for a given `item_id` at a point in time, t (with t ranging over the time range from the backtest period and i ranging over all items).
- $\hat{y}_{i,t}$ is the mean forecast predicted for a given `item_id` at a point in time, t.
- n is the number of data points in the time series associated with a given `item_id`.

As the formula hints, this metric is highly influenced by outliers: the MAPE is useful when your time series differ significantly over time. Compared to the WAPE, the MAPE is also unnormalized, making it useful when you want to consider time series with large values and others with small values equally.

Mean absolute scaled error (MASE)

When your dataset is seasonal, the cyclical property of your time series may be better captured by this metric, which considers the seasonality by integrating it into a scaling factor. The formula to derive this metric over a given backtesting window for a given time series is the following:

$$MASE_i = \frac{\frac{1}{n} \cdot \Sigma_t |y_{i,t} - \hat{y}_{i,t}|}{\frac{1}{n-m} \cdot \Sigma_{t=m+1}^n |y_{i,t} - y_{i,t-m}|}$$

Here, we have the following:

- $y_{i,t}$ is the actual value observed for a given `item_id` at a point in time, t (with t ranging over the time range from the backtest period and i ranging over all items).

- $\hat{y}_{i,t}$ is the mean forecast predicted for a given `item_id` at a point in time, t.

- n is the number of data points in the time series associated with a given `item_id`.

- m is the seasonality value: when m is equal to 1, the denominator of this formula is actually the mean absolute error of the *naïve forecast method* (which takes a forecast equal to the previous timestep). Amazon Forecast sets this value, m, depending on the forecast frequency selected.

When your time series have a significant change of behavior over different seasons, using this metric as the one to optimize for can be beneficial. This metric is scale-invariant, making it easier to compare different models for a given `item_id` time series or compare forecast accuracy between different time series.

Root mean square error (RMSE)

Like the WAPE, this accuracy metric is also a method that computes the deviation made by a predictor with regard to the actual values (the real observations). In the case of the RMSE, we average a squared error over time and over different items (the household in our case). This metric doesn't differentiate between these, meaning the RMSE does not assume any preference between which point or item the model predicted better. It is always a positive number and the smaller it is, the better the model.

The formula to derive this metric over a given backtesting window is as follows:

$$RMSE = \sqrt{\frac{1}{n \times T} \sum_{i,t} (\hat{y}_{i,t} - y_{i,t})^2}$$

Here, we have the following:

- $y_{i,t}$ is the actual value observed for a given `item_id` at a point in time, t (with t ranging over the time range from the backtest period and i ranging over all items).

- $\hat{y}_{i,t}$ is the mean forecast predicted for a given `item_id` at a point in time, t.

- $n \times T$ is the number of data points in a given backtest window (n being the number of items and T the number of time steps).

As you can see in the preceding formula, the RMSE squares the errors (also called the **residuals**), which gives more importance to large errors when computing this metric. A few wrong predictions can have a negative impact on the RMSE. This metric is very useful in use cases where you do not have the luxury of getting a few predictions wrong.

Weighted quantile loss (wQL)

The WAPE and RMSE are computed using the mean forecast. wQL is a metric that measures the accuracy of a forecasting model at a given quantile. In the Amazon Forecast console, you will, for instance, see *wQL[0.1]* as a label for the quantile loss computed for the forecast type *0.1*.

The formula to derive this metric over a given backtesting window and a given quantile, τ, is as follows:

$$wQL[\tau] = 2 \cdot \frac{\sum_{i,t} \left[\tau \cdot max\left(y_{i,t} - q_{i,t}^{(\tau)}, 0 \right) + (1 - \tau) \cdot max\left(q_{i,t}^{(\tau)} - y_{i,t}, 0 \right) \right]}{\sum_{i,t} |y_{i,t}|}$$

Here, we have the following:

- $y_{i,t}$ is the actual value observed for a given `item_id` at a point in time, t (with t ranging over the time range from the backtest period and i ranging over all items).

- $q_{i,t}^{(\tau)}$ is the τ quantile predicted for a given `item_id` at a point in time, t.

- τ is a quantile that can take one of the following values: 0.01, 0.02…, 0.98, or 0.99.

On the numerator of the previous formula, you can see the following:

- $\tau \cdot max\left(y_{i,t} - q_{i,t}^{(\tau)}, 0\right)$ is strictly positive when the predictions are below the actual observations. This term penalizes under-forecasting situations.

- On the other hand, $(1-\tau) \cdot max\left(q_{i,t}^{(\tau)} - y_{i,t}, 0\right)$ is strictly positive when the predictions are above the actual observations. This term penalizes over-forecasting situations.

Let's take the example of *wQL[0.80]*. Based on the preceding formula, this metric assigns the following:

- A larger penalty weight to under forecasting: $0.8 \cdot max\left(y_{i,t} - q_{i,t}^{(0.8)}, 0\right)$
- A smaller penalty weight to over forecasting: $(1-0.8) \cdot max\left(q_{i,t}^{(0.8)} - y_{i,t}, 0\right)$

Very often, in retail, being understocked for a given product (with the risk of missed revenue because of an unavailable product) has a higher cost than being overstocked (having a larger inventory). Using *wQL[0.8]* to assess the quality of a forecast may be more informative to make supply-related decisions for these products.

On the other hand, a retailer may have products that are easy for consumers to substitute. To reduce excess inventory, the retailer may decide to understock these products because the occasional lost sale is overweighed by the inventory cost reduction. In this case, using *wQL[0.1]* to assess the quality of the forecast for these products might be more useful.

Now that you have a good understanding of which metrics Amazon Forecast computes, let's see how you can use this knowledge to analyze your model accuracy and try and improve it.

Understanding your model accuracy

Some items might be more important than others in a dataset. In retail forecasting, 20% of the sales often accounts for 80% of the revenue, so you might want to ensure you have a good forecast accuracy for your top-moving items (as the others might have a very small share of the total sales most of the time). In every use case, optimizing accuracy for your critical items is important: if your dataset includes several segments of items, properly identifying them will allow you to adjust your forecast strategy.

In this section, we are going to dive deeper into the forecast results of the first predictor you trained in *Chapter 4, Training a Predictor with AutoML*. In *Chapter 6, Generating New Forecasts*, I concatenated all the forecast files associated with the AutoML model trained in *Chapter 4, Training a Predictor with AutoML*. Click on the following link to download my Excel file and follow along with my analysis:

```
https://packt-publishing-timeseries-on-aws-michaelhoarau.
s3.eu-west-1.amazonaws.com/part1-amazon-forecast/london_
energy_automl_forecast_results.xlsx
```

In the following steps, you are going to perform a detailed accuracy analysis to understand where your model can be improved. As an exercise, feel free to reproduce these steps either directly from this Excel spreadsheet or in a Jupyter notebook if you're comfortable writing Python code to process data:

1. Let's compute the WAPE metric for each time series and plot them by decreasing value. We can observe that a few items (less than 20) have a WAPE greater than 5%.

Figure 7.4 – Household time series with a high WAPE

2. As they are very few, you can then analyze each of these to understand whether this comes from a specific segment of customers. For instance, you could have a look at one of the metadata fields (the `transport_work_from_home` field one, for instance) and observe how this field is distributed throughout the whole dataset and compare this to the distribution of this field for items that have a high WAPE.

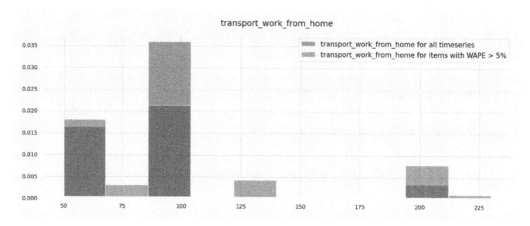

Figure 7.5 – transport_work_from_home variable overlaps with the MAPE

Both distributions overlap significantly, so this field (alone) does not help distinguish between time series with a good WAPE and others with a high WAPE. Diving deeper into this approach goes beyond the scope of this book, but you could apply traditional clustering techniques to try and identify potential conditions that make it harder to forecast energy consumption in this population.

3. Similarly, computing and plotting the correlation of the fields present in your item metadata dataset with an individual WAPE doesn't show any strong linear correlation.

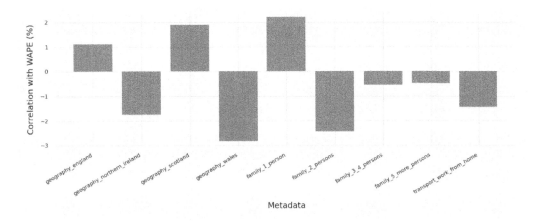

Figure 7.6 – Item metadata correlation with the WAPE

In situations where strong correlations are detected, you might decide to segment these populations and build several predictors that are best suited for each segment.

4. You could then plot the actual values of a few selected signals and compare the values a signal took during training with the actual values taken during the forecast window we used for testing. Here is a plot of the energy consumption for household MAC000636:

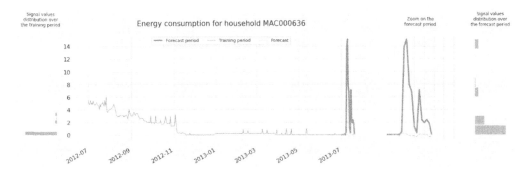

Figure 7.7 – Household time series with a high WAPE

In this figure, you can uncover one of the key reasons why the forecast (the hardly visible dotted line on the bottom right, also seen in the zoomed area) is far away from the actual values (the thick line making a high peak on the right). This is probably because there is significant behavior drift between the data seen by the predictor at training time (the thin line on the left) and what you can witness over the forecast window. This is further highlighted by the histograms exposing the distribution of the time series values over the training period (on the left) and the forecast period (on the far right).

As you can see, drift in your time series data can have severe consequences on the accuracy of your model for some of your time series and this can have a critical impact on the trust your end users will develop for the predictions of your forecasts. In the next section, we will discuss how this can be tackled from an operational perspective.

Model monitoring and drift detection

As was made clear in the previous section, in addition to error analysis, you should also make sure to monitor any potential shifts in your data. To do this, you could follow this process:

1. Build and store a dataset with the training data of all the time series that you want to use to build a predictor.

2. Compute the statistical characteristics of your dataset at a global level (for example, average, standard deviation, or histograms of the distribution of values).

3. Compute the statistical characteristics of your dataset at a local level (for each time series).

4. Train your predictors with these initial datasets and save the performance metrics (wQL, MAPE, and RMSE).

5. Generate a new forecast based on this predictor; you will only get the predictions here and have no real data to compare them with yet.

6. When new data comes in, compute the same statistical characteristics and compare them with the original values used at training time.

7. Now that you have new data, compute the metrics to measure the performance of the previous forecast and compare them with these actual results.

8. You can display these statistics next to the predictions for your analysts to make the appropriate decisions. This will help them better trust the results generated by Amazon Forecast.

Once you have this process set up, you will be able to organize regular reviews to analyze any shifts in the data or any drift in the performance of your forecasts to decide when is a good time to amend your training datasets and retrain a fresh predictor.

Serverless architecture orchestration

Until now, you have been relying heavily on the AWS console to perform all your actions, such as training predictors, generating forecasts, and querying or visualizing forecast results. In this section, you are going to use one of the solutions from the **AWS Solutions Library**.

The AWS Solutions Library contains a collection of cloud-based architecture to tackle many technical and business problems. These solutions are vetted by AWS and you can use these constructs to assemble your own applications.

The solution you are going to implement is called *Improving Forecast Accuracy with Machine Learning* and can be found by following this link:

```
https://aws.amazon.com/solutions/implementations/improving-
forecast-accuracy-with-machine-learning/
```

After a high-level overview of the components that will be deployed in your account, you are going to use this solution to build the same predictor that you built in *Chapter 5, Customizing Your Predictor Training*.

Solutions overview

When you deploy the *Improving Forecast Accuracy with Machine Learning* solution, the following serverless environment is deployed in the AWS cloud:

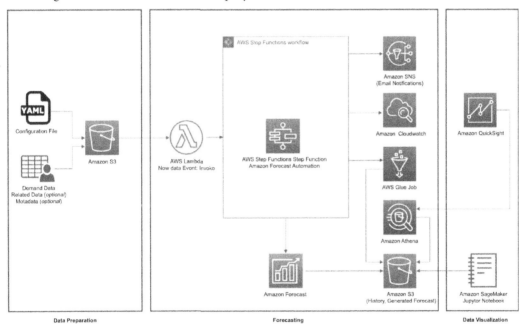

Figure 7.8 – Improving Forecast Accuracy with Machine Learning solution components overview

As you can see in the previous diagram, this solution has three main components:

- A **Data Preparation** component
- A **Forecasting** component
- And a **Data Visualization** component

Let's dive into each of these components.

Data preparation component

The data preparation part assumes you already have your dataset prepared in the format expected by Amazon Forecast. For instance, you must already have a target time series dataset. Optionally, you can have a related time series dataset and a metadata dataset.

To follow along with this section, you can download the following archive directly from this location and unzip it:

```
https://packt-publishing-timeseries-on-aws-michaelhoarau.
s3-eu-west-1.amazonaws.com/part1-amazon-forecast/energy_
consumption_serverless.zip
```

This archive contains the following:

- One file with a `.ipynb` extension: this is a Jupyter notebook that you will use for visualization later in this chapter.
- One YAML file that you will use to configure the solution.
- Three CSV files containing the target time series data, the related time series data, and the item metadata.

The solution needs a forecast configuration file in YAML format. YAML is often used for configuration files and is similar to JSON but less verbose and more readable when the nesting levels are not too deep.

Amazon Simple Storage Service (**Amazon S3**) is used to store the configuration file and your datasets.

Forecasting component

The forecasting part of the solution is mainly built around the following:

- **AWS Lambda**: Serverless Lambda functions are used to build, train, and deploy your machine learning models with Amazon Forecast. Lambda functions are just pieces of code that you can run without having to manage an underlying infrastructure (the service is called **serverless**).

- **AWS Step Functions** uses a state machine to orchestrate all the Lambda functions together. In the following diagram, you can see the different steps this state machine will go through when running:

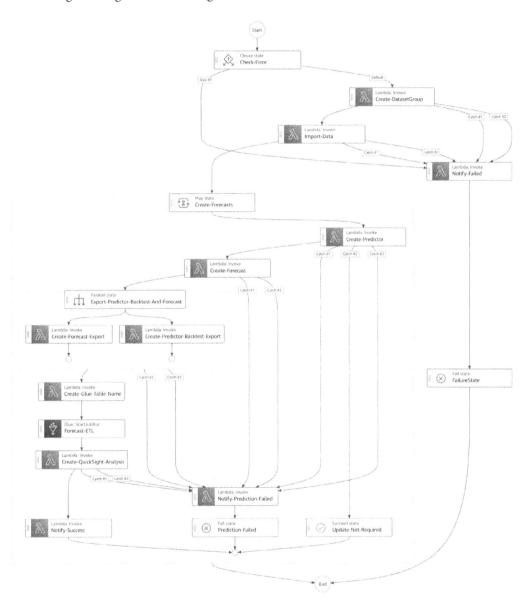

Figure 7.9 – Forecast state machine overview

- **Amazon Forecast** is the key machine learning service used to train your predictors and generate new forecasts.

- **Amazon Simple Notification Service** (**Amazon SNS**): Amazon SNS is used to notify you of the results of the step functions by email.

In addition to the preceding components, the forecasting part of the solutions also uses the following services under the hood:

- **Amazon CloudWatch**: This service is used to log every action performed by the solution. This is especially useful to understand what's happening when your workflow fails.

- **AWS Glue**: This solution uses an AWS Glue job to build an aggregated view of your forecasts, including raw historical data, backtesting exports, and forecast results.

- **Amazon Athena**: This service allows you to query Amazon S3 with standard SQL queries. In this solution, Amazon Athena will be used to query the aggregated views built by the previous AWS Glue job.

- **Amazon S3**: This is used to store the generated forecasts.

Data visualization component

The data visualization components deployed by the solutions allow you to explore your forecast using either of the following:

- **Amazon SageMaker** if you're a data scientist that is comfortable with manipulating your data with Python

- **Amazon QuickSight** if you're a data analyst that is more comfortable with using a business intelligence tool to build dashboards from the analysis generated by the solution on a per-forecast basis

Now that you're familiar with the different components used by this solution, you are going to deploy it in your AWS account.

Solutions deployment

To deploy this solution in your AWS account, you can follow the steps given here:

1. Navigate to the solution home page at `https://aws.amazon.com/solutions/implementations/improving-forecast-accuracy-with-machine-learning/` and scroll down to the middle of the page to click on the **Launch in the AWS Console** button.

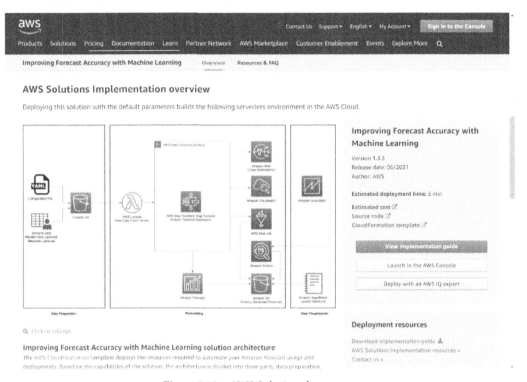

Figure 7.10 – AWS Solutions home page

2. You will be brought to the CloudFormation service home page. If you are not logged into your account, you will have to sign in before you're redirected to CloudFormation.

3. CloudFormation is a service used to deploy any AWS service with a template written in either JSON or YAML format. This allows you to configure services with code instead of building everything by clicking through multiple service consoles. Click on the **Next** button on the bottom right.

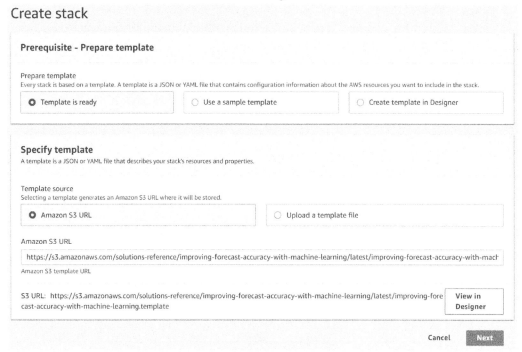

Figure 7.11 – Creating the CloudFormation stack

4. On the stack details page, enter a stack name. I chose `energy-consumption-forecast-stack` for mine.

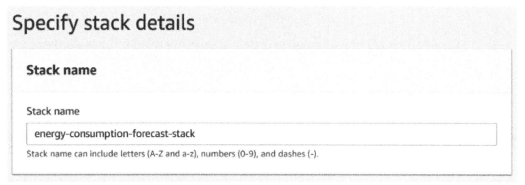

Figure 7.12 – CloudFormation stack name

5. In the stack parameters, you will fill in your email address in **Email**, leave the QuickSight visualization option empty, and select **Yes** to deploy a Jupyter notebook. Leave all the other options as is and click **Next**.

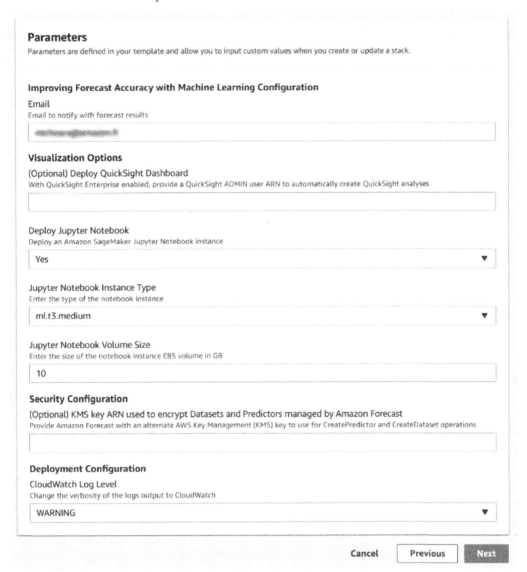

Figure 7.13 – CloudFormation parameters

6. On the next screen, you will have the opportunity to configure advanced options. You can leave all these values as their defaults, scroll down the screen, and click **Next** again.

7. On the last screen, you can review all the options and parameters selected and scroll down to the very bottom. Click on both the check-boxes and click on **Create stack**.

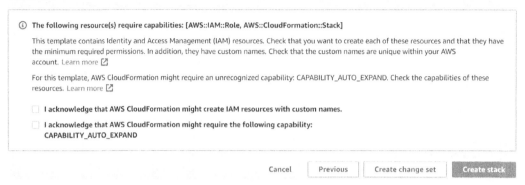

Figure 7.14 – Creating the CloudFormation stack

8. This will bring you to a CloudFormation stack creation screen where you can see your stack deployment in progress.

Figure 7.15 – Stack creation started

9. At the end of the process, you can navigate to the **Outputs** tab of the template deployment. Take note of the ForecastBucketName value under this tab.

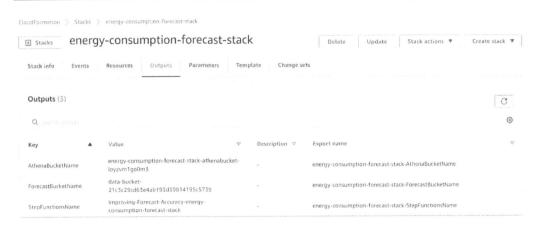

Figure 7.16 – CloudFormation stack outputs

10. Once you're through the CloudFormation stack creation, you will also receive an email asking you to confirm your subscription to a notification topic. This SNS topic will be used to send you notifications about the forecasting process. Click on the **Confirm subscription** link in this email.

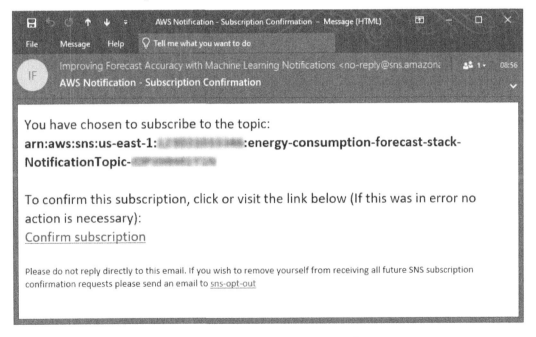

Figure 7.17 – Notification subscription confirmation

Your solution is now deployed. It's time to configure it to match our energy consumption prediction use case.

Configuring the solution

The *Improving Forecast Accuracy with Machine Learning* solution is configured with a YAML file that you will need to upload to the S3 bucket you took note of earlier (*Step 9* of the *Solutions deployment* section). The file you will use will contain an introduction section configured as follows:

```
Household_energy_consumption:
  DatasetGroup:
    Domain: CUSTOM
```

You then configure the different datasets to be used. Here is the section for the target time series dataset:

```
  Datasets:
    - Domain: CUSTOM
      DatasetType: TARGET_TIME_SERIES
      DataFrequency: D
      TimestampFormat: yyyy-MM-dd
      Schema:
        Attributes:
          - AttributeName: item_id
            AttributeType: string
```

Next, you will describe how the predictor will be trained:

```
  Predictor:
    MaxAge: 604800
    PerformAutoML: False
    ForecastHorizon: 30
    AlgorithmArn: arn:aws:forecast:::algorithm/CNN-QR
    FeaturizationConfig:
      ForecastFrequency: D
    TrainingParameters:
      epochs: "100"
      context_length: "240"
      use_item_metadata: "ALL"
      use_related_data: "FORWARD_LOOKING"
```

Last but not least, you will define which forecast types you are interested in:

```
Forecast:
  ForecastTypes:
    - "0.10"
    - "0.50"
    - "0.90"
```

You will find a copy of the complete YAML file in the archive downloaded earlier.

Navigate to the Amazon S3 bucket you took note of earlier and upload this YAML file to this bucket. Also, click on **Create folder** and create a folder named `train`. Your S3 bucket root looks like the following (a folder named `glue` was created during the initial deployment and should already be present):

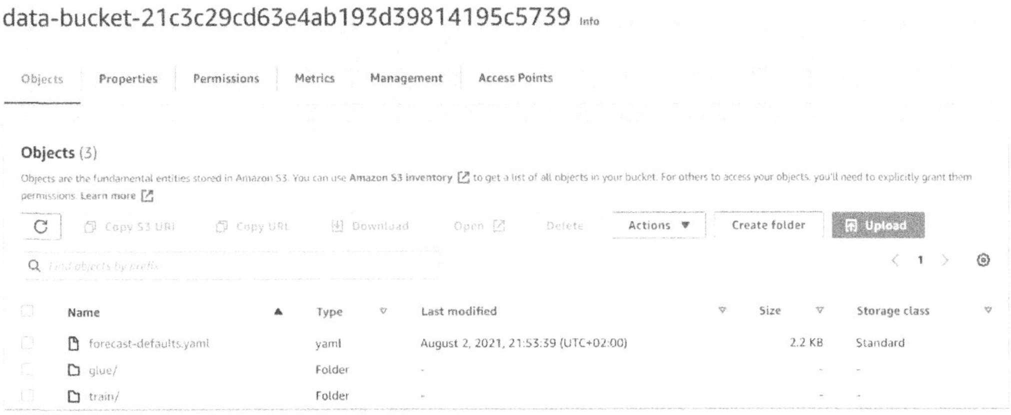

data-bucket-21c3c29cd63e4ab193d39814195c5739 Info

Figure 7.18 – S3 bucket initial configuration

Your solution is now configured and ready to be used!

Using the solution

After deploying the *Improving Forecast Accuracy with Machine Learning* solution, you are now ready to use it. In this section, you will learn how to trigger and monitor the main workflow run by the solution and how to visualize the results.

Monitoring the workflow status

Navigate to the train directory of your S3 bucket and upload the three CSV files you extracted in the *Data preparation component* section.

The solution is automatically triggered; if you want to know how your process is progressing, you can use the AWS Step Functions console. To visualize this progress, you can follow these steps:

1. Log into your AWS console and search for `Step Functions` in the search bar at the top.

2. Click on **AWS Step Functions** to go to the service home page. On this page, click on the **State machines** link at the top of the left menu bar.

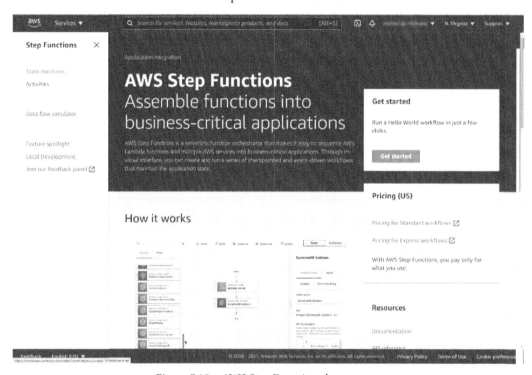

Figure 7.19 – AWS Step Functions home page

3. You will land on a page listing all the workflows visible from your AWS account. If this is your first time using the service, your list will only contain the state machine deployed by the solution.

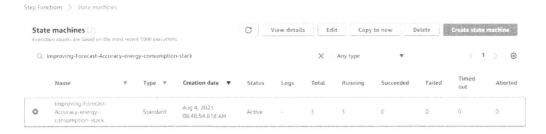

Figure 7.20 – Step Functions state machine list

4. Click on the `Improving-Forecast-Accuracy-energy-consumption` `-stack` link to visualize all the executions of this workflow. You should see three ongoing executions, one for each file uploaded. Click on one with a **Running** status.

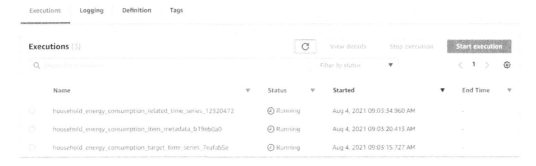

Figure 7.21 – State machine executions list

5. You will see the workflow status with the current step (**Import-Data**) and the past successful ones (**Check-Error** and **Create-DatasetGroup**) highlighted.

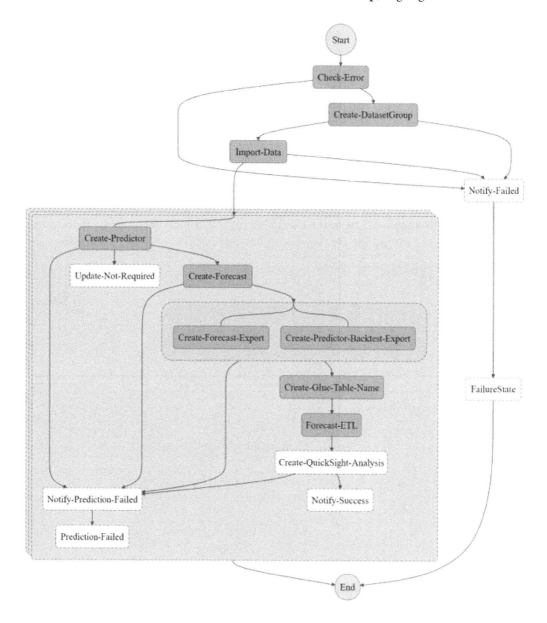

Figure 7.22 – Graph inspector for the current workflow execution

This graph is updated live and is useful for debugging any issues happening in the process. Once you're familiar with the solution, you usually don't need to open the Step Functions console anymore.

Visualizing the results

Once all the workflows are run successfully, you will receive a notification by email and you can then visualize your predictor results. Follow these steps to this effect:

1. Log into your AWS console and search for SageMaker in the search bar at the top.

2. Click on **Amazon SageMaker** to go to the service home page. On this page, click on the **Notebook instances** link in the left menu bar.

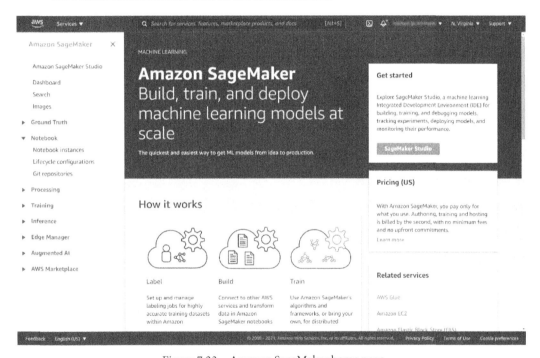

Figure 7.23 – Amazon SageMaker home page

3. You will land on a page listing all the notebook instances visible from your AWS account. If this is your first time using the service, your list will only contain the notebook instance deployed by the solution.

Figure 7.24 – Amazon SageMaker notebook instances list

4. Click on the **Open JupyterLab** link to access your instance; you will be redirected to the JupyterLab environment. On the left, you have a directory structure. Drag and drop the .ipynb file you downloaded earlier at the beginning of this section to this directory structure area. Then, double-click on the EnergyConsumptionVisualization.ipynb notebook name to open it in the main interface on the right.

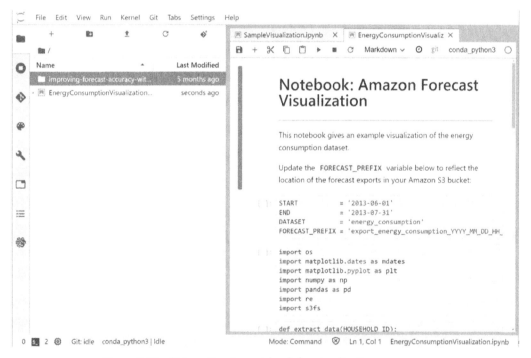

Figure 7.25 – Using a Jupyter notebook for visualization purposes

5. Jupyter notebooks are structured in successive cells. Update the first cell so that your code matches the name of your dataset group and the location of the forecast exports:

```
START            = '2013-06-01'
END              = '2013-07-31'
DATASET          = 'household_energy_consumption'
FORECAST_PREFIX  = 'export_energy_consumption_XXXX'
```

6. From the top menu bar, select **Run** and then **Run all cells** to run the whole notebook.

7. Scroll down to the bottom of the notebook to visualize some of the results. For instance, here are the results for the MAC001259 household:

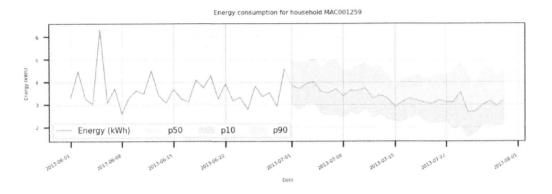

Figure 7.26 – Visualizing energy consumption for a household

Cleanup

Once you are done experimenting with this solution, you can delete all the resources created to prevent any extra costs from being incurred. Follow these steps to clean your account of the solution resources:

1. Log into your AWS console and search for `CloudFormation` in the search bar at the top.

2. Click on **AWS CloudFormation** to go to the service home page. Click on **Stacks** in the left menu bar to see the list of CloudFormation stacks deployed in your account.

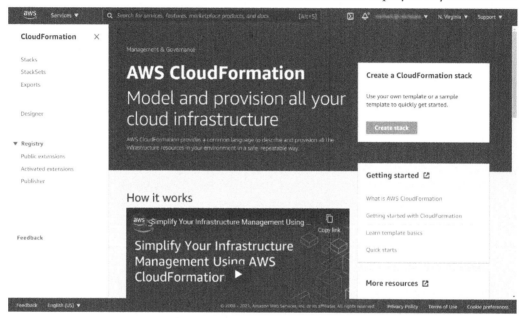

Figure 7.27 – AWS CloudFormation service home page

3. In the search bar at the top of the **Stacks** table, you can enter `energy-consumption` if you don't find your stack right away.

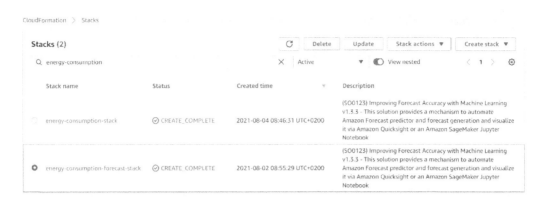

Figure 7.28 – AWS CloudFormation stacks list

4. Select energy-consumption-forecast-stack and click on the **Delete** button at the top.

The deletion process starts and after a few minutes, your account is cleaned up. The Amazon S3 bucket created by this solution will be emptied and deleted by this process. However, if you created other buckets and uploaded other files during your experimentation, you will have to navigate to the Amazon S3 console and delete these resources manually.

Summary

In this chapter, you dived deeper into the forecast accuracy metrics and learned how you can perform some analysis to better understand the performance of your predictors. In particular, you uncovered the impact any behavior changes in your datasets (data drift) can have on the accuracy of a forecasting exercise. You also learned how you can move away from using the console to integrate Amazon Forecast results into your business operations thanks to a serverless solution vetted by AWS and actively maintained.

Congratulations! This chapter concludes the part dedicated to forecasting with Amazon Forecast. In the next chapter, you will start your journey into time series anomaly detection!

Section 2: Detecting Abnormal Behavior in Multivariate Time Series with Amazon Lookout for Equipment

In this section, you will learn how to train a model that spots anomalies in multivariate sensor data and create a scheduler to monitor your equipment. You will also read about the insights **Amazon Lookout for Equipment** can deliver to help you improve your anomaly detection and prediction practice.

This section comprises the following chapters:

- *Chapter 8, An Overview of Amazon Lookout for Equipment*
- *Chapter 9, Creating a Dataset and Ingesting Your Data*
- *Chapter 10, Training and Evaluating a Model*
- *Chapter 11, Scheduling Regular Inferences*
- *Chapter 12, Reducing Time to Insights for Anomaly Detections*

8
An Overview of Amazon Lookout for Equipment

In this chapter, you will learn what **Amazon Lookout for Equipment** can do, how it works, and the kinds of applications it's better suited for. You will also understand, at a high level, how to prepare your dataset and how to integrate the service results into your own business process.

Along with **Amazon Forecast** and **Amazon Lookout for Metrics** (which you will learn about in the last part of this book), Amazon Lookout for Equipment is one of the **artificial intelligence (AI)**-/**machine learning (ML)**-managed services dedicated to problems that are structured around time series data. Amazon Lookout for Equipment is an anomaly detection service that can provide valuable insights into industrial equipment and predictive maintenance teams.

In this chapter, we're going to cover the following main topics:

- What is Amazon Lookout for Equipment?
- What are the different approaches to tackle anomaly detection?
- The challenges encountered with multivariate time series data

- How does Amazon Lookout for Equipment work?

- How do you choose the right applications?

Technical requirements

No hands-on experience in a language such as **Python** or **R** is necessary to follow along with the content of this chapter. However, we highly recommend that you follow along in the AWS console, where you can access the Amazon Lookout for Equipment service.

If you already have an AWS account, you can connect to the AWS console, click on the search bar at the top, and enter `Lookout for Equipment` in the **Services** section. Then, click on **Amazon Lookout for Equipment** to bring up the landing page of the service console.

If you don't have an AWS account, you will need to create one before you can log in to your console. To create an AWS account and log in to the Amazon Forecast console, please refer to the *Technical requirements* section of *Chapter 2, An Overview of Amazon Forecast*.

Now you are ready to use Amazon Lookout for Equipment!

What is Amazon Lookout for Equipment?

Amazon Lookout for Equipment is one of the AI/ML-managed services available on the AWS Cloud platform. This service leverages the data from sensors on your industrial equipment and automatically trains unsupervised ML models based on the specific data from this equipment without the requirement of any ML expertise. Amazon Lookout for Equipment analyzes your incoming sensor time series data to flag early warning signs (such as events) that could lead to an anomaly or a failure in your equipment or manufacturing process. Amazon Lookout for Equipment is **asset agnostic**. This means that beyond the time series data, you do not need to provide the characteristics of the process or equipment (for example, the make and model of the equipment, the units of measure of the time series data, the age of the asset, and more) that you are monitoring to use the service.

Managed services are services where only end-users bring their data and configure the parameters to suit their needs. All the other tasks, *considered to be undifferentiated heavy lifting*, are performed on the users' behalf by the service. This includes the automation of all the infrastructure management. As an Amazon Lookout for Equipment user, you don't have to provision and manage virtual machines, configure user accounts, implement security, plan for scalability if your request volume increases, or decommission unused resources.

In the case of AI/ML managed services, some data preparation, ingestion tasks, and model management activities are also performed under the hood, allowing you to focus primarily on the problem to solve. Amazon Lookout for Equipment is a scalable, managed service that automates the whole end-to-end anomaly detection pipeline from data ingestion to model deployment and serving inference results. Additionally, the service deals with data preparation under the hood. Amazon Lookout for Equipment can perform the following functions:

- It can fill *missing values* in your datasets for you.

- It can deal with *misaligned timestamps* (that is, time series that don't share a common date time index between them).

- It can *prepare the time series* so that it can be ingested by multiple algorithms. Amazon Lookout for Equipment can prepare the appropriate time series dataset for both deep learning or statistical models suitable for anomaly detection.

- It can *compute a smart threshold* based on your historical time series data to decide whether a given data point should be flagged as an anomaly or not. Many unsupervised approaches require you to provide a contamination level, that is, the ratio of outliers or anomalies present in the dataset. This contamination level is used to define a threshold for the decision function that will determine whether a given data point is normal or not. Unfortunately, this is a parameter that you have to provide, and that will likely depend on your datasets. Changing this value can yield significant changes in the result, making the approach difficult to scale beyond one use case. Amazon Lookout for Equipment abstracts away this challenge for you.

- It can perform *hyperparameter tuning* to find the best parameters for you.

Now that you have a good understanding of what Amazon Lookout for Equipment can do for you, let's dive deeper into the challenges arising with anomaly detection when you want to tackle it without using this type of service.

What are the different approaches to tackle anomaly detection?

Before we dive into Amazon Lookout for Equipment, first, we are going to look at a few definitions. In this section, you will read about the different types of anomalies before getting a high-level overview of the different methods you can use to build your own anomaly detection models.

What is an anomaly?

An **anomaly** in a time series is usually defined as an observation or sequence of observations that do not follow the expected behavior of the series. For example, you could have point anomalies (in other words, single events that are only recorded at a single timestamp):

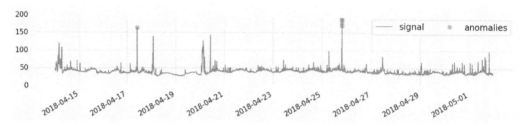

Figure 8.1 – Single-event anomalies

Additionally, you might have a sequence of data points that can be viewed as a suspicious event with a longer time range:

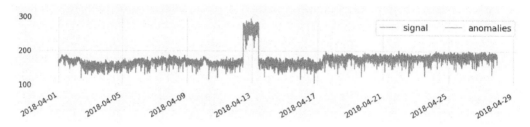

Figure 8.2 – Event range anomalies

These sequences of anomalies are more challenging to identify than point anomalies as they can vary in duration.

Additionally, you might have a whole time series that is considered an anomaly: the ECG200 dataset is often used as a benchmark for time series classification. The *electrical activity recorded during human heartbeats* can be labeled as *normal* or *ischemia* (myocardial infarction). Each time series, as a whole, is either characterized as normal or abnormal, as shown in the following screenshot:

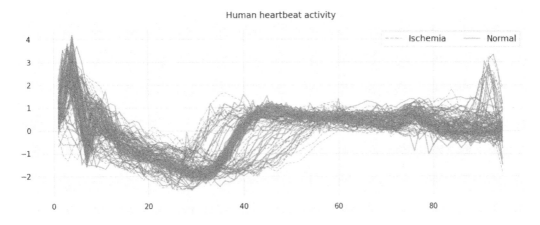

Figure 8.3 – Heartbeat activity for 100 patients (the ECG200 dataset)

In the remaining part of this chapter, we are going to focus on single-event and event range anomalies, as time series classification is not the purpose of Amazon Lookout for Equipment. Such classification can be performed through dimensionality reduction or dissimilarity techniques.

Now, let's take a look at the different families of approaches you can leverage to build anomaly detection systems.

Model-based approaches

Model-based methods detect anomalies by computing the distance between an actual observation (or a set of observations for a multivariate dataset) and its expected value. An observation, y_t (which can either be a single value in the univariate case or a vector in the multivariate case), is considered an anomaly if its distance from the expected value, $\hat{y}_t$, is greater than a given threshold, τ. Each method has its own way of computing this threshold and the expected values of a given time series.

Estimation models

Estimation models use past and future values of y_t. Examples of estimation model-based methods use median or median absolute deviation to compute $\hat{y}_t$. Other methods model univariate time series data using smoothing methods such as B-splines, kernels, exponentially weighted moving averages, slope constraints, and Gaussian mixture models (https://doi.org/10.1109/SPW.2017.9). You can find an implementation of the Gaussian mixture in scikit-learn at https://scikit-learn.org/stable/modules/generated/sklearn.mixture.GaussianMixture.html.

Isolation forest algorithms can be applied to a whole time series to assign an anomaly score to each observation. It is then up to you to define the appropriate threshold that will help you isolate the anomalies of interest for your business case. An example implementation of isolation forest can be found in scikit-learn at `https://scikit-learn.org/stable/modules/generated/sklearn.ensemble.IsolationForest.html`.

A robust variant of isolation forest can also be found in the built-in **SageMaker Random Cut Forest algorithm** at `https://docs.aws.amazon.com/sagemaker/latest/dg/randomcutforest.html`.

In a multivariate setting, an autoencoder is a type of neural network that learns the normal behavior of a set of signals and generates large reconstruction errors when encountering anomalies. As such, autoencoders can be considered a semi-supervised approach; this is because you only need to ensure the model is fed with a time series that has no anomalies (you don't need to precisely label each anomaly).

Prediction models

These models only use past values of y_t. This family of methods can be used to stream data where future values are not known when inference is requested. Several statistical and neural network methods have been devised in this family, as follows:

- For instance, some methods leverage ARIMA models under the hood to fit the data and predict the expected values of the time series.

- DeepAnT is an example of a deep learning model (`https://doi.org/10.1109/ACCESS.2018.2886457`) from this family. DeepAnT can be leveraged on both univariate and multivariate time series. To model both the temporal dependency and the correlation between multiple time series of a dataset, the **Contextual Hidden Markov Model (CHMM)** has been devised.

- Extreme value theory is leveraged in the **Streaming Peak-over-Threshold (SPOT)** and DSPOT (that is, SPOT with drift) methods for univariate time series (please refer to `http://dx.doi.org/10.1145/3097983.3098144`) and in **Variational Autoencoders (VAEs)** for multivariate cases. Extreme value theory allows these models to automatically select the right threshold value to mark observations as normal or anomalies.

Other anomaly detection methods

Other univariate and multivariate methods have been designed to capture anomalies based on different representations (or encodings) of both univariate and multivariate datasets, as follows:

- **Density-based methods**: These types of methods classify any given observation as an outlier if less than N observations lie within a certain distance from them. When dealing with time series data, several authors have suggested slicing the time series into successive sliding windows to take the temporality of such data into account.

- **Histogram-based methods**: The histogramming technique creates a compact representation of a time series by replacing the time series with an HB histogram with B bins. For instance, it is possible to collapse the values of consecutive data points into a single value (for example, their average).

- **Dissimilarity-based methods**: These multivariate methods have been devised to measure the pairwise dissimilarity between multivariate points. For instance, you can measure the similarity of each consecutive vector and classify any anomalies when the dissimilarity is higher than a certain threshold.

Using univariate methods with a multivariate dataset

In the previous review, we hinted at several methods that have been expressly built for multivariate datasets. However, given that a multivariate time series dataset is an assembly of many univariate time series, you can also apply any of the univariate methods discussed in the preceding section. However, note that the dependencies between the different signals of a multivariate dataset would be lost, leading to methods where the dataset is simplified from multiple (potentially) correlated time series into a lower number of independent univariate time series.

Dimensionality reduction methods can be applied to achieve this outcome before you apply your univariate anomaly detection technique of choice to discover multivariate anomalies.

Now that we have reviewed a selection of approaches to tackle anomaly detection in a time series, we will focus on the specific challenges you might encounter when dealing with multivariate time series.

The challenges encountered with multivariate time series data

You can find both single-event and event range anomalies across multivariate time series data. However, the multivariate nature of your problems also gives you more context, and you could start seeing some anomalies because the relationships between the different signals start to diverge from their normal conditions. Let's dive deeper into the following figure (also *Figure 8.2*):

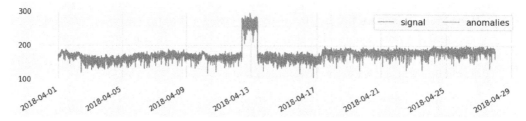

Figure 8.4 – Event range anomalies

This signal is actually part of a multivariate dataset with 51 sensors collecting data from a pump in a water treatment facility. Let's plot this same signal along with a second one, as follows:

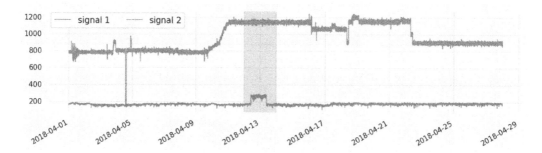

Figure 8.5 – Multivariate time series anomalies

As you can see, when adding this contextual information, you might not label the highlighted area as an anomaly, as this might be the normal behavior of signal 1 (the one at the bottom), when signal 2 (at the top) shifts from an average of 800 to an average of 1,150. On the other hand, it appears as though something is happening around April 17, so you might have to expand this context and plot other signals to confirm this hunch.

As you can see, defining anomalies in a multivariate setting now becomes very challenging as it requires you to build a holistic view of every single signal while keeping in mind the relationship of each signal with every other signal. This is where the capability of deep learning algorithms to uncover complex non-linear relationships between multiple time series signals comes in handy!

Now you are ready to dive into how Amazon Lookout for Equipment can help you to tackle all of these challenges.

How does Amazon Lookout for Equipment work?

In this section, you will learn how Amazon Lookout for Equipment works by first looking at the different concepts manipulated by the service. Then, you will dive deeper into how these concepts are orchestrated together to build anomaly detection models. This section will then end with an overview of the pricing model used by this service.

Defining the key concepts

To build anomaly detection models, Amazon Lookout for Equipment deals with the following concepts and resources:

- **Tags**: A tag is the name of a time series and can be linked to a sensor, an equipment-monitored condition, or a process variable. In this chapter, we will use the terms **tags**, **signals**, and **sensors** indifferently.

- **Datasets**: A dataset is a container to host your time series data. The Amazon Lookout for Equipment algorithms use these datasets to train their models. Each dataset is defined by a schema where you can define the list of time series tags.

- **Components**: When defining the data schema of a dataset, you have the ability to group tags into components. This is an artificial construct that has no impact on the modeling process. However, it will give you the ability to easily train models on subsets of sensors linked to different components. Depending on what you are trying to model, you can use the component level to structure your sensors into different pieces of equipment on a single manufacturing line, regroup them in different facilities, or choose to organize them depending on their unit of measure.

- **Labels**: Although Amazon Lookout for Equipment only uses unsupervised approaches, you can also feed the training process with known time ranges, where you understand the time series behavior is not representative of the normal operating modes of your asset or process. Usually, these labels cover historical maintenance periods or known anomalous ranges that will be used to rank the tested algorithms at training time (please refer to the *Amazon Lookout for Equipment workflow overview* section in this chapter).

- **Models**: Amazon Lookout for Equipment has access to more than 28,000 combinations of models and hyperparameter configurations. The service has access to this bank of models when selecting the one that is more suitable for your dataset given the presence of labels or no labels. The algorithm choice is abstracted away from you, and the applied science team behind Amazon Lookout for Equipment tirelessly researches new algorithms and combinations to enrich this model bank.

- **Schedulers**: Once a model has been trained, you have the ability to schedule regular inferences every 5, 10, 15, 30, or 60 minutes. The inference scheduler will wake up at the chosen interval to look for new data in a certain location on Amazon S3, run it through your trained model, and store the inference results back on Amazon S3 where they will be available for further processing.

Now, let's take a look at how all these concepts are used by Amazon Lookout for Equipment to train and run anomaly detection models.

Amazon Lookout for Equipment workflow overview

Building an unsupervised anomaly detection process involves two steps:

1. We start by looking at historical time series to model the normal behavior of your equipment or process as characterized by this data. This establishes the baseline of the asset.

2. Then, we use this knowledge to flag any deviation in the relationships between the multivariate time series as an anomaly.

As depicted in the following diagram, Amazon Lookout for Equipment provides an approach to tackle the two preceding steps:

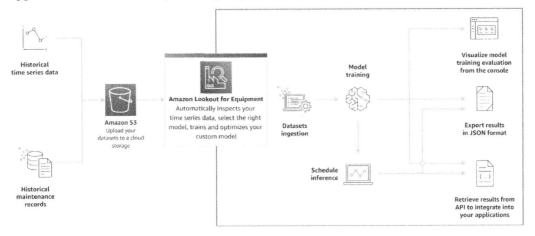

Figure 8.6 – An overview of Amazon Lookout for Equipment

Let's dive into this diagram to explain the different steps you have to go through to use Amazon Lookout for Equipment:

- **Uploading and ingesting data into the service**: This will be thoroughly detailed in *Chapter 9, Creating a Dataset and Ingesting Your Data*. Amazon Lookout for Equipment can use data that is located in **Amazon Simple Storage Service** (**S3**; a scalable data storage infrastructure used to store any kind of object or dataset). At ingestion time, Amazon Lookout for Equipment inspects your data and returns any errors that might prevent the proper training of an anomaly detection model (such as missing signals concerning your dataset schema or signals with too few values).

- **Training a model**, as described in *Chapter 10, Training and Evaluating a Model*: Depending on the performance obtained, you can iterate over the data ingestion and training steps a few times to achieve the desired performance.

- Once you have a model that you are happy with, you can start *scheduling inferences for it*. When you configure and start a scheduler, Amazon Lookout for Equipment will regularly wake it up to feed it with newly available data. The inference results will be returned to Amazon S3 for further postprocessing.

You should now have a high-level understanding of how you can leverage this service to integrate it into your own anomaly detection systems. The last piece of information you will need is a clear understanding of the pricing model so that you can better optimize the way you use this service.

Pricing

As with many AWS services, you only pay for what you use with no upfront commitment. Although the cost of the service is minimal to build a **proof of concept** (especially if you can benefit from the free tier), there are three dimensions to consider when operationalizing an anomaly detection pipeline with Amazon Lookout for Equipment. These are as follows:

- **Storage**: Data is ingested and prepared to ensure the fastest training time by Amazon Lookout for Equipment. Storage is priced for each GB of historical data ingested in the service to train your model. There is no ingestion charge for the data used for inferencing.

- **Training hours**: Each time you train a new custom model based on your data, you are billed for the number of hours of training. Amazon Lookout for Equipment will provide the appropriate number of compute resources to train multiple models in parallel and pick the best one more quickly. For instance, if your model is ready within an hour and the service has provisioned a compute resource that is 4 times the baseline, the actual number of hours billed will be equivalent to the number of compute resources actually provisioned (that is, 4 hours).

- **Inference hours**: You are billed for each hour of inference that a scheduler is running for, regardless of the configured frequency. The inference charges are rounded up to the nearest hour.

If this is the first time you use Amazon Lookout for Equipment with any given account, you have access to a free tier that will allow you to use the service for free for 1 month. During this period, you will not be charged if you use the following services:

- **Storage**: Less than 50 GB of historical data ingestion

- **Training hours**: Less than 250 training hours

- **Inference hours**: Less than 168 hours of scheduled inference

AWS service developers work relentlessly at reducing the operational costs of the services, and price reductions happen regularly. At the time of writing, the pricing of these components are as follows:

- **Storage**: $0.20 per GB

- **Training hours**: $0.24 per hour

- **Inference hours**: $0.25 per hour

For the most up-to-date pricing, you can check the Amazon Lookout for Equipment pricing page:

```
https://aws.amazon.com/lookout-for-equipment/pricing/
```

This pricing overview ends my presentation of Amazon Lookout for Equipment. In the next section, you will look at the different requirements your applications need to satisfy to successfully leverage the capability of this service.

How do you choose the right applications?

You have successfully framed your ML project as an anomaly detection problem, and you have collected some historical time series datasets. So, is Amazon Lookout for Equipment a good candidate to deliver the desired insights? Let's review some considerations that will help you to determine whether Amazon Lookout for Equipment is suitable for your anomaly detection scenario:

- Latency requirements
- Dataset requirements
- Use case requirements

Latency requirements

With Amazon Lookout for Equipment, *training must happen in the cloud*. If your data is not available in cloud storage such as Amazon S3, the first step will be to transfer it there.

At prediction time, *inference will also happen in the cloud*. You will need to send your most recent data to the cloud, and the trained model will be generated and also stored in the cloud. As inference happens in the cloud, you will depend on the network latency between your local systems and the internet. If you need anomaly detections in near real time to feed optimization algorithms in a factory, Amazon Lookout for Equipment will likely be the wrong choice, and you should explore building a custom anomaly detection model that you can deploy at the edge (for instance, leveraging **Amazon SageMaker** and its **Edge Manager** feature to compile, deploy, and manage ML models on local machines).

Dataset requirements

To train a model, you will need all your time series signals to have *at least 180 days worth of data*. On top of this, you will probably want to evaluate your model. We recommend having at least 9 months to 1 year of data to comfortably train and evaluate an anomaly detection model with Amazon Lookout for Equipment. If some of your time series have too much missing data, you might trigger an error as you will have less than 180 days of data available to train your model.

Too much missing data will also block the process at ingestion time. If you provide labeled time ranges for past maintenance periods or known anomalous periods, you will also want to take these into consideration, as these periods will be removed from the data for both the training and evaluation periods. Each signal must have at least 50% of the data present in both the training period and the evaluation period.

Last but not least, your data must have a *compatible time interval*. Although Amazon Lookout for Equipment can deal with datasets that have been left with their raw sampling rate, the service can resample your data from 1-second to 1-hour intervals, with the most common intervals being 1 minute or 5 minutes. High-frequency datasets (for example, sensor data collected at a sampling rate of 10 milliseconds) will require you to aggregate the data to ensure your training data is below 1.5 million rows over 6 months (as mentioned previously, the minimum range is 6 months).

On the other end of the spectrum, if your use case only provides data at a sampling rate that is higher than 1 hour, Amazon Lookout for Equipment might have a hard time spotting early warning events, as this frequency will cut off the many weak signals the service feeds from to detect any useful events.

Use case requirements

Throughout this chapter, you read through multiple anomaly detection examples. Additionally, you saw how much heavy lifting Amazon Lookout for Equipment is performing on your behalf. However, there are situations and use cases for which Amazon Lookout for Equipment is not the best match:

- **Univariate data**: Amazon Lookout for Equipment gives its best when it can establish a baseline relationship by looking at multiple interrelated time series data.

- **Equipment is not operating continuously**: Amazon Lookout for Equipment was built for industrial processes driven by continuously running equipment and low variability in operating conditions. If your process runs with industrial rotating machines such as turbines, compressors, motors, and pumps, Amazon Lookout for Equipment will likely be a good match. If your process runs sporadically (for example, a car that is parked most of the time, a manually operated piece of equipment, or a CNC machine with a highly variable process), the predictive power of the intrinsic time series collected on these processes will be less likely picked up by Amazon Lookout for Equipment. As a rule of thumb, the more variations your normal operations go through, the more challenging it is for your system to be modeled by such a service.

- **Batch processes**: Framing batch data so that it can be leveraged by Amazon Lookout for Equipment is an additional preprocessing step that involves the appropriate domain expertise to guide the feature engineering step. Batch processes are not good candidates for Amazon Lookout for Equipment out of the box. However, if your feature engineering can be scaled across multiple production lines, products, and factories, you can automate this step and feed these calculated fields to Amazon Lookout for Equipment.

- **Less than 6 months of data**: Historical process and equipment data must be available for at least 6 months to train an Amazon Lookout for Equipment model. If you want to evaluate the trained model, you might also need a few more weeks' worth of data.

- **When known anomalies are not available**: If you want to evaluate the capability of the service to capture anomalies that are important for your business process, you need to ensure that the examples of such anomalies are present at least in the evaluation time range (and, ideally, in both the training and evaluation time ranges). If you know there are some anomalies but are not able to label them precisely, you can still use the service to help you identify them more precisely.

Now you should have a good understanding of how to frame your anomaly detection problem to leverage Amazon Lookout for Equipment. Additionally, you can use this section to identify how to enrich your existing datasets to successfully use this service (such as labeling anomaly ranges, adding more sensors, or extracting a longer period of data).

Summary

Amazon Lookout for Equipment is an AI-/ML-managed service running in the cloud. It leverages multiple algorithms to perform anomaly detection on multivariate datasets while abstracting away all the ML decisions you need to take when building your own custom models (for example, questions such as *How do I set the threshold to actually capture the anomalies I'm interested in?*).

The service is also fully unsupervised. This means that you do not need to spend valuable time to label massive amounts of multivariate time series data. Amazon Lookout for Equipment makes it easy to build whole farms of models that can be applied to each of your individual assets. This allows the service to learn the specific behavior that each asset has developed over the course of the year depending on how it has been manufactured, operated, and maintained.

In this chapter, you learned about the many approaches multivariate anomaly detection can take and the challenges Amazon Lookout for Equipment tackles on your behalf. You discovered the key constructs manipulated by the service and should also have a good understanding of which applications are good candidates to leverage Amazon Lookout for Equipment.

In the next chapter, we will create our first anomaly detection project by creating a dataset and ingesting some time series data.

9
Creating a Dataset and Ingesting Your Data

In the previous chapter, you learned about anomaly detection problems and some ways to tackle them. You also had an overview of Amazon Lookout for Equipment, an AI-/ML-managed service designed to build anomaly detection problems in multivariate, industrial time series data.

The goal of this chapter is to teach you how to create and organize multivariate datasets, how to create a JSON schema to prepare the dataset ingestion, and how to trigger a data ingestion job pointing to the S3 bucket where your raw data is stored.

In addition, you will also have a high-level understanding of all the heavy lifting the service is performing on your behalf to save as much data preparation effort as possible (imputation, time series alignment, resampling). You will also understand what kind of errors can be raised by the service and how to work around them.

In this chapter, we're going to cover the following main topics:

- Preparing a dataset for anomaly detection purposes
- Creating an Amazon Lookout for Equipment dataset

- Generating a JSON schema

- Creating a data ingestion job

- Understanding common ingestion errors and workarounds

Technical requirements

No hands-on experience in a language such as **Python** or **R** is necessary to follow along with the content of this chapter. However, we highly recommend that you read this chapter while connected to your own AWS account and open the Amazon Lookout for Equipment console to run the different actions on your end.

To create an AWS account and log in to the Amazon Lookout for Equipment console, you can refer yourself to the technical requirements of *Chapter 2, An Overview of Amazon Forecast*.

In the companion GitHub repository of this book, you will find a notebook that will show you the detailed steps to prepare the dataset we are going to use from now on. *This preparation is optional* to follow along with this chapter. At your first reading, I recommend that you download the prepared dataset from the following link:

```
https://packt-publishing-timeseries-on-aws-michaelhoarau.
s3.eu-west-1.amazonaws.com/part2-amazon-lookout-for-equipment/
lookout-for-equipment.zip
```

From there, you can log in to the AWS console and follow along with this chapter without writing a single line of code.

At a later reading, feel free to go through the preparation code to understand how to prepare a dataset ready to be consumed by Amazon Lookout for Equipment. You will find a notebook with all this preparation on the companion GitHub repository of this book:

```
https://github.com/PacktPublishing/Time-series-Analysis-on-
AWS/blob/main/Chapter09/chapter9-preparing-l4e-dataset.ipynb
```

This notebook will help you understand the format expected to build a successful model.

Preparing a dataset for anomaly detection purposes

Before you can train an anomaly detection model, you need to prepare a multivariate time series dataset. In this section, you will learn how to prepare such a dataset and how to allow Amazon Lookout for Equipment to access it.

Preparing the dataset

The dataset we are going to use is a cleaned-up version of the one that can be found on Kaggle here:

`https://www.kaggle.com/nphantawee/pump-sensor-data/version/1`

This dataset contains known time ranges when a pump is broken and when it is operating under nominal conditions. To adapt this dataset so that it can be fed to Amazon Lookout for Equipment, perform the following steps:

1. Download the raw time series dataset. This data contains 5 months' worth of data at a 1-minute sampling rate with several events of interest. The original dataset ranges from **2018-04-01** to **2018-08-31**.

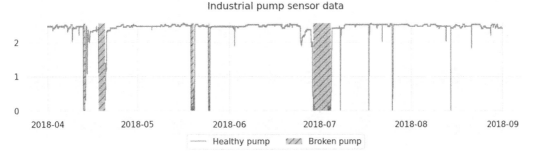

Figure 9.1 – Industrial pump dataset overview

2. Amazon Lookout for Equipment requires a minimum of 6 months of data to train a model. To obtain a sufficiently long period of time while having some anomalies to verify, I applied a new date time index using the same number of data points and start date, but applied a 5-minute sampling rate. This yielded the equivalent of 25 months' worth of data ranging from **2018-04-01** to **2020-05-04**.

3. Use the `machine_status` column to identify the time ranges during which the pump was broken. I compiled these ranges into a DataFrame with the start and end date time for each event.

	start	end
0	2018-05-30 01:30:00	2018-06-03 08:15:00
1	2018-06-24 14:25:00	2018-07-06 09:40:00
2	2018-11-27 04:25:00	2018-12-02 17:50:00
3	2018-12-26 14:25:00	2018-12-29 16:55:00
4	2019-06-19 01:55:00	2019-07-19 05:10:00
5	2019-08-03 12:50:00	2019-08-04 16:20:00
6	2019-10-30 09:55:00	2019-10-31 16:15:00

Figure 9.2 – Anomalous ranges overview

4. Two sensors were also missing a lot of data (`sensor_15` and `sensor_50`). For the purpose of this tutorial, I removed these two columns from the dataset altogether.

5. Create a single CSV file for each sensor and host each of them inside a dedicated folder. In the end, the dataset structure obtained will be as follows:

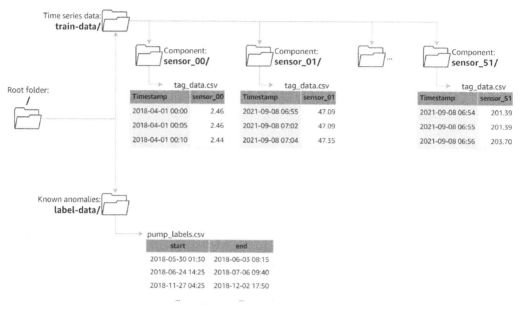

Figure 9.3 – Pump dataset structure overview

No other specific preprocessing was necessary and you will now upload this prepared dataset in a location where Amazon Lookout for Equipment can access it.

Uploading your data to Amazon S3 for storage

You can download the archive I prepared directly from the following location:

```
https://packt-publishing-timeseries-on-aws-michaelhoarau.
s3.eu-west-1.amazonaws.com/part2-amazon-lookout-for-equipment/
lookout-for-equipment.zip
```

Download this archive and unzip it. You should have the following:

- 50 CSV files (located in the `train-data` folder) containing the time series data for 50 sensors

- One CSV file (named `pump_labels.csv` and located in the `label-data` folder) containing the label data with the known periods where anomalies are expected

- One JSON file (named `schema.txt`) that contains the schema you are going to use later when creating the dataset

In the next section, you are going to create an Amazon S3 bucket, upload your dataset there, and give Amazon Lookout for Equipment permission to access this data.

Creating an Amazon S3 bucket

Equipped with our prepared datasets, let's create a bucket on Amazon S3 and upload our data there:

1. If you went through the *Technical requirements* prerequisites at the beginning of this chapter, you should already be logged in to your AWS console, otherwise, fire up your favorite browser and log in to your AWS console.

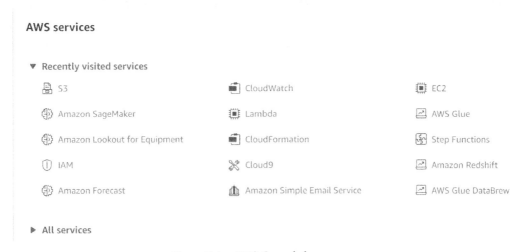

Figure 9.4 – AWS Console home page

2. At the top left of your console, you will see a **Services** drop-down menu that will display all the available AWS services. In the **Storage** section, look at the **S3** service and click on its name to go to the S3 console.

3. From here, we are going to click on the **Create bucket** button located at the top of your bucket list section.

Figure 9.5 – Amazon S3 console landing page

4. You are brought to the bucket creation page.

General configuration

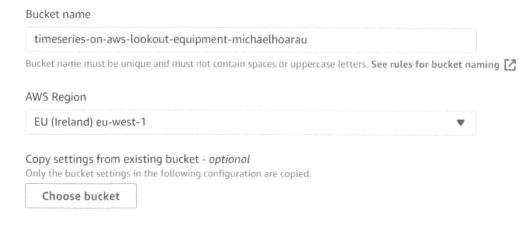

Bucket name

timeseries-on-aws-lookout-equipment-michaelhoarau

Bucket name must be unique and must not contain spaces or uppercase letters. **See rules for bucket naming**

AWS Region

EU (Ireland) eu-west-1

Copy settings from existing bucket - *optional*
Only the bucket settings in the following configuration are copied.

Choose bucket

Figure 9.6 – Amazon S3 bucket creation form

5. Choose a name for your bucket. This name must be unique across the whole S3 service. I will call mine `timeseries-on-aws-lookout-equipment-michaelhoarau`. That should be unique enough.

6. Select an AWS Region from where your data will be fetched by Amazon Lookout for Equipment. I selected the **Europe (Ireland)** region for mine.

> **Important Note**
>
> At the time of writing this book, Amazon Lookout for Equipment is only available in the following regions: US East (N. Virginia), Asia Pacific (Seoul), and Europe (Ireland). Make sure you select one of these regions to create your bucket or you won't be able to ingest your data into Amazon Lookout for Equipment.

7. You can keep all the other fields at their default values and click on **Create bucket**. You will be brought back to the S3 home page and you should see your newly created bucket in the buckets listing. A green message at the top of the window will also confirm that your bucket was created successfully.

Your Amazon S3 bucket is now created and you can start uploading your files to this location.

Uploading your dataset to Amazon S3

To upload your dataset, complete the following steps:

1. Click on the name of the bucket you just created in the buckets list that appears on the S3 home page.

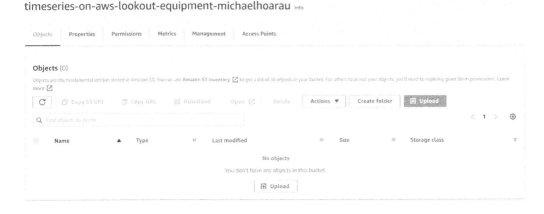

Figure 9.7 – Amazon S3 empty objects listing from your new bucket

This page lists all the objects available in this bucket: it is empty for now.

2. From here, click on the **Upload** button at the top of the objects list. You will be brought to the upload page where you can either click on the **Add files** button or drag and drop all the CSV files unpacked from the archive you previously downloaded. They should be located in two directories named `train-data` and `label-data`. You can drag and drop these two folders directly in your browser window. You don't need to upload the `schema.txt` file.

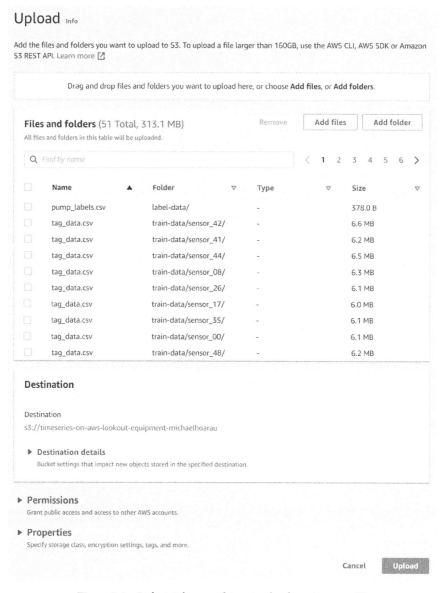

Figure 9.8 – Industrial pump dataset upload on Amazon S3

3. Leave all the other fields at their default values, scroll to the bottom of the screen, and click on **Upload** to start uploading the files. There is a total of 313 MB and it may take a while depending on your internet upload bandwidth. An upload status page is displayed while the transfer is in progress.

4. Once this is done, you can click on the **Exit** button to be brought back to the objects list at the root of your bucket.

Figure 9.9 – Industrial pump dataset upload completed

Once your upload is complete, you should see two folders in the objects list, one for the label data and the other (`train-data`) containing the time series sensor data you are going to use for training a model.

5. Click on each of the folder names and copy their S3 URI (their address in Amazon S3) where you will be able to access it later (in a notepad on your desktop, for instance); the S3 URI of these folders in Amazon S3 takes the following format:

```
s3://BUCKET_NAME/FOLDER_NAME/
```

For instance, my `train-data` folder S3 URI is the following:

```
s3://timeseries-on-aws-lookout-equipment-michaelhoarau/
train-data/
```

We will need the `train-data` link at ingestion time and the `label-data` link when training a new model. Let's now give access to this S3 bucket to Amazon Lookout for Equipment.

Giving Amazon Lookout for Equipment access to your S3 bucket (optional)

By default, the security mechanisms enforced between different AWS services will forbid any service other than Amazon S3 from accessing your data. From your account, you can upload, delete, or move your data from the bucket you just created. Amazon Lookout for Equipment, however, is a different service and will not be able to access this data. We need to specify that it can access any data in this bucket.

You can configure this access directly from the Amazon Lookout for Equipment console during the ingestion step. However, if you want to have more control over the roles and the different accesses created within your account, you can read through this section. Otherwise, feel free to skip it and come back here later.

To enable access to your S3 bucket to the Amazon Lookout for Equipment service, we are going to use the AWS **Identity and Access Management (IAM)** service to create a dedicated **IAM role**:

1. At the top left of your console, click on the **Services** drop-down menu and search for the **Security, Identity, and Compliance** section. Click on the IAM service name to go to this service console.

2. On the left panel menu, click on **Roles** and then click on the **Create role** button on the top left of this screen.

3. On the **Create role** screen, select **AWS service** as the type of trusted entity.

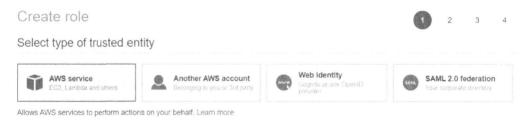

Figure 9.10 – IAM role creation – trusted entity type selection

4. In the following section (**Choose a use case**), locate **SageMaker** and click on the service name.

> **Note**
>
> Not all AWS services appear in these ready-to-use use cases, and this is why we are using Amazon SageMaker (another AWS Managed Service). In the next steps, we will adjust the role created to configure it specifically for Amazon Lookout for Equipment.

5. Click on the **Next** button until you reach the last step (**Review**). Provide a name and a description of your role (I called it `LookoutEquipmentIndustrialPumpDataAccess`).

Figure 9.11 – IAM role creation – Review step

6. Click on **Create role**. Your role is created and you are presented with a summary of your role. At the top of this screen, you will see a **Role ARN** (**Amazon Resource Name**) field. Copy this ARN and paste it somewhere handy. We will need it when we ingest your data into the service.

   You are brought back to the list of roles available in your account. In the search bar, search for the role you just created and choose it from the returned result.

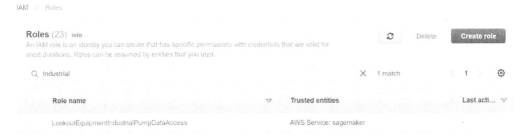

Figure 9.12 – Selecting your IAM access role

7. Click on the cross at the far right of the **AmazonSageMakerFullAccess** managed policy to remove the permission for this role (we only need this role to have access to Amazon S3 data).

8. Click on **Add inline policy** and then on the **JSON** tab. Then fill in the policy with the following document (update the name of the bucket with the one you created earlier):

```
{
    "Version": "2012-10-17",
    "Statement": [
        {
            "Effect": "Allow",
            "Action": [
                "s3:ListBucket",
                "s3:GetObject",
                "s3:PutObject"
            ],
            "Resource": [
                "arn:aws:s3:::<<YOUR-BUCKET>>/*",
                "arn:aws:s3:::<<YOUR-BUCKET>>"
            ]
        }
    ]
}
```

9. Give a name to your policy (for instance, `LookoutEquipmentS3Access`) and then click on **Create policy**.

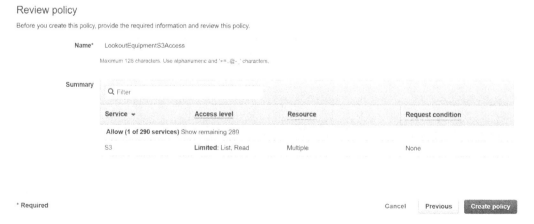

Figure 9.13 – Reviewing the S3 access policy

10. On the **Trust relationships** tab, choose **Edit trust relationship**.

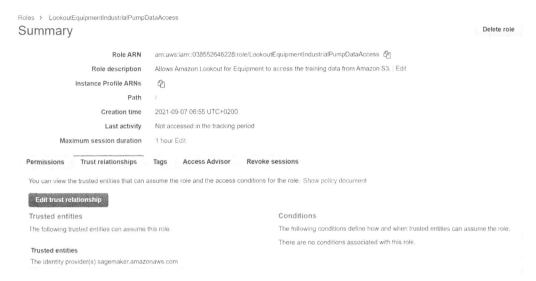

Figure 9.14 – Editing the trust relationship

11. Under the policy document, replace the whole policy with the following document and click on the **Update trust policy** button on the bottom right:

```
{
    "Version": "2012-10-17",
    "Statement": [
      {
        "Sid": "",
        "Effect": "Allow",
        "Principal": {
          "Service": "lookoutequipment.amazonaws.com"
        },
        "Action": "sts:AssumeRole"
      }
    ]
}
```

When Amazon Lookout for Equipment tries to read the datasets you just uploaded in S3, it will request permissions from IAM by using the role we just created:

- The trust policy allows Lookout for Equipment to assume this role.

- The inline policy specifies that Lookout for Equipment is authorized to list and access the objects in the S3 bucket you created earlier.

You are now ready to ingest your dataset into Amazon Lookout for Equipment.

Creating an Amazon Lookout for Equipment dataset

As mentioned in *Chapter 8, An Overview of Amazon Lookout for Equipment*, a dataset is a convenient way to organize your time series data stored as CSV files. These files are stored in an Amazon S3 bucket and organized in different folders.

Each dataset is a container that can contain one or several components that groups tags together. In S3, each component will be materialized by a folder. You can use datasets and components to organize your sensor data depending on how your industrial pieces of equipment are organized themselves.

For instance, you can use the dataset level to store all the tags from a factory and then each component to group all the tags relative to a given production line (across multiple pieces of equipment) or a given piece of equipment.

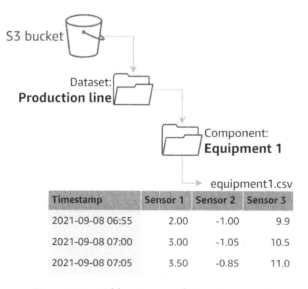

Figure 9.15 – Folder structure factory/equipment

In this configuration, each component contains several sensors in the same CSV file. Depending on how your sensor data is generated, you may have to align all the timestamps so that you can join all your sensor data in a single CSV file sharing a common timestamp column.

An alternative is to match each piece of equipment with a dataset and then store each sensor in its own component.

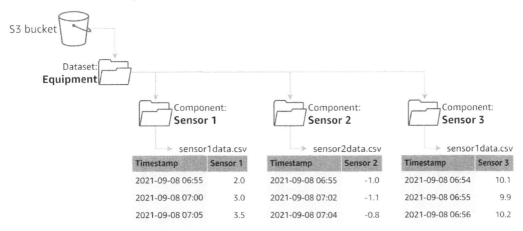

Figure 9.16 – Folder structure equipment/sensors

In this configuration, the timestamps for each sensor do not need to be aligned. This timestamp alignment will be dealt with on your behalf at ingestion time by Amazon Lookout for Equipment.

For the industrial pump dataset, throughout this tutorial, you will use the second format described previously, to remove the need for any preprocessing. To create your first anomaly detection project with Amazon Lookout for Equipment, complete the following steps:

1. Log in to your AWS console and search for Lookout for Equipment in the search bar at the top.

2. Click on **Amazon Lookout for Equipment** to go to the service home page.

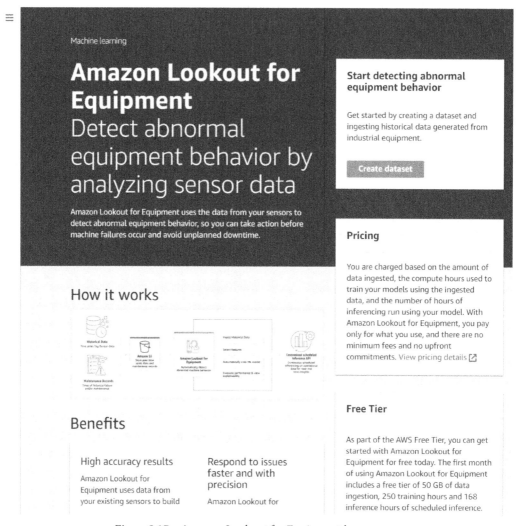

Figure 9.17 – Amazon Lookout for Equipment home page

3. On this page, you can either click on the **Create dataset** button on the right side of the screen or click the hamburger icon (the one with three horizontal lines) on the top left to open the left panel, where you can click on **Datasets**. You will land on a page listing all the datasets visible from your AWS account. If this is your first time using the service, your list will be empty and you can click on the **Create dataset** button at the top right of the list to bring up the dataset creation page.

4. On this screen, you are asked to give a name to your dataset (let's call it
    `industrial-pump`) and a data schema. In the dataset archive you downloaded in
    the initial technical requirements paragraph from this chapter, I provided a `schema.`
    `txt` file. Open it and copy and paste its content into the dataset schema widget.

Dataset details

Dataset name

industrial-pump

The name can have up to 200 characters, and it must be unique. Valid characters: A-Z, a-z, 0-9, _, and -
(hyphen).

Data schema   Info

The data schema is metadata that describes your dataset to Lookout for Equipment. It contains the
folder name for each .csv file (Component), the header names in each .csv file (Name), and the data
type for each column (Type).

```
 1 ▾ {
 2 ▾     "Components": [
 3 ▾         {
 4               "ComponentName": "sensor_43",
 5 ▾             "Columns": [
 6 ▾                 {
 7                       "Name": "Timestamp",
 8                       "Type": "DATETIME"
 9                   },
10 ▾                 {
11                       "Name": "sensor_43",
12                       "Type": "DOUBLE"
13                   }
14               ]
15           },
16 ▾         {
17               "ComponentName": "sensor_07",
18 ▾             "Columns": [
19 ▾                 {
20                       "Name": "Timestamp",
21                       "Type": "DATETIME"
22                   },
23 ▾                 {
24                       "Name": "sensor_07",
25                       "Type": "DOUBLE"
26                   }
```

Data encryption   Info

Your data is encrypted by default with a key that AWS owns and manages for you. To
choose a different key, customize your encryption settings.

☐ Customize encryption settings (advanced)

Figure 9.18 – Dataset creation details

5. Scroll down to the bottom of the screen and click **Create** to create your dataset.

The dataset is created and you are brought to the dataset dashboard. Before you actually ingest your data, let's take a short pause to look at the dataset schema.

Generating a JSON schema

To create a dataset in Amazon Lookout for Equipment, you need to describe the list of sensors it contains. You will do this by writing a data schema in JSON format. In this section, you will learn how to write one manually and how to generate one automatically.

Dataset schema structure

The data schema to describe an Amazon Lookout for Equipment dataset is a JSON string that takes the following format:

```
{
    "Components": [
        {
            "ComponentName": "string",
            "Columns": [
                { "Name": "string", "Type": "DOUBLE" |
    "DATETIME" },
                ...
                { "Name": "string", "Type": "DOUBLE" |
    "DATETIME" }
            ]
        },
        ...
    ]
}
```

The root item (Components) of this JSON string lists all the components of the dataset. Then, each component is a dictionary containing the following:

- The name of the component as a string (ComponentName).

- The list of all columns in this component (Columns).

- Each column of a component is a dictionary with the name of the column (Name) and its type, which can either be DOUBLE or DATETIME. The latter is reserved for the timestamp columns of the dataset.

Writing such a schema from scratch can be hard to get right, especially for datasets that contain several dozen, if not hundreds, of signals shared between multiple components. In the next section, I will show you how to programmatically generate a data schema file.

Using CloudShell to generate a schema

Building a schema from scratch manually is a highly error-prone activity. In this section, you are going to use the CloudShell service to run a script that will build this schema automatically from an S3 path you provide it. Let's go through the following instructions:

1. Log in to your AWS console.

2. At the top right of your console, make sure the Region selector is set to one of the regions where Amazon Lookout for Equipment is available: either **Europe (Ireland)**, **US East (N. Virginia)**, **or Asia Pacific (Seoul)**.

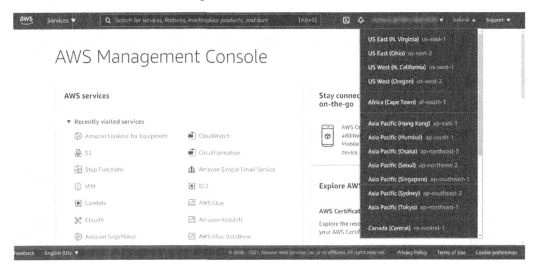

Figure 9.19 – AWS console region selector

3. Once your region is selected, click on the **CloudShell** icon located not far to the left of the region selector.

Figure 9.20 – Locating the CloudShell icon

4. When clicking on the CloudShell icon, a new tab is opened in your browser. If you don't have a CloudShell session already opened, you should see a blue ribbon stating that your environment is in preparation. After a minute, your environment is ready and you are presented with a Linux command prompt.

Figure 9.21 – Your CloudShell environment is ready!

5. Now, run the following commands in this terminal (don't forget to replace <<YOUR_BUCKET>> with the name of your own bucket):

```
python3 -m pip install --quiet s3fs pandas
```

```
wget https://github.com/PacktPublishing/Time-Series-
Analysis-on-AWS/blob/main/Chapter09/create_schema.py
```

```
python3 create_schema.py
s3://<<YOUR_BUCKET>>/ train-data/
```

After a few seconds this script will output a long JSON string starting with
{ "Components" : .... You can now copy this string when you need to create a dataset
based on this time series dataset.

> **Note**
> After running the first line from the preceding code, you might see some error
> messages about pip dependencies. You can ignore them and run the dataset
> generation script.

You have seen how you can create a Lookout for Equipment dataset and how you can
generate a schema with a script. Let's now ingest actual data in our dataset.

Creating a data ingestion job

At the end of dataset creation, you are automatically brought to the dataset dashboard.

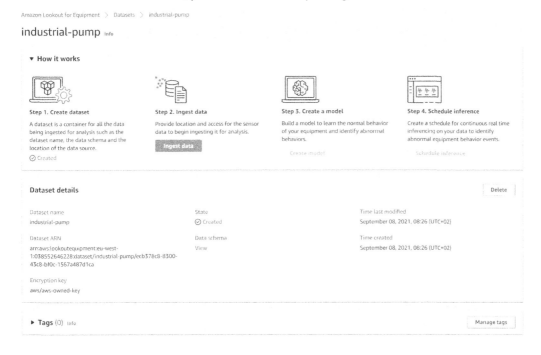

Figure 9.22 – Dataset dashboard after creation

From here, you can click the **Ingest data** button in the **Step 2** column and start configuring the data ingestion job.

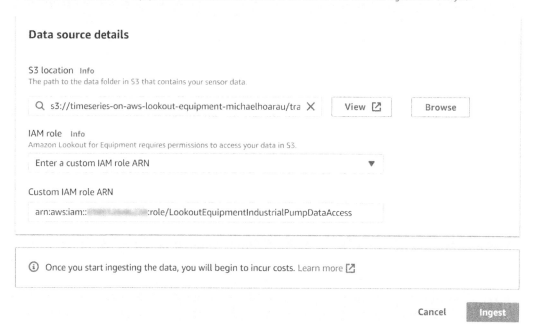

Ingest Data

Provide Amazon Lookout for Equipment with location and access to the sensor data so it can ingest it for analysis.

Figure 9.23 – Data ingestion job configuration

When configuring the ingestion, the job details you must define are as follows:

- **S3 location**: The S3 location of the training data where the time series are located. In *step 5* of the *Uploading your dataset to Amazon S3* section, you copied the S3 URI of your training data. Paste it into this field.

- In the **IAM role** field, select **Enter a custom IAM role ARN** and paste the ARN of the `AmazonForecastEnergyConsumption` role that you created earlier in the IAM service. The format of the ARN should be `arn:aws:iam::<ACCOUNT-NUMBER>:role/LookoutEquipmentIndustrialPumpDataAccess`, where `<ACCOUNT-NUMBER>` needs to be replaced with your AWS account number.

Once you're done, you can click on **Ingest** to start the ingestion process. Your process starts and can last around 5-6 minutes depending on the GB of data to be ingested. During the ingestion process, Amazon Lookout for Equipment checks your data, performs some missing value filling on your behalf, aligns the timestamps, and prepares the sequence of time series so that they are ready to be used at training time by the multiple algorithms the service can run.

Understanding common ingestion errors and workarounds

When ingesting data, Amazon Lookout for Equipment performs several checks that can result in a failed ingestion. When this happens, you can go back to your dataset dashboard and click on the **View data source** button. You will then access a list of all the ingestion jobs you performed.

Figure 9.24 – Data ingestion history

This screen lists all the ingestion jobs you performed. When ingestion fails, the **Success** icon is replaced by a **Failed** one and you can hover your mouse on it to read about what happened. There are three main sources of errors linked to your dataset. Two of them can happen at ingestion time, while the last one will only be triggered when you train a model:

- The S3 location where the time series data is not the right one.

- The data file for a given tag/sensor is not found.

- You have too many missing values in a given sensor.

Let's dive into each of these issues.

Wrong S3 location

The S3 location you used when you configured your ingestion job may not be the right one. Remember that your dataset can contain several components. The S3 URI you should mention is the root folder that contains the folders materializing these components. This is a common mistake when you have only one component.

When you see this error, you just need to relaunch the ingestion process and set the correct S3 location before attempting the ingestion again.

Component not found

When you ingest your data, Amazon Lookout for Equipment matches the data structure as being available in S3 with the data schema you used when configuring your dataset. If a component is missing (an entire folder), if a tag is missing from a given component, or if a tag is misplaced and positioned in the wrong component file, you will find this error.

Double-check the file structure in your S3 bucket and make sure it matches the schema used at dataset creation time (each folder must match a component name that is case-sensitive and each CSV file must contain exactly the sensors as listed under this component in the dataset schema).

If your file structure is correct, you may have to do the following:

1. Delete the dataset.
2. Regenerate a schema based on your current file structure.
3. Recreate a new dataset with the new data schema.
4. Reattempt the ingestion.

Missing values for a given time series

If you did not generate the dataset programmatically, you may have had no opportunity to look into your time series data. Some of this data might miss a significant portion of its data points or be empty altogether (an unused or malfunctioning sensor for instance). When you train a model with Amazon Lookout for Equipment, you must choose a training start date and end date. Lookout for Equipment will check whether all the sensors have at least one data point present in this time period and forward fill any missing values.

If a time series is completely empty (100% m the model will fail to train. When this happens,

- If this is a data generation issue, regenerate you reattempt ingestion.

- If you have good knowledge of the process that genera to fill these values, you can update the time series for this and reattempt ingestion.

- If you want to remove this signal altogether, you will have to dele build a new schema that doesn't include this sensor data, create a n the new schema, and reattempt ingestion.

Now that you understand the key issues that may happen with your dataset, it is th conclude this chapter and move to the fun part – training and evaluating a model!

Summary

In this chapter, you learned how you should organize your dataset before you can train an anomaly detection model with Amazon Lookout for Equipment. You also discovered the dataset we are going to use in the next few chapters and you performed the first tasks necessary to train a model, namely, creating a dataset and ingesting your time series data in it.

With the help of this chapter, you should now have an understanding of what can go wrong at this stage with a few pointers to the main errors that can happen at ingestion time.

In the next chapter, we are going to train and evaluate our first anomaly detection model.

issing values) in the selected training range,
you have the following possibilities:

r data, upload it in S3, and

tes this data and know how
sensor, upload them to S3,

te your dataset,
w dataset with

me to

10
Training and Evaluating a Model

In the previous chapter, you familiarized yourself with a multivariate industrial water pump dataset and learned how to configure data with **Amazon Lookout for Equipment**. You also ingested your dataset in the service and learned about the main errors that can arise during this step.

In this chapter, you will use the datasets you prepared and ingested previously to train a multivariate anomaly detection model. You will learn how to configure your model training and the impact each parameter can have on your results. You will also develop an understanding of the key drivers that can increase your training duration. At the end of this chapter, we will walk through the evaluation and diagnostics dashboard to give you the right perspective about the quality of the outputs.

In this chapter, we're going to cover the following main topics:

- Using your dataset to train a model
- Organizing your models
- Choosing a good data split
- Evaluating a trained model

Technical requirements

No hands-on experience with a language such as **Python** or **R** is necessary to follow this chapter's content. However, we highly recommend that you read this chapter while connected to your AWS account and open the Amazon Lookout for Equipment console to run the different actions on your end.

To create an AWS account and log into the Amazon Lookout for Equipment console, you can refer to the *Technical requirements* section of *Chapter 2, An Overview of Amazon Forecast.*

Using your dataset to train a model

In the previous chapter, you created an Amazon Lookout for Equipment dataset and ingested your first time series dataset in it. You are now ready to train an **anomaly detection model**.

Training an anomaly detection model

To train an anomaly detection model with Amazon Lookout for Equipment, follow these steps:

1. Log into your AWS console and search for Lookout for Equipment in the search bar at the top.

2. Click on **Amazon Lookout for Equipment** to go to the service's home page:

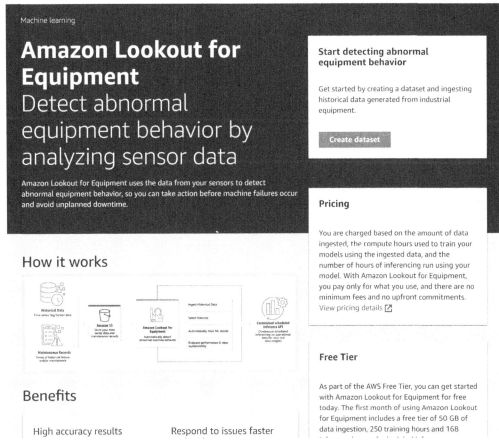

Figure 10.1 – The Amazon Lookout for Equipment home page

3.   On this page, you can click on the hamburger icon (the one with three horizontal lines) at the top left to open the left panel, where you can click on **Datasets**. You will land on a page listing all the datasets that are visible from within your AWS account. You should see the dataset you created earlier (we named it `industrial-pump`). Click on your dataset's name:

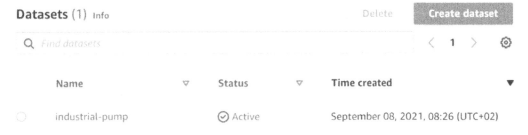

Figure 10.2 – Datasets list

4. This will bring you to your dataset dashboard, where you can click on the **Create model** button:

Figure 10.3 – Dataset details

5. The model creation form has several sections. Let's go through each of them in detail. The **Model details** section lets you enter a name for your model and select an optional encryption key to access your data. Leave the **Customize encryption settings** box unchecked and enter `pump-anomaly-detection-model` for your **Model name**:

Model details

Model name

```
pump-anomaly-detection-model
```

The name can have up to 200 characters, and it must be unique. Valid characters: A-Z, a-z, 0-9, _, and - (hyphen).

Data encryption   Info

Your data is encrypted by default with a key that AWS owns and manages for you. To choose a different key, customize your encryption settings.

☐ Customize encryption settings (advanced)

Figure 10.4 – Model creation details

6. The next section lets you select which **Fields** you would like to use to train your model. In this case, you are going to use all the fields. To do this, you will need to click on the checkbox positioned in the header (**1**), navigate through each page (using the pagination controls) (**2**), and make sure the header checkbox is checked on each page:

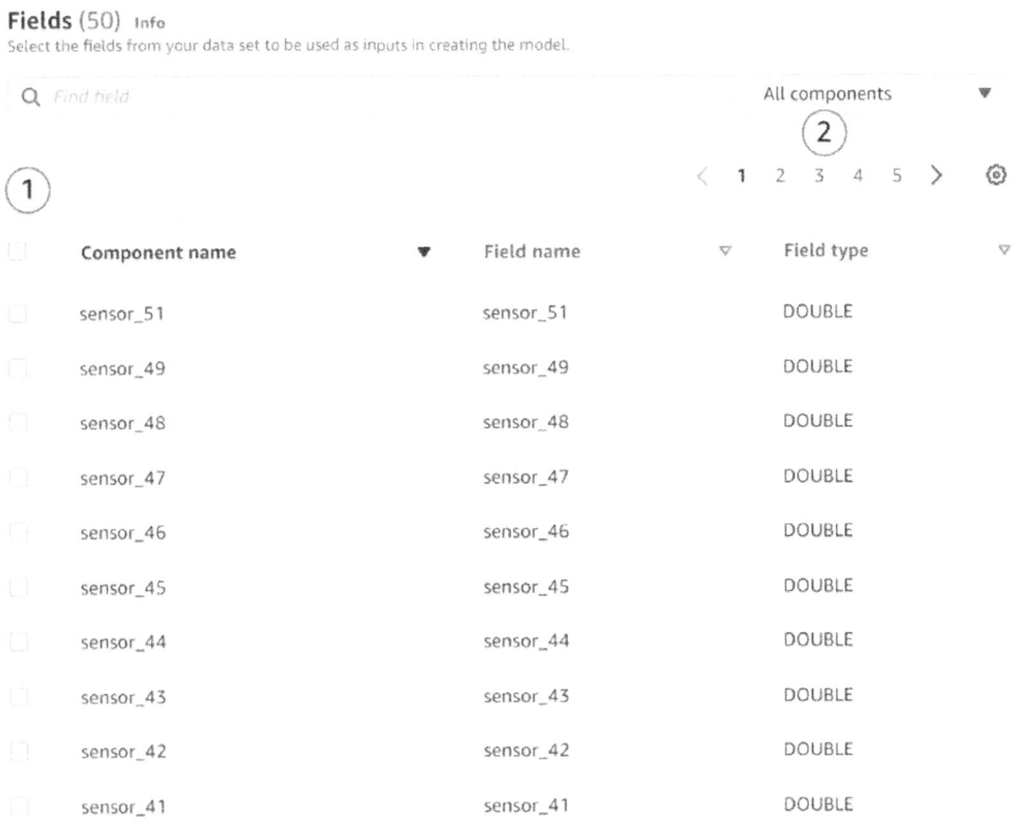

Fields (50) Info
Select the fields from your data set to be used as inputs in creating the model.

Q Find field		All components ▼

(**2**)

(**1**)   ‹ 1 2 3 4 5 › ⚙

☐ Component name ▼	Field name ▽	Field type ▽
sensor_51	sensor_51	DOUBLE
sensor_49	sensor_49	DOUBLE
sensor_48	sensor_48	DOUBLE
sensor_47	sensor_47	DOUBLE
sensor_46	sensor_46	DOUBLE
sensor_45	sensor_45	DOUBLE
sensor_44	sensor_44	DOUBLE
sensor_43	sensor_43	DOUBLE
sensor_42	sensor_42	DOUBLE
sensor_41	sensor_41	DOUBLE

Figure 10.5 – Model creation fields

7. The next section, **Historical maintenance events**, will let you point Amazon Lookout for Equipment to your label CSV file. When configuring this parameter, you must define the S3 location of the label data where the time series data is located. Click **Browse** to find your label data location:

Historical maintenance event (labels) data – *optional*   Info

Label data will be used to help with train the model. It is a list of time ranges within which the machine abnomaly exists.

S3 location   Info

The path to the data folder in S3 that contains your label data.

| Q 1eseries-on-aws-lookout-equipment-michaelhoarau/label-data   ✕ | View ☐ | Browse |

Please choose a folder, not a file

IAM role   Info

Amazon Lookout for Equipment requires permissions to access your data in S3.

| Enter a custom IAM role ARN   ▼ |

Custom IAM role ARN

| arn:aws:iam:: ▓▓▓▓▓▓▓▓ :role/LookoutEquipmentIndustrialPumpDataAccess |

Figure 10.6 – Selecting a historical anomalous event file

From the popup that appears, click the **label-data** folder name:

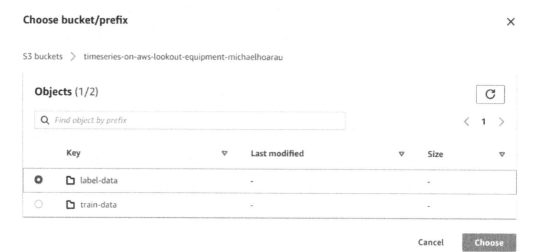

Figure 10.7 – Selecting the location of label-data

Then, select **Enter a custom IAM role ARN** and paste the ARN of the
`LookoutEquipmentIndustrialPumpDataAccess` role that you created in
Chapter 9, Creating a Dataset and Ingesting Your Data, using the IAM service. The
format of the ARN should be `arn:aws:iam::<ACCOUNT-NUMBER>:role/`
`LookoutEquipmentIndustrialPumpDataAccess`, where <ACCOUNT-
NUMBER> needs to be replaced with your AWS account number.

> **Important Note**
>
> Although you will see this historical event file often called the *labels file*, this
> denomination has nothing to do with the type of machine learning algorithms
> that are used by Amazon Lookout for Equipment as they are all fully
> *unsupervised* ones. For more details about how this labels file is used, check out
> the *How is the historical events file used?* section, later in this chapter.

8. The **Training and evaluation settings** section will let you define the time split and
    the sample rate at which your data will be downsampled by the service:

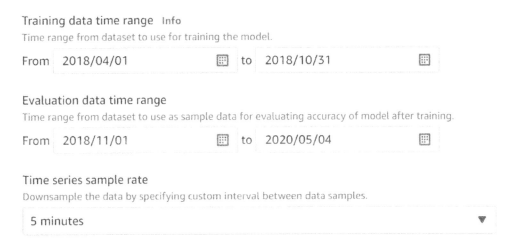

Figure 10.8 – Defining the training and evaluation split

When you're configuring this section, you must define the following:

a) **Training data time range**: This is the time range the service will use to train the model. For our industrial pump dataset, you can use `2018/04/01` to `2018/10/31`.

> **Important Note**
> At the time of writing this book, the training range must at least be 90 days long. If your training range is shorter than this, the training process will fail.

b) **Evaluation data time range**: This is the time range the service will use to evaluate a trained model. For our dataset, you can use `2018/11/01` to `2020/05/04`.

c) **Time series sample rate**: You can either use the original sample rate of your dataset or request Amazon Lookout for Equipment to downsample your data with a custom interval that can go from 1 second to 1 hour. Let's use `5 minutes`.

> **Important Note**
> The sample rate choice impacts the training time – the smaller the sample rate, the longer the training will take. However, resampling your time series data also acts as a filter that keeps the highest frequency of your data out. If the anomalous events you are looking for are located in these higher frequencies, choosing a sample rate that is too coarse will filter them out and Amazon Lookout for Equipment will have a harder time finding them. If you have 6 to 12 months of data, a resampling rate of 5 minutes or 10 minutes is a reasonable starting point. Depending on the training time and the results of your model evaluation, you can retrain another model with a different sample rate and compare the output.

9. The last section of interest is the optional **Off-time detection** section. We will not use this section for this example. See the *Deep dive into the off-time detection feature* section, later in this chapter, to get more details about this section.

10. Scroll down to the bottom of the page and click on the **Create** button. Your model training will be launched.

You should now have ongoing training in progress: based on the size of the dataset and the parameters that you have configured, it should take less than 1 hour to train your first anomaly detection model with Amazon Lookout for Equipment. In the meantime, you can read about the way historical events and off-time sensors are used.

How is the historical event file used?

As a reminder, your historical event file (or labels files) looks like this:

	start	end
0	2018-05-30 01:30:00	2018-06-03 08:15:00
1	2018-06-24 14:25:00	2018-07-06 09:40:00
2	2018-11-27 04:25:00	2018-12-02 17:50:00
3	2018-12-26 14:25:00	2018-12-29 16:55:00
4	2019-06-19 01:55:00	2019-07-19 05:10:00
5	2019-08-03 12:50:00	2019-08-04 16:20:00
6	2019-10-30 09:55:00	2019-10-31 16:15:00

Figure 10.9 – Anomalous ranges overview

This label file provides insight into past events to Amazon Lookout for Equipment. Although all the algorithms that are used by the service are unsupervised, Amazon Lookout for Equipment uses these *optional* labels to train its models more accurately and efficiently. Leveraging its bank of more than 28,000 combinations of parameters and algorithms, Amazon Lookout for Equipment can use this label file to find the optimal model that finds abnormal behaviors within these time windows.

How does Amazon Lookout for Equipment use this data? Let's look at the first row and let's see how it's interpreted:

- The second timestamp (**2018-06-03** at **8:15:00**) can be a maintenance event or when the abnormal behavior was noticed by someone.

- The first timestamp (**2018-05-30** at **1:30:00**) indicates when the abnormal behavior is expected to have started.

This window will be used by Amazon Lookout for Equipment to look for signs of an upcoming event leading to an anomaly. Let's look at the events that are part of our industrial pump dataset:

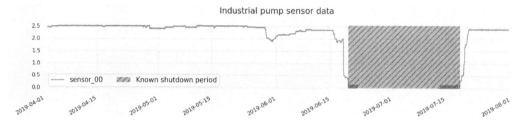

Figure 10.10 – Historical event example

In the previous plot, you can see the following:

- The hashed area highlights the known shutdown period provided with the original dataset. This period has a range going from **2019-06-19 14:00** to **2019-07-18 17:10**.

- On this signal, you can see that something already looks off before the period marked and as soon as 20 days before (starting around **2019-06-01**).

- On this same signal, you can also see that this equipment goes through a restart or healing period after the event.

Depending on the quality of the predictions and how long a forewarning you can get for a given event, one strategy to improve your model could be to expand the label ranges. For instance, the label for the event shown in the preceding screenshot could be enlarged to go from **2019-05-29** up to **2019-07-22**:

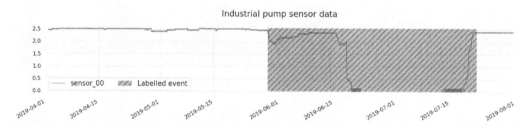

Figure 10.11 – Historical event updated label

As an exercise, I recommend that you have a look at the time series data and try to identify any good labels of the historical event that were provided with the original dataset. Once you have trained your first model, you can train a second version with your updated label file and compare the results.

Deep dive into the off-time detection feature

This optional section lets you tell Amazon Lookout for Equipment which sensors it can use to decide that equipment is going through a shutdown. When your piece of equipment has long shutdown periods (regular or not), it is usually required to remove the signals from these periods as they are not relevant for finding any anomalies.

When creating a new model, the **Off-time detection** section is located at the bottom of the screen, before the **Tags definition** section:

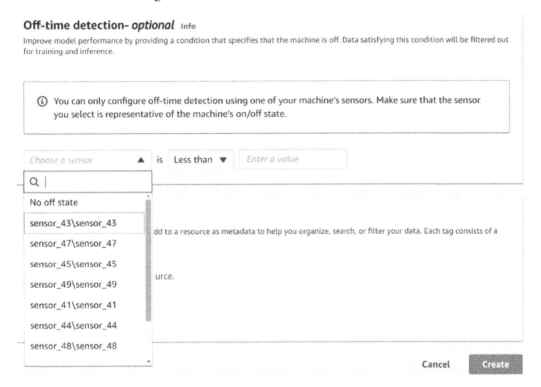

Figure 10.12 – The Off-time detection feature

To use this feature, simply fill in the following fields:

- **Sensor**: This dropdown list will be populated with the list of fields that you selected for this model. Each sensor will have a label of component name\tag name, as defined in the schema corresponding to the dataset that was used to train the model. In our case, we put each sensor in a component with the same name and each item of the dropdown list has a duplicated label (for instance, sensor_43\sensor_43).

- **Rule**: The rule can either be `less than` or `greater than`.

- **Value**: Enter an integer or float value.

Let's say your equipment is a rotating machine and that `sensor_43` measures the rotation speed in RPM. You know that any rotation speed *less than 100 RPM* means your equipment is either off or currently shutting down. To tell Amazon Lookout for Equipment this, you will configure the **Off-time detection** section by writing a rule stating that `sensor_43\sensor_43` is `less than 100 RPM`.

Once a condition has been met, all the data satisfying it will be discarded to train a model. Similarly, at inference time, all the data satisfying this condition will be filtered out.

Now that you know how the labels data and the off-time detection feature are used to train an anomaly detection model, let's look at the different ways you can organize your collection of models.

Model organization best practices

Amazon Lookout for Equipment includes the following hierarchy of artifacts within a given AWS account:

- The **dataset** is the highest level of the hierarchy; a dataset is defined by an immutable data schema that's defined at creation time.

- When defining the data schema, the different tags can be regrouped in different **components**: a component must match a folder in your S3 training dataset.

- Each dataset can be used to train multiple **models** and each model can use all the sensors available in the dataset (as defined in the schema) or only a selection of those.

- The lower level of this hierarchy is the **sensor** time series (also called **tag**, **signal**, or **field**).

> **Note**
>
> A higher level of this hierarchy is the AWS account/user. Although more heavy lifting will be required to set up the appropriate permission, you can build a solution where multiple AWS accounts would use Amazon Lookout for Equipment across your organization, depending on their geographical location, for instance.

Depending on the root level or your industrial data organization, you can use this hierarchy in different ways:

- If you have multiple sites/factories/shop floors:

  - Store all the data of a factory at the dataset level; a dataset can contain up to 3,000 sensors across all components. You will have as many datasets as you have factories.

  - Use the components to regroup the sensors of different production areas or production lines. A dataset can contain up to 3,000 components.

  - Use specific tag naming conventions to identify different pieces of equipment within a given production area/line.

  - A model can then use all the sensors from a component (production line anomaly) or a subselection of tags associated with a given piece of equipment. A model can use up to 300 sensors at once.

- If you are focused on a single factory:

  - If you have less than 3,000 signals, you can store all your time series in a single dataset. If not, you can use the dataset level to store the sensor data linked to different production areas or production lines.

  - Use the components to regroup the sensors of a given piece of equipment.

  - Build a model per component of interest (depending on the piece of equipment you want to monitor) or for the whole dataset if you want to monitor a given process or production line.

- If you are focused on a single piece of equipment:

  - Use the dataset to store all the data of this single piece of equipment.

  - Use the component to model the different subsystems of this piece of equipment.

  - Build a model per component (to monitor individual subsystems) or for the whole dataset (to monitor the piece of equipment at once).

Note that if the amount of data you have allows it, I recommend not splitting your data according to different periods (a dataset for 2021, another for 2020, and so on) as this will prevent you from building models across your different periods. When you create a new model, you can define the training start and end date, along with the evaluation start and end date. You can then either use the AWS tagging mechanisms to store the time or add a date-time string to your model naming convention to recognize it easily.

Now that you have an idea of the different ways you can organize your dataset, let's look at how to choose the best split possible between your training and evaluation data.

Choosing a good data split between training and evaluation

When you're choosing a data split between your training and evaluation periods, you need to consider the following constraints or recommendations:

- The first constraint to consider is the requirement to have *at least 90 days in the training range*. At the time of writing, Amazon Lookout for Equipment considers that it needs at least this period to model the normal operating behavior of a piece of industrial equipment. This physical behavior is independent of the granularity at which the sensor data is collected.

- Ideally, the training range should include all the normal operating behaviors of your process or equipment. If a new behavior is only seen during the evaluation range, then there will be a high chance that Amazon Lookout for Equipment will flag it as an anomaly.

> **Important Note**
>
> Make sure that you don't have severe level shifts in some of your sensors (for instance, sensors that stopped working over a long time): although this has more to do with how to select good signals to build a model, we recommend that you remove any signals that display long periods of shutdown time as it will make it harder for you to select a train/evaluation split that includes both behaviors.
>
> In addition, although a malfunctioning sensor is an anomaly you may want to correct, you don't want these malfunctions to impair your capability to capture more complex equipment or process anomalies.

- In addition, your training range should include some occurrences of anomalies (precisely delimited in time or not) if possible.

- Once you have set aside this minimum amount of training data (at least 180 days, as many normal operating modes as possible, and a few anomalies), you can start positioning the split to start the evaluation range. Ideally, this evaluation range will include some known anomalies so that you can evaluate the relevance of the events that are detected by Amazon Lookout for Equipment.

Once you have a trained model and are using it in production, your equipment or process may display a new normal operation model (by new, I mean not seen at training time). As we discussed previously, Lookout for Equipment may flag these periods as anomalies. To prevent this from happening, you will need to update your training dataset and adjust your training/evaluation split to ensure that the new normal modes are captured during model training.

Now that you know how to split your dataset, let's look at the insights provided by Amazon Lookout for Equipment when it evaluates a trained model.

Evaluating a trained model

Once a model has been trained, you can evaluate its relevance by looking at the evaluation results. In this section, we are going to do the following:

- Provide an overview of the model evaluation dashboard
- Deep dive into the model performance section and how to interpret it
- Deep dive into the event diagnostics section and how to interpret it

Let's start with the evaluation dashboard overview.

Model evaluation dashboard overview

To access this dashboard for any given model, follow these steps:

1. Log into your AWS console and search for Lookout for Equipment in the search bar at the top.

2. Click on **Amazon Lookout for Equipment** to go to the service's home page.

3. On this page, you can click on the hamburger icon (the one with three horizontal lines) at the top left to open the left panel, where you can click on **Datasets**. You will land on a page listing all the datasets that are visible in your AWS account. You should see the dataset you created earlier (we named it industrial-pump). Click on your dataset's name.

4. This will bring you to your dataset dashboard, where you can click on the **View models** button:

Figure 10.13 – Dataset dashboard when at least one model has been trained

5. You will see a list of all the trained models based on this dataset. In your case, you should only have one, so click on its name to access this model's dashboard.

6. A trained model dashboard is divided into four parts:

    I.   The model details section tells you, among other things, the model's name, the date it was created, and how long it took to train:

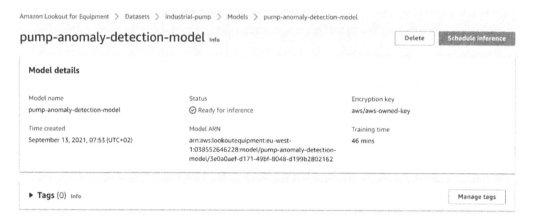

Figure 10.14 – Trained model dashboard – Model details

    II. The model performance overview section. This will be covered in more detail in the *Interpreting the model performance dashboard's overview* section, later in this chapter:

Model performance Info

Overview

5/5 abnormal equipment behavior events detected within label ranges, with an average forewarning time of 187 hrs 25 mins.

28 abnormal equipment behavior events detected outside the label ranges, with an average duration of 46 hrs 41 mins.

Want to improve model performance? Learn more

Evaluation data time range
From Nov 01, 2018 to May 04, 2020

Training data time range
From Apr 01, 2018 to Oct 31, 2018

Data sample rate
5 minutes

Abnormal equipment behavior events

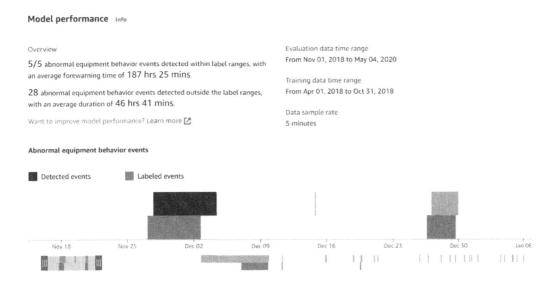

Figure 10.15 – Trained model dashboard – Model performance

III. A single event diagnostic that unpacks the details associated with a detected anomaly that you clicked on in the previously detected event strip chart. You will learn more about this in the *Using the events diagnostics dashboard* section, later in this chapter:

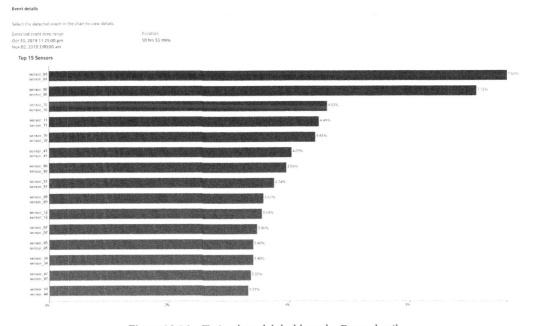

Figure 10.16 – Trained model dashboard – Event details

IV. The last section contains a reminder of the sensors that you selected to train this model and if it used any label data containing known historical events:

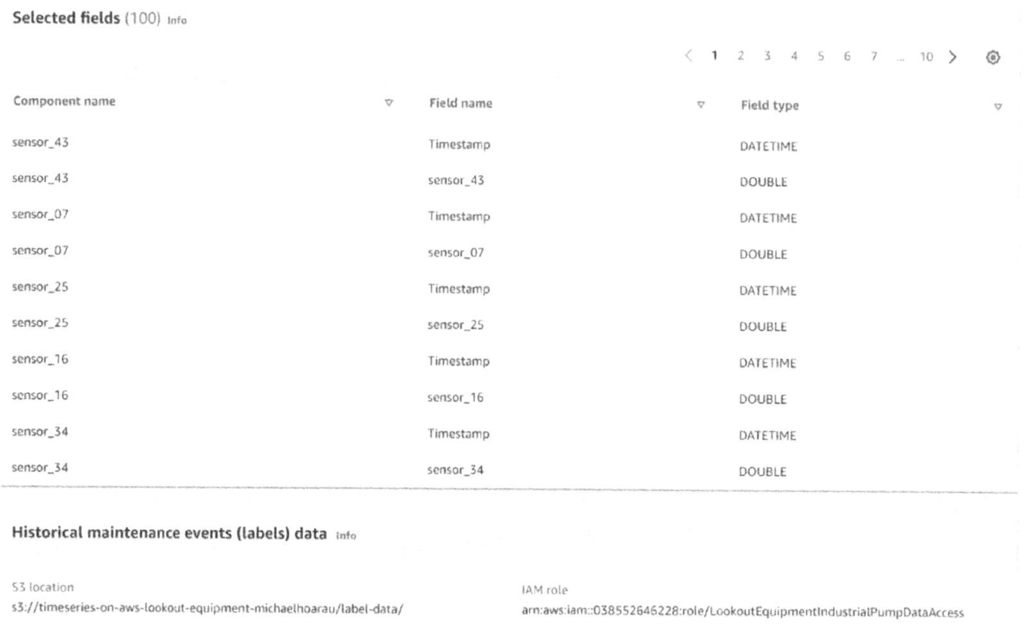

Selected fields (100) Info

⟨ 1 2 3 4 5 6 7 .. 10 ⟩ ⊚

Component name ▽	Field name ▽	Field type ▽
sensor_43	Timestamp	DATETIME
sensor_43	sensor_43	DOUBLE
sensor_07	Timestamp	DATETIME
sensor_07	sensor_07	DOUBLE
sensor_25	Timestamp	DATETIME
sensor_25	sensor_25	DOUBLE
sensor_16	Timestamp	DATETIME
sensor_16	sensor_16	DOUBLE
sensor_34	Timestamp	DATETIME
sensor_34	sensor_34	DOUBLE

Historical maintenance events (labels) data Info

S3 location
s3://timeseries-on-aws-lookout-equipment-michaelhoarau/label-data/

IAM role
arn:aws:iam::038552646228:role/LookoutEquipmentIndustrialPumpDataAccess

Figure 10.17 – Trained model dashboard – Model configuration reminders

Now that you know about the outputs of a model that's been trained by Amazon Lookout for Equipment, let's dive into the model performance and event diagnostics sections to see how you can derive meaningful insights from them.

Interpreting the model performance dashboard's overview

This section of the model performance dashboard contains the following information:

- How many known abnormal events (as provided in the historical events file) are captured by Amazon Lookout for Equipment. An **abnormal event** is considered detected if at least one anomaly detection is triggered by Amazon Lookout for Equipment. In our case, we mentioned five events in our historical abnormal event file and all of these were detected.

- How long before each known historical event (part of the label file) it takes Amazon Lookout for Equipment to detect something. This measure is averaged over all the known events located in the evaluation period and is labeled as the **Average forewarning time**.

- How many events are detected outside of the label ranges, along with their average duration.

- A strip chart containing the known events and the detected ones. The strip chart contains an overall view of the whole evaluation period and a slider you can use to zoom in on any area of interest. The zoomed area will appear at the top:

Figure 10.18 – Trained model dashboard – Detected events

Anomaly detection accuracy is challenging to assess in most industrial environments where precise historical anomalies may not be captured. Traditionally, in machine learning, any event that's detected outside of the known ones can be considered a false positive. In industrial anomaly detection, such an event could be one of the following:

- A **false positive**; that is, looking at the average duration of all detected events and comparing it with a given event can help filter it out if it looks sporadic or isolated.

- A **precursor event**, which may lead to an equipment or process anomaly, should the event be discarded. Establishing a procedure to react only when events frequency and/or average duration stays above a certain threshold can help orient the investigation effort of your shop floor operators, process engineers, or reliability teams accordingly.

- An **unknown event** – in other words, an event that was not captured in the labels file with the historical event. Double-checking what happened at that time can help you tell if this event was relevant or not.

- An **unknown normal operating mode**. This may also be a normal behavior that Amazon Lookout for Equipment did not see during training time.

Next, we will look at how to use events diagnostics dashboard.

Using the events diagnostics dashboard

If Amazon Lookout for Equipment detects any events in the evaluation period, you will be able to click on any of them in the model performance strip chart to unpack the magnitude at which the top signals contributed to this event. At the top of the event details section of the model evaluation dashboard, you will see the following:

Event details

Select the detected event in the chart to view details.

Detected event time range   Duration
Nov 27, 2018 7:10:00 pm   158 hrs 40 mins
Dec 04, 2018 9:50:00 am

Figure 10.19 – Event details

In this header, you can find the time range and the duration of the selected event. The sensor importance chart is plotted after these event details as a horizontal bar chart:

Top 15 Sensors

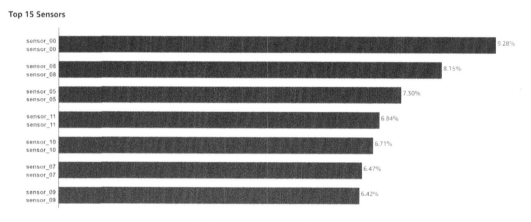

Figure 10.20 – Event details – Top sensors

This chart displays up to 15 sensors. For each sensor, you can see the following:

- The component and the name of the sensor as the label for each horizontal bar on the left-hand side.

- A horizontal bar with the top contributor sensors by decreasing magnitude.

- A percentage number on the right, indicating how much a given sensor is contributing to a detected event according to Amazon Lookout for Equipment.

> **Note**
> Although this chart displays no more than 15 sensors, the Service API allows you to programmatically query the sensor importance for every sensor present in your dataset.

If you were to sum up the total contribution for every sensor, you would find 100% contribution. This means that you can easily compare the contribution of any sensor to what would have happened if every sensor was contributing equally. Let's take the example of our industrial pump dataset. This dataset includes 50 sensors. For any given event, if each sensor had the same contribution as the other, the sensor importance should be 100% / 50 = 2%. In *Figure 10.20*, you can see that **sensor_00** has a contribution magnitude of 9.28%, which is significantly higher than the 2% average. In addition, you can also see that the top 7 sensors (out of the 50 provided) already have a contribution magnitude of more than 50% for this particular event. This knowledge is very useful if you wish to have a maintenance team focus on the right location in an industrial environment.

Since this difference is significant from a statistical point of view, you may find it interesting to start investigating the piece of equipment or process step this sensor is attached to.

There are several ways you can use this raw information to derive more insights to manage your equipment or process:

- If you used the data schema components to regroup your sensors according to a process step, a piece of equipment, or a subsystem, you can sum their feature importance and group them by component. You could then build another horizontal bar chart showing the importance of each component concerning any selected event.

- You can also plot the evolution over time of the sensor importance for each tag. This kind of plot can help you understand which signals are consistently top contributors for a group of events and will provide more robust insight that you can leverage in your anomaly investigation.

- In addition, the plot evolution can visually display different patterns that a skilled process engineer could help you use to perform some anomaly classification. The following screenshot shows an example of a sensor evolution plot for another dataset:

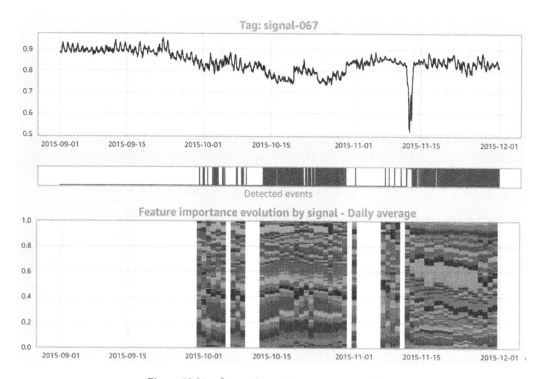

Figure 10.21 – Sensor importance post-processing

> **Note**
>
> To learn more about how you can build such dashboards, check out *Chapter 12, Reducing Time to Insights for Anomaly Detections.*

In the preceding screenshot, from top to bottom, you can see the following:

- A line plot for a given signal. You can easily see a dip shortly before November 15 where it looks like an anomaly occurred.

- A strip chart with the events detected by Amazon Lookout for Equipment. You can see that it fires some events before the actual anomaly and that these events appear as soon as mid-October. An investigation of the equipment around that time may have helped prevent the anomaly on November 15.

- A feature importance evolution over time. The sensor contributions are only visible when an event is detected. Here, you can easily see that the patterns of the events that were detected before, during, and after the anomaly are very different.

As you can see, learning how to post-process the outputs from Amazon Lookout for Equipment can yield rich insights that can help facilitate proactive inspection or maintenance of your manufacturing process or industrial equipment.

Summary

In this chapter, you learned how to train your first anomaly detection model with Amazon Lookout for Equipment. Using the dataset you created in the previous chapter, you were able to configure and train a model.

One of the key things you learned from this chapter is how Amazon Lookout for Equipment leverages provided optional labels. Although the service only uses unsupervised models under the hood, these label ranges are used to rank the ones that are best at finding abnormal behaviors located within these ranges.

Last but not least, we took a deep dive into how to read the evaluation dashboard of a trained model and how valuable it can be to go beyond the raw results that are provided by the service.

In the next chapter, you are going to learn how to use your trained model to run regularly scheduled inferences on fresh data.

11
Scheduling Regular Inferences

In the previous chapter, you trained a model and visualized the events it was able to detect over an evaluation period. Once **Amazon Lookout for Equipment** has trained a model, you can configure and start an inference scheduler that will run your data against it. This scheduler will wake up regularly, look for CSV files in a location on Amazon S3, open the right ones, and run them with your trained model to predict whether anomalous events are present in your new data. This process is called **inference**.

In this chapter, you will learn how to manage such schedulers and how to use the predictions obtained. In other words, you will learn how to use a deployed version of your model and use it in production.

In this chapter, we're going to cover the following main topics:

- Using a trained model
- Configuring a scheduler
- Preparing a dataset for inference
- Extracting the inference results

Technical requirements

No hands-on experience in a language such as **Python** or **R** is necessary to follow along with the content from this chapter. However, we highly recommend that you read this chapter while connected to your own AWS account and open the Amazon Lookout for Equipment console to run the different actions on your end.

To create an AWS account and log in to the Amazon Lookout for Equipment console, you can refer to the technical requirements of *Chapter 2, An Overview of Amazon Forecast.*

Using a trained model

The following diagram illustrates how Amazon Lookout for Equipment works at inference time:

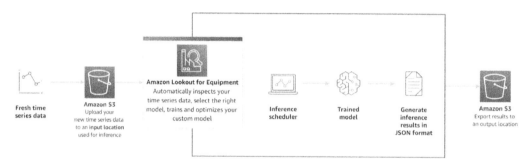

Figure 11.1 – Inference scheduler overview

Let's dive into the different steps of this pipeline:

1. New time series are generated: depending on your use case, you might collect new sensor data directly from your piece of equipment or directly access a piece of software such as a **historian**.

2. As you did at training time, you will need to push this fresh data to a location on Amazon S3 (you will see in the following *Configuring a scheduler* section how this location is configured).

3. Your inference scheduler will be configured to run regularly (for instance, every five minutes or every hour). Each time it wakes up, it will look for fresh data and run it against your trained model. Once the model generates new results, the scheduler will store it in JSON format.

4. At the end of each scheduler run, the inference results will be stored in another location on Amazon S3, where you will be able to retrieve them and post-process them further.

Once you have the inference results from a given model, you can use them to feed a business intelligence dashboard or send them back as notification to a mobile application targeted at a process engineer or shop floor operator. Data scientists can also use these insights as features to feed to other machine learning models they may have built further down the road.

Now that you have a high-level understanding of how you can use an Amazon Lookout for Equipment scheduler in your own inference pipeline, let's see how you actually configure one using the AWS console.

Configuring a scheduler

In *Chapter 9*, *Creating a Dataset and Ingesting Your Data*, you prepared and ingested time series data in Amazon Lookout for Equipment. In *Chapter 10*, *Training and Evaluating a Model*, you used your dataset to train a new anomaly detection model. In this section, you are going to use this trained model to schedule regular inferences.

To configure a new scheduler once a model is trained, you will need to do the following:

- Prepare your Amazon S3 bucket with an input and output location that will be used by your scheduler.

- Configure and start your scheduler.

Let's dive into each of these in detail.

Preparing your Amazon S3 bucket

To prepare your Amazon S3 bucket for an Amazon Lookout for Equipment scheduler, follow these steps:

1. If you went through the *Technical requirements* section at the beginning of this chapter, you should already be logged in to your AWS console, otherwise, fire up your favorite browser and log in to your AWS console.

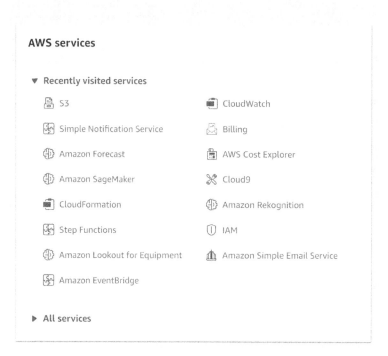

Figure 11.2 – AWS Management Console home page

2. As can be seen in *Figure 11.2*, at the top left of your console, you will see a **Services** drop-down menu that will display all the available AWS services. Click on this dropdown to bring up a menu with all the AWS services. In the **Storage** section of this menu, look for the **S3** service and click on its name to go to the S3 console. You should see a new screen with a list of buckets available in your account. You should see the bucket you created in *Chapter 9, Creating A Dataset and Ingesting Your Data*. Mine was called `timeseries-on-aws-lookout-equipment-michaelhoarau`. Click on the name of your bucket to see what's inside. You should see two folders (`label-data` and `train-data`). Click on the **Create folder** button.

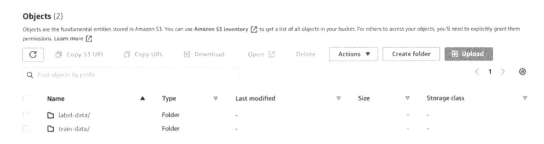

Figure 11.3 – Amazon S3 bucket content

3.   Let's name your folder `inference-data` and click on **Create folder** to finish this process.

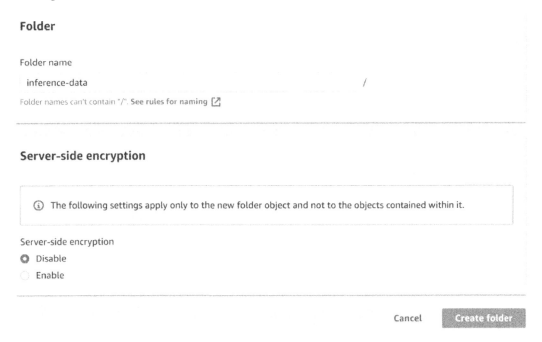

Figure 11.4 – Creating the inference data folder

4.   You will be brought back to the root level of your bucket where you will see a new directory (the one named `inference-data`) that you just created. Click on this folder name and proceed the same way to create two additional subdirectories located under the `inference-data` one: a directory called `input` and the other called `output`.

Your S3 bucket is now ready to be monitored by an Amazon Lookout for Equipment inference scheduler. Let's configure it.

Configuring your scheduler

Now that your S3 bucket is prepared, you can configure a new inference scheduler for Amazon Lookout for Equipment. To achieve this, you will need to go through the following steps:

1. Log in to your AWS console and search for `Lookout for Equipment` in the search bar at the top.

2. Click on **Amazon Lookout for Equipment** to go to the service home page.

Figure 11.5 – Amazon Lookout for Equipment home page

3. On this page, you can click on the hamburger icon (the one with three horizontal lines) on the top left to open the left panel, where you can click on **Datasets**. You will land on a page listing all the datasets visible from your AWS account. You should see the datasets you created earlier (we named it `industrial-pump`). Click on your dataset name.

Datasets (1) Info   Delete   **Create dataset**

Q Find datasets   ‹ 1 ›   ⚙

Name ▽	Status ▽	Time created ▽
industrial-pump	⊘ Active	September 08, 2021, 08:26 (UTC+02)

Figure 11.6 – Datasets list

4. This will bring you to your dataset dashboard where you can click on the **Schedule inference** button:

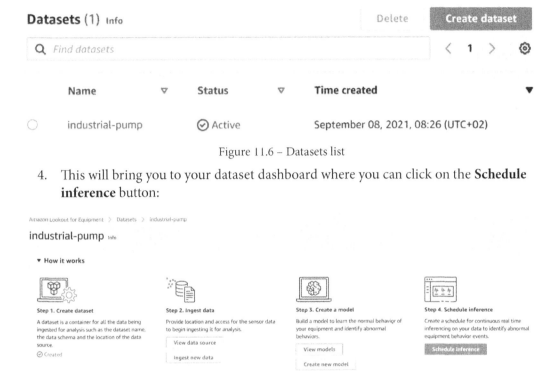

Figure 11.7 – Dataset details

5. The scheduler configuration form has several sections. Let's go through each of them in detail. In the first part, you will enter an inference scheduler name for your scheduler (`pump-scheduler` for instance), select which model you want to run inference for (`pump-anomaly-detection-model`), and what the S3 location for the input data is. When configuring this parameter, you will enter the S3 location for the input directory that you created earlier (you can fill in the S3 path manually or click **Browse** to look for it).

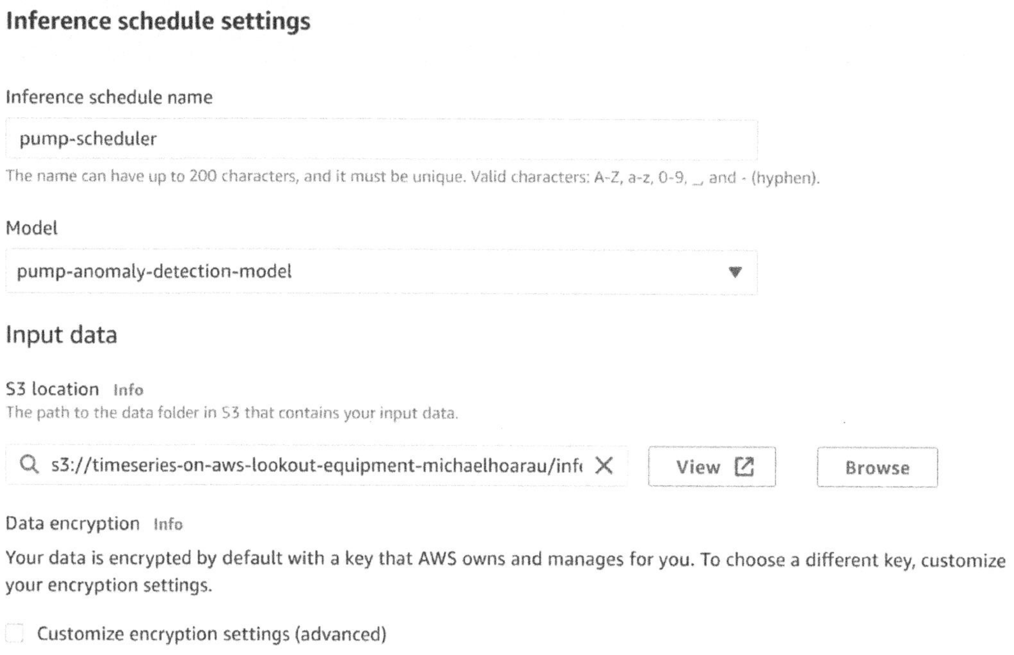

Inference schedule settings

Inference schedule name

pump-scheduler

The name can have up to 200 characters, and it must be unique. Valid characters: A-Z, a-z, 0-9, _, and - (hyphen).

Model

pump-anomaly-detection-model ▼

Input data

S3 location Info
The path to the data folder in S3 that contains your input data.

| Q s3://timeseries-on-aws-lookout-equipment-michaelhoarau/inf(✕ | View 🗗 | Browse |

Data encryption Info

Your data is encrypted by default with a key that AWS owns and manages for you. To choose a different key, customize your encryption settings.

☐ Customize encryption settings (advanced)

Figure 11.8 – Scheduler configuration overall settings

6. In the next section, you will specify how the scheduler should expect the input data to be formatted.

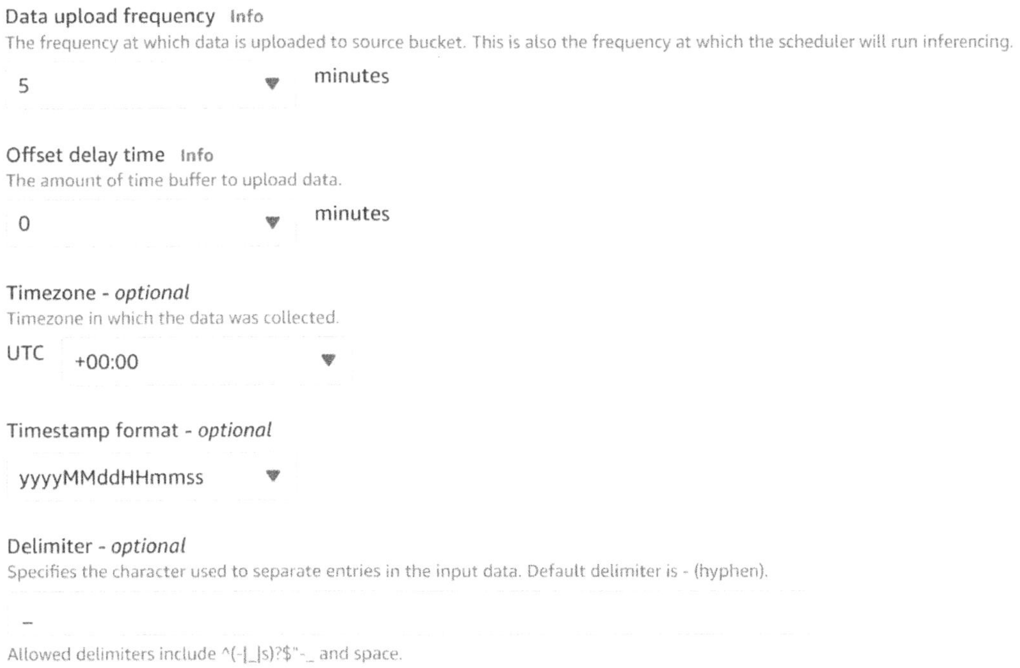

Data upload frequency Info
The frequency at which data is uploaded to source bucket. This is also the frequency at which the scheduler will run inferencing.

| 5 | ▼ | minutes |

Offset delay time Info
The amount of time buffer to upload data.

| 0 | ▼ | minutes |

Timezone - *optional*
Timezone in which the data was collected.

| UTC | +00:00 | ▼ |

Timestamp format - *optional*

| yyyyMMddHHmmss | ▼ |

Delimiter - *optional*
Specifies the character used to separate entries in the input data. Default delimiter is - (hyphen).

| _ |

Allowed delimiters include ^(-|_|s)?$"-_ and space.

Figure 11.9 – Scheduler input data format

In our case, you will set the following parameters:

- Use a data upload frequency of 5 minutes.

- Set the expected timestamp format as yyyyMMddHHmmss.

- Set the delimiter as the underscore character: _.

- Leave all the other parameters at their default values.

> **Note**
>
> You can specify the time zone in which the timestamp for the new data is recorded. To prevent any delicate debugging, I recommend, if possible, working only in the UTC time zone and making sure your data generation pipeline enforces this.

This input configuration tells the Amazon Lookout for Equipment scheduler to look for new CSV files located in an `input` folder on Amazon S3. Each CSV file will have the following format:

`<COMPONENT>_yyyyMMddHHmmss.csv`

Here, `<COMPONENT>` is the name of the component as defined in the dataset data schema (see *Chapter 9*, *Creating a Dataset and Ingesting Your Data*). The component and the timestamp are delimited by an underscore (_) (as defined in the **Delimiter** parameter you just set). The timestamp located in this filename also takes the (`yyyyMMddHHmmss`) format you just configured and will be set to the time at which the file was generated.

7. In the next section, you configure the output location where the inference results will be stored. When configuring this parameter, enter the S3 location for the output directory that you created earlier (you can fill in the S3 path manually or click **Browse** to look for it).

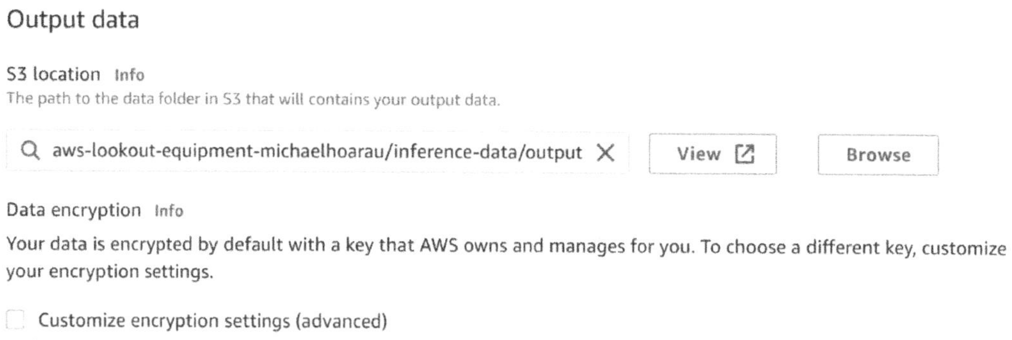

Output data

S3 location Info
The path to the data folder in S3 that will contains your output data.

Q aws-lookout-equipment-michaelhoarau/inference-data/output ✕ | View ☐ | | Browse |

Data encryption Info

Your data is encrypted by default with a key that AWS owns and manages for you. To choose a different key, customize your encryption settings.

☐ Customize encryption settings (advanced)

Figure 11.10 – Scheduler output data configuration

8. You will then need to fill in the role that Amazon Lookout for Equipment will use to access the data in the S3 locations configured earlier for the input and output data. Select **Enter a custom IAM role ARN** and paste the ARN of the `LookoutEquipmentIndustrialPumpDataAccess` role that you created in *Chapter 9, Creating a Dataset and Ingesting Your Data*, using the IAM service. The format of the ARN should be `arn:aws:iam::<ACCOUNT-NUMBER>:role/LookoutEquipmentIndustrialPumpDataAccess`, where `<ACCOUNT-NUMBER>` needs to be replaced by your AWS account number. Click on **Schedule inference** to create your scheduler.

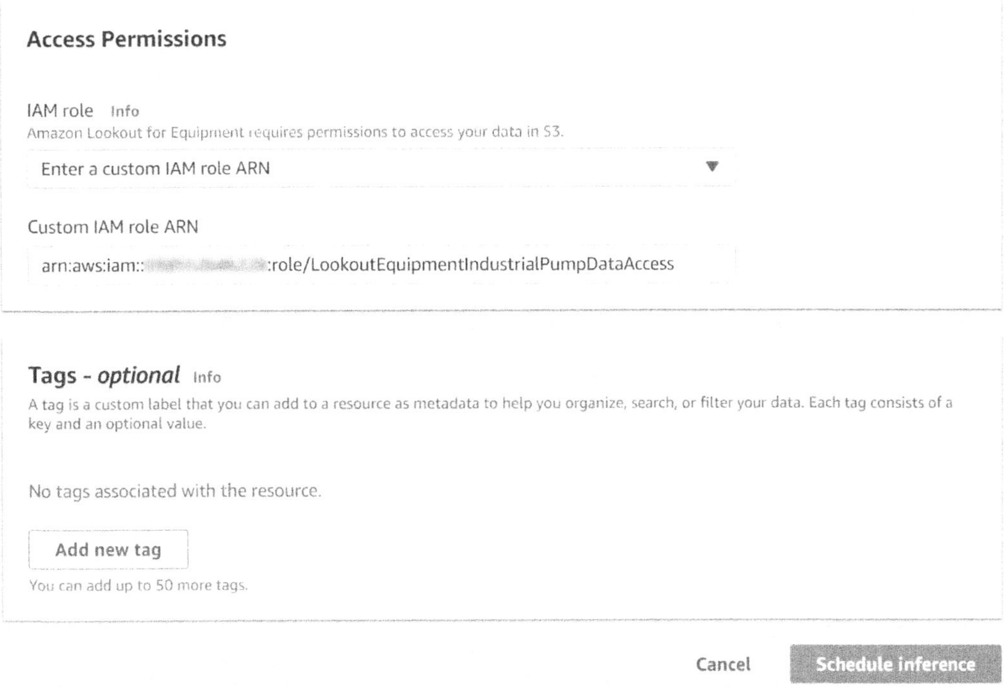

Access Permissions

IAM role   Info
Amazon Lookout for Equipment requires permissions to access your data in S3.

Enter a custom IAM role ARN   ▼

Custom IAM role ARN

arn:aws:iam:: ▓▓▓▓ :role/LookoutEquipmentIndustrialPumpDataAccess

Tags - *optional* Info
A tag is a custom label that you can add to a resource as metadata to help you organize, search, or filter your data. Each tag consists of a key and an optional value.

No tags associated with the resource.

Add new tag

You can add up to 50 more tags.

Cancel   Schedule inference

Figure 11.11 – Scheduler S3 access permission

9. You are brought back to the model dashboard. Under the model details section, click on the **Inference schedule** tab to bring up the scheduler dashboard.

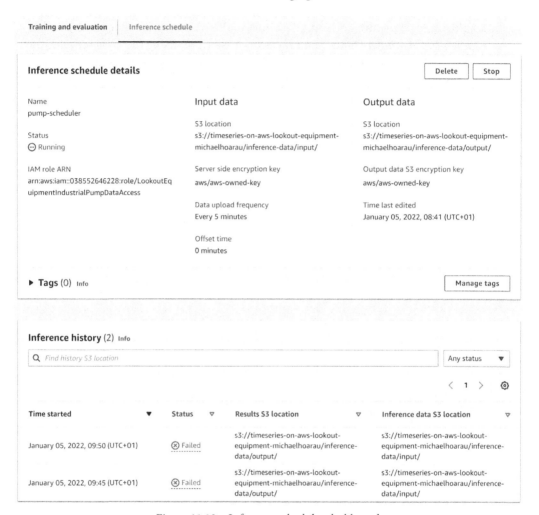

Figure 11.12 – Inference scheduler dashboard

Note that after a few minutes (at least 5 as we configured the scheduler to run every 5 minutes), you will see some failed inference execution in the **Inference history** section of this dashboard. This is perfectly normal, as no new data has been pushed in the input location that this scheduler is monitoring. Let's now generate some suitable input data!

Preparing a dataset for inference

An Amazon Lookout for Equipment inference schedule runs on a tight schedule. You just configured one to be run every 5 minutes. Let's say you just finished this configuration at 10:38. The next times the scheduler will run are 10:40, 10:45, 10:50... until you stop the scheduler. In this section, you will do the following:

- Learn what happens when a scheduler wakes up.
- Use CloudShell to prepare some inference data ready to be processed by your scheduler.

Understanding the scheduled inference process

Let's say your scheduler wakes up at 10:40 on September 24, 2021. This scheduler will first look for every CSV file in your input location with a timestamp corresponding to this time in their name: 20210924104000.

As a reminder, the dataset schema you used when creating your initial dataset was the following:

Data schema Info

The data schema is metadata that describes your dataset to Lookout for Equipment. It contains the folder name for each .csv file (Component), the header names in each .csv file (Name), and the data type for each column (Type).

```
 1  {
 2     "Components": [
 3       {
 4          "ComponentName": "sensor_43",
 5          "Columns": [
 6            {
 7               "Name": "Timestamp",
 8               "Type": "DATETIME"
 9            },
10            {
11               "Name": "sensor_43",
12               "Type": "DOUBLE"
13            }
14          ]
15       },
16       {
17          "ComponentName": "sensor_07",
18          "Columns": [
19            {
20               "Name": "Timestamp",
21               "Type": "DATETIME"
22            },
23            {
24               "Name": "sensor_07",
25               "Type": "DOUBLE"
26            }
```

Figure 11.13 – Dataset schema

We put each sensor into its own component. As a result, the scheduler will scout the input location on S3 for files whose names start with `sensor_43_` (remember that the delimiter we selected was the underscore character), `sensor_07_`, and so on.

If we put these two pieces of information together (expected component name and expected timestamp), a scheduler waking up at `10:40` on `September 24, 2021` will look for the following files:

- `sensor_00_20210924104000.csv`

- `sensor_01_20210924104000.csv`

- `...`

- `sensor_50_20210924104000.csv`

As we had 50 components defined in our datasets, it will expect to find 50 CSV files following the same naming scheme.

> **Important Note**
>
> If a component does not have any value at any given timestamp, the scheduler will still look for a file for it. You will have to put an empty file (just the header with no other row) for this component to prevent a scheduler execution from failing.
>
> Also note that if a given component does not have any value at a given timestamp, Amazon Lookout for Equipment will forward fill the sensor values for this component based on the last existing value found in the previous timestamps. At the time of writing, this forward filling process should go up to 12 hours in the past.

Once Amazon Lookout for Equipment finds these files, it will open them and look for new data with a timestamp ranging from the previous scheduler execution and the current one. For instance, when opening the `sensor_43_20210924104000.csv` file, it will extract *only* the rows where the timestamps are between `2021-09-24 10:35:00` and `2021-09-24 10:40:00`. Every other row will be discarded.

> **Important Note**
>
> To consider that some data may be flowing from one CSV file to another, Amazon Lookout for Equipment opens three files for each component. The one corresponding to the wake-up time (`10:40` in our previous example), the one before (corresponding to `10:35`), and the one after (corresponding to `10:45`). It will look for rows with the appropriate timestamps (still between `2021-09-24 10:35:00` and `2021-09-24 10:40:00`) in these three files and discard everything else.

As you can see, to properly test the scheduler you configured earlier, you will need to generate some CSV files with the precise timestamps corresponding to your scheduler execution times. This is what you are going to generate, using a script that you will run from CloudShell.

Preparing the inference data

Preparing inference data manually can be a highly error-prone activity. In this section, you are going to use the CloudShell service to run a script that will generate this data and push it to Amazon S3 for you. Let's go through the following instructions:

1. Log in to your AWS console.

2. At the top right of your console, make sure **Region selector** is located in one of the regions where Amazon Lookout for Equipment is available; either **Europe (Ireland)**, **US East (N. Virginia)**, or **Asia Pacific (Seoul)**.

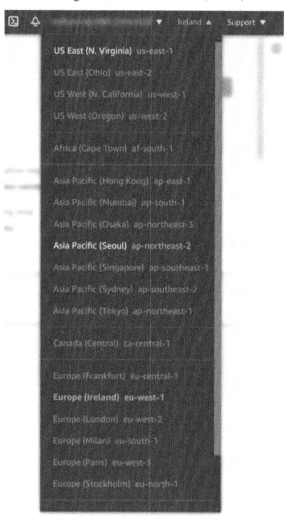

Figure 11.14 – AWS console region selector

3. Once your region is selected, click on the **CloudShell** icon located not far to the left of the region selector.

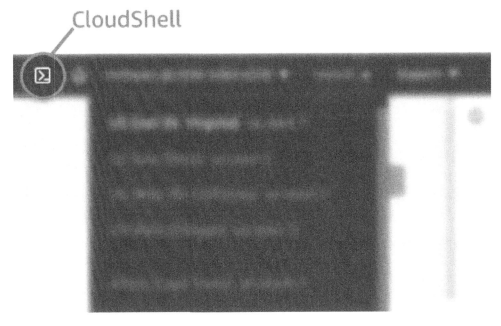

Figure 11.15 – Locating the CloudShell icon

4. When clicking on the **CloudShell** icon, a new tab is opened in your browser. If you don't have a CloudShell session already opened, you should see a blue ribbon stating that your environment is in preparation. After a minute, your environment is ready and you are presented with a Linux command prompt.

Figure 11.16 – Your CloudShell environment is ready!

5. Now, run the following commands in this terminal (don't forget to replace `<<YOUR_BUCKET>>` with the name of your own bucket before you copy the following piece of code):

```
python3 -m pip install --quiet pandas
```

```
wget https://packt-publishing-timeseries-on-aws-
michaelhoarau.s3.eu-west-1.amazonaws.com/part2-amazon-
lookout-for-equipment/lookout-for-equipment.zip
```

```
unzip lookout-for-equipment.zip
```

```
wget https://github.com/PacktPublishing/Time-Series-
Analysis-on-AWS/blob/main/Chapter11/generate_inference_
data.py
```

```
python3 generate_inference_data.py
```

```
aws s3 cp --recursive inference-data/input/ s3://<<YOUR_
BUCKET>>/inference-data/input/
```

This script downloads the original training data and extracts a snippet from it to generate 15 minutes' worth of inference data (enough for three successful executions). Once your data is uploaded, go back to the scheduler dashboard to confirm that the next scheduler run is successful. If everything went well, you should see your last execution run marked as successful.

Figure 11.17 – Successful scheduler run

6. You can let your scheduler run thrice (as the generator from *step 5* produces enough inference data for 15 minutes) before stopping it (this will stop the incurring cost of the scheduler). To do this, on the scheduler dashboard, you can just click on the **Stop** button, located at the top right of this section.

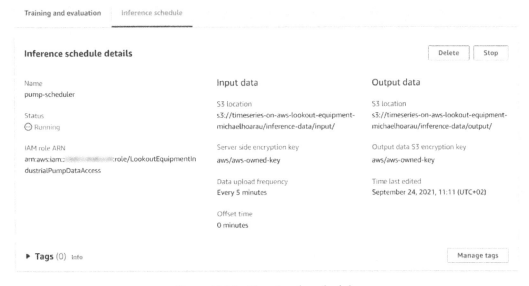

Figure 11.18 – Stopping the scheduler

At this stage, you have successfully run a scheduler. Now let's see how you can download and visualize the results.

Extracting the inference results

In the previous section, you let your scheduler run thrice. The results from any successful inference will be stored in the output location on S3 that you configured at the beginning of this chapter. Let's download one of these files and look at its content:

1. Log in to your AWS console.

2. At the top left of your console, you will see a **Services** drop-down menu that will display all the available AWS services. In the **Storage** section, look for the **S3** service and click on its name to go to the S3 console.

3. Navigate to your bucket and then to `inference-data` and finally to `output`. Each inference execution creates a new directory named after the timestamp at which the scheduler woke up.

Figure 11.19 – Inference scheduler output content

4. In this directory, you will find a single file named `results.jsonl`. This is a JSON-line file. Click the checkbox next to its name and click on the Download button.

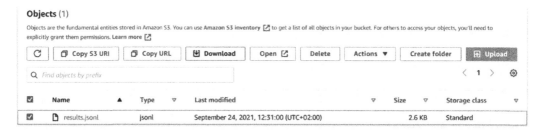

Figure 11.20 – Inference scheduler JSON-line result file

5. Once this file is downloaded on your local computer, open it with a text editor to inspect its content:

```
{
    "timestamp": "2021-09-24T10:30:00.000000",
    "prediction": 1,
    "prediction_reason": "ANOMALY_DETECTED",
    "diagnostics": [
        {"name": "sensor_43\\sensor_43", "value":
0.08642},
        {"name": "sensor_07\\sensor_07", "value":
0.00526},
        {"name": "sensor_25\\sensor_25", "value":
0.00049},
        [...]
```

```
          {"name": "sensor_42\\sensor_42", "value":
 0.11554}
      ]
 }
```

Each line in this file is a proper JSON object that contains the following fields:

- timestamp: The timestamp of the data point that was sent to the trained model to get the associated prediction.

- prediction: This field will either be 1 (an anomaly is detected) or 0 (no anomaly is detected).

- prediction_reason: This is a text equivalent of the prediction field. At the time of writing this book, the only values this field can take are ANOMALY_DETECTED or NO_ANOMALY_DETECTED.

> **Note**
>
> Both the prediction_reason and prediction fields provide the same information with a different format. Initially, only the prediction field was provided. The prediction_reason field was added later to provide a forward compatibility with future features to be deployed. For instance, the service might provide additional insights about the classification of the anomaly in the future. These pieces of information will be provided in text format, whereas the prediction field will stick to 0 and 1 values. If you intend to automate a workflow based on the presence of an anomaly or not, I recommend that you use the prediction field and not prediction_ reason.

- diagnostics: When an abnormal behavior is detected and the prediction is 1, this field will contain a diagnostics list. The diagnostics field is a list with the name of the sensors and the weight of each sensor's contribution in indicating this abnormal behavior. For each sensor, two fields are available: the name field (with the name of the sensor including the component it's attached to) and the value field (with the sensor's contribution to the prediction value).

Each run of the scheduler will generate a single results.jsonl file. You can concatenate all of them to build real-time dashboards showing the latest events detected, or you can react to the presence of a prediction value of 1 to trigger notifications. In *Chapter 12, Reducing Time to Insights for Anomaly Detections*, you will see an example showing how you can visualize these results in a more user-friendly way, to accelerate the decision-making processes associated with any anomaly detection systems.

Summary

In this chapter, you learned how to use a trained model to schedule regular inferences. You learned how to prepare an S3 bucket and how to configure an inference scheduler to monitor said bucket.

This chapter was also important to help you understand the sequence of actions a scheduler runs when it wakes up: this will be critical when you will need to prepare your input data so that it can be detected and used appropriately. You also learned where the results of the inference are stored and how you can interpret them.

In the next chapter, you are going to dive deep into how you can interpret the results of Amazon Lookout for Equipment anomaly detection models and reduce the time it takes to process these insights.

12
Reducing Time to Insights for Anomaly Detections

In the previous chapters, you learned how to prepare multivariate datasets, how to train and evaluate an anomaly detection model, and how to configure an inference scheduler. To get the most from Amazon Lookout for Equipment, you can partner with a data engineer or a data scientist who will help you improve your model performance and go further in the post-processing of results.

The main objectives of this chapter are to point you in the right direction to visualize and monitor your models. This will be very valuable to detect any drift that would trigger either retraining or further investigation. In addition, you will learn how to build an automation pipeline, which will be critical to iterate as fast as possible without having to manually navigate through multiple console screens.

In this chapter, we're going to cover the following main topics:

- Improving your model's accuracy
- Processing the model diagnostics

- Monitoring your models

- Orchestrating each step of the process with a serverless architecture

Technical requirements

No hands-on experience in a language such as **Python** or **R** is necessary to follow along with the content from this chapter. However, we highly recommend that you read this chapter while connected to your own AWS account and open the different AWS service consoles to run the different actions on your end.

To create an AWS account and log in to the Amazon Lookout for Equipment console, you can refer to the technical requirements of *Chapter 2, An Overview of Amazon Forecast.*

Improving your model's accuracy

In *Chapter 10, Training and Evaluating a Model,* you trained an anomaly detection model and visualized the outputs over an evaluation period. Depending on what your business objectives are, here are several areas you may want to improve the obtained results:

- *Too many false positives*: After evaluating the events triggered by Amazon Lookout for Equipment against reality, you might see some events as false positives you would like to discard.

- *Too many false negatives*: In some cases, you might know about some anomalous events that were not detected in the evaluation period.

- *No or too short forewarning time*: Sometimes, anomalies are detected but too late and you want to get a longer forewarning time so that your end users have enough time to take the appropriate mitigation actions.

Reducing the occurrences of these situations will increase the trust your end user puts in the insights provided by the service and increase the added value you get from it. Every situation, piece of equipment, or industrial process is different and you will likely have to work closely with a subject matter expert to improve your anomaly detection models. Here are a few areas of investigation I have found useful when it comes to anomaly detection/prediction model improvement:

- Reducing the number of signals

- Using the off-time conditions

- Selecting the best signals

Let's start by looking at how you can reduce the number of signals to train a model.

Reducing the number of signals

Amazon Lookout for Equipment can build models with up to 300 signals. However, the more time series signals you use, the more likely you will generate some multivariate noise, making it difficult for a machine learning model to capture what is a normal operating condition and what is the normal variability of a given process.

If you start training with many signals, identify which signals are often present in the signals ranking from the Amazon Lookout for Equipment dashboard and try to train with the top 15 or 30 signals. In the following screenshot, you can see that the top 12 signals have a 50% contribution to a particular event that lasted more than 50 hours. Looking at other significant events in your evaluation period will help you select the signals that keep coming up whenever an event is detected.

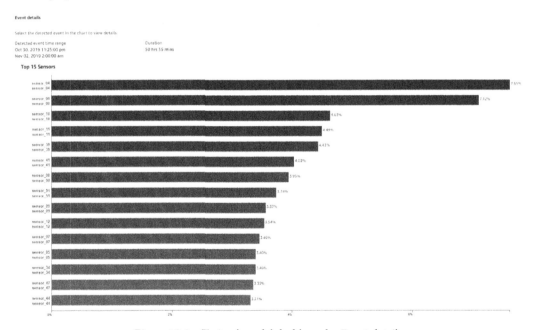

Figure 12.1 – Trained model dashboard – Event details

You may also keep only the signals whose feature importance is higher than the average. If you have 50 signals, 100% / 50 = 2% is actually the feature importance each signal would have if they were contributing equally to any given event. Any signal with a significantly higher contribution than 2% will be a good candidate to keep for a second version of your model.

Using the off-time conditions

When training a model, Amazon Lookout for Equipment allows you to select a signal that will be used to identify when a process or a piece of equipment is off, as shown in the following screenshot:

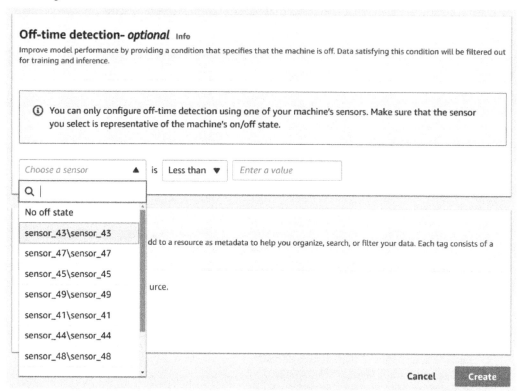

Figure 12.2 – Off-time detection feature

When you configure this parameter, Lookout for Equipment will remove the signals from these periods as they are not relevant to find any anomalies. If you leave this data while training, the periods where your asset or process is down will likely be marked as anomalies and you will end up with many false positives.

Selecting the best signals

Not all time series signals have good predictive power when it comes to anomaly detection. Plot and visualize the top signals that contribute to your most important events. Look especially for signals that support the following behavior:

- **Many missing values**: This might indicate a sensor failure or a data collection issue. Although this may be a valid situation to investigate, you may want to drop these sensors when your train a new model.

- **Constant values**: This situation is very similar to the previous ones. Signals with constant values do not add any value to the modeling. However, if such a signal were to start evolving differently in the future, this would be easily picked up by Amazon Lookout for Equipment. Consider dropping this type of signal if you are confident this won't happen.

- **Categorical data**: In most anomaly detection settings, many false positives will be triggered if your categories are imbalanced. I recommend not using these signals as is. You might want to use them for additional preprocessing or to engineer new features of interest.

- **Chaotic behavior**: Some measurements may be all over the place without any steady behavior that's easy to capture. These kinds of signals add a lot of noise that makes it hard for an anomaly detector to separate what is normal from abnormal. Consider dropping these signals.

- **Monotonically increasing**: This might indicate a measurement such as operating hours or be linked to how long an asset has been running. I recommend that you avoid using these types of sensors.

- **Seasonal data**: Some signals may be impacted by seasonality. In this case, make sure you include enough data in the training period to visualize a whole cycle. For instance, if your data displays yearly seasonality, consider training over at least a year to capture this behavior.

- **Level shifts**: When the evaluation period displays *normal* operating modes that are different from the training period, Amazon Lookout for Equipment will likely fire up many anomalies. Consider changing the train/evaluation split to capture the additional operating modes of interest.

Once you are happy with the signals you have discarded, you can train a new model while using most of the training period and reducing the evaluation period to 1 day (this is the minimum you can set at the time of writing this book). This will ensure your model is built with the freshest data at inference time.

Processing the model diagnostics

When you train an anomaly detection model with Amazon Lookout for Equipment, you can visualize the results obtained over an evaluation period. These results are available in the console and you can also query an API to integrate and further post-process these results for your own needs.

At inference time, the inference scheduler reads new data from an input location on Amazon S3 and outputs the model results in an output location. Each inference execution creates a new directory named after the timestamp at which the scheduler woke up and each directory contains a single file in JSON Lines format. In *Chapter 11, Scheduling Regular Inferences*, you learned how to locate, download, and interpret the results contained in these files.

In this section, you will use a CloudFormation template that will deploy a CloudWatch dashboard that you can use to visualize training and inference results from Amazon Lookout for Equipment. You will then see how you can use these dashboards. The last part of this section will be dedicated to using these dashboards to derive more insights from the raw Lookout for Equipment results.

Deploying a CloudWatch-based dashboard

As a first step, make sure you log in to the AWS Console. Once this is done, and depending on the AWS region where you are using Amazon Lookout for Equipment, you can click on one of the following links to start the deployment process:

- US East (N. Virginia): `https://tinyurl.com/vp3da3t2`

- Europe (Ireland): `https://tinyurl.com/vj3kcdx5`

- Asia Pacific (Seoul): `https://tinyurl.com/44e4ua48`

After you have clicked on one of the previous links, you will be brought to the **Create stack** screen from the **AWS CloudFormation** console. To continue with your deployment, follow these steps:

1. Start by clicking **Next** at the bottom of the first screen.

2. On the parameters page, you will have to fill in the following:

   - **Stack name**: Let's call our stack `LookoutEquipmentDashboard`.

   - **SnapshotBucket**: A name for the bucket where the dashboard snapshots and temporary files will be collected. Remember that your bucket name must be unique across all the accounts of the AWS Cloud. Add a random string at the end of the name you choose if you get an error telling you your bucket already exists at deployment time.

   - **SnapshotRuns**: The frequency (daily or weekly) at which the inference dashboard snapshot will be taken and sent by email.

   - **TargetEmail**: The email where the snapshots will be sent.

3. The target email must be registered in **Amazon Simple Email Service** (**SES**). To do this, take the following steps:

   I. Open a new tab or window in your browser and navigate to the SES console. You can use the **Services** dropdown located at the top of any AWS Console page and search for **Amazon Simple Email Service** in the **Business Applications** section.

   II. In the left menu, click on **Verified identities** and then click on **Create identity**.

   III. Select **Email address** and fill in the address you want to use. Click **Create identity**.

   IV. You will shortly receive an email in your inbox: click on the link to verify your address.

4. Once you have registered your email address, go back to the tab with your CloudFormation parameters and click the **Next** button.

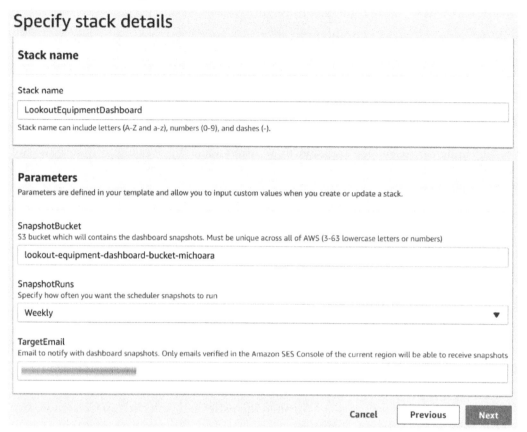

Figure 12.3 – Parameters for the Lookout for Equipment dashboard deployment

5. The next page will also be fine with the default values. Click **Next** to proceed to the **Review** page. Scroll again to the bottom, check the box to enable the template to create new IAM resources, and then click on **Create stack**.

6. CloudFormation will take a few minutes to create all the resources on your behalf. Once it is completed, you will see a green **CREATE_COMPLETE** message next to the name of the stack (on the left panel of the CloudFormation console), indicating that the deployment is completed, as shown in the following screenshot:

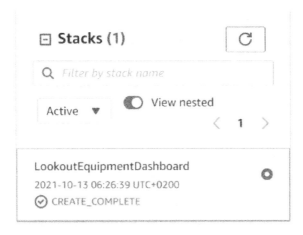

Figure 12.4 – Template deployed

After deployment, the following resources will have been deployed in your account.

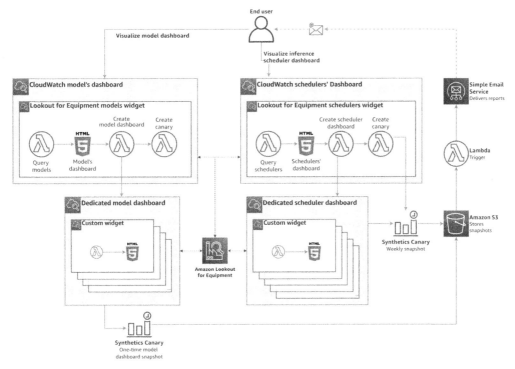

Figure 12.5 – Lookout for Equipment dashboard deployment overview

Now that the template is deployed, you can start using it immediately.

Using the Lookout for Equipment dashboards

Once the template is deployed, use the **Services** drop-down menu on the top left of the screen to bring up the list of AWS services. In the **Management & Governance** section, look for the **CloudWatch** service and click on its name to go to its console. There, click on the **Dashboards** link on the left menu bar. This will bring you to a page with a list of all the CloudWatch dashboards you have access to in your account, as shown in the following screenshot. You should find two new dashboards that you are going to use to visualize your Amazon Lookout for Equipment models and schedulers.

Figure 12.6 – New CloudWatch dashboards

You can use the dashboard with a name starting with **Lookout-for-Equipment-Models** to manage the models trained in Amazon Lookout for Equipment in your account. The other dashboard will let you do the same with any schedulers configured in your account.

Using the model dashboard

Click on the dashboard with a name starting with **Lookout-for-Equipment-Models**. This will open a dashboard summarizing all the models that exist in your account.

> **Important Note**
> This dashboard uses the **CloudWatch Custom Widget** feature, which calls a Lambda function in the background to display custom plots. The first time you open such a dashboard, you will see a warning message asking you if you trust these functions before executing them. Click on the **Execute them all** button located at the top right of the dashboard to run these functions and plot the widget's content.

By default, only the last 50 models trained in the past 3 months are shown, as follows:

Dataset	Model	Training status	Model dashboard	
chiller	chiller-model	SUCCESS	Create	View
deep-dive-demo-expander	deep-dive-demo-expander-model	SUCCESS	Create	View
demonstration	demonstration-model	SUCCESS	Create	View
equipment-asset1	model-asset1-63b165be-b431-4ce8-94fd-8bed71b21e33	FAILED	No model found	
equipment-asset2	model-asset2-2f959ce3-c6e8-49f8-9d91-c36f7a24b4d1	FAILED	No model found	
my_dataset	my_model	SUCCESS	Create	View
-	my_model2	SUCCESS	Create	View
-	my_model3	FAILED	No model found	

Figure 12.7 – Lookout for Equipment model dashboard

> **Important Note**
> Ensure you are running this CloudWatch dashboard in the same AWS region where you created your models.

You can use the date picker on the top right of your screen to limit the models shown. This date picker will use the model training date to filter which ones to display. In this widget, your models' information will be displayed as follows:

- The first column will list all the *datasets* from the current AWS region in your account.

- The *model names* are listed in the second column. If several models are built using the same dataset, the dataset name is shared between them and is not repeated.

- In the third column, a *training status* will let you know whether this model was successfully trained. Only successful training will give you access to the actions of the fourth column.

- The last column gives you two possible actions to perform on successfully trained models:

  - You can request the *creation of a specific dashboard* for a trained model. This will create a new CloudWatch dashboard specifically for this model and will also configure and start a **CloudWatch Synthetics** canary that will send you a dashboard screenshot to the email you configured when you deployed the CloudFormation template. The dedicated model dashboard and the Synthetics creation can take a few seconds. Then the model list dashboard will be refreshed and the **View** button will be enabled.

  - The **View** button is enabled when a dashboard exists for a given model (the **Create** button will then be disabled). Click on this button to navigate to this model's specific CloudWatch dashboard.

When you click on the **View** button of any trained model, you are brought to another CloudWatch dashboard dedicated to this model. Several widgets will be preconfigured for each of these dashboards:

- Model details

- Detected anomalies

- Aggregated signal importance

- Signal importance evolution

To read more about the insights you can derive thanks to these widgets, check out the *Post-processing detected events results in building deeper insights* section.

Using the scheduler dashboard

From the CloudWatch dashboard home page, click on the dashboard with a name starting with **Lookout-for-Equipment-Schedulers**: this will open a dashboard summarizing all the schedulers that exist in your account. As with the model dashboard, only the last 50 schedulers created in the current AWS region in the past 3 months are shown by default, as shown in the following screenshot:

Lookout for Equipment - Schedulers list ☑

Model	Scheduler	Status	Scheduler dashboard
demonstration-model	demonstration-scheduler	Start	View
my_model	my_scheduler	Start	Create dashboard
well-1622A3-2020-06-12	scheduler-1	Start	Create dashboard

Figure 12.8 – Lookout for Equipment scheduler dashboard

From this dashboard, you can either **Start** or **Stop** the schedulers.

Important Note

Bear in mind that running schedulers incurs costs: do not forget to stop a scheduler that you have no more use for.

As with the trained models' evaluation, you can also request the creation of a specific dashboard dedicated to a scheduler. When you create a scheduler's dashboard, you also create a CloudWatch Synthetics canary that will send you a weekly (or daily) dashboard screenshot to the email you configured when you deployed the CloudFormation template. This canary is configured by default to run every Monday morning at 6 a.m. UTC (or on every workday morning at 6 a.m. UTC if you chose the daily option).

The CloudWatch dedicated dashboard and Synthetics canary can take a few seconds to create, then the scheduler list dashboard will be refreshed, and the **View** button will be enabled.

When you click on the **View** button of an existing inference scheduler, you are brought to another CloudWatch dashboard dedicated to this scheduler. A couple of widgets are preconfigured:

- Scheduler details
- Last execution diagnostics

In the following section, you will read more about the insights you can derive from these widgets.

Post-processing detected events results in building deeper insights

In this section, you will read about the kind of insights you can derive from post-processing the raw results delivered by Amazon Lookout for Equipment.

Model details

This widget just gives you a reminder of the dataset name, the training period, and the evaluation period, as shown in the following screenshot:

pump-anomaly-detection-model | Model details

Dataset	Training start	Training end	Evaluation start	Evaluation end
industrial-pump	2018-04-01 00:00:00	2018-10-31 00:00:00	2018-11-01 00:00:00	2020-05-04 00:00:00

Figure 12.9 – Model details example

Detected anomalies

The detected anomalies are displayed for the evaluation period of the selected model. The dropdown at the top of the widget lets you select which signal you want to plot above the **Detected anomalies** ribbon to help you relate a given time series behavior with the actual events detected by Amazon Lookout for Equipment.

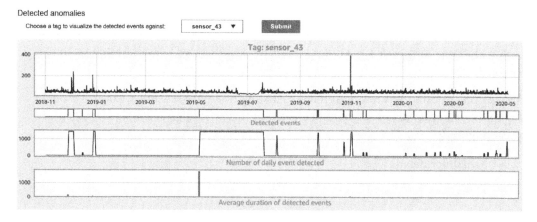

Figure 12.10 – Detected anomalies example

This widget also plots the following:

- The number of daily events detected: In some situations, you will see the number of events gradually increase before reaching a maximum value. This may be a good indicator of a potential future anomaly.

- The average duration of the detected events.

Aggregated signal importance

This horizontal bar chart aggregates the average importance of up to 15 signals *across the evaluation period*.

While the native console from Amazon Lookout for Equipment lets you click on every event detected to plot the associated signal importance, this plot lets you understand whether there is a systematic bias toward the same sensors when any event is detected.

In the following screenshot, you can see that **sensor_51** is contributing, on average, a lot more than the other signals to the events detected. Plotting this signal will help you understand why this particular sensor has such a large contribution. It may also be an indicator that the sensor behavior is quite noisy and should be removed to train a more robust model.

Aggregated signal importance

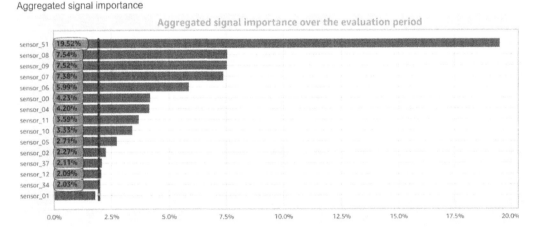

Figure 12.11 – Aggregated signal importance example

The vertical dotted line (located around 2% in the preceding screenshot) materializes the value that each signal importance would have if they were all equally contributing to every anomaly detected. The dataset illustrated here had 50 signals. If every signal was contributing the same way, they would each be ranked at approximately 1/50 = 2.0%. We can now say that the higher contributions from the top 5 signals are definitely statistically significant.

Every signal higher than the black dotted line will have a red bar, whereas the other ones will have a green bar.

Signal importance evolution

The last widget plots the evolution of the feature importance of each signal over time. When numerous events are detected, this plot can become very crowded. At this stage, the feature importance is aggregated at the daily level to help better understand the dynamics of each signal, as shown in the following screenshot:

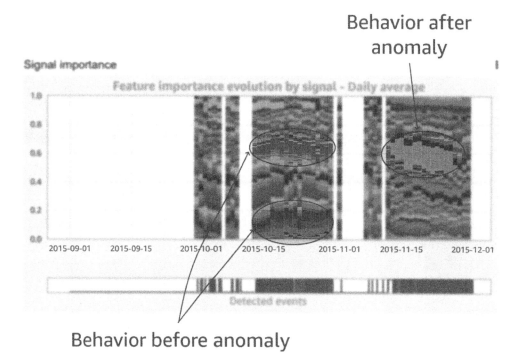

Figure 12.12 – Signal importance evolution example

In the preceding screenshot you can see the following:

- During the period ranging from 2015-10-15 to 2015-11-01, you can actually see a different dynamic than during the last period.

- This widget will help you understand whether it is possible to match the signal contributions' relationships to different types of failure. Using these as high-quality features leading to anomaly classification will help you further reduce the analysis time for your end users.

Scheduler details

This widget reminds you of the scheduler name and how it is configured.

It also details what it expects as an input (the format and location of the input CSV file to run the inference with). This can be useful when you run into issues with a scheduler that doesn't seem to find your fresh data.

demonstration-scheduler | Inference scheduler details

Input	s3://sagemaker-lookout-equipment-demo/demo/inference-data/input/
Output	s3://sagemaker-lookout-equipment-demo/demo/inference-data/output/
File format	*<component>*_yyyyMMddHHmmss.csv
Next execution	• Current time is **2021-10-13 05:50:31** • Next execution time: **2021-10-13 05:55:00** • Next file: ***<component>*_20211013055000.csv** • Timestamps must be between **2021-10-13 05:50:00** and **2021-10-13 05:54:59**
Last execution	• Executed **12** times • Last execution time: **2021-08-31 13:30:00** • Last successful execution: **2021-08-31 13:30:00**

Figure 12.13 – Scheduler details example

Last execution diagnostics

This widget displays the signal ranking for the last anomaly caught by Amazon Lookout for Equipment, as shown in the following screenshot:

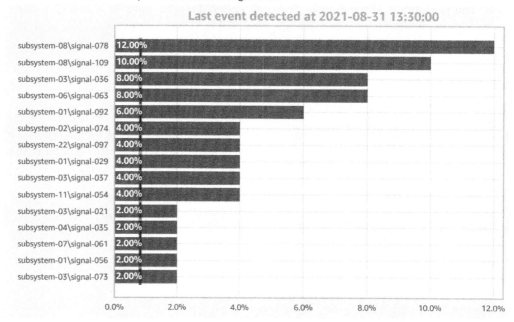

Figure 12.14 – Last execution diagnostics example

With these dashboards, you are now equipped to visualize your Lookout for Equipment results quickly and derive valuable insights to help you improve the way you operate the monitored assets or processes. Let's now have a look at some of the best practices you can leverage to monitor your models and detect any drift once your models are deployed.

Monitoring your models

You should also make sure to monitor any potential shift in your data. To do this, you can follow this process:

1. Build and store a dataset with the training data of all the time series that you want to use to build an anomaly detection model.

2. Compute the statistical characteristics of each time series (for example, average, standard deviation, and histograms of the distribution of values).

3. Train your models with these initial datasets and save the performance metrics (how well they capture the anomalies you are interested in).

4. When new data comes in, compute the same statistical characteristics and compare them with the original values used at training time.

5. You can display these statistics next to the predictions for your analysts to take the appropriate decisions. This will help them better trust the results generated by Amazon Lookout for Equipment. In particular, visualizing a potential distribution shift from training to inference time will help pinpoint whether the model should be retrained with new, fresh data or whether something must actually be investigated from a process perspective.

Once you have this process set up, you will be able to organize regular reviews to analyze any shift in the data or any drift in the performance of your anomaly detection models to decide when is a good time to amend your training datasets and retrain a fresh model.

Automating your training process will be key to making this continuous improvement task as painless as possible. In the next section, you will configure a pipeline that will be able to automatically orchestrate this process.

Orchestrating each step of the process with a serverless architecture

In the preceding chapters, you have been working mainly with the Amazon Lookout for Equipment console, building each step mostly manually. In this section, you will learn how you can build an automatic workflow that will take care of all these steps and inform you when it is finished. You will implement and deploy the components shown in the following screenshot:

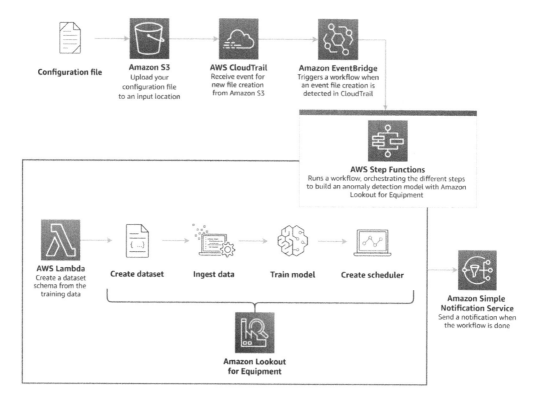

Figure 12.15 – Amazon Lookout for Equipment automation diagram

To achieve this, we will focus on the implementation of each key part of this architecture diagram. Namely, we will dive into the following:

1. First, you will get an overview of the **AWS Step Functions** orchestration service.

2. Then you will build the key components of your Step Functions workflow (leveraging an **AWS Lambda** function and orchestrating the different **Amazon Lookout for Equipment** tasks).

3. To trigger your workflow automatically, you will need to know about other AWS cloud services. We will go through a high-level description of **AWS CloudTrail** and **Amazon EventBridge** and you will configure them to enable the automatic trigger of your Step Functions workflow when a new file is uploaded in an Amazon S3 bucket containing your training data.

4. Finally, you will use **Amazon Simple Notification Service**, which will send you an email when your workflow is done (either successfully or not).

You will have the option to implement most of these components yourself so that you get a good understanding of each of these components and how they are articulated with each other.

Assembling and configuring the AWS components

In this section, you will learn how to build and configure each service to automate your anomaly detection training workflow. Let's start with an overview of the different services that you will need to use (beyond **Amazon Lookout for Equipment** and **Amazon S3**, with which you are already familiar):

- **AWS Step Functions**: This is a low-code visual workflow service that you can use to orchestrate AWS services and automate any business process. Using this service, you can manage failures, service integrations, and focus on your business logic. You are going to use this service to orchestrate the different steps needed to build a dataset, train a model, and configure an inference scheduler.

- **AWS Lambda**: This is a computing service that lets you run your code without provisioning and managing any underlying services or infrastructure. You will write a Lambda function that will build the dataset schema based on the actual training data located in an Amazon S3 bucket.

- **AWS CloudTrail**: This service monitors and records account activity across all your infrastructure and services. It records every API call so that you can react to them. You will configure a trail that will monitor your S3 bucket and trigger an event when a new configuration text file is uploaded at the root of your bucket.

- **Amazon EventBridge**: This serverless event bus makes it easy to connect event-driven applications using events generated by your applications or any AWS services. You will use EventBridge to trigger your workflow or send a notification whenever this workflow goes through a status change.

- **Amazon Simple Notification Service**: This messaging service can be used to send messages between applications or between applications and persons. You will use this service to send notifications whenever your training and deployment workflow goes through a status change.

Equipped with this overview, you can now head safely into the first step of your automation journey: assembling the model training and deployment workflow.

Building the anomaly detection workflow

Let's now build the following part of our automation architecture:

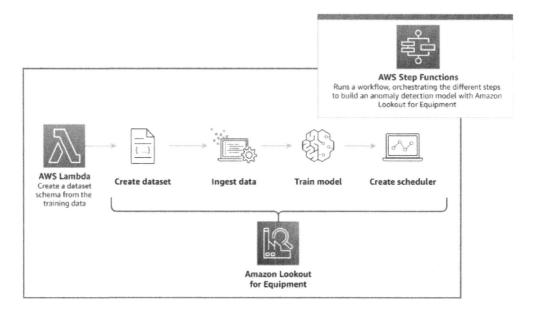

Figure 12.16 – Automation pipeline, focusing on the Step Functions

First, we need to create the Lambda function, which will be used to build a data schema to create a dataset in Amazon Lookout for Equipment. As an input, the step function will receive the location of the data and this location will be passed to the AWS Lambda function. This Lambda function will need the same access to the data located in S3 as Amazon Lookout for Equipment. Let's start by updating your access role.

Updating the access role

You will need to update the IAM role you created in *Chapter 9, Creating a Dataset and Ingesting Your Data*, and you will then need to create your Lambda function. To do all of this, follow these steps:

1. If you went through the *Technical requirements* prerequisites at the beginning of this chapter, you should already be logged in to the AWS console, otherwise, fire up your favorite browser and log in to the AWS console.

2. At the top left of your console, you will see a **Services** drop-down menu that will display all the available AWS services. In the **Security, Identity & Compliance** section, look for the **IAM** service and click on its name to go to the IAM console. On the left menu bar, click on the **Roles** menu and then search for your `LookoutEquipmentIndustrialPumpDataAccess` role in the list on the right.

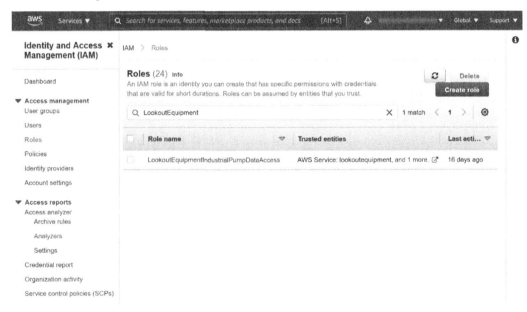

Figure 12.17 – IAM role list

3. Click on the name of your role and then click on the **Trust relationships** tab. Then, click on the **Edit trust relationship** button.

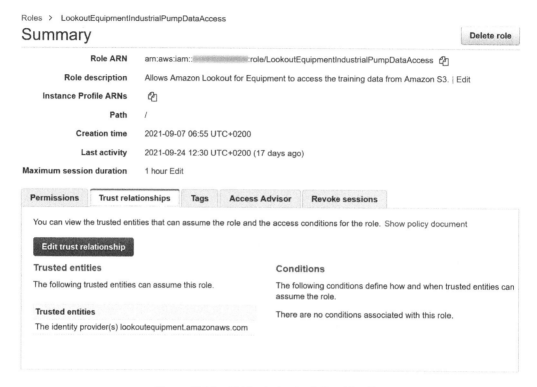

Figure 12.18 – IAM role trust relationships list

4. Update the policy document from your role with the following code. Notice the additional service (`lambda.amazonaws.com`) that must be allowed to assume this role and access your data in Amazon S3:

```
{
    "Version": "2012-10-17",
    "Statement": [
        {
            "Sid": "",
            "Effect": "Allow",
            "Principal": {
                "Service": [
                    "lookoutequipment.amazonaws.com",
                    "lambda.amazonaws.com"
```

```
            ]
        },
            "Action": "sts:AssumeRole"
        }
    ]
}
```

5. Click on the **Update trust policy** button. This will bring you back to the role overview.

Your role is now up to date and ready to be used by the AWS Lambda service.

Creating the Lambda function

You can now create the first component of your workflow, namely, a Lambda function that will create the appropriate data schema in JSON format for an input location on Amazon S3. To do so, you will need to follow these steps:

1. Use the **Services** drop-down menu at the top left of the screen to bring up the list of AWS services. In the **Compute** section, look for the **Lambda** service and click on its name to go to the AWS Lambda console. By default, you should see a list with all the functions available in your account, otherwise, click on the **Functions** item in the left menu bar. Then, click on the **Create function** button.

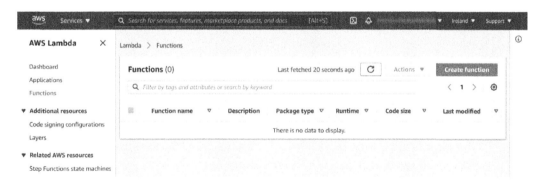

Figure 12.19 – AWS Lambda console landing page

2. Next, you will author a new function from scratch (called `create-lookout-equipment-schema`) and you will fill in the following fields on the function creation page:

    - **Function name**: Let's call this function `create-lookout-equipment-schema`.

    - **Runtime**: You will use **Python 3.9**.

    - Select **Use an existing role** for **Execution role**.

    - In the **Existing role** dropdown, select the `LookoutEquipmentIndustrialPumpDataAccess` role you updated earlier.

    At the bottom right of this screen, you will find a **Create function** button; click on it to go to the next page.

3. On the next page, at the top right of the **Code source** section, there is an **Upload from** drop-down list. Click on it and select **Amazon S3 location**.

Figure 12.20 – Uploading a Lambda function from Amazon S3

4. In the window appearing there, enter the following URL pointing to the code this function will run and click on the **Save** button:

    ```
    s3://packt-publishing-timeseries-on-aws-michaelhoarau/
    part2-amazon-lookout-for-equipment/create-lookout-
    equipment-schema.zip
    ```

> **Important Note**
> Make sure to be in the same region as your initial S3 bucket when creating your Lambda function with this zip package. If not, you will see a region-related error.

5. You are then brought back to the **Code** tab from your Lambda function, where your source code should be updated. Click on the **Configuration** tab and then on the **Edit** button at the top right.

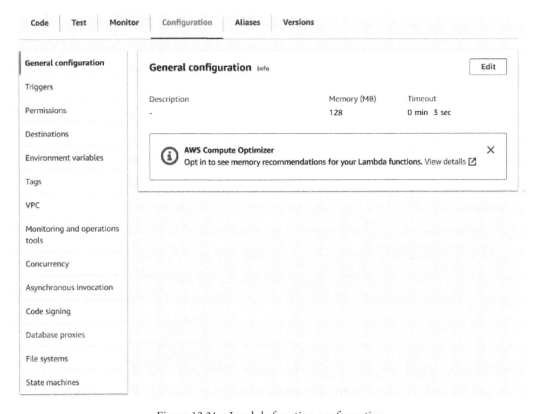

Figure 12.21 – Lambda function configuration

6. Enter 256 MB for **Memory** and select 10 seconds for Timeout. This should be enough for the processing that happens in this function (mainly opening the first row of several CSV files to look for their header content). Then, click on the **Save** button.

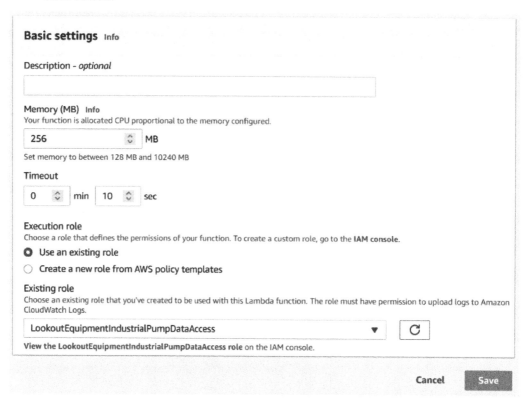

Basic settings Info

Description - *optional*

Memory (MB) Info
Your function is allocated CPU proportional to the memory configured.

| 256 | ⌃⌄ | MB |

Set memory to between 128 MB and 10240 MB

Timeout

| 0 | ⌃⌄ | min | 10 | ⌃⌄ | sec |

Execution role
Choose a role that defines the permissions of your function. To create a custom role, go to the **IAM console**.

⦿ Use an existing role

◯ Create a new role from AWS policy templates

Existing role
Choose an existing role that you've created to be used with this Lambda function. The role must have permission to upload logs to Amazon CloudWatch Logs.

| LookoutEquipmentIndustrialPumpDataAccess | ▼ | ↻ |

View the **LookoutEquipmentIndustrialPumpDataAccess** role on the IAM console.

Cancel   Save

Figure 12.22 – Lambda function basic settings

7. When you are back to the Lambda function overview, click on the **Copy ARN** button located at the top right of the screen and paste it into a text file that you will keep handy for the next section (where you will create a workflow starting with this function). Your ARN will have a format similar to this: `arn:aws:lambda:eu-west-1:<<ACCOUNT-ID>>:function:create-lookout-equipment-schema` (where `<<ACCOUNT-ID>>` will be replaced by the ID of your AWS account).

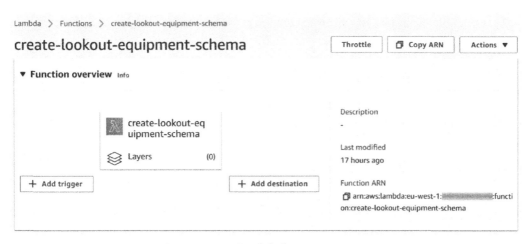

Figure 12.23 – Lambda function overview

We have now configured a Lambda function and can now configure the actual workflow.

Building the workflow

We will build the actual workflow, using the AWS Step Functions service. To do so, let's follow these steps:

1.   Use the **Services** drop-down menu at the top left of the screen to bring up the list of AWS services. In the **Application Integration** section, look for the **Step Functions** service and click on its name to go to the AWS **Step Functions** console. Click on the hamburger menu (the three horizontal lines) at the top left of the window and then click on the **State machines** tab and finally, on the **Create state machine** button.

Figure 12.24 – State machines list

2. On the **Define state machine** screen, select **Write your workflow in code** at the top and select the **Standard** type.

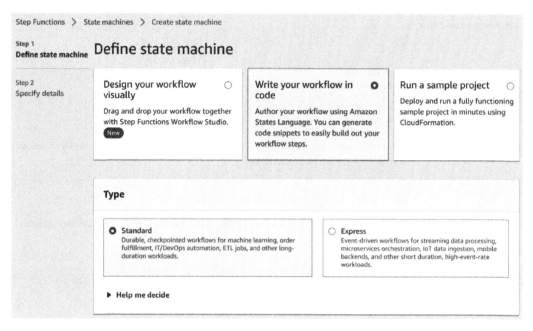

Figure 12.25 – State machine definition

3. Download the following file:

    https://packt-publishing-timeseries-on-aws-michaelhoarau.
    s3.eu-west-1.amazonaws.com/part2-amazon-lookout-for-
    equipment/lookout-equipment-automation-step-function.json

4. Open the preceding text file and search for the following string: <<LAMBDA_ ARN>>. Replace this string with the ARN of the Lambda function you copied previously (at the end of the Lambda function definition).

5. Copy the whole content of your text file (with the updated Lambda function ARN) into the **Definition** area of your state function. The workflow on the right is updated with the actual flow of the state machine.

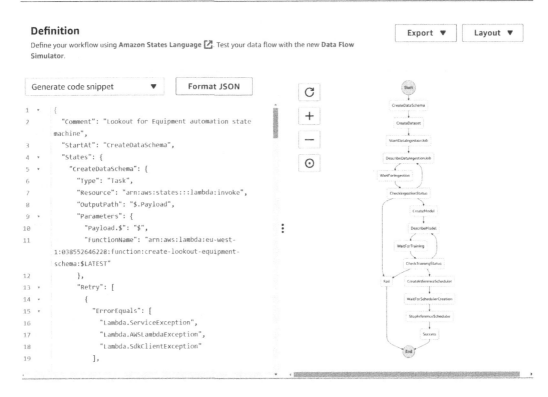

Figure 12.26 – State machine definition

6. Click on the **Next** button located at the bottom right. This will bring up a second screen where you will be able to specify other details for your workflow.

7. On the next screen, you can specify a name for your state machine. I called mine `LookoutEquipmentAutomationPipeline`. Leave all the other fields as their default values and click on the **Create state machine** button located at the bottom of your screen.

8. This will bring you to a screen with the details of your newly created state machine. Click on the **Edit role in IAM** button at the top to update the role used by the state machine so that it can call the Amazon Lookout for Equipment API function.

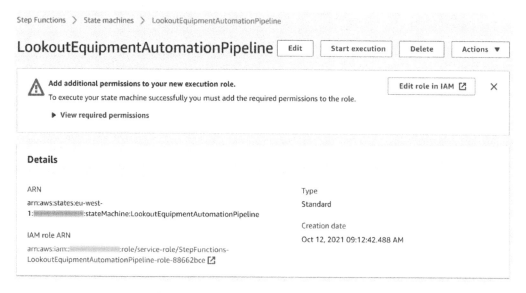

Figure 12.27 – State machine details

9. The default role created by the AWS Step Functions service will have the ability to call the Lambda function but is not authorized to call the Amazon Lookout for Equipment API (as a reminder, for security reasons, AWS services only have permissions that you explicitly give them). On the Roles **Permissions** tab, click on **Attach policies**.

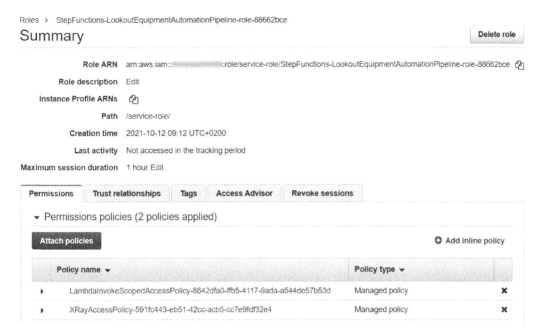

Figure 12.28 – State machine default role definition

10. Search for the `LookoutEquipment` string in the **Filter policies** field at the top of the screen and check the box next to **AmazonLookoutEquipmentFullAccess**. Then, click on the **Attach policy** button located at the bottom of the screen:

Figure 12.29 – Attaching a new policy to the state machine role

In this section, you performed the following tasks:

1. You updated the role you already used to access data in Amazon S3 to allow a Lambda function to assume this role.

2. Then, you created a Lambda function that is used to create a valid data schema ready to be used by Amazon Lookout for Equipment to create a new dataset.

3. You then proceeded to create a state machine (or workflow) in AWS Step Functions to orchestrate the different steps in your automation pipeline.

4. You finished the process by making sure your workflow has all the permissions it needs to call Lambda functions and Amazon Lookout for Equipment API methods.

You will now set up an automatic trigger to react to a new file uploaded to an S3 bucket: this trigger will launch the workflow you just defined.

Configuring the automatic trigger

We will now build the following part of our automation pipeline:

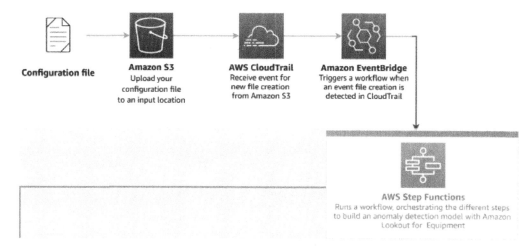

Figure 12.30 – Automation pipeline, focusing on the trigger step

You already have an Amazon S3 bucket that you have been using to store your training and inference data. We are going to create a trail in AWS CloudTrail that will log every event happening in this bucket. To do this, follow these steps:

1. Use the **Services** drop-down menu at the top left of the screen to bring up the list of AWS services. In the **Management & Governance** section, look for the **CloudTrail** service and click on its name to go to its console. From the service dashboard, click on the **Create trail** button.

2. For **Trail name**, enter `LookoutEquipmentAutomationS3Event`.

3. Disable the **Log file SSE-KMS encryption** checkbox if you do not want to encrypt the log files of the trail (if you do, you will have to provide an encryption key). Scroll down to click on the **Next** button.

4. On the second step of the trail creation, uncheck the **Management events** checkbox and check the **Data events** checkbox.

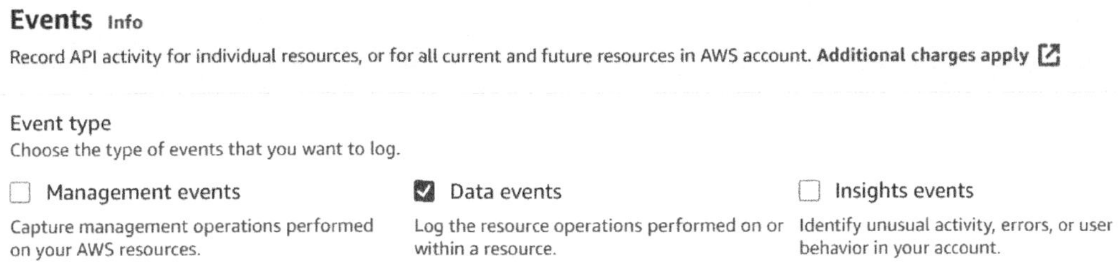

Events Info

Record API activity for individual resources, or for all current and future resources in AWS account. **Additional charges apply** [↗]

Event type
Choose the type of events that you want to log.

☐ Management events	✅ Data events	☐ Insights events
Capture management operations performed on your AWS resources.	Log the resource operations performed on or within a resource.	Identify unusual activity, errors, or user behavior in your account.

Figure 12.31 – Events type selection for new trail creation

5. In the **Data event** section of the screen, select **S3** for **Data event source** and uncheck the **Read** and **Write** checkboxes for **All current and future S3 buckets**. Then, under **Individual bucket selection**, fill in the name of your bucket and add / `config-` after your bucket name. In my case, I will use the following value for this parameter: `timeseries-on-aws-lookout-equipment-michaelhoarau/ config-`. This will tell CloudTrail that we only want to monitor events associated with the uploading of a file with a name that starts with `config-` and located at the root of our bucket. Then, just check the **Write** boxes (we only want to detect when a new file is created).

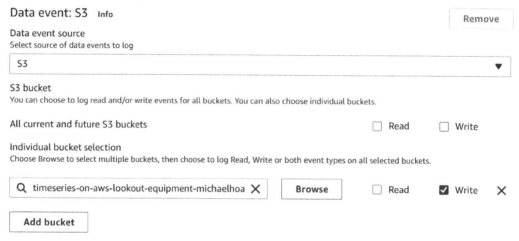

Figure 12.32 – Data event configuration

6. Scroll down and click on the **Next** button at the bottom. As the last step, scroll all the way down and click on **Create trail**.

Now that a trail has been configured, all the events captured in this trail are also sent to **Amazon EventBridge**.

Configuring Amazon EventBridge

Let's now navigate to Amazon EventBridge to actually catch this event and trigger our workflow:

1. Use the **Services** drop-down menu at the top left of the screen to bring up the list of AWS services. In the **Application Integration** section, look for the **Amazon EventBridge** service and click on its name to go to its console. From the service home page, click on the **Create rule** button.

2. Give a name to your rule: `Lookout Equipment Pipeline Trigger`.

3. In the **Define pattern** section, select the **Event pattern** radio button and then **Pre-defined pattern by service**. Select **AWS** for the **Service provider** field, **Simple Storage Service (S3)** for **Service name**, and **Object Level Operations** for **Event type**:

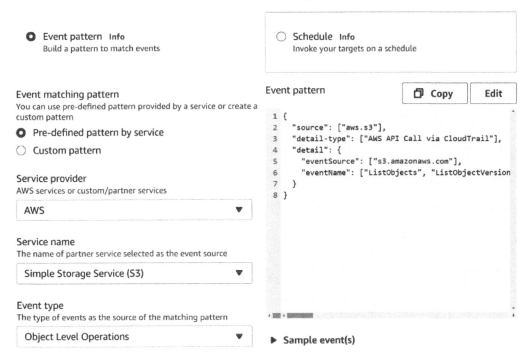

Figure 12.33 – EventBridge pattern definition

4. Select the **Specific operation(s)** radio button and select the **PutObject** operation from the drop-down list. Then, select **Specific bucket(s) by name** and fill in the name of your bucket (`timeseries-on-aws-lookout-equipment-michaelhoarau` in my case).

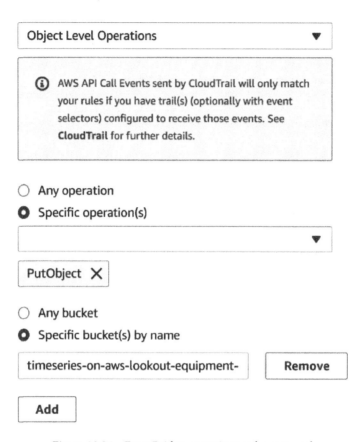

Figure 12.34 – EventBridge operations to be captured

5. Scroll down to the **Select targets** section of the screen. Select **Step Functions state machine** for **Target** and choose `LookoutEquipmentAutomationPipeline` in the **State machine** dropdown. Leave all the other parameters untouched (including the new role creation).

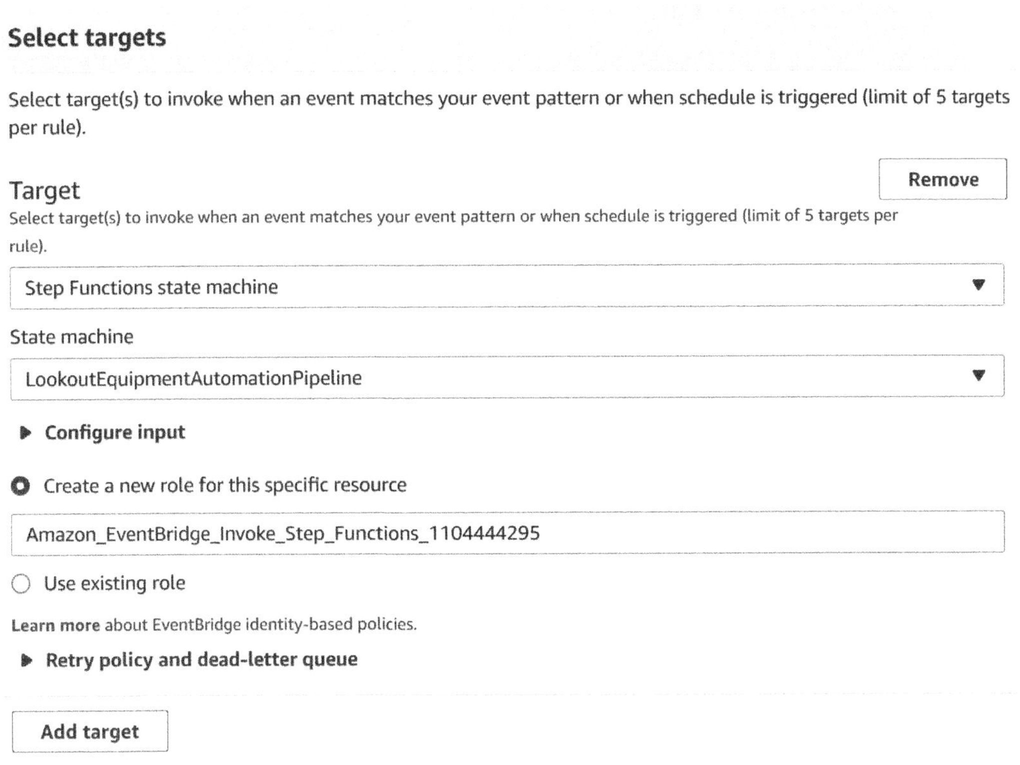

Select targets

Select target(s) to invoke when an event matches your event pattern or when schedule is triggered (limit of 5 targets per rule).

Target

Select target(s) to invoke when an event matches your event pattern or when schedule is triggered (limit of 5 targets per rule).

Remove

```
Step Functions state machine                                              ▼
```

State machine

```
LookoutEquipmentAutomationPipeline                                        ▼
```

▶ **Configure input**

⦿ Create a new role for this specific resource

```
Amazon_EventBridge_Invoke_Step_Functions_1104444295
```

○ Use existing role

Learn more about EventBridge identity-based policies.

▶ **Retry policy and dead-letter queue**

```
Add target
```

Figure 12.35 – EventBridge target selection

6. Scroll to the bottom of the screen and click on the **Create** button.

Your trigger is now ready. The last step is to set up a notification once the step function is done.

Configuring the notification

We will now build the last part of our architecture, the notification service configuration. To achieve this final task, you will once again use Amazon EventBridge and use it to send a message to an **Amazon Simple Notification Service** (**SNS**) queue each time your workflow status changes. To do this, you can take these actions:

1. Use the **Services** drop-down menu at the top left of the screen to bring up the list of AWS services. In the **Application Integration** section, look for **Simple Notification Service** and click on it to go to its console. From the service home page, set **Topic name** to LookoutEquipmentWorkflowStatusUpdate and click on the **Next step** button.

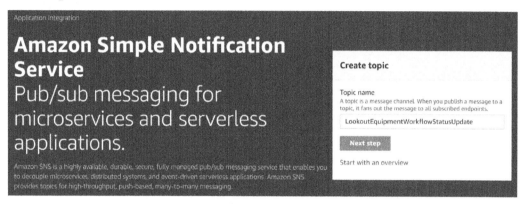

Figure 12.36 – Creating a new SNS topic

2. On the next screen, leave all the fields as their default values, scroll down to the bottom of the page, and click on the **Create topic** button. Your topic will be created and a summary dashboard will be displayed. In the **Subscriptions** section, click on **Create subscription**.

3. In the **Details** section of the **Create subscription** screen, enter **Email** for **Protocol** and your email address for **Endpoint**.

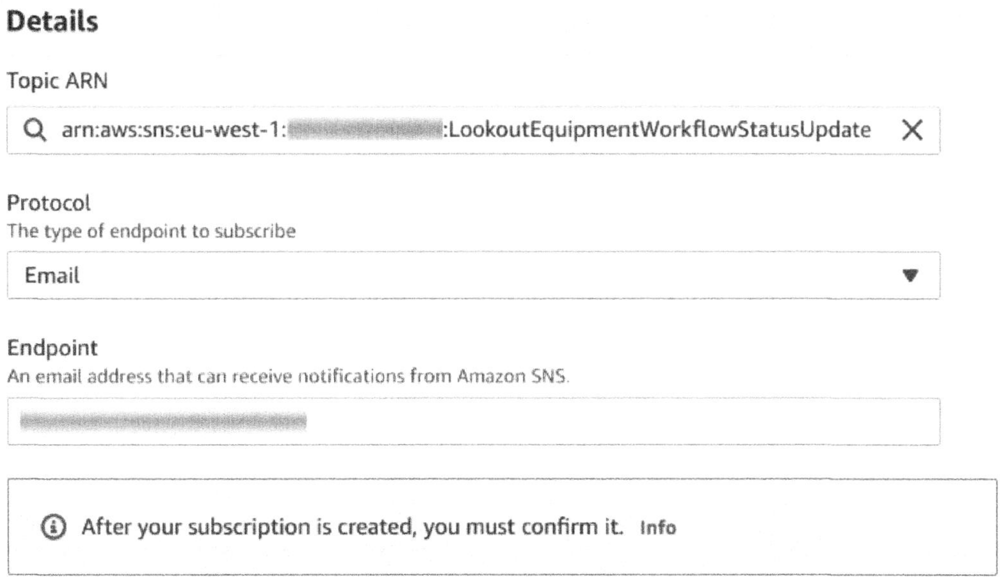

Details

Topic ARN

Q arn:aws:sns:eu-west-1:▓▓▓▓▓▓▓▓:LookoutEquipmentWorkflowStatusUpdate   ✕

Protocol
The type of endpoint to subscribe

| Email   ▼ |

Endpoint
An email address that can receive notifications from Amazon SNS.

▓▓▓▓▓▓▓▓▓▓▓▓▓▓▓▓▓▓▓

ⓘ After your subscription is created, you must confirm it. **Info**

Figure 12.37 – Creating a subscription to an existing SNS topic

4. Scroll down and click on the **Create subscription** button. You will receive an email after a few seconds with the subject titled *AWS Notification – Subscription Confirmation*. Click on the **Confirm subscription** link that you will find in this message: your email address is now subscribed to this SNS topic. This means that any message sent to this topic will be delivered to your email address.

Now that your notification delivery is configured, you will go back into Amazon EventBridge to connect your workflow status change to this topic. To do this, follow these steps:

1. Use the **Services** drop-down menu at the top left of the screen to bring up the list of AWS services. In the **Application Integration** section, look for the **Amazon EventBridge** service and click on its name to go to its console. From the service home page, click on the **Create rule** button.

2. Give a **Name** to your rule: `LookoutEquipmentPipelineStatusChange`.

3. In the **Define pattern** section, select the **Event pattern** radio button and
    then **Pre-defined pattern by service**. Select **AWS** for **Service provider**,
    Step Functions for **Service name**, and **Step Functions Execution Status
    Change** for **Event type**. Then, select **Specific state machine ARN(s)** and
    enter the ARN of the workflow you created earlier. This ARN will have
    the following format: `arn:aws:states:eu-west-1:<<ACCOUNT_`
    `ID>>:stateMachine:LookoutEquipmentAutomationPipeline`, where
    `<<ACCOUNT_ID>>` is your AWS account ID.

4. Scroll down to the **Select targets** section of the screen. Select **SNS Topic** for **Target**
    and choose `LookoutEquipmentWorkflowStatusUpdate` in the **Topic**
    dropdown. Leave all the other parameters untouched (including the new role
    creation).

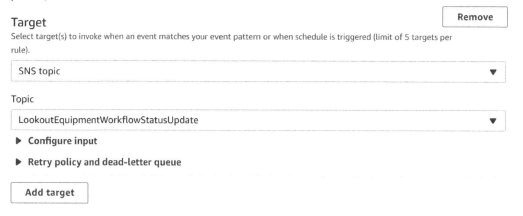

Figure 12.38 – Event target definition

5. Click on the **Create** button at the bottom of the page to create your event.

Your notifications are now ready to be triggered. Let's test your pipeline!

Testing the pipeline

Your automation pipeline is ready – let's test it! Open your favorite text editor and write
the following in it:

```
{
    "train_prefix": "train-data/",
```

```
    "label_prefix": "label-data/",
    "sampling_rate": "PT5M",
    "dataset_name": "pump",
    "model_name": "pump_model",
    "scheduler_name": "pump_scheduler",
    "access_role": "LookoutEquipmentIndustrialPumpDataAccess",
    "training_start": "2018-04-01",
    "training_end": "2018-10-31",
    "evaluation_start": "2018-11-01",
    "evaluation_end": "2020-05-04"
}
```

Then, to test your pipeline, you will follow these steps:

1. Save this file under the name `config-example.txt` (or any name that starts with `config-`).

2. Connect to the AWS Console and navigate to the Amazon S3 service. Find your bucket and click on its name.

3. Upload the text file you just created at the root of your bucket. Your bucket files list should look similar to the following screenshot:

Figure 12.39 – Amazon S3 bucket files list

4. Navigate to the AWS Step Functions console and click on the name of the state machine you created earlier. In the **Executions** list section, you should see an execution with the **Running** status. Click on this execution.

5. In the **Graph inspector** section, you should see your process running and, after a while, your process should be successful with all the steps highlighted and marked as successful.

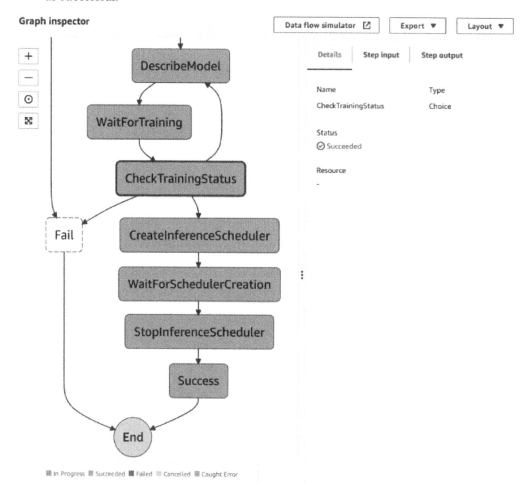

Figure 12.40 – Successful automation pipeline

6. Check your email. You should have received two new messages, one when your workflow started running, and the other when the workflow was done.

> **Note**
>
> We did not customize the content of the notification email: they are rather nondescript for a non-developer as you receive the actual JSON payload as a raw notification. In an actual production system for business users, you might want to customize these emails to make them more user friendly. You would achieve this by expanding the **Configure input** section when you define the target in Amazon EventBridge. There, you can select **Input transformer** to transform this JSON raw data into an actual English sentence.

Congratulations for reaching the end of this section! You now have all the tools to automate a whole anomaly detection pipeline for your industrial time series!

Summary

In this final chapter dedicated to Amazon Lookout for Equipment, you learned how to build dashboards that will be useful to get detailed visualizations of your model and inference results. You also built your first automation pipeline, to let the AWS orchestration services do all the heavy lifting for you while you focus on the model results.

This chapter was especially important to understand how to improve your anomaly detection models and how to automate most of the tasks to iterate as fast as possible.

In the next chapter, you will switch to another anomaly detection managed service, but dedicated to business metrics instead of industrial time series: Amazon Lookout for Metrics.

Section 3: Detecting Anomalies in Business Metrics with Amazon Lookout for Metrics

In this last section, you will focus on operational and business metrics and train an anomaly detector for univariate time series data. You will also create automated alerts to send notifications whenever an anomaly is detected in your live data.

This section comprises the following chapters:

13

An Overview of Amazon Lookout for Metrics

In this chapter, you will learn what Amazon Lookout for Metrics is designed for, how it works, and the kind of situations it is best suited for. By the end of this chapter, you will also have a good command of the underlying concepts manipulated by Amazon Lookout for Metrics (dataSPACE sources, datasets, detectors, alerts, and anomalies).

Along with Amazon Forecast and Amazon Lookout for Equipment, Amazon Lookout for Metrics is one of AWS' **artificial intelligence (AI)/machine learning (ML)** managed services dedicated to problems structured around time series data. Amazon Lookout for Metrics is an anomaly detection service dedicated to finding and diagnosing outliers in business and operational metrics.

In this chapter, we're going to cover the following main topics:

- Recognizing different types of anomalies

- What is Amazon Lookout for Metrics?

- How does Amazon Lookout for Metrics work?

- Identifying suitable metrics for monitoring

- Choosing between Lookout for Equipment and Lookout for Metrics

Technical requirements

No hands-on experience with a language such as **Python** or **R** is necessary to work with the content of this chapter. However, we highly recommend that you follow along in the AWS Console, from where you can access the Amazon Lookout for Metrics service.

If you already have an AWS account, you can connect to the AWS Console, click on the search bar at the top, enter `Lookout for Metrics` in the services section, and then click on **Amazon Lookout for Metrics** to bring up the landing page of the service console.

To create an AWS account and log in to the Amazon Lookout for Metrics console, you can refer to the *Technical requirements* section of *Chapter 2, An Overview of Amazon Forecast*.

You should now be ready to use Amazon Lookout for Metrics! But before we dive into an overview of the service, let's first have a look at the challenges posed by detecting anomalies in business metrics.

Recognizing different types of anomalies

Before we dive into Amazon Lookout for Metrics, I recommend that you read a few definitions first. If you need a refresher about what different types of anomalies look like in time series data, you can read the *What are the different approaches to tackle anomaly detection?* section at the beginning of *Chapter 8, An Overview of Amazon Lookout for Equipment*. This paragraph will give you an overview of the different types of anomalies we can find in time series data, along with a description of the different approaches we can use when building a custom outlier or anomaly detection system from scratch.

If you head over to the Amazon Lookout for Metrics home page (`https://aws.amazon.com/lookout-for-metrics`), you will read that it uses ML techniques to automatically detect anomalies that are defined as outliers from the norm. Amazon Lookout for Metrics looks for deviations in live or real-time univariate time series data. The keyword in this description is **outlier**. In statistics, an outlier is a value that differs significantly from other observations. Not all outliers are anomalies though:

- **The outlier can be an anomaly**: If you are monitoring the sales figures for multiple products on your e-commerce website and see a sudden spike of warm scarves in the middle of summer, you may safely assume this is not normal behavior. Making the decision to add more scarves to your inventory at this time of the year may not be a reasonable decision based on this unique data point.

- **The outlier can be an expected value**: In the previous example of an e-commerce website, you might see a spike for many products before Christmas or around Thanksgiving. These sales values may differ significantly from the median value of your usual sales figures, but they are expected. If you provide enough data (several years) to an ML model, it might start learning about this exceptional behavior and won't react to it. On the contrary, if your sales do not spike around Thanksgiving in a given year, this may well be called an outlier (and definitely an anomaly!).

- **The outlier can belong to a different population**: Let's say you are selling smart weather stations that people can put in their gardens or on their balconies. You also provide a mobile application where your customers can actually see the temperatures (among other data) from every weather station in the city. If you're in France in the fall, you expect daily temperatures to range from 5°C to 10°C in the morning. If you see some locations with temperatures ranging between 20°C and 22°C, an outlier detection system will definitely spot them. However, after investigation, you might find out that some customers position their weather station in their child's bedroom to make sure they keep comfortable. In this case, these values are neither outliers nor anomalies, they are just part of a sample (customers using the weather station in their house) that differs from the rest of your population (customers using the weather station outside).

Amazon Lookout for Metrics detects outliers and gives you the explainability tools to help you make decisions about outliers and anomalies with a consideration of these different possible alternatives. Let's now dive into what Amazon Lookout for Metrics does.

What is Amazon Lookout for Metrics?

Amazon Lookout for Metrics is one of the AI/ML managed services available on the AWS cloud platform. This service finds anomalies in your live real-time data, helps you pinpoint their root causes, and continuously improves by collecting your feedback. This service connects to your data sources and lets you create detectors that will monitor values from your data sources. Amazon Lookout for Metrics develops an understanding of your data over time to better capture anomalies. You can either let the service learn from the live data it starts analyzing when you connect a datasource (this training period might take from a few minutes to a day), or provide some historical training data to kickstart the learning process. Under the hood, Lookout for Metrics can leverage multiple algorithms and will select the best one based on your data.

Managed services are services where the end users only provide their data and configure some parameters to suit their needs. All the other tasks, *considered undifferentiated heavy lifting*, are performed on the users' behalf by the service. This includes the automation of all the infrastructure management. As an Amazon Lookout for Metrics user, you don't have to provision and manage virtual machines, configure user accounts, take care of security, plan for scalability if your request volume increases, or decommission unused resources.

In the case of AI/ML managed services, some data preparation, ingestion tasks, and model management activities are also performed under the hood, allowing you to focus primarily on the problem to be solved. Amazon Lookout for Metrics is a scalable managed service that automates the whole end-to-end anomaly detection pipeline from data ingestion to model deployment and serves inference results. The service also deals with data preparation under the hood. Amazon Lookout for Metrics can perform the following functions on your behalf:

- *Pick the best algorithm* based on your data characteristics: your data is unique and one single anomaly detection algorithm won't fit all types of data. Amazon Lookout for Metrics will learn your data behavior (is it sparse or spiky, or does it have some seasonality?) and choose the appropriate algorithm and model parameters based on these characteristics.

- *Perform hyperparameter tuning* to find the best parameters for you when the selected algorithm requires it.

- *Prepare the time series* so that they can be ingested by multiple algorithms: Amazon Lookout for Metrics can prepare time series sequences to feed a range of statistical and deep learning models.

- *Automatically consider the human-in-the-loop feedback* that end users can provide when they flag an anomaly as correct or not. Human feedback is immediately reflected in the Amazon Lookout for Metrics model in real time. By automating this step and providing an easy way to incorporate feedback, Amazon Lookout for Metrics reduces the risk of alert fatigue or missed anomalies.

- *No manual retraining decisions*: Amazon Lookout for Metrics *automatically takes the decision to retrain* its model on your behalf. The retraining process is automated and a model will retrain on its own when it detects the need. This doesn't require any human intervention, letting you focus more time on analyzing the results and providing timely feedback on Amazon Lookout for Metrics' insights. This dynamic way of working allows Amazon Lookout for Metrics to adapt to changing cycles in your business or operation data, discover and match seasonal trend changes to reduce false alerts, and improve accuracy over time.

- *Build root cause analysis reports* to provide actionable results users can provide feedback on.

Now that you have a good understanding of what Amazon Lookout for Metrics can do for you, let's dive deeper into how this service works.

How does Amazon Lookout for Metrics work?

In this section, you will learn how Amazon Lookout for Metrics works by first looking at the different concepts manipulated by the service. You will then dive deeper into how these concepts are orchestrated together to build **detectors** (this is what Lookout for Metrics calls its anomaly detection models). This section will then end with an overview of the pricing model used by this service.

Key concept definitions

To build models able to spot anomalies in your data, Amazon Lookout for Metrics uses the following concepts and resources:

- **Detector**: Amazon Lookout for Metrics trains ML models to detect outliers in your data. Such a model is called a *detector* in this service. A detector continuously learns from your data so that it gets better at understanding the normal behavior and any expected variability.

- **Datasource**: A datasource is a service that provides time series data that a detector can analyze. Each datasource must provide timestamped records with each record containing both metrics and (optionally) dimensions (the definition of these two concepts follows in this list). Amazon Lookout for Metrics can connect to multiple AWS services as well as third-party services able to integrate with **Amazon AppFlow** (Salesforce and Google Analytics being two examples).

- **Dataset**: Once a detector is connected to your datasource, it ingests a copy of your data and prepares it for analysis. The data ingested by Amazon Lookout for Metrics is stored in a *dataset*. A detector analyzes live continuous data to detect anomalies while learning your data's behavior from historical data. A dataset will contain both historical and continuous data.

- **Measure**: Each row in your dataset is called a **record** and a record can contain multiple key-value pairs (or labeled values) called **fields**. To be usable with Lookout for Metrics, your dataset must have at least *one timestamp field* and at least *one field to monitor*. The monitored field is called a **measure**.

- **Dimensions**: When choosing which field of your dataset will be a suitable measure to monitor, you can also select up to five additional fields that will be used to group measures based on the values of these additional fields. These fields are called *dimensions*. Let's say you are monitoring the sales of a given product across a country: `sales number` will be your measure. If you select another field that contains the city where the sales were made, `city` will be the dimension that will allow Lookout for Metrics to consider `sales number in Paris`, `sales number in New York`, and so on, as independent time series to monitor.

- **Metrics**: Once you have connected your detector to a datasource, you must select certain fields that will be your dataset's measures and additional ones that will be your dimensions. Each combination of measures and dimensions is called a *metric*. In the previous example, `sales number in Paris` and `sales number in New York` were metrics.

- **Severity score**: When an anomaly is detected by Amazon Lookout for Metrics, it ranks it using a *severity score*. This score is a number between 0 and 100, which is an indication of how far from the expected range a given metric value is.

- **Alert**: When a detector spots an anomaly, you can trigger an alert that will have a target such as a notification in an **Amazon Simple Notification Service (SNS)** topic, or more complex processing using an **AWS Lambda** function. This alert is sent when the severity score of an anomaly crosses a certain threshold (that you can configure): the alert will contain the record of the anomaly and you will be able to process it with the language of your choice (using AWS Lambda) or connecting it to any Amazon SNS subscriber that supports webhooks with this service (such as Slack).

- **Feedback**: When an anomaly is detected by a detector, it creates a report with the anomaly details. These details include all the metrics with unexpected values and packages them up in the Amazon Lookout for Metrics console. From there, you can provide your feedback on how relevant this anomaly is for each metric concerned. This feedback is immediately integrated into the model to improve its accuracy.

Let's now have a look at how all these concepts are used by Amazon Lookout for Metrics to train and run anomaly detection models.

Amazon Lookout for Metrics workflow overview

You do not need to provide any past labels to Amazon Lookout for Metrics to be able to start detecting anomalies in your dataset: the service can start its detection immediately in an unsupervised fashion using only your new live data (the model is trained online and keeps learning as it observes more and more data from your datasource). If you have historical data, you can bootstrap the training by providing it to Amazon Lookout for Metrics. In addition, when the first anomalies are detected, the service switches to semi-supervised mode by asking for your feedback about the detected anomalies and feeds your answers back to the service to gradually improve the model.

The following diagram illustrates how Amazon Lookout for Metrics orchestrates all these tasks together:

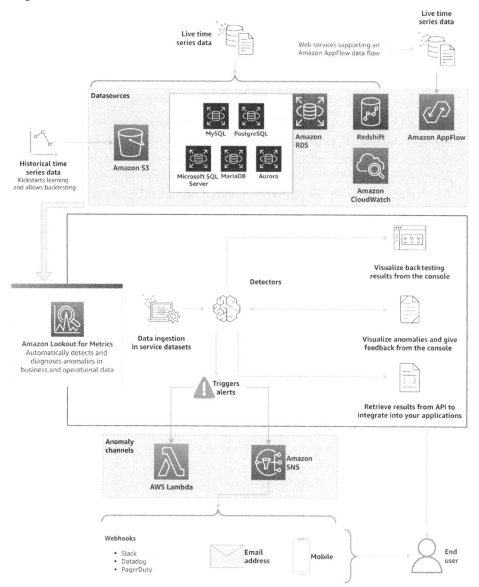

Figure 13.1 – Amazon Lookout for Metrics overview

Let's dive into this illustration to explain the different steps you have to go through to use Amazon Lookout for Metrics:

1. Connecting your data to a service that Amazon Lookout for Metrics can use as a datasource for either historical data or live data:

    A. Your *historical data* can be pushed to Amazon S3. If you want to use historical data to bootstrap Amazon Lookout for Metrics model training, you can only use Amazon S3 as a datasource to build a detector.

    B. Your *live time series data* can be available in a database hosted on Amazon **Relation Database Service** (**RDS**) or from Amazon Redshift (the data warehouse service from AWS). You can also use a metric coming from the AWS log service (Amazon CloudWatch) or collect your data from Amazon AppFlow. The latter can be connected to one of your business applications able to support an Amazon AppFlow data flow.

> **Note**
>
> At the time of writing this book, the compatible business applications that support an Amazon AppFlow data flow are the following: Amplitude, Dynatrace, Google Analytics, Infor Nexus, Marketo, Salesforce, ServiceNow, Singular, Trendmicro, Veeva, and Zendesk.

2. Once your data is available in your datasource of choice, you can use Amazon Lookout for Metrics to connect to it, configure your measures and dimensions (that is, define the metrics you want to monitor), and start your detector. Depending on the granularity of your measures, it may take up to a day for Amazon Lookout for Metrics to understand your data's behavior and start detecting anomalies.

3. Once a detector has seen enough data, it will start sending anomalies that you can review: you can give your feedback right from the service console so that Amazon Lookout for Metrics can improve its detector with a human-in-the-loop continuous improvement process. The service console will also allow you to further investigate anomalies by delivering root cause analysis, enabling you to quickly take better actions when an anomaly is triggered.

4. You can also configure alerts to receive notifications or trigger an application automation process by connecting Amazon SNS or AWS Lambda, respectively, as targets for Amazon Lookout for Metrics alerts.

You should now have a high-level understanding of how you can integrate this service into into your own anomaly detection practice. The last piece of the puzzle is to understand the pricing model so that you can better optimize the way you use this service.

Pricing

As with many AWS services, you only pay for what you use with no upfront commitment. Although the cost of the service is minimal to build a **proof of concept** (especially if you can benefit from the Free Tier), there is only one dimension to consider to operationalize an anomaly detection pipeline with Amazon Lookout for Metrics: the number of metrics a detector analyzes during a given month. You will be billed irrespective of the frequency at which your metrics are analyzed: whether your metric issues data once per hour or once per day, you will still be billed for a single metric.

If this is the first time you have used Amazon Lookout for Metrics with any given account, you have access to the Free Tier, which allows you to use the service for free for one month. During this period, there will be no charge for analyzing up to 100 metrics.

AWS service developers work relentlessly at reducing the operational costs of the services and price reductions happen regularly. At the time this book was written, your Amazon Lookout for Metrics usage is billed according to the following tiered pricing:

- First 1,000 metrics: $0.75 per metric

- From 1,000 to 5,000 metrics: $0.50 per metric

- From 5,000 to 20,000 metrics: $0.25 per metric

- From 20,000 to 50,000 metrics: $0.10 per metric

- Every metric beyond the 50,000th one will be billed at $0.05.

For the most up-to-date pricing, you can check the Amazon Lookout for Metrics pricing page at `https://aws.amazon.com/lookout-for-metrics/pricing/`.

Note that depending on how you use Amazon Lookout for Metrics, other charges may occur. This will happen, for instance, if you do any of the following:

- Create alerts using **Amazon SNS**.

- Create custom actions with **AWS Lambda** functions.

- Use **AWS AppFlow** to import data into a Lookout for Metrics dataset.

For more details about the pricing models of these services, check out their respective pricing pages:

- Amazon SNS: `https://aws.amazon.com/sns/pricing/`

- AWS Lambda: `https://aws.amazon.com/lambda/pricing/`

- AWS AppFlow: `https://aws.amazon.com/appflow/pricing/`

This pricing overview ends my presentation of Amazon Lookout for Metrics. In the next section, you will have a look at the different requirements your applications need to satisfy to successfully leverage the capability of this service.

Identifying suitable metrics for monitoring

You have successfully framed your ML project as an anomaly or outlier detection problem and you may have collected some historical time series datasets. Is Amazon Lookout for Metrics a good candidate to deliver your desired insights? Let's review some considerations that will help you understand whether Amazon Lookout for Metrics is suitable for your anomaly detection scenario, namely, the following:

- Dataset requirements
- Use case requirements

Dataset requirements

Unlike many other AI services (within AWS or not), Amazon Lookout for Metrics can get started without any data points: you won't receive any detected anomalies until there is enough information to perform a cold start detection (for instance, if your data has daily intervals, you will need to wait for at least 14 days to start receiving inference results from Amazon Lookout for Metrics) but you can start building your pipeline and your applications without having to wait for enough data to train a model, as happens with other AI services.

In addition, Amazon Lookout for Metrics leverages several algorithms under the hood (from simple statistical models to the more data-hungry deep learning ones) and the service will automatically switch from a simple algorithm to a more complex one when you have enough data available.

Amazon Lookout for Metrics is a univariate service: each metric is monitored individually and each detector can monitor up to five metrics. Each detector will generate actionable results with root cause analysis that helps you spot the relationships between these metrics when an anomaly happens.

If you have more than five metrics to analyze, you will need to build multiple detectors though. If you have a multivariate dataset and know that anomalies can arise based on evolving relationships between multiple variables, then Amazon Lookout for Metrics won't be able to capture this type of event.

Use case requirements

You saw how much heavy lifting Amazon Lookout for Metrics performs on your behalf. There are, however, situations and use cases for which Amazon Lookout for Metrics is not the best match, such as the following:

- **Multivariate data**: Amazon Lookout for Metrics focuses on univariate data while using multiple dimensions to group your data. Any given detector can tackle up to five metrics that will be monitored independently. When you select dimensions, Amazon Lookout for Metrics will create subgroups of measures that will also be monitored separately. If the relationship between multiple interrelated time series data must be considered to detect anomalies of interest for your business case, this service won't be able to uncover them.

- **Fast processes**: When you create a detector, you have to choose an interval for the data it will monitor, which can range from 5 minutes to a day. A detector only processes the records with timestamps consistent with the interval range selected or aggregates the data in the interval if you choose an aggregation method. If your original data (without any aggregation) needs to be processed at a faster pace, Amazon Lookout for Metrics will only be able to capture anomalies that lie in the lower frequency bands of your time series data (that is, anomalies that can be detected in a period higher than 5 minutes). Failure detection in industrial pieces of equipment based on high-frequency sensor data won't be a suitable use case for Amazon Lookout for Metrics.

> Tip
>
> You can use Amazon Lookout for Metrics to detect drift in your univariate time series data: as you can only process time intervals ranging from 5 minutes to a day, this should work well if you expect your data to change over the course of a few days or less. If the shift is very slow (for instance, over the course of a few months), Amazon Lookout for Metrics may have a harder time catching them though. At the other end of the spectrum, if your data drifts quickly (over a few minutes or less), then you won't be able to use this service to detect them.

- **Using log files as input**: Although log files are heavily time-based, using freeform text log files as data sources for Lookout for Metrics is not a good match. You will have to preprocess your data and structure it in an input format recognized by Amazon Lookout for Metrics (CSV or JSON Lines files located in Amazon S3, for instance) to be able to detect something. You will also have to preprocess the freeform text into easy-to-process events: you might be able to capture diagnostic codes to replace the freeform text, for instance.

- **Anomaly predictions**: Amazon Lookout for Metrics can detect anomalies in live data. However, it cannot provide anomaly predictions by telling when an anomaly will likely occur based on recent patterns.

- **Anomalies that build over time**: Some anomalies can gradually appear and grow in importance over time. Amazon Lookout for Metrics can detect anomalies that happen over the course of a few hours or days. If you're monitoring a metric that degrades over the course of several weeks or even months, the service will have a hard time picking this behavior up.

You should now have a good understanding of how to frame your anomaly detection problem to leverage Amazon Lookout for Metrics. You can also use this section to identify how to enrich your existing datasets to successfully use this service (for instance, transforming freeform text files into diagnostic codes or aggregating your data at a suitable time interval during data preparation).

Choosing between Lookout for Equipment and Lookout for Metrics

The first part of this book was dedicated to Amazon Forecast, while the second focused on Amazon Lookout for Equipment. This chapter helped you start your journey with Amazon Lookout for Metrics. In addition to these three AI/ML managed services, the AWS cloud platform offers many options to process your time series data and gain valuable insights from them. The following mind map illustrates these different options at a fine-grained level:

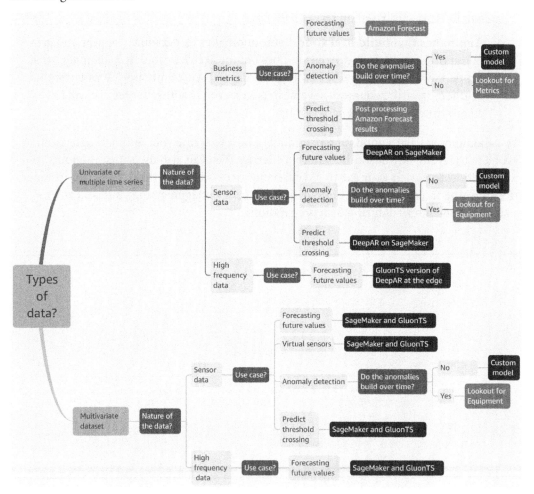

Figure 13.2 – Simplified mind map for time series analysis on AWS

Now that you have a more or less deep overview of the three managed services previously mentioned, let's have a look at the different decisions points that will help you choose between them:

1. If you have a *multivariate dataset* and want to perform *anomaly detection* or prediction, head over to **Amazon Lookout for Equipment**.

2. If you have *univariate* or *multiple times series*, do the following:

   A. If you want to *forecast* business metrics, use **Amazon Forecast**.

   B. If you want to perform *anomaly detection* (no prediction), then use **Amazon Lookout for Metrics**. If your *anomalies build up over time*, try **Amazon Lookout for Equipment**, although the service will shine with multivariate datasets.

3. For *any other use cases*, you may have to combine multiple services or leverage other algorithms, libraries, and models you can build on the **Amazon SageMaker** platform.

If you want a more detailed view of this mind map with more details about other use cases and other AWS services and libraries, you can download a detailed high-resolution mind map by following this link:

```
https://packt-publishing-timeseries-on-aws-michaelhoarau.
s3.eu-west-1.amazonaws.com/time series-on-AWS-decision-tree.
png
```

Summary

Amazon Lookout for Metrics is an AI/ML managed service that can detect outliers in your dataset and provide root cause analysis to help you collect insights from your univariate or multiple time series data.

In this chapter, you learned how to frame an anomaly detection problem suitable for Amazon Lookout for Metrics and discovered the key concepts employed by the service (datasets, detectors, metrics, measures, and dimensions). This chapter was important to help you develop a good understanding of which applications will be good candidates to be solved with Amazon Lookout for Metrics. We also covered how you can improve your anomaly detection framing approach to benefit the most from the undifferentiated heavy lifting that this service can deliver on your behalf.

In the next chapter, we are going to connect Amazon Lookout for Metrics to a dataset and configure our first detector.

14
Creating and Activating a Detector

In the previous chapter, we identified the type of anomaly detection problems that are of interest when dealing with business or operational metrics structured as univariate time series. In this chapter, we are taking a dive into using **Amazon Lookout for Metrics** with an e-commerce dataset that contains the evolution of the number of views and revenues over the course of a year. This dataset is hosted publicly by **Amazon Web Services** on the Amazon Lookout for Metrics public sample repository:

```
https://github.com/aws-samples/amazon-lookout-for-metrics-
samples/blob/main/workshops/RI2021/ml_ops/datasets
```

By the end of this chapter, you will have a good understanding of this dataset and you will know how to ingest it into Amazon Lookout for Metrics and use it for both backtesting and live detection purposes.

In this chapter, we're going to cover the following main topics:

- Preparing a dataset for anomaly detection purposes
- Creating a detector
- Adding a dataset and connecting a data source
- Understanding the backtesting mode
- Configuring alerts

Technical requirements

No hands-on experience in a language such as **Python** or **R** is necessary to follow along with the content from this chapter. However, we highly recommend that you read this chapter while connected to your own AWS account and open the Amazon Lookout for Metrics console to run the different actions on your end.

If you already have an AWS account, you can connect to the AWS console, click on the search bar at the top, enter `Lookout for Metrics` in the services section, and click on **Amazon Lookout for Metrics** to bring up the landing page of the service console.

To create an AWS account and log in to the Amazon Lookout for Metrics console, you can refer to the *Technical requirements* section of *Chapter 2, An Overview of Amazon Forecast*.

You are now ready to use Amazon Lookout for Metrics!

Preparing a dataset for anomaly detection purposes

Throughout this chapter and the next one, we are going to focus on an e-commerce dataset in which we will detect potential anomalies and identify some root causes to help us investigate the problems and deliver a faster route to remediation.

In the sub-sections that follow, we are going to look at the following steps in detail:

1. Download the e-commerce dataset and split your data into a training dataset (that you will use for backtesting purposes) and a testing dataset (that you will use to monitor simulated live data to understand how the continuous mode of Amazon Lookout for Metrics works).

2. Upload your prepared CSV files to **Amazon Simple Store Service (S3)** for storage. Amazon S3 lets you store files and is often used as a file datastore for many AWS services such as Amazon Lookout for Metrics.

3. Authorize Amazon Lookout for Metrics to access your data in Amazon S3. This is optional as you can let Amazon Lookout for Metrics do it for you while you ingest new data. However, this will give you better control over the authorization aspects and can help you debug permission errors in your future work with Amazon Lookout for Metrics.

4. Use backtesting to train a detector on your dataset and switch to continuous mode to monitor live data.

Let's now start by downloading the dataset and getting an overview of its content.

Collecting the dataset

We are going to use the following dataset as an e-commerce dataset hosted by AWS on the Amazon Lookout for Metrics GitHub samples repository:

```
https://github.com/aws-samples/amazon-lookout-for-metrics-
samples/blob/main/workshops/RI2021/ml_ops/datasets/ecommerce.
zip.
```

Once unzipped, this archive contains both a dataset to be used for backtesting purposes (`input.csv`) and a `live` folder structured in a way that Amazon Lookout for Metrics can understand it to detect anomalies in it.

> **Note**
>
> At the time of writing this book, the demonstration live data extends until the end of February 2022. This dataset is regularly updated by the maintainers of this repository and should be updated regularly to ensure that the demo content you can find in this location stays up to date.

The backtest part of this dataset contains the number of daily views and revenue for a fictitious e-commerce website that sells globally. The data included exposes the number of views and revenue for each marketplace (organized by country code) and for each consumer platform (web, mobile app, or mobile web). The backtest data is available from 2021-01-01 to 2022-01-18. Here, for instance, is the revenue collected for the US marketplace from mobile web customers:

Figure 14.1 – Revenue from mobile web customers for the US market

Within this synthetic dataset, you will notice some artificial anomalies have been added here and there (for instance, around 2021-02-07 on the preceding plot). This dataset is ready to be ingested in Amazon Lookout for Metrics. Let's start by uploading it to Amazon S3.

Uploading your data to Amazon S3 for storage

In this section, you will create an Amazon S3 bucket used to store your raw dataset before ingesting it into Amazon Lookout for Metrics. You will then proceed with the actual dataset upload.

Amazon S3 bucket creation

Equipped with our prepared datasets, let's create a bucket on Amazon S3 and upload our data there as follows:

1. If you went through the technical requirements prerequisites at the beginning of this chapter, you should already be logged in to your AWS console, otherwise, fire up your favorite browser and log in to your AWS console.

2. At the top left of your console, you will see a **Services** drop-down menu that will display all the available AWS services. In the **Storage** section, look for the **S3** service and click on its name to go to the S3 console. From here, we are going to click on the **Create bucket** button located at the top of your buckets list section.

3. You are now on the bucket creation page. Choose a name for your bucket. This name must be unique across the whole S3 service. I will call mine `timeseries-on-aws-forecast-michael-hoarau`. That should be unique enough. Also, select an AWS region where your data will be fetched from by Amazon Lookout for Metrics. I selected the **Europe (Ireland)** region for mine.

General configuration

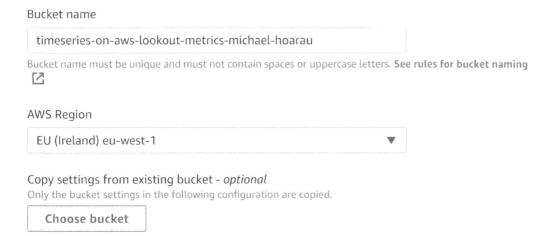

Figure 14.2 – Amazon S3 bucket creation form

> **Important Note**
>
> At the time of writing this book, Amazon Forecast is only available in the following regions: US East (N. Virginia), US East (Ohio), US West (Oregon), Asia Pacific (Singapore), Asia Pacific (Sydney), Asia Pacific (Tokyo), Europe (Frankfurt), Europe (Ireland), and Europe (Stockholm). Make sure you select one of these regions to create your bucket or you won't be able to ingest your data into Amazon Lookout for Metrics.

4. You can keep all the other fields at their default values and click on the **Create bucket** button located at the bottom right of the screen. You are brought back to the S3 home page and you should see your newly created bucket in the buckets listing. A green message at the top of the window will confirm that your bucket was successfully created.

Your Amazon S3 bucket is now created, so we can start uploading our CSV files to this location.

Uploading your dataset to Amazon S3

To upload your dataset, complete the following steps:

1. Click on the name of the bucket you just created in the buckets list that appears on the S3 home page. This page lists all the objects available in this bucket. If you already used it previously (when going through the *Chapter 2, An Overview of Amazon Forecast or Chapter 8, An Overview of Amazon Lookout for Equipment*

2. chapters earlier in this book), you may already have some objects listed here. Otherwise, it will be empty, as shown in the following screenshot:

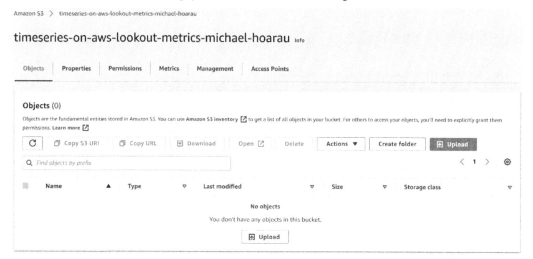

Figure 14.3 – Amazon S3 empty objects listing from your new bucket

3. From here, click on the **Create folder** button and enter `lookout-for-metrics` for the **Folder name** field. Then, click on the **Create folder** button at the bottom of this page.

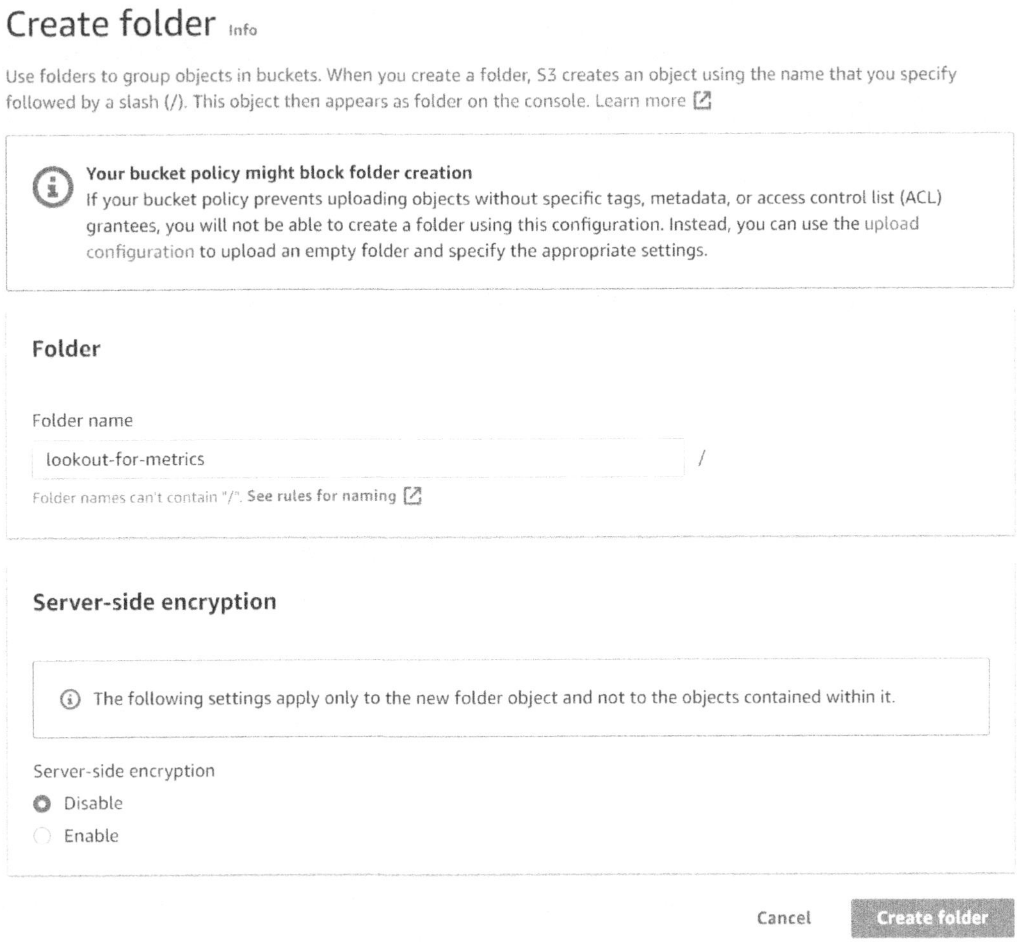

Create folder Info

Use folders to group objects in buckets. When you create a folder, S3 creates an object using the name that you specify followed by a slash (/). This object then appears as folder on the console. Learn more ⬚

ⓘ **Your bucket policy might block folder creation**
If your bucket policy prevents uploading objects without specific tags, metadata, or access control list (ACL) grantees, you will not be able to create a folder using this configuration. Instead, you can use the upload configuration to upload an empty folder and specify the appropriate settings.

Folder

Folder name

```
lookout-for-metrics                                          /
```

Folder names can't contain "/". **See rules for naming** ⬚

Server-side encryption

ⓘ The following settings apply only to the new folder object and not to the objects contained within it.

Server-side encryption
● Disable
○ Enable

Cancel   **Create folder**

Figure 14.4 – Creating a new folder for hosting Amazon Lookout for Metrics data

4. You will be brought back to the objects listing page of your bucket. Click on the name of the folder you just created. From here, click on the **Upload** button at the top of the objects list. You will be brought to the upload page where you can either click on the **Add files** button or drag and drop the CSV files unpacked from the archive you downloaded previously.

Upload Info

Add the files and folders you want to upload to S3. To upload a file larger than 160GB, use the AWS CLI, AWS SDK or Amazon S3 REST API. Learn more 🔗

> Drag and drop files and folders you want to upload here, or choose **Add files**, or **Add folders**.

Files and folders (6553 Total, 12.5 MB)   Remove | Add files | | Add folder |

All files and folders in this table will be uploaded.

Q Find by name   ‹ **1** 2 3 4 5 6 7 ... 656 ›

	Name ▲	Folder ▽	Type ▽	Size ▽
☐	20210101_000000.csv	live/20210101/0000/	text/csv	1.0 KB
☐	20210101_010000.csv	live/20210101/0100/	text/csv	975.0 B
☐	20210101_020000.csv	live/20210101/0200/	text/csv	1015.0 B
☐	20210101_030000.csv	live/20210101/0300/	text/csv	1.0 KB
☐	20210101_040000.csv	live/20210101/0400/	text/csv	997.0 B
☐	20210101_050000.csv	live/20210101/0500/	text/csv	1011.0 B
☐	20210101_060000.csv	live/20210101/0600/	text/csv	1000.0 B
☐	20210101_070000.csv	live/20210101/0700/	text/csv	973.0 B
☐	20210101_080000.csv	live/20210101/0800/	text/csv	1.0 KB
☐	20210101_090000.csv	live/20210101/0900/	text/csv	1.0 KB

Destination

Destination

s3://timeseries-on-aws-forecast-michael-hoarau/lookout-for-metrics/

▶ **Destination details**
  Bucket settings that impact new objects stored in the specified destination.

▶ **Permissions**
Grant public access and access to other AWS accounts.

▶ **Properties**
Specify storage class, encryption settings, tags, and more.

Cancel   Upload

Figure 14.5 – E-commerce dataset upload on Amazon S3

5. Leave all the other fields at their default values, scroll to the bottom of the screen, and click on **Upload** to start uploading the files. There is a total of 12.5 MB and 6,553 files to upload. This may take a while depending on your internet upload bandwidth. An upload status page is displayed while the transfer is in progress.

> **Note**
>
> If you feel the transfer of 6,553 files is too slow using the browser, I recommend using the **AWS Command Line Interface** to optimize your upload speed: `https://docs.aws.amazon.com/cli/latest/userguide/install-cliv2.html`. Another option would be to use **AWS CloudShell** to open a command line in your browser while connected to your console: `https://docs.aws.amazon.com/cloudshell/latest/userguide/welcome.html`.

6. Once this is done, you can click on the **Exit** button to be brought back to the objects list at the root of your newly created folder.

Once your upload is complete, you should see two subfolders in your objects listing, one called `backtest` and the other named `live`.

Giving access to your data to Amazon Lookout for Metrics

By default, the security mechanisms enforced between different AWS services will forbid any service other than Amazon S3 to access your data. From your account, you can upload, delete or move your data from the bucket you just created. Amazon Lookout for Metrics, however, is a different service and will not be able to access this data. We need to specify that Amazon Lookout for Metrics can access any data in this bucket.

> **Note**
>
> You can configure this access directly from the Amazon Lookout for Metrics console during the ingestion step. However, if you want to have more control over the roles and the different accesses created within your account, you can read through this section. Otherwise, feel free to skip it and come back here later.

To enable access to your S3 bucket to the Amazon Lookout for Metrics service, we are going to use the **AWS Identity and Access Management (IAM)** service to create a dedicated IAM role as follows:

1. At the top left of your console, click on the **Services** drop-down menu and search for the **Security, Identity, and Compliance** section. Click on the IAM service name to go to this service console.

2. On the left panel menu, click on **Roles** and then click on the **Create role** button on the top left of this screen.

3. On the **Create role** screen, select **AWS service** as the type of trusted entity:

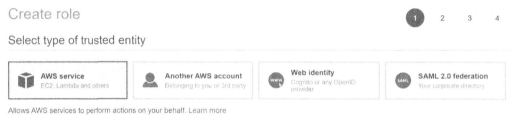

Figure 14.6 – IAM role creation – Trusted entity type selection

4. In the following section (**Choose a use case**), locate **Forecast** and click on the service name.

5. In the last section (**Select your use case**), select **Allows Amazon Forecast to access data in S3**.

Important Note

At the time of writing this book, Amazon Lookout for Metrics does not have a ready-to-use use case in the IAM service. This is why you are selecting **Forecast** in the previous two steps. You can adjust the role created later to match the service for which you want to configure access.

---

6. Click on the **Next** button until you reach the last step (**Review**). Give a name and a description to your role (I called it `LookoutMetricsAccessRole`).

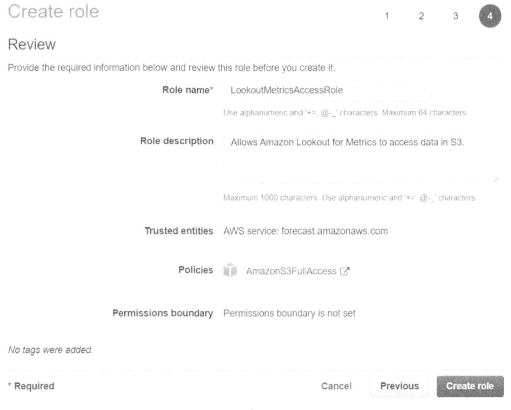

Figure 14.7 – IAM Role creation – Review step

7. Click on **Create role**. Your role is created and a success message is displayed at the top of the screen where you can click on the name of your role. You are then presented with a summary of your role. At the top of this screen, you will see a **Role ARN (Amazon Resource Name)** field. Copy this ARN and paste it somewhere handy. We will need it when we ingest your data into the service.

8. Now, you will adjust this role to limit access to your S3 bucket specifically. To do this, locate the **AmazonS3FullAccess** row in the **Permission policies** section and remove it by clicking on the **X** icon on the right. A confirmation box will ask you to confirm that you actually want to detach this policy from this role. Click on the **Detach** button to confirm this.

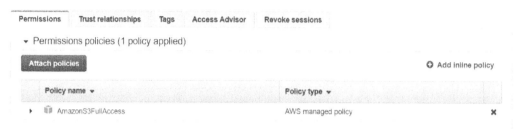

Figure 14.8 – IAM Role creation – Detaching the full access policy

9. Next, click on the **Add inline policy** link and then on the **JSON** tab. Copy and paste the following policy document in the editor. Don't forget to adjust the <<YOUR-BUCKET>> string to match the name of the bucket you created earlier:

```
{
    "Version": "2012-10-17",
    "Statement": [
        {
            "Effect": "Allow",
            "Action": [
                "s3:ListBucket",
                "s3:GetBucketAcl"
            ],
            "Resource": [
                "arn:aws:s3:::<<YOUR-BUCKET>>"
            ]
        },
        {
            "Effect": "Allow",
            "Action": [
                "s3:GetObject",
                "s3:GetBucketAcl"
            ],
            "Resource": [
```

```
                    "arn:aws:s3:::<<YOUR-BUCKET>>/*"
              ]
          }
      ]
  }
```

10. Scroll down to the bottom of the policy definition screen and click on the **Review policy** button.

11. Give a name to your policy (for instance, `LookoutMetricsDatasetAccess`) and click on **Create policy**.

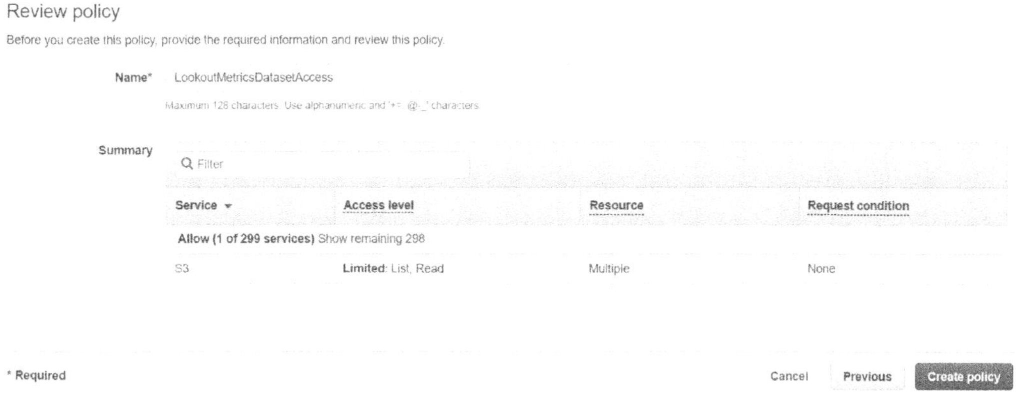

Review policy

Before you create this policy, provide the required information and review this policy.

Name*	LookoutMetricsDatasetAccess
	Maximum 128 characters. Use alphanumeric and '+=,.@_-' characters.

Summary			
Q Filter			
Service ▾	Access level	Resource	Request condition
Allow (1 of 299 services) Show remaining 298			
S3	Limited: List, Read	Multiple	None

* Required   Cancel   Previous   Create policy

Figure 14.9 – IAM role creation – Adding a least privilege access policy

12. Let's now adjust this role to match the right service (Amazon Lookout for Metrics instead of Amazon Forecast). To do this, click on the **Trust relationships** tab and then on the **Edit trust relationship** button. In the **Edit trust relationship** policy document, paste the following JSON document and click on the **Update Trust Policy** button:

```
{
    "Version": "2012-10-17",
    "Statement": [
        {
            "Sid": "",
            "Effect": "Allow",
            "Principal": {
                "Service": [
                    "sns.amazonaws.com",
                    "lookoutmetrics.amazonaws.com"
```

```
                ]
            },
            "Action": "sts:AssumeRole"
        }
    ]
}
```

13. Your trust relationships should now look like this:

Figure 14.10 – IAM role creation – Updated trust relationship

When Amazon Lookout for Metrics will try to read the datasets you just uploaded in S3, it will request permissions from IAM by using the role we just created. The policy you defined to give access to your S3 bucket is what IAM will use to authorize Amazon Lookout for Metrics to access your dataset. On the other hand, the trust relationship you defined will allow other services (such as Amazon SageMaker) to run Amazon Lookout for Metrics APIs for you. You may have noticed that we also added the SNS service to the trust relationships.

Later in this chapter, you will use **Amazon Simple Notification Service (SNS)** to create a notification when severe anomalies are detected. We will use this trust relationship to give Amazon Lookout for Metrics the ability to call Amazon SNS APIs.

You are now ready to connect your dataset to Amazon Lookout for Metrics.

Creating a detector

As mentioned in *Chapter 13, An Overview of Amazon Lookout for Metrics*, a detector is a machine learning model that monitors your dataset to find anomalies and help you analyze their impact. To create your first detector, complete the following steps:

1. Log in to your AWS console and search for `Lookout for Metrics` in the search bar at the top.

2. Click on **Amazon Lookout for Metrics** and go to the home page.

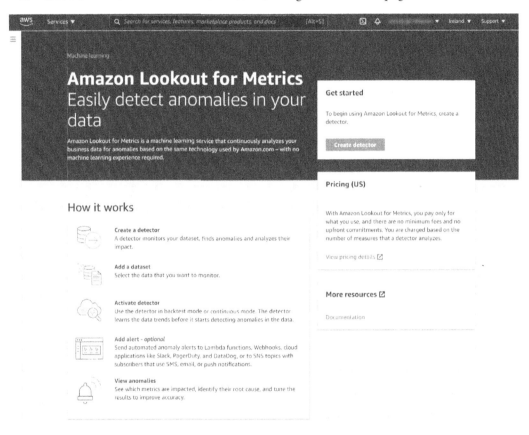

Figure 14.11 – Amazon Lookout for Metrics home page

3. On this page, you can either click on the **Create detector** button on the right side of
    the screen or click the hamburger icon (the one with three horizontal lines) on the
    top left to open the left panel, where you can click on **Detectors**. You will land on a
    page listing all the detectors visible from your AWS account. If this is your first time
    using the service, your list will be empty (as shown in the following screenshot).
    Click on the **Create detector** button at the top right.

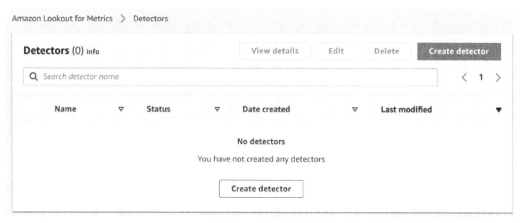

Figure 14.12 – Amazon Lookout for Metrics detectors list

4. Following a reminder to check the AWS region you are going to create a detector in, you are asked to provide a name for your detector (let's call it `sales-anomaly-detector`), an optional description, and the amount of time between each analysis (1-hour intervals). Leave all the other options at their default values, scroll down to the bottom of the screen, and click on the **Create** button.

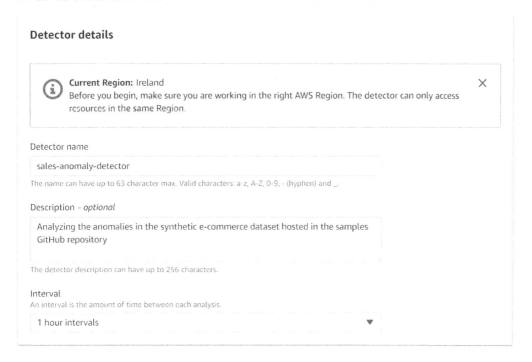

Figure 14.13 – Amazon Lookout for Metrics detector creation screen

You are brought to the detector dashboard screen where you can see the first step completed (**Create a detector**). A success message is also shown in a green ribbon at the top of the dashboard.

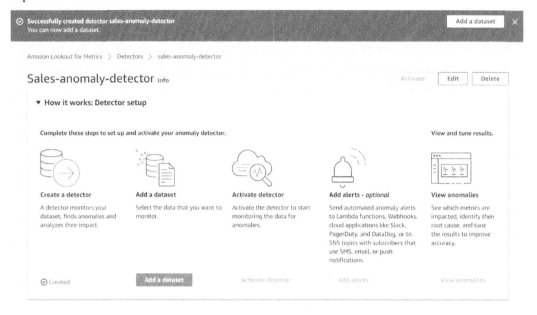

Figure 14.14 – Detector dashboard at creation time

Your detector is now ready and configured, so it is time to connect it to your dataset to start detecting anomalies!

Adding a dataset and connecting a data source

We are going to ingest our data into Amazon Lookout for Metrics to start detecting anomalies in it. To do this, complete the following steps:

1. On the detector dashboard, click on the **Add a dataset** button.

2. In the **Basic information** section, just give a name to your dataset (I called mine ecommerce-dataset).

Basic information

Name

| ecommerce-dataset |

The dataset name must have 1 to 63 characters. Valid characters= a-z, A-Z, 0-9, - (hyphen) and _.

Description - *optional*

| *Description of my datasource and interval* |

The detector description can have up to 256 characters.

Timezone - *optional*
The timezone is used to interpret timestamps in your data.

| *Choose a time zone*   ▼ |

Figure 14.15 – Dataset basic information

3. In the **Datasource details** section, we are going to start the backtest mode to find anomalies in historical data. To do this, select **Amazon S3** in the **Datasource** dropdown and then select **Backtest** for **Detector mode**.

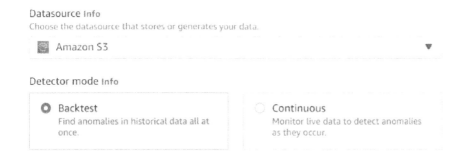

Datasource details
Read data from an Amazon S3 bucket that you manage or from a datasource that integrates with Amazon Lookout for Metrics.

Datasource Info
Choose the datasource that stores or generates your data.

| 🖳 Amazon S3   ▼ |

Detector mode Info

| ◉ Backtest | ○ Continuous |
| Find anomalies in historical data all at once. | Monitor live data to detect anomalies as they occur. |

Figure 14.16 – Datasource details – Backtest mode selection

4. Then, you will point Amazon Lookout for Metrics to your input dataset where you have your historical data. If you followed the dataset upload section earlier in this chapter, the S3 path to your historical data will have the following format: `s3://<<YOUR-BUCKET>>/lookout-for-metrics/backtest/input.csv`. Use this path to fill the **Historical data** field and leave all the other parameters at their default values as they are valid.

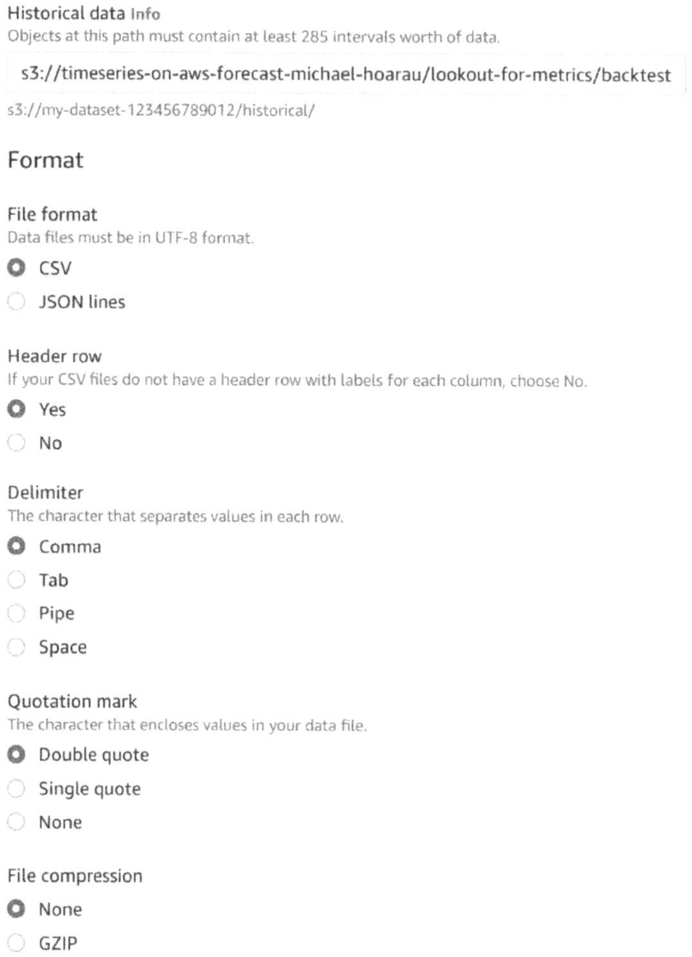

Historical data Info
Objects at this path must contain at least 285 intervals worth of data.

> s3://timeseries-on-aws-forecast-michael-hoarau/lookout-for-metrics/backtest

s3://my-dataset-123456789012/historical/

Format

File format
Data files must be in UTF-8 format.

- ● CSV
- ○ JSON lines

Header row
If your CSV files do not have a header row with labels for each column, choose No.

- ● Yes
- ○ No

Delimiter
The character that separates values in each row.

- ● Comma
- ○ Tab
- ○ Pipe
- ○ Space

Quotation mark
The character that encloses values in your data file.

- ● Double quote
- ○ Single quote
- ○ None

File compression

- ● None
- ○ GZIP

Figure 14.17 – Datasource details – Historical data configuration

5. The last step is to specify **Permissions**. Select **Enter the ARN of a role** in the **Service role** section and then paste the ARN of the role you created earlier. Your role ARN should have the following format, `arn:aws:iam::<<YOUR-ACCOUNT-ID>>:role/LookoutMetricsAccessRole`, where `<<YOUR-ACCOUNT-ID>>` will be replaced by the ID of your AWS account.

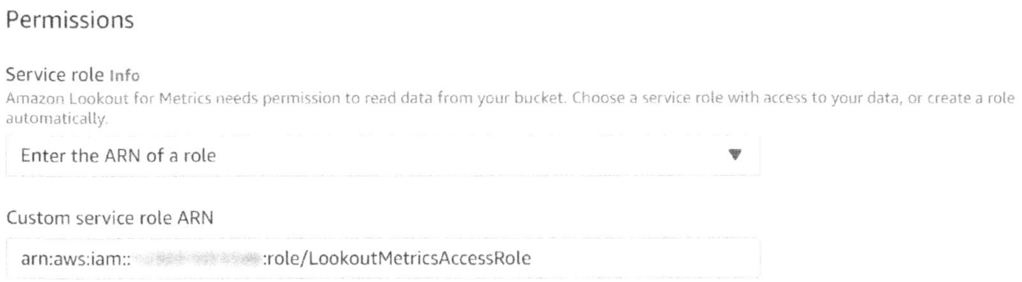

Permissions

Service role Info

Amazon Lookout for Metrics needs permission to read data from your bucket. Choose a service role with access to your data, or create a role automatically.

Enter the ARN of a role ▼

Custom service role ARN

arn:aws:iam:: ~~~~ :role/LookoutMetricsAccessRole

Figure 14.18 – Datasource details – Permission definition

> **Note**
>
> As an alternative, you can also directly create a suitable role at this stage by selecting **Create a role** in the **Service role** dropdown. Amazon Lookout for Metrics will ask you to specify which Amazon S3 bucket you would like to give some permissions for and a role will be created on your behalf.

6. Scroll down to the bottom of the screen and click on **Next**. Amazon Lookout for Metrics tries to access your data and validate your dataset. Once validation is complete, you get a success dialog box where you can click on **OK** to continue.

7. On the next page, you will map the different fields of your dataset to the **Measures** and **Dimensions** of Amazon Lookout for Metrics. Let's start by adding two measures (you can have up to five of them). Your detector will track these fields of your CSV file for anomalies. You will map the views and revenue columns of your CSV file with Amazon Lookout for Metrics measures. For each of these fields, you will also request the service to perform a **SUM** aggregation across all dimensions.

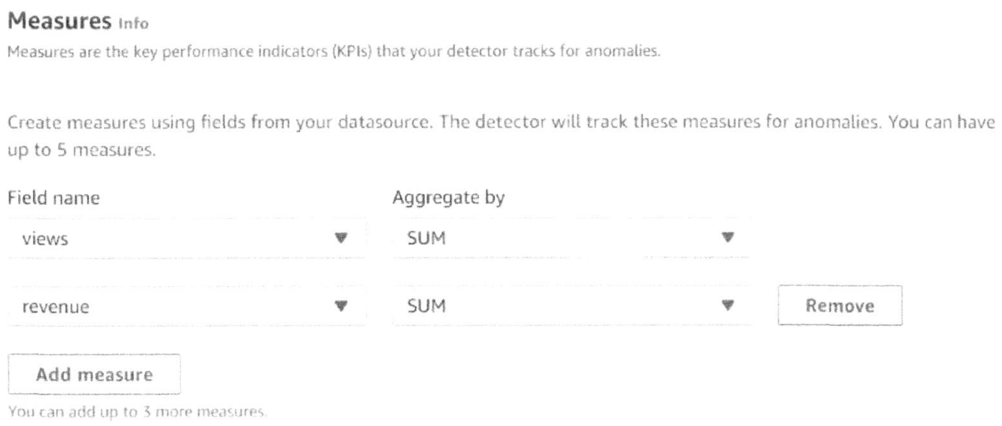

Measures Info

Measures are the key performance indicators (KPIs) that your detector tracks for anomalies.

Create measures using fields from your datasource. The detector will track these measures for anomalies. You can have up to 5 measures.

Field name		Aggregate by		
views ▼		SUM ▼		
revenue ▼		SUM ▼		Remove

Add measure

You can add up to 3 more measures.

Figure 14.19 – Defining the measures in your dataset

Important Note

At the time of writing this book, Amazon Lookout for Metrics will just ignore time series with missing data. At this time, you will have to check that all the data exists and handle missing data before the service performs any analysis (you can put 0 for a missing data point, for instance).

---

8. You will then define two dimensions by telling Amazon Lookout for Metrics that it can aggregate data across the different values for the **platform** and **marketplace** fields present in your dataset.

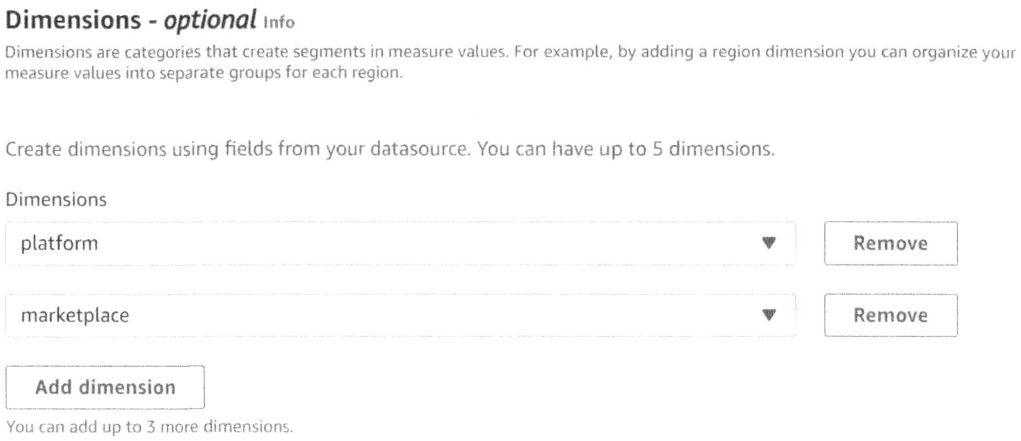

Dimensions - *optional* Info

Dimensions are categories that create segments in measure values. For example, by adding a region dimension you can organize your measure values into separate groups for each region.

Create dimensions using fields from your datasource. You can have up to 5 dimensions.

Dimensions

| platform | ▼ | Remove |

| marketplace | ▼ | Remove |

Add dimension

You can add up to 3 more dimensions.

Figure 14.20 – Defining the dimensions in your dataset

9. The last field to map is the timestamp. Select the **timestamp** column from your dataset and let Amazon Lookout for Metrics detect the format for you.

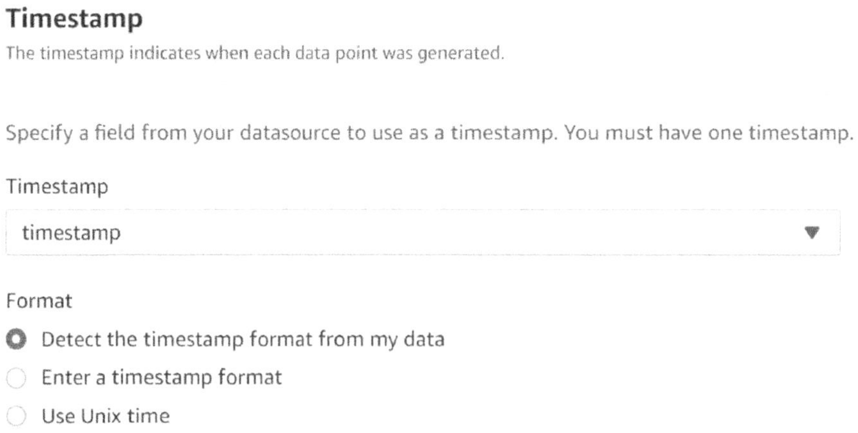

Timestamp

The timestamp indicates when each data point was generated.

Specify a field from your datasource to use as a timestamp. You must have one timestamp.

Timestamp

| timestamp | ▼ |

Format

◉ Detect the timestamp format from my data

◯ Enter a timestamp format

◯ Use Unix time

Figure 14.21 – Defining the timestamp in your dataset

10. At the bottom of the screen, click on the **Next** button to review your data source configuration. If you're happy with the configuration of your dataset, click **Save and activate** to start detecting anomalies in this dataset. A dialog box is displayed to remind you that you're in backtest mode and that you will begin incurring costs once you start your detector. Type `confirm` in the dialog box and then click on **Activate**.

You are brought back to your detector dashboard, where you can see that you're in backtest mode and that your detector is learning from this initial dataset.

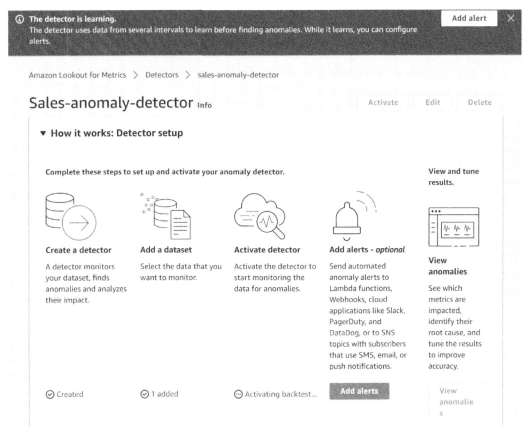

Figure 14.22 – Activating the dataset in backtest mode

You can see that your detector is currently activating its backtest mode. After a while, it will switch to a **Backtest in progress** status and later to **Backtest complete**. Some anomalies may have been detected and you will see how you can visualize them in *Chapter 15, Viewing Anomalies and Providing Feedback*.

Understanding the backtesting mode

When you add a dataset for backtest purposes, Amazon Lookout for Metrics uses it to analyze your data over multiple intervals to identify patterns and learn about expected variations. The backtest mode allows your detector to learn about your data before it starts processing continuous data. When you provide historical data, Amazon Lookout for Metrics uses 70% to learn from it and 30% to run a backtest.

The amount of data Amazon Lookout for Metrics can use to learn from historical data depends on the interval you configured when you added the dataset. The service will only look for up to 2,500 previous intervals that must fall within a certain timeframe:

- For 5-minute intervals, the previous intervals have to lie within the last 3 months.

- For 10-minute intervals, this timeframe will be 6 months.

- For 1-hour intervals, this timeframe will be 3 years.

- For 1-day intervals, this timeframe will be 5 years.

If you do not provide historical data and only live data, Amazon Lookout for Metrics will look into the live data location for past intervals. If it finds some, it will use this data to learn from it and this will reduce the time needed to start detecting anomalies in your live data.

Configuring alerts

Amazon Lookout for Metrics finds anomalies in your data. Depending on the severity of the anomalies detected, the service can send some notifications either to a Lambda function or to an SNS topic:

- **AWS Lambda**: This is a computing service that lets you run your code without provisioning and managing any underlying services or infrastructure. You can write a lambda function that will process any event generated by Amazon Lookout for Metrics to react to detected anomalies.

- **Amazon SNS**: This messaging service can be used to send messages between applications or between applications and persons (for instance, by sending text messages to an end user). You can use this service to send a notification whenever your detector finds an anomaly worthy of being reported.

To add an alert to a detector, complete the following steps:

1. Open the Amazon Lookout for Metrics service home page and click on **Detectors** in the left-hand menu bar. Then, select your detector and click on **Alerts** in the left menu bar. You should be presented with a list of alerts configured for your detector. At this stage, this list will be empty. Click on the **Add alert** button in the top-right corner of this screen.

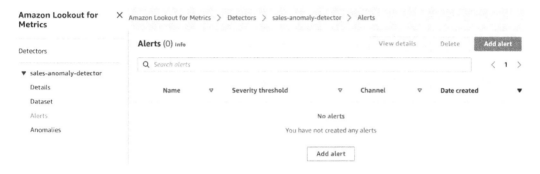

Figure 14.23 – List of configured alerts for a detector

2. On the **Alert details** page, fill in the following details for your alert:

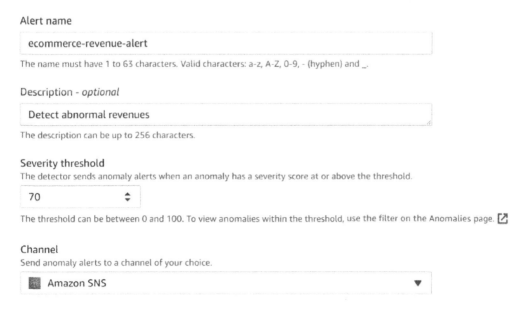

Figure 14.24 – Configuring alert details

You will need to enter the following mandatory details to define your alerts:

- **Alert name**: Let's call our alert `ecommerce-revenue-alert`.

- **Severity threshold**: Leave the default value of `70%`. The severity level is a measure of the criticality of a detected anomaly. In *Chapter 15, Viewing Anomalies and Providing Feedback*, you will have the opportunity to learn more about severity levels.

- **Channel**: You will choose Amazon SNS as the delivery channel.

3. In the **SNS topic** section, click on **Create a topic** to bring a new window into your browser. This will open the Amazon SNS service home page. Click on **Topics** in the left menu bar and then on the **Create topic** button in the top right. Select the **Standard** type and enter a name for your topic (for instance, `revenue-anomalies-topic`).

Details

Type Info
Topic type cannot be modified after topic is created

○ FIFO (first-in, first-out)
- Strictly-preserved message ordering
- Exactly-once message delivery
- High throughput, up to 300 publishes/second
- Subscription protocols: SQS

◉ Standard
- Best-effort message ordering
- At-least once message delivery
- Highest throughput in publishes/second
- Subscription protocols: SQS, Lambda, HTTP, SMS, email, mobile application endpoints

Name

    revenue-anomalies-topic

Maximum 256 characters. Can include alphanumeric characters, hyphens (-) and underscores (_).

Display name - *optional*
To use this topic with SMS subscriptions, enter a display name. Only the first 10 characters are displayed in an SMS message. **Info**

    My Topic

Maximum 100 characters, including hyphens (-) and underscores (_).

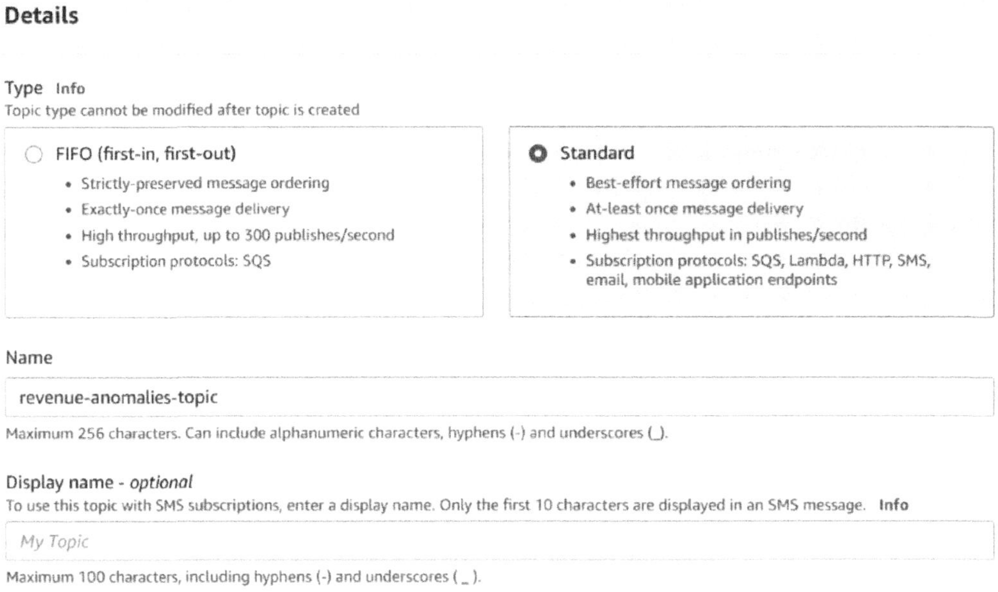

Figure 14.25 – Amazon SNS topic creation

4. Leave all the other fields at their default values, scroll down to the bottom of the screen, and click on **Create topic**. You are brought to the topic details screen. Scroll down and click on the **Create subscription** button in the **Subscriptions** tab.

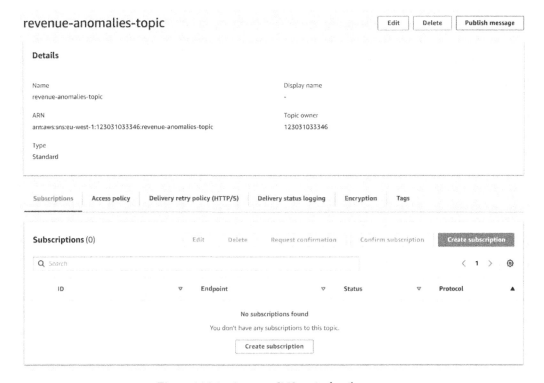

Figure 14.26 – Amazon SNS topic details screen

5. In the subscription creation details, select **Email** for the **Protocol** field and fill in your email address. Then, click on **Create subscription**. You will receive an email within a few minutes and you will need to click on the link provided to confirm your subscription to this topic. By default, any message posted on this topic will be sent to your email address.

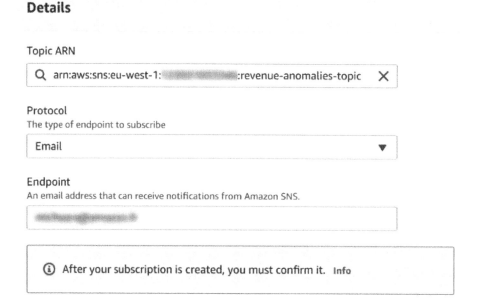

Details

Topic ARN

Q   arn:aws:sns:eu-west-1: ▓▓▓▓▓▓▓ :revenue-anomalies-topic   ✕

Protocol
The type of endpoint to subscribe

Email   ▼

Endpoint
An email address that can receive notifications from Amazon SNS.

▓▓▓▓▓▓▓▓▓▓▓

ⓘ After your subscription is created, you must confirm it. Info

Figure 14.27 – Amazon SNS topic subscription configuration

6. Your topic is now created and you can go back to the Amazon Lookout for Metrics alerts creation window. Click on the refresh button next to the **SNS topic** dropdown. You should now see your topic in the list and you can select it. For **Service role**, select **Enter the ARN of a role** and paste a **Custom service role ARN**. Your role ARN will have the following format, `arn:aws:iam::<<YOUR-ACCOUNT-ID>>:role/LookoutMetricsAccessRole`, where `<<YOUR-ACCOUNT-ID>>` will be replaced by the ID of your AWS account.

SNS topic Info

Choose an Amazon SNS topic and a role that gives the detector permission to send notifications to it.

SNS topic

arn:aws:sns:eu-west-1: ⬛⬛⬛⬛⬛⬛ :r... ▼   [C]   [Create a topic 🗗]

Choose a topic in the current Region or create one.

Service role Info

Choose a service role with access to your topic, or create a role automatically.

Enter the ARN of a role   ▼

Custom service role ARN

arn:aws:iam:: ⬛⬛⬛⬛⬛⬛ :role/LookoutMetricsAccessRole

Figure 14.28 – Amazon SNS topic selection for the alert

> **Note**
> As an alternative, you can also directly create a suitable role at this stage by selecting **Create a role** in the **Service role** dropdown. Amazon Lookout for Metrics will ask you to specify which Amazon SNS topic you would like to give some permissions for and a role will be created on your behalf.

7. Scroll down to the bottom of this screen and click on **Add alert** to create this alert.

Your alert is created and you can see it in the alerts list of your detector.

Figure 14.29 – Amazon Lookout for Metrics alerts associated with a given detector

Congratulations! You have successfully trained a detector and configured an alert to warn you whenever it detects an anomaly. Time to close up this chapter!

Summary

In this chapter, you learned how to prepare your historical data so that Amazon Lookout for Metrics can use it to perform backtesting. You also developed a good understanding of the e-commerce dataset that we will continue to use throughout this part dedicated to anomaly detection. You also got initial hands-on experience of Amazon Lookout for Metrics as you learned how to create a detector and how to connect it to a data source. You also learned how to configure an alert so that you can react when an anomaly is detected.

This chapter was key to understanding and manipulating the key concepts used by Amazon Lookout for Metrics (detectors, data source, alerts).

In the next chapter, you are going to switch your detector into a live detection mode and you are going to learn how to visualize the detected anomalies and provide feedback to the service.

15
Viewing Anomalies and Providing Feedback

In the previous chapter, you configured and trained your first detector with historical data you used in backtest mode. You also learned how to trigger an alert by connecting Amazon Lookout for Metrics with Amazon **Simple Notification Service** (**SNS**). In this chapter, you will learn how to review detected anomalies.

By the end of this chapter, you will have a good command of the anomalies dashboard and understand the key concepts Amazon Lookout for Metrics uses to rank and qualify anomalies. You will also learn how to use the impact analysis dashboard to provide feedback about the quality of detections.

In this chapter, we're going to cover the following main topics:

- Training a continuous detector
- Reviewing anomalies from a trained detector
- Interacting with a detector

Technical requirements

No hands-on experience with a language such as **Python** or **R** is necessary to follow along with the content from this chapter. However, we highly recommend that you read this chapter while connected to your own AWS account and open the different AWS service consoles to run the different actions on your end.

To create an AWS account and log into the Amazon Lookout for Metrics console, you can refer to the technical requirements in *Chapter 2, An Overview of Amazon Forecast*.

Training a continuous detector

In the previous chapter, you configured a detector in backtest mode. You will now configure the same detector in live mode. You already created a role and uploaded all the necessary data. To review these steps and make sure you have everything ready, you can review the detector creation steps in *Chapter 14, Creating and Activating a Detector*.

Configuring a detector in continuous mode

To build your live detector, complete the following steps:

1. Log into your AWS console and search for `Lookout for Metrics` in the search bar at the top. Then, click on **Amazon Lookout for Metrics** and go to the service home page.

2. Click on the **Create detector** button on the right side of the screen. You will land on a page listing all the detectors visible from your AWS account. Click on the **Create detector** button at the top right.

3. After a reminder to check the AWS region you are going to create a detector in, you are asked to provide a name for your detector (let's call it `sales-anomaly-live-detector`), an optional description, and the amount of time between each analysis (`1-hour intervals`). Leave all the other options as their default values, scroll down to the bottom of the screen, and click on the **Create** button. You are brought to the detector dashboard screen, where you can see the first step completed (**Create a detector**). A success message is also shown in a green ribbon at the top of the dashboard.

4. Click on the **Add a dataset** button. In the **Basic information** section, just give a name to your dataset (I called mine `ecommerce-dataset`). In the **Datasource details** section, we are going to select **Continuous** mode to find anomalies in live data. To do this, select **Amazon S3** in the **Datasource** dropdown and then select **Continuous** for **Detector mode**:

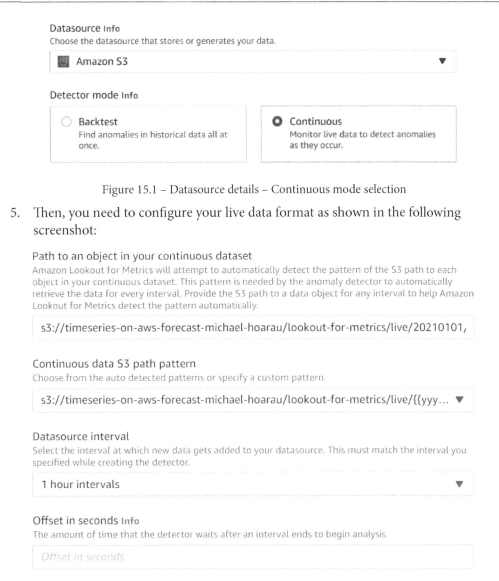

Figure 15.1 – Datasource details – Continuous mode selection

5. Then, you need to configure your live data format as shown in the following screenshot:

Figure 15.2 – Datasource details – Continuous data configuration

Fill these fields in with the following information:

- **Path to an object in your continuous dataset**: If you followed the dataset upload section from *Chapter 14, Creating and Activating a Detector*, the first file of your live data will have the following format: `s3://<<YOUR-BUCKET>>/lookout-for-metrics/live/20210101/0000/20210101_000000.csv`, where `<<YOUR-BUCKET>>` will be replaced by the name of the bucket you created in the previous chapter. Amazon Lookout for Metrics will attempt to detect the common pattern of the S3 path of each object of your live dataset.

- **Continuous data S3 path pattern**: Select the following format: `s3://<<YOUR-BUCKET>>/lookout-for-metrics/live{{yyyyMMdd}}/{{HHmm}}/`.

- **Datasource interval**: Select `1 hour intervals` in the dropdown. This value must match the interval used when creating your detector.

6. We want this detector to benefit from the presence of historical data to learn faster. Point Amazon Lookout for Metrics to your input dataset where you have your historical data. If you followed the dataset upload section in *Chapter 14, Creating and Activating a Detector*, the S3 path to your historical data will have the following format: `s3://<<YOUR-BUCKET>>/lookout-for-metrics/backtest/input.csv`. Use this path to fill the **Historical data** field and leave all the other parameters as their default values, as they are valid.

7. The final step is to specify **Permissions**: select `Enter the ARN of a role` in the **Service role** section and then paste the ARN of the role you created earlier. Your role ARN should have the following format: `arn:aws:iam::<<YOUR-ACCOUNT-ID>>:role/LookoutMetricsAccessRole`, where `<<YOUR-ACCOUNT-ID>>` should be replaced with the ID of your AWS account.

8. Scroll down to the bottom of the screen and click on **Next**. Amazon Lookout for Metrics tries to access your data and validate your dataset. Once validation is complete, you get a success dialog box where you can click on **OK** to continue.

9. On the next page, you will map the different fields of your dataset to **Measures** and **Dimensions**. A continuous detector is configured the same way as in backtest mode: use `views` and `revenue` as measures (with **SUM** aggregation), `platform` and `marketplace` as dimensions, and `timestamp` as the timestamp of your dataset.

10. At the bottom of the screen, click on the **Next** button to review your datasource configuration. If you're happy with the configuration of your dataset, click **Save and activate** to start detecting anomalies in this dataset. A dialog box is displayed to remind you that you will begin incurring costs once you start your detector. Type `confirm` in the dialog box and click on **Activate**.

Your live detector is now ready. I would recommend that you also attach an alert to it. Feel free to replicate the steps you went through at the end of the previous chapter to do so on your new detector.

After a while, your detector will be activated and will start searching for new files in the S3 location you configured as a datasource for continuous detection.

Preparing data to feed a continuous detector

When you configured a detector in backtest mode in the previous chapter or when you used historical data settings to configure your continuous detector in the previous section, you pointed Amazon Lookout for Metrics to a single S3 location where you can put all the files from your historical data. The e-commerce dataset comes with a single `input.csv` file that contains all the data from 01/01/2021 to 18/01/2022 (at the time of writing), but you are free to structure your dataset in multiple files if you'd prefer. For instance, your historical data may come in monthly chunks: `input-2020-01.csv` (with all metrics for January 2020 contained in this file), `input-2020-02.csv`, and so on. As a reminder, here is an excerpt from the `input.csv` file used by a detector to learn from historical data:

platform	marketplace	timestamp	views	revenue
pc_web	us	01/01/2021 00:00	298	89,4
pc_web	uk	01/01/2021 00:00	476	142,8
pc_web	de	01/01/2021 00:00	152	45,6
pc_web	fr	01/01/2021 00:00	405	121,5
pc_web	es	01/01/2021 00:00	113	33,9
pc_web	it	01/01/2021 00:00	153	45,9
pc_web	jp	01/01/2021 00:00	161	48,3
mobile_web	us	01/01/2021 00:00	438	131,4
mobile_web	uk	01/01/2021 00:00	536	160,8
mobile_web	de	01/01/2021 00:00	231	69,3
mobile_web	fr	01/01/2021 00:00	220	66
mobile_web	es	01/01/2021 00:00	283	84,9
mobile_web	it	01/01/2021 00:00	691	207,3
mobile_web	jp	01/01/2021 00:00	222	66,6
mobile_app	us	01/01/2021 00:00	498	149,4
mobile_app	uk	01/01/2021 00:00	218	65,4
mobile_app	de	01/01/2021 00:00	387	116,1
mobile_app	fr	01/01/2021 00:00	687	206,1
mobile_app	es	01/01/2021 00:00	197	59,1
mobile_app	it	01/01/2021 00:00	169	50,7
mobile_app	jp	01/01/2021 00:00	566	169,8

Figure 15.3 – Historical data excerpt

On the other hand, a *continuous detector* will search for a new file each time it wakes up to process a given time interval. Your detector was configured to wake up on an hourly basis, so it expects a new file to be present at the top of every hour (notwithstanding an offset you can configure to account for processing time).

The folder structure used when you uploaded your data in Amazon S3 is the following:

```
s3://<<YOUR-BUCKET>>/lookout-for-metrics/
    live/20210101/0000/20210101_000000.csv
    live/20210101/0100/20210101_010000.csv
    live/20210101/0200/20210101_020000.csv
    ...
    live/20220118/2200/20220118_220000.csv
    live/20220118/2300/20220118_230000.csv
```

In this dataset, data for each 1-hour interval is stored in a single CSV file at a path that is named according to the interval. The files (there can be several) located under the `live/20210101/0000/` path will contain the data generated for the 1-hour interval starting at midnight on January 1, 2021.

When you define the continuous data S3 path pattern, you can let Amazon Lookout for Metrics guess which patterns it should follow by pointing it to a given object or you can configure it manually with a path template. Such a template can contain different keys configured with double curly brackets. For instance, the path template for the continuous data described previously is the following:

```
s3://<<YOUR-BUCKET>>/lookout-for-metrics/live/{{yyyyMMdd}}/
{{HHmm}}
```

These letters in double curly brackets represent parts of the S3 path that can change depending on date and time (yyyy stands for the current four-digits year, MM for a double-digit month in the year, and so on). Follow this link to learn about the placeholder keys you can use in your path template:

```
https://docs.aws.amazon.com/lookoutmetrics/latest/dev/
detectors-dataset.html#detectors-dataset-pathkeys
```

The structure of each individual file located under a given location is the same as the historical data format. It can be either JSON Lines or CSV. Here is the full content of one of the files:

platform	marketplace	timestamp	views	revenue
pc_web	us	17/11/2021 08:00	364	109,2
pc_web	uk	17/11/2021 08:00	360	108
pc_web	de	17/11/2021 08:00	600	180
pc_web	fr	17/11/2021 08:00	383	114,9
pc_web	es	17/11/2021 08:00	123	36,9
pc_web	it	17/11/2021 08:00	203	60,9
pc_web	jp	17/11/2021 08:00	313	93,9
mobile_web	us	17/11/2021 08:00	291	87,3
mobile_web	uk	17/11/2021 08:00	549	164,7
mobile_web	de	17/11/2021 08:00	340	102
mobile_web	fr	17/11/2021 08:00	812	243,6
mobile_web	es	17/11/2021 08:00	344	103,2
mobile_web	it	17/11/2021 08:00	228	68,4
mobile_web	jp	17/11/2021 08:00	151	45,3
mobile_app	us	17/11/2021 08:00	204	61,2
mobile_app	uk	17/11/2021 08:00	163	48,9
mobile_app	de	17/11/2021 08:00	589	176,7
mobile_app	fr	17/11/2021 08:00	196	58,8
mobile_app	es	17/11/2021 08:00	224	67,2
mobile_app	it	17/11/2021 08:00	113	33,9
mobile_app	jp	17/11/2021 08:00	122	36,6

Figure 15.4 – File content example for live data

This file is located under `s3://<<YOUR-BUCKET>>/lookout-for-metrics/live/20211117/0800/20211117_080000.csv` and contains all the measures captured between 8 a.m. and 9 a.m. on November 17, 2021. Let's now have a look at how Amazon Lookout for Metrics exposes the results when a detector finds an anomaly.

Reviewing anomalies from a trained detector

In this section, we are going to review the different dashboards Amazon Lookout for Metrics provides to help you understand the state of your detectors and the anomalies they detected.

Detector details dashboard

In the previous chapter, you trained a detector in backtest mode and you also built a second one using continuous mode. Once a backtest job is complete, you will see the detector status change on its dashboard as follows:

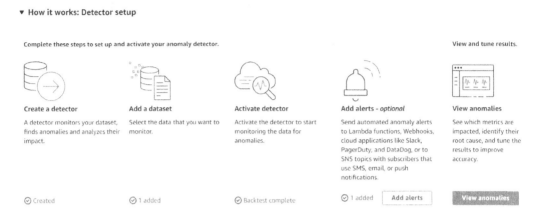

Figure 15.5 – Completed backtest status

On this main dashboard, you can see a **Backtest complete** status under the **Activate detector** step. This means that your historical data has been analyzed. For a continuous detector such as the one you configured and trained in the previous section, you will instead see **Learning…** and then **Activated**.

If you scroll down to the bottom of this screen, you will have more details about the backtest job under the **Backtest data properties** tab:

Figure 15.6 – Backtest job data properties

The historical data you used in the previous chapter to train your detector starts on January 1, 2021; however, a Lookout for Metrics backtesting job only uses up to 3,000 intervals. As your detector was configured to deal with 1-hour intervals, this means the data range considered by the backtesting job will go from **May 29, 2021** to **Oct 1, 2021** (*125 days x 24 hours = 3,000 intervals*). Of this range, 70% was used to learn the behavior of your data (from **May 29** to **Aug 24**), while 30% was used to try and detect some anomalies (from **Aug 24** to **Oct 1**).

A detector running in continuous mode will have a **Data validation** tab instead of a **Backtest data properties** tab:

Data validation	Detector log	Tags

Data validation results

Time validation started	Total number of rows processed	Number of invalid rows
Nov 17, 2021 05:00 CET	21	0
		Number of dropped rows
		0

Figure 15.7 – Data validation in continuous mode

This tab shows how many rows were processed by your continuous detectors and if any of them were invalid or dropped.

The **Detector log** tab is fed by live detectors. If you click on this tab while reviewing your continuous detector dashboard, you will see something similar to the following:

Detector log Info

Q Filter   < 1 2 >

Run status	Start time
⊘ COMPLETED	Nov 17, 2021 04:00 UTC
⊘ COMPLETED	Nov 17, 2021 03:00 UTC
⊘ COMPLETED	Nov 17, 2021 02:00 UTC
⊘ COMPLETED	Nov 17, 2021 01:00 UTC
⊘ COMPLETED	Nov 17, 2021 00:00 UTC
⊘ COMPLETED	Nov 16, 2021 23:00 UTC
⊘ COMPLETED	Nov 16, 2021 22:00 UTC
⊘ COMPLETED	Nov 16, 2021 21:00 UTC
⊘ COMPLETED	Nov 16, 2021 20:00 UTC
⊘ COMPLETED	Nov 16, 2021 19:00 UTC

Figure 15.8 – Continuous detector log

If a file is missing, this tab will display an error stating which file it is so that you can investigate further. Let's now have a look at the **Anomalies** dashboard.

Anomalies dashboard

While you're on your detector dashboard (either in backtest or continuous mode), click on **Anomalies** on the left-hand menu bar to bring up the **Anomalies** dashboard:

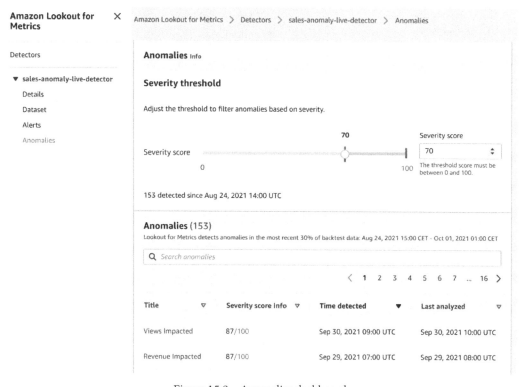

Figure 15.9 – Anomalies dashboard

Based on the understanding of your data behavior by your trained detector, the latter will mark unexpected changes in your metrics as anomalies that will be visible on this dashboard. At the top, you can see a **Severity threshold** widget that you can use to filter out the anomalies you are interested in:

Severity threshold

Adjust the threshold to filter anomalies based on severity.

Severity score

70

Severity score

70

0   100

The threshold score must be
between 0 and 100.

Figure 15.10 – Using the severity score threshold to filter the anomalies

By default, this threshold is set to 70%, meaning that any anomaly with a severity score higher than 70% will be listed in the second part of the dashboard. You can use the slider to list more or less severe anomalies. The severity score indicates how far the datapoint is outside of the expected range based on the data that the detector has analyzed.

The second part of the **Anomalies** dashboard is a list of all the anomalies with a severity score higher than the previously configured threshold, as shown in the following screenshot:

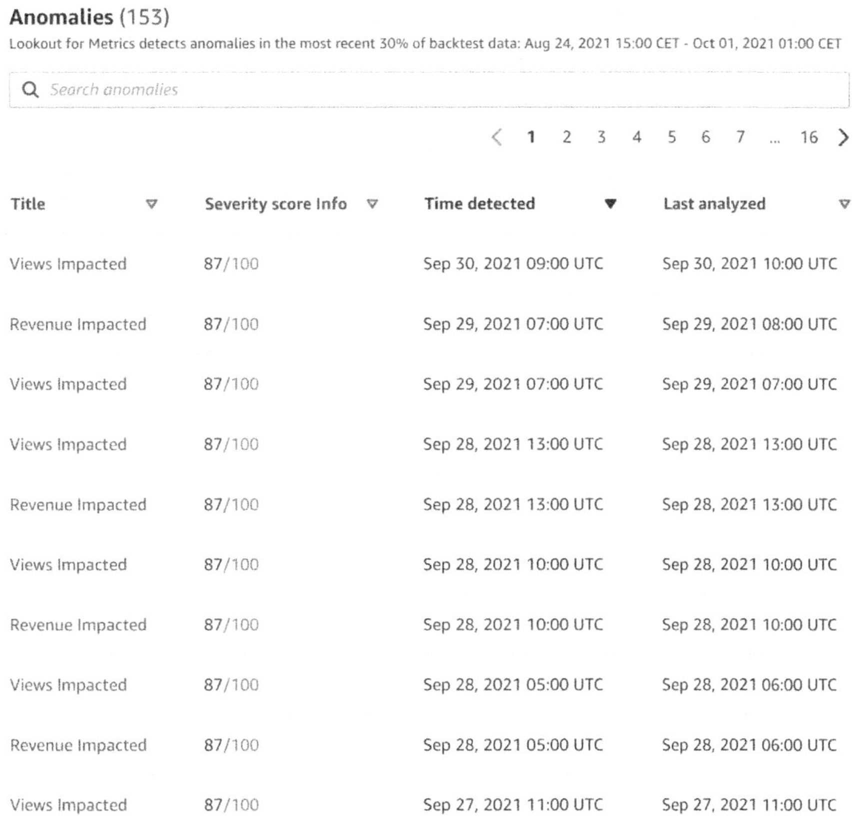

Anomalies (153)

Lookout for Metrics detects anomalies in the most recent 30% of backtest data: Aug 24, 2021 15:00 CET - Oct 01, 2021 01:00 CET

Q Search anomalies

⟨ **1** 2 3 4 5 6 7 ... 16 ⟩

Title ▽	Severity score Info ▽	Time detected ▼	Last analyzed ▽
Views Impacted	87/100	Sep 30, 2021 09:00 UTC	Sep 30, 2021 10:00 UTC
Revenue Impacted	87/100	Sep 29, 2021 07:00 UTC	Sep 29, 2021 08:00 UTC
Views Impacted	87/100	Sep 29, 2021 07:00 UTC	Sep 29, 2021 07:00 UTC
Views Impacted	87/100	Sep 28, 2021 13:00 UTC	Sep 28, 2021 13:00 UTC
Revenue Impacted	87/100	Sep 28, 2021 13:00 UTC	Sep 28, 2021 13:00 UTC
Views Impacted	87/100	Sep 28, 2021 10:00 UTC	Sep 28, 2021 10:00 UTC
Revenue Impacted	87/100	Sep 28, 2021 10:00 UTC	Sep 28, 2021 10:00 UTC
Views Impacted	87/100	Sep 28, 2021 05:00 UTC	Sep 28, 2021 06:00 UTC
Revenue Impacted	87/100	Sep 28, 2021 05:00 UTC	Sep 28, 2021 06:00 UTC
Views Impacted	87/100	Sep 27, 2021 11:00 UTC	Sep 27, 2021 11:00 UTC

Figure 15.11 – Filtered anomalies with a high enough severity score

For each anomaly of this list, you can quickly check the following:

- **Title**: When you configured your detector and your dataset, you selected the **Views** and **Revenue** variables as measurements. On this **Anomalies** list, you will see anomalies that have an impact on either of these variables. The title of the anomaly mentions the impacted measure (for example, **Views impacted**).

- **Severity score**: The severity score of each anomaly ranging from 0 to 100.

- **Time detected**: The timestamp at which the anomaly occurs.

- **Last analyzed**: The timestamp at which the detector finds this anomaly (the detector may find an anomaly several hours or days after the anomaly actually occurs).

Click on the title of the first anomaly to dig into what caused this anomaly. This will bring up a screen with three sections: an overview, the dimension values, and the metric graph.

Anomaly overview

The first section of the anomaly details dashboard is the **Anomaly overview** section:

Anomaly overview

Severity score Info	Start time detected	Last analyzed	Detection interval
87/100	Sep 30, 2021 09:00 UTC	Sep 30, 2021 10:00 UTC	1 hour intervals

Figure 15.12 – Anomaly overview

In this section, you have a reminder of the severity score (**87/100**), the timestamp of the anomaly (**Sep 30, 2021 9:00 UTC**), the timestamp of the detection (**Sep 30, 2021 10:00 UTC**), and the detection interval of the detector (**1 hour intervals**).

Dimension values

The second section displays the dimensions detected as anomalous using the following representation:

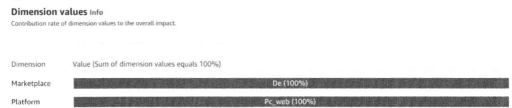

Figure 15.13 – Impact analysis for a given anomaly

Our dataset has two dimensions: **Marketplace** and **Platform**. In the preceding figure, you can see that the anomalous metrics were recorded in Germany (in this dataset, the marketplace uses two letters for each country: in this case, De stands for Deutschland) for users navigating on your website with a browser from a PC (with a **Pc_web** platform).

For each dimension, a percentage is associated with each possible value: on the previous anomaly shown, the detector only detected an issue for the marketplace dimension when it was set to De (Germany), hence the 100% value associated with it. If the anomaly was detected across multiple geographies for the number of views, Amazon Lookout for Metrics would group them together and the percentage associated with each dimension would be displayed in the extent the anomaly impacts each marketplace.

Here is another example with an anomaly detected across multiple metrics:

Figure 15.14 – Anomaly impacting multiple metrics

In this example, you can see five bars for the marketplace dimension: with Germany and the UK at 19% and the US at 13%, this means that the number of views in Germany and the UK is more impacted by this specific anomaly than the number of views in the US. When considering the platform dimension, the balanced ratio between mobile app, mobile web, and desktop web points to a cross-platform issue.

Metric graphs

The final section of the detailed anomaly overview contains the metric graphs:

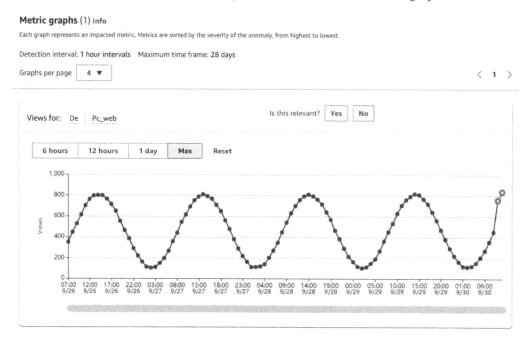

Metric graphs (1) Info

Each graph represents an impacted metric. Metrics are sorted by the severity of the anomaly, from highest to lowest.

Detection interval: **1 hour intervals**　Maximum time frame: **28 days**

Graphs per page　4 ▼　　　　　　　　　　　　　　　　　〈 1 〉

Views for:　De　｜　Pc_web　　　　　　　　　Is this relevant?　Yes　No

6 hours　12 hours　1 day　**Max**　Reset

Figure 15.15 – Metric graphs

On this graph, you can see a quick visualization of one of the metrics impacted by the anomaly you selected. The datapoints that triggered the anomaly are highlighted in blue and have a bold edge: the last two points in the preceding graph are marked as such in this example. You can also change the extent of the visualization (in this example, **6 hours**, **12 hours**, **1 day**, or **Max**).

Now that you have seen how a detector displays an anomaly it finds, you will learn how to interact with these events.

Interacting with a detector

In this section, you are going to learn how you can interact with a detector, namely, how to get human-readable notifications and how to provide feedback once an anomaly has been issued.

Delivering readable alerts

If you configured an alert on the live detector you created at the beginning of this chapter (see the *Training a continuous detector* section for more details), you may have already received some of the alerts as emails, but you may have been surprised by the default format of the alerts. The alert contains a lot of information in a JSON document, which is a great format to connect applications but is not easy to consume for us humans. Here is an example of such a JSON document:

```
{
  "alertName": "ecommerce-revenue-alert-009a9443-d34a-41af-
b782-f6e409db55c2",

  "alertEventId": "arn:aws:lookoutmetrics:eu-west-
1:123456789012:Alert:ecommerce-revenue-alert-009a9443-
d34a-41af-b782-f6e409db55c2:event/3bf090ef-5437-4262-920c-5-
12d311c1503",

  "anomalyDetectorArn": "arn:aws:lookoutmetrics:eu-west-1:
123456789012:AnomalyDetector:sales-anomaly-detector",

  "alertArn": "arn:aws:lookoutmetrics:eu-west-
1:123456789012:Alert:ecommerce-revenue-alert-009a9443-d34a-
41af-b782-f6e409db55c2",

  «alertDescription»: null,

  «impactedMetric»: {

    «metricName»: «revenue»,

    «dimensionContribution»: [

      {

        «dimensionName»: «Marketplace»,

        «dimensionValueContributions»: [

          {

            «dimensionValue»: «DE»,

            «valueContribution»: 100

          }

        ]

      },

      {...
```

To provide a more readable message to your end users, I recommend using the following module hosted by AWS:

```
https://lookoutformetrics.workshop.aws/en/addtional_labs/
alerts.html
```

This workshop lab will provide you with a CloudFormation template you can deploy in your account and a walk-through to configure the Amazon Lookout for Metrics alerts using a Lambda function. Once you're set, the emails you receive when an anomaly is detected will contain templated email content written in plain English (instead of a raw JSON file). The content will look like this (I highlighted the key parameters that will change depending on the notification):

```
An anomaly in revenue was detected on November 17 2021 at
08:00.
1 time series was impacted.
TimeSeries: 1 was impacted on the following dimensions and
values:
        Marketplace - GERMANY
        Platform - PC Web
The Anomaly score was: 76.58
```

You are now ready to easily react whenever a detector finds an anomaly worthy of your time. Let's have a look at how to provide feedback to Amazon Lookout for Metrics.

Providing feedback to improve a detector

When you click on an anomaly in the **Anomalies** dashboard and scroll down to the last section of the detailed anomaly overview, you can find the metric graphs shown in *Figure 15.15*.

Beyond the metric visualization, at the top right of this widget, you can also provide feedback to Amazon Lookout for Equipment by telling it if this sharp increase in the number of views from PC web users in Germany is relevant or not.

In the future, this detector will consider your feedback when determining the severity score for anomalies deemed similar.

Summary

In this chapter, you learned about the tools Amazon Lookout for Metrics gives you to analyze the anomalies detected by a detector. In particular, you learned how to use the **Anomalies** dashboard and how to provide feedback to the service when an anomaly is detected.

This chapter was also important in helping you understand how to configure a detector in continuous mode to enable live data monitoring. You also read about using complementary content to make the service easier to use by delivering alerts in a human-readable format, making these insights even more actionable.

This is the last chapter of this section: by now, you should have a complete understanding of Amazon Lookout for Metrics and know how you can use it to perform anomaly detection on your business metrics.

You have now reached the end of this book: I hope you have enjoyed discovering what you can do with time series data using different AWS services and that you learned enough to help you get started with your own AI projects related to time series analysis. In this book, you learned how to use managed AI services that allowed you to build, train, and deploy machine learning models without having a developer background. There is a lot more to get your teeth into should you want to get more hands-on with these services and the other capabilities AWS offers when it comes to extracting business value from your time series data. Don't hesitate to head over to the AWS Samples GitHub repository (`https://github.com/aws-samples`) if you'd like to get a sense of what can be done by programmatically interacting with these services!

Index

Other Books You May Enjoy

If you enjoyed this book, you may be interested in these other books by Packt:

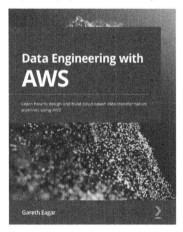

Data Engineering with AWS

ISBN: 9781800560413

- Understand data engineering concepts and emerging technologies
- Ingest streaming data with Amazon Kinesis Data Firehose
- Optimize, denormalize, and join datasets with AWS Glue Studio
- Use Amazon S3 events to trigger a Lambda process to transform a file
- Run complex SQL queries on data lake data using Amazon Athena
- Load data into a Redshift data warehouse and run queries
- Create a visualization of your data using Amazon QuickSight
- Extract sentiment data from a dataset using Amazon Comprehend

Serverless Analytics with Amazon Athena

ISBN: 9781800562349

- Secure and manage the cost of querying your data
- Use Athena ML and User Defined Functions (UDFs) to add advanced features to your reports
- Write your own Athena Connector to integrate with a custom data source
- Discover your datasets on S3 using AWS Glue Crawlers
- Integrate Amazon Athena into your applications
- Setup Identity and Access Management (IAM) policies to limit access to tables
- and databases in Glue Data Catalog
- Add an Amazon SageMaker Notebook to your Athena queries
- Get to grips with using Athena for ETL pipelines

Packt is searching for authors like you

If you're interested in becoming an author for Packt, please visit authors. packtpub.com and apply today. We have worked with thousands of developers and tech professionals, just like you, to help them share their insight with the global tech community. You can make a general application, apply for a specific hot topic that we are recruiting an author for, or submit your own idea.

Share Your Thoughts

Now you've finished *Time series analysis on AWS*, we'd love to hear your thoughts! Scan the QR code below to go straight to the Amazon review page for this book and share your feedback or leave a review on the site that you purchased it from.

https://packt.link/r/1-801-81684-0

Your review is important to us and the tech community and will help us make sure we're delivering excellent quality content.

Made in the USA
Monee, IL
20 November 2022

18188151R00254